T0221012

TRUSTWORTHY CLOUD COMPUTING

TRUSTWORTHY CLOUD COMPUTING

VLADIMIR O. SAFONOV
St. Petersburg University

WILEY

Library of Congress Cataloging-in-Publication Data:

Names: Safonov, V. O. (Vladimir Olegovich), author.
Title: Trustworthy cloud computing / Vladimir O. Safonov.
Description: Hoboken, New Jersey : John Wiley & Sons, Inc., [2016] | Includes
    bibliographical references and index.
Identifiers: LCCN 2015036885 | ISBN 9781119113508 (cloth)
Subjects: LCSH: Cloud computing.
Classification: LCC QA76.585 .S34 2016 | DDC 004.67/82–dc23 LC record available at http://lccn.loc.gov/2015036885

Typeset in 10/12pt TimesLTStd by SPi Global, Chennai, India

CONTENTS

PREFACE

The book I am presenting to the readers now is my third book published with John Wiley & Sons. During all my professional life and work, this has been the best publishing opportunity, and I greatly appreciate it. My first Wiley book [1] published in 2008 is on aspect-oriented programming and its use in trustworthy software development. My second Wiley book published in 2010 is on compilers and on applying the principles of trustworthiness for compilers.

With this new book, I continue my trustworthy computing series with a book on the novel area of cloud computing, which is very attractive for many computer users – both end users and software development professionals.

First, let me explain the meaning of the picture on the front cover. It corresponds to yet another tradition I follow in my Wiley books – the use in the front covers of my personally made photos of my native city of St. Petersburg and its suburbs, such views that can be regarded as having some allegorical meaning related to the book content. This is done to familiarize foreign readers with the beauties of St. Petersburg, in addition to teaching them novel approaches in IT. Please see my two previous Wiley books for the other examples of allegorical St. Petersburg views – the Atlants [1] and the Rostral Columns [2].

On the front cover of this book there is a picture of *Urania*, the Greek antique muse of astronomy, soaring in the clouds, that can be regarded as a classical style allegory of cloud computing. This beautiful sculpture stands in Pavlovsk, a suburb of St. Petersburg, in its world famous park. The sculpture, as many other beautiful statues in the Pavlovsk park, was cast by French sculptor E. Gastecloux in 1796 from the antique Greek original. Urania is the muse of all precise sciences and their areas, including such a modern area as cloud computing, covered in my book. Urania, as well as the whole Pavlovsk park where she stands, has greatly inspired me and many other scientists to our creative works for many years.

This book is a synthesis of my ideas, experience, and results in two modern fields – trustworthy computing and cloud computing. Actually, the book, either directly or indirectly, summarizes my work in most areas of my competence since the mid-1970s when I started my professional activity as a computer scientist and software engineer: programming languages, compiler development, hardware architecture and operating systems, software architecture and programming technologies (including aspect-oriented programming), Java and .NET platforms, parallel programming, trustworthy computing, and now cloud computing.

In addition, I am one of the originators of active and broad university teaching of cloud computing in Russian universities, for the first turn, in my native St. Petersburg State University where I have been working since 1977. I am the author of two Russian books [3,4] and three Internet courses in Russian [5–7] on cloud computing and Microsoft Azure cloud platform. All of them are quite popular in Russia; my Internet courses have several hundred online students.

The book can be used as a university textbook as a basis for the one-semester university course I recommend for graduate teaching programs. It contains many practical examples of cloud computing and a number of testing questions and exercises at the end of each chapter, which help acquire the material. In addition, the book companion Web site http://www.vladimirsafonov.org/cloud contains presentations, examples of cloud projects, and many other teaching resources related to the topics of the book. Surely the book can be also used for self-education in cloud computing by software practitioners.

The book covers some results of our advanced research related to cloud computing and application of aspect-oriented programming to refactoring cloud applications. In this respect, the book can be considered as a research monograph.

Now it is time for wide learning, using, and enhancing the area of cloud computing as one of the most prospective IT approaches – not only to software development, but, in general, to a new kind of worldwide use of computing resources, both software and data, via a structured collection of Web interfaces, without the need for extra software installations on client computers. A Web browser and access to the Internet are enough to use the *cloud*, as this structured collection of Web interfaces is called, which provides access to a huge amount of computing resources, software, and data running on powerful server computers of big *data* centers. Deep interest among many million people, including me, in cloud computing is one of the reasons why I wrote this book.

As compared to many other cloud computing books that cover mostly the general concepts and the business aspects of cloud computing, my book should be considered as a thorough scientific analysis of cloud computing architectures and the ways to make them trustworthy.

Here is an overview of the book content.

A short introduction covers key ideas, motivations, and concepts of cloud computing and explains its novelty and perspectives of its applications.

Chapter 1 is a detailed description of the principles and concepts of cloud computing and the related concepts of software architecture, such as service-oriented architectures (SOA), multitenancy, and software as a service (SaaS). Cloud computing architecture is very complicated, so its internal logic requires understanding many modern software architectural principles.

Chapter 2 overviews the most widely known cloud computing platforms and gives the readers a feel and understanding of a variety of approaches to cloud by several major companies – Amazon, IBM, Oracle, Google, HP, Salesforce. From this chapter the readers can extract not only ideas and principles but also practical methods of using various cloud platforms.

Chapter 3 is an introduction to trustworthy computing, a paradigm and initiative proposed and implemented by Microsoft since 2002. Now trustworthy computing is one of the foundations of developing modern software, including cloud platforms and cloud applications. The four "pillars" of trustworthy computing are security, reliability, privacy, and business integrity [1].

Chapter 4 is a bridge between trustworthy computing and cloud computing. It explains why it is so important to make cloud computing trustworthy, and describes the principles of how to do it in different aspects: eliminate the psychological barrier between the cloud and the users; develop a friendly user interface for the cloud; analyze and mitigate possible types of attacks on the cloud and cloud applications; develop and use the appropriate hardware to enable fast, scalable, and reliable cloud computing; use the appropriate features of operating systems to make the cloud trustworthy; load balancing the cloud to reasonably distribute its workload between datacenters; use the appropriate principles to develop fault-tolerant cloud services – in particular, use aspect-oriented programming as one of the software paradigms helpful for refactoring cloud applications.

As a major, practical part of the book, Chapter 5 considers in detail, just as an example of implementation of the above cloud computing principles, the cloud computing platform Microsoft Azure. It is not the first cloud platform in the history of IT (the first one was Amazon's EC2, now referred to as Amazon AWS). But now Microsoft Azure is one of the most widely spread cloud computing platforms all over the world. The chapter covers both the principles of the Azure platform and the details of its various features, so the chapter can be considered and studied separately by those readers already familiar with the basic concepts of the cloud and desiring to learn and use Microsoft Azure.

The Conclusions summarizes the perspectives of cloud computing and covers some novel cloud computing projects, such as the InterCloud IEEE Standard and TClouds project by the European Union.

The Appendix contains examples of trustworthy cloud computing services developed for Microsoft Azure.

VLADIMIR O. SAFONOV
St. Petersburg, Russia
August 2015

ACKNOWLEDGMENTS

Thanks a lot to many people who contributed to the creation of the book.

For the first turn, I would like to thank John Wiley & Sons as the greatest publishing company in the world for the wonderful opportunities to publish and disseminate my books. In particular, many thanks to Brett Kurzman and Alex Castro as my immediate Wiley contacts. Also, thanks a lot to many other Wiley people who helped to create and publish my previous two Wiley books. I consider Wiley as a template of the best publishing quality, working with people, understanding, help, and friendship.

I would like to thank my beloved wife and university colleague Adel Safonova a lot for the deep understanding and great interest to all my works, lots of advice, care, help, and support, and in particular for making excellent photos of St. Petersburg and suburbs I used in all my Wiley books.

I would like to memorialize one of the greatest IT persons I have ever known, Professor Lawrence Bernstein from Stevens University of Technology who passed away in 2012. All my books can be considered as devoted to his holy memory. I consider Larry to be one of my greatest teachers, tutors, supporters, and friends, the person who believed in me and my proposals when I first came to Wiley. Larry was the editor of the Wiley Quantitative Computing Series for years. Two of my previous Wiley books were published as parts of his series. The role of Professor Larry Bernstein in their publication, his great help, attention, advice is invaluable. My book can be regarded as continuation of his Wiley book series.

Thanks very much to Microsoft Research for their support to my works, in particular, to Microsoft Windows Azure in Education team who provided to me and my students a number of grants since 2011 to enable our access to the Microsoft Azure cloud computing platform. Without their help this book and my Russian Azure books and courses could not be created.

Thanks a lot to Alexander Gavrilov who worked at the Microsoft Russia university relations team for many years for his great help in getting access to Microsoft Azure and supporting my activity on the creation of my Azure books and courses.

Thanks a lot to Mark Russinovich from Microsoft, the Azure technical fellow, for his inspiring books and presentations on Windows and Microsoft Azure internals, in particular, at the Microsoft TechEd Europe conferences I visited.

Thanks to my book proposal reviewers who helped me to pay attention to some new cloud computing books.

Thanks a lot to my disciples – former students, students, and doctoral students who expressed keen interest in cloud computing, learned it, and developed a number of interesting Microsoft Azure cloud services as their graduate papers and term papers. Some of them are used as appendices to my book.

Special thanks to Dmitry Grigoriev, my talented disciple who proved his candidate of sciences dissertation on aspect-oriented programming and our Aspect.NET toolkit under my supervision – now an associate professor of our university chair – and to his wife and university colleague Anastasia Grigorieva, for their advanced research work on using Aspect.NET [1] for refactoring cloud applications for Microsoft Azure platform covered in Chapter 4.

INTRODUCTION

To get better acquainted with the subject of the book, let us first understand what the key ideas and motivations of cloud computing are, why it is so attractive, popular, prospective, hot, and fashionable worldwide, what are the issues of the cloud approach and directions of its future development, and what kind of interest and activity relative to cloud computing different categories of people demonstrate right now.

THE CLOUD AS AN INNOVATIVE CHANGE OF COMPUTING PARADIGM

The metaphor of the cloud, depicting a symbol of the Internet or any other network, appeared long ago, probably in the 1960s when the first networks appeared. However, a picture of the cloud itself is not enough to explain the key ideas of cloud computing. To understand the motivation and the essence of cloud computing better, let us consider how the viewpoint on using computers to make computations or to get access to some data has changed over the years. The key questions are as follows: what is the best way to use computer services, what is required from the user (client) to do that, and what is the center of the computation in different approaches to it?

In the 1950s, computers were isolated "monsters," each occupying a large hall, requiring huge amounts of electric power, water, or air cooling, a brigade of people taking care of the computer hardware and software, and serving as intermediary between the computer and its users. The only way to use a computer was to get full personal access to it for some time, to solve just a single task at each moment; the interfaces between the computer and the user were very poor, such as punched cards or punched tapes as program and data input media and engineering control panels where the content of the computer memory was displayed by hundreds of LEDs, each depicting a bit of information. No networking was used to connect computers and their users to each other.

In the 1960s, the first operating systems appeared, which allowed the users to share the computer resources – CPU, memory, input/output devices – between several users and several tasks. Also, in the late 1960s, the first computer networks appeared, such as ARPANET. Such innovations allowed the clients to use computing resources in the shared mode, and, even more important, to use networking to transfer information from one computer to the other.

In the 1970s, networking technologies, hardware, and protocols developed rapidly. The number of computers connected to networks increased, from several dozens in the 1960s to several thousands in the 1970s. Ethernet and TCP/IP protocols were developed as the basis for the future worldwide network – the Internet whose birth goes back to the early 1980s.

So the computing paradigm has changed from the isolated use of a single computer to solve a single task to the use of the client computer resources, along with the other computing resources available via some network, to solve a set of everyday tasks. It became possible to avoid keeping all computing resources on the client computer. However, much effort was still required from the clients, related to many extra software and/or hardware installations and settings. Even in order to use a set of office applications needed every day for creating, printing, and exchanging documents, such as Microsoft Office, this set of applications needed to get installed on the client computer, which required extra disk space of the client computer and extra working time of the computer user.

THE BASIC IDEA OF THE CLOUD AND ITS ADVANTAGES

Developers and users of computing technologies, over several decades, have come a long way from local computations on isolated machines to the use of local area, regional area, and global area networking and, finally, to the *clouds* – full virtualization of resources based on the only "window to the world" of computations – a Web browser through which all the cloud resources are available.

The basic idea of cloud computing is as follows: to help the client to avoid any extra installations on his or her computer and to consume a ready-to-use structured set of virtualized computing Web services, both software and data (*"the cloud"*), via Web browser, without any extra requirements to cloud client computers. Only a computer with an operating system, a Web browser, and access to the Internet are necessary from any client to use the power of cloud computing.

Speaking in more general terms, *cloud computing* is now a more and more popular innovative approach to *virtualization* of computing resources, platforms, and infrastructures based on using via the Web a set of powerful computers, and a huge amount of software and databases stored on the computers of the cloud provider's *datacenters*.

This approach is really innovative, since it radically changes the viewpoint of the software developer on the use of resources. Instead of the time-consuming and effort-consuming approaches of the past, such as, "I'll install these and that programs and data on my computer and will solve this task (the installation may require several days, and a serious upgrade or even a replacement of the computer could be required)," we can now use the modern cloud approach: "I'll subscribe to the cloud services of the XXX company for six months and will solve with the help of cloud resources all my necessary problems, using the cloud when and where it will be comfortable for me, communicating to the cloud from my smartphone or from my laptop."

Please feel the difference between the above two approaches. Due to the use of the cloud, the user is freed from routine and mundane work and switches to creative activity. When the user becomes the author of useful software cloud applications, he or she will be able to use the cloud for publishing his or her own software.

So the metaphor of the cloud, with cloud computing, now acquires a new sense. Before the cloud era, the center of organizing computations was a client computer or, in some cases, a local area network. The Internet was used just as a source of useful information or useful software applications that should be *downloaded* from the Internet and installed on the client computer. Now, with cloud computing, the cloud (part of the Internet) becomes itself a powerful tool of organizing and performing computations, and the client computer (via a Web browser) is used as a tool to control the computations and to visualize the results.

The advantages of such approach are obvious: the set of computing resources, referred to as the cloud, can be implemented on powerful server computers located in the *datacenters* without the clients' participation, and the only thing the cloud clients should do is to consume cloud services via the Web, using their browsers and any kind of computing devices, from desktop or laptop computers to mobile devices such as smartphones, to solve their everyday tasks using the cloud. No installations on client computers and no extra client resources are required.

So, looking from the client side, cloud computing provides just unlimited opportunities. Any client, a specialist in any problem domain (e.g., a doctor, a scientist, or a teacher), can use the cloud in his or her everyday activity, due to the cloud's Web interface being available for use either from a mobile device or from a laptop computer – this is all that is needed from the client. So the following prospective picture of the near future can be imagined: all computing resources are structured and available from the clouds, and everybody is using the appropriate cloud in their everyday activity.

This approach to computing is radically different from the previous ones used in the history of IT: no need to carry a computing center with you every day, no need to learn and perform subtle networking settings typical of client operating systems – just a smartphone and access to the cloud are enough to get all necessary computing resources.

Thus, two very important principles are being implemented, due to cloud computing: *pervasive use of computers* in everyday activity and *user-centric computing*. The latter principle means that a comfortable *working environment* is implemented for any user to work in the cloud, the same working environment, irrespective of the

kind of computing device the client is using. More traditional approaches to computing actually require the user to be part of the existing computer system he or she uses
and perform specific settings to be able to work under proper conditions. Speaking
in a straightforward manner, cloud computing enables the principle of *computer for
the user, rather than the user for the computer.*

ISSUES OF THE CLOUD APPROACH AND OF ITS LEARNING

No matter how attractive the cloud approach is, a number of initial questions arise in a
moment when you realize the idea of the cloud. Question number one is *security* and
reliability of the cloud, that is, *cloud computing trustworthiness.* Please note that it
closely relates to the title and the motto of my book. Not only software cloud services
are located on server computers in the datacenters implementing the cloud but any
kind of the client data (including confidential information) has to be also stored in the
cloud. The question arises as to how secure it is. Is there any guarantee that the client's
private data will not be somehow stolen from the cloud datacenter computers? Storing
private data on a private computer, intuitively, looks more secure. But this intuition
is wrong: now *every* computer is subject to cyber attacks via the Internet or any other
network the computer is using [1].

Question number two is *performance* and *scalability* of the cloud: How fast will
this Web browser interface be to the cloud? How many users will the public cloud
handle at each moment without any failures, hangings, or substantial time delays?
This set of concerns also relates to the *trustworthiness* of the cloud: the clients just
would not use non-reliable, non-scalable, or too slow a cloud.

From the viewpoint of the developers and the providers of the cloud, there are
several problems to solve. First, implementation of a public cloud to be consumed
by many million users requires giant computing resources that cost a lot of money,
requires a lot of office space (some datacenters occupy large multistoried buildings),
and consumes a lot of electric power. Second, the architecture of the cloud should
enable its *elasticity* – adaptability to the fast changing number of users (up to several
million). Third, cloud *security* should be guaranteed, which is a serious problem in
the present circumstances of danger of cyber attacks.

From the *student* viewpoint of those who are eager to quickly learn the cloud architecture and start using the cloud, there is also a serious issue. The cloud architecture
is very complicated and requires thorough learning. As we see later on in this book,
the architecture of the cloud consists of many *layers* and *tiers* of cloud hardware and
software, which makes it non-evident (as compared, e.g., to a simple class hierarchy
typical of an ordinary object-oriented application).

There is yet another cloud learning issue related to changing the viewpoint to computations in cloud computing. Traditional computations operate with data in memory
or external memory in the form of *variables, arrays, records, and databases* that have
evident ways of naming, structuring, and handling. In cloud computing, an elementary unit of data or software is represented not by a variable, array, or database located
in virtual or external memory, but by a *Web site* with its specific URL address whose

format is characteristic of the cloud platform being used. Since the elements of the cloud storage are accessible via Web interfaces, they have to be accessed via URL addresses. Most software developers, even experienced ones, are not accustomed to such methods of computing.

ELEMENTS OF THE CLOUD APPROACH ALREADY IN USE

There are several kinds of cloud features we all use every day and it has already become quite traditional for us, so that we often do not realize that we are already using cloud technologies. The first one is *cloud disks (cloud memory)*. Modern operating systems, for example, Windows 8/8.1, provide such features as *Dropbox* – a cloud disk space that can be used to back up the data stored on your computer. Many other toolkits, such as *SkyDrive* or *Yandex.disk*, provide an opportunity to create a named item of cloud disk space to share some piece of information with your colleagues, without the need for sending those data by email, just by sending a *Web reference* to the cloud disk space item you created. So, in fact, cloud disks are the first step to overall use of cloud technologies and making them ubiquitous. Using cloud disks in everyday practice greatly extends our opportunities to store and share big data over the Internet.

Another opportunity for a modern user is to use free *cloud analogs of office applications*. For example, to create or read a Microsoft Office file (*.docx, .xslx, .pptx*, etc.), it is not necessary to buy and install Microsoft Office. It is quite enough to use the Web site http://www.live.com, which provides a free cloud analog of Microsoft Office. Using this cloud office application, which has become quite popular right now, you can create, for example, a Word file, keep it in the cloud, and use it whenever needed, without spending your computer disk space to save it. Yet another set of examples of free cloud services are Web interfaces to *email servers*, e.g., *Google mail (Gmail.com), Hotmail.com*, or *Mail.ru*.

So using free cloud analogs of office applications extends our opportunities of document processing.

These are just a few examples to prove the usability of the cloud computing approach in many everyday situations of using computers.

NEXT STEPS OF CLOUD DEVELOPMENT AND THEIR ISSUES

To briefly formulate the next related set of tasks for cloud and cloud application developers, the next step is to create a comfortable cloud-based working environment for everyday use by any kind of specialists of various problem domains – from doctors to scientists, teachers, or just children or housekeepers. This is a challenging task for software developers, for the first turn, for students eager to learn, use, and enhance the cloud.

The problems of cloud trustworthiness outlined above are yet another set of challenging tasks for cloud developers. The cloud should be simpler, should have intuitively evident user interface, and should have a simple and logical system of naming the elements of the cloud (represented as a set of Web sites).

The first cloud was developed by Amazon in 2008 – *Amazon Elastic Cloud 2 (Amazon EC2)*, now called *Amazon AWS*. This date can be considered to be the origin of the cloud. Since then, there has been a boom in cloud computing. Many major and even smaller companies who realized the advantages of the cloud approach and have enough resources started to develop their own clouds (see Chapter 2). However, it became clear in practice that developing and supporting a *public cloud* (which may be available to million users at each moment) is a task only realistic for big companies with huge resources. A more realistic task for a small company is to develop and support a *private cloud*, the cloud available only to the employees of the cloud owner company, since implementing such a cloud requires only several computers with midlevel computing resources. So, for any company, the first step of cloud development is to create the company's private cloud.

Realizing that the cloud is a method to greatly increase the number of users and their applications, software companies started to port their software products to the cloud, that is, to develop cloud analogs of popular applications. However, they faced many problems, since straightforward porting of any software code to the cloud is impossible because of the radically different paradigm of cloud computing considered above: cloud software should operate *Web sites* as elementary units of information available in the cloud. So porting software products to the cloud may require dramatic changes in their architecture, up to full redesign and rewriting.

Many cloud software solutions have been developed recently in various problem domains. One of the interesting examples is *Windows Intune* [6] – a cloud solution for Microsoft Azure cloud for creating a network of personal computers and mobile devices (e.g., belonging to employees of some company) controlled by the cloud.

INTEREST IN CLOUD AMONG DIFFERENT CATEGORIES OF SPECIALISTS AND COMMUNITIES

As for actual or potential cloud users, many of them are in the process of making a decision to start using the cloud in their everyday activity and to choose the amount of resources to spend on using the cloud, and need proper advice on that matter and understanding of the cloud specifics. One of the goals of my book and of many other books on cloud is to provide enough information for such cloud users. For them, the first task is to choose the type of cloud to use – a *public cloud*, a *private cloud*, a *hybrid* cloud – a combination of the above, or a *community cloud* that unites professionals in some domain, for example, IT specialists.

IT researchers are now trying to tie their research to cloud computing, since this is a way to get more funding in the form of grants. From this viewpoint, the area of cloud computing gives plenty of opportunities: it requires solving many nontrivial problems of software and hardware architecture, resource allocation and management, software trustworthiness, networking, and so on.

Annually, hundreds of conferences are held on cloud computing – both business style, discussing the ways to better apply clouds in business activities, and scientifically oriented. For example, the biggest annual IT conference, *Microsoft TechEd,* with several thousand participants every year, provides a lot of information on cloud computing. In 2013, the Microsoft TechEd Europe Conference in Madrid (June 2013) I visited had two special sessions on cloud computing, *Modern Datacenter* and *Windows Azure Application Development*, with about a hundred talks in each. A number of journals have been recently founded on cloud computing, for example, *IEEE Transactions on Cloud Computing*. Special scientific communities are created on cloud computing, for example, *IEEE Cloud Computing Community,* of which I have been a member for a few years. It distributes interesting novel information on the cloud.

As for *teaching* cloud computing ant its use in education, both in high schools and in universities, I should say that it is just starting. There are not so many universities where courses on cloud computing are taught now. Our St. Petersburg University is one of the pioneers of teaching and using cloud computing in Russia. The interest of students in cloud computing is deep. Each educational year several of my students develop their term projects and graduate projects using cloud computing. The results of our research and teaching activity in this area are covered in this book and in my Russian books and Internet courses [3–7]. At our university, I teach cloud computing as part of the basic course on networking for the second year students, and also as part of yet another bachelor level course on models and architectures of software and knowledge (for the fourth year students), as an example of modern innovative approach to software development and use. This year I am starting my new university course titled "Cloud computing" as a graduate one-semester course for masters degree students majoring in the mathematical foundation of informatics. In any case, I combine my theoretical lectures on cloud computing with practice, based on Microsoft Azure cloud platform. Thanks very much to Microsoft Research who provides free academic access to Microsoft Azure to my students for the whole educational semester, enough to learn everything and develop a term or graduate project in the cloud.

There are many *cloud computing books* available on the market. For example, among the best ones are the books [8–12]. However, the limitations of most other cloud computing books are their business orientation, brief formulation of basic concepts of cloud computing, lack of scientific analysis, and, therefore, poor suitability for teaching. The authors of some of the cloud computing books prefer to use the following scenario: overview the basic cloud computing paradigms and concepts, emphasize the importance of cloud computing for business, and estimate the cost of using clouds. This is good but not enough, especially for teaching cloud computing.

What is needed for cloud computing literature, especially for university teaching, is detailed and understandable explanation and scientific analysis (using examples and analogies) of very complicated cloud architectures; examples of working cloud services; concrete information on widely spread cloud platforms (Google cloud, IBM Bluemix Cloud, Microsoft Azure cloud, Oracle Cloud, etc.) suitable for practical use, along with an overview of their key concepts. I hope my book will be helpful in this respect.

In addition, I wish for the authors of cloud computing books to make their books more interesting, attractive, and desirable to read, rather than dull and full of structured itemized definitions of basic concepts and technical acronyms that make books difficult to read. My feeling of cloud computing is that it is so attractive, exciting, and innovative that it deserves learnable and reasonably emotional books that inspire young people to their own inventions and developments in this new area.

To complete this short introduction and to proceed to more detailed consideration of cloud computing and their trustworthiness, I wish the readers to feel the advantages and perspectives of the "universe of cloud computing" by practice with some cloud computing platform. Most cloud developer companies (e.g., Oracle and Microsoft) provide complimentary trial access to their clouds for 1 month.

EXERCISES TO INTRODUCTION

EI.1 What are the key ideas of cloud computing and its advantages?

EI.2 Overview the evolution of approaches to computing during the 1950s, from local computing on isolated non-networked machines to cloud computing.

EI.3 What kind of software and connections are required from a client for using the cloud?

EI.4 What kind of software tool enables the interface between the client and the cloud?

EI.5 Please define cloud computing in the most general way you know.

EI.6 What is a datacenter?

EI.7 What kinds of clouds do you know? What is public cloud, private cloud, hybrid cloud, and community cloud?

EI.8 How is an elementary item of information represented and addressed in cloud computing?

EI.9 What was the name of the first cloud computing platform and by which company was it developed?

EI.10 What kind of issues of cloud computing do you know?

EI.11 What kind of cloud tools and applications are already in everyday use right now?

EI.12 What is Windows Intune?

EI.13 Please describe the kind of issues a software developer experiences when he or she is trying to port his or her application to the cloud and why.

EI.14 Please name the journals on cloud computing you know.

1

PRINCIPLES AND CONCEPTS OF CLOUD COMPUTING

1.1 KINDS OF MODERN SOFTWARE ARCHITECTURES

Before diving into cloud computing itself, let us consider some important concepts and kinds of modern software architectures and analyze the place of cloud computing in this scheme.

Here are some typical kinds of modern software:

- Client–server systems
- Web services and Web applications
- Integrated distributed software solutions
- Built-in systems
- Real-time systems
- Software for mobile devices
- Software for wearable computers
- Middleware (midlevel software)
- Software for cloud computing and datacenters
- Software for computer clusters
- Software for virtualization
- Software for information management
- Software for knowledge management
- Software for scientific computing.

In general, modern software architectures tend to get more and more complicated.

Trustworthy Cloud Computing, First Edition. Vladimir O. Safonov.
© 2016 John Wiley & Sons, Inc. Published 2016 by John Wiley & Sons, Inc.

Client–server system paradigm and architecture have become widely spread for decades. A client–server system consists of a server or set of servers and a set of clients, connected to a local area network. The following kinds of servers are used in most local networks: *application* server, *Web* server, *email* server, *database* server, *file* server, and so on [13].

Internet (Web) applications are intended for use on the net. Currently the majority of them are developed on .NET [14] or Java [15] platforms, though some software developers still prefer to write Internet applications in older languages such as C. In modern Web programming, languages with *dynamic types* are widely used – JavaScript, Python, and Ruby. Their characteristic features are the dynamic change and construction of new types at runtime, which is comfortable, since it reflects the dynamic nature of Web applications and Web sites.

Internet applications are classified into *client side* applications (e.g., Web browsers) and *server side* applications (e.g., Web services).

Integrated software solutions are distributed software systems for information processing and supporting the business and functioning of enterprises, companies, banks, or universities. The characteristic features of integrated software solutions are modules for authentication and authorization of users, modules for accessing databases, modules for networking, and modules for implementing the business logic of the company. Integrated solutions can be developed using several programming languages.

Built-in systems are software for specialized microprocessors controlling various kinds of specific devices, from nuclear reactors to freezers, cardiostimulators, electric power transmission systems, and cars. The characteristic requirement of such software is fixed *response time* interval with some critical upper limit that is dramatic to satisfy for usability, reliability, and security of the whole system and the controlled object in general, or even for continuing the life of some living organism to be controlled. The typical requirement to the basic working cycle of such a system is the absence of interrupts, which could cause critically undesirable time delays.

Software for mobile devices is one of the most modern and widely used kinds of software. Its specific characteristics are the use of limited amount of resources (for the first turn, limited memory size) and the need to take into account a variety of models of mobile devices (differences of their screens and control keys) when implementing the graphical user interface of mobile applications. Currently, most of the software for mobile devices is developed on the Java platform; an especially popular mobile platform now is Google Android.

As an exotic but real-life example, consider the *software for wearable computers*. Such specialized computers are built into specific kinds of wear or uniform (e.g., space suits) that they monitor the state, health, and behavior of a human, and give expert recommendations to him or her. This class of software also has strict limitations on the computing resources used.

Middleware (or *mid-level software*) is a kind of communication software present in the software architectural scheme between the client and the server and supporting their networking communication protocols. A typical modern example of middleware is communication software for sending and receiving *instant messages* between mobile devices, and laptop and desktop computers.

Software for datacenters is yet another modern kind of software. Its most important components are powerful server-side operating system, middleware to support networking communications, and database management systems (e.g., Microsoft SQL Server).

Software for virtualization is a modern software intended for the installation and use of *virtual machines* on real computer hardware, with the purpose of extending computing features, using other kinds of operating systems, or using software developed for other hardware platforms. Examples of such software are *Microsoft Virtual PC* and a new toolkit *Microsoft Hyper-V hypervisor*.

Software for cloud computing consists of various kinds of server-side operating systems (e.g., Windows Server or Linux) and other software that supports the use of cloud resources (applications and data) by the cloud clients. It is considered in more detail subsequently in this chapter.

Software for knowledge management plays a more and more important role now, in relation to Web intellectualization and popularity of *intelligent software solutions* that contain modules of logical assessment of the computation results, in addition to computational modules. Examples of knowledge management software are the *Protégé* knowledge management system developed at Stanford University [16] implementing the ontology management language OWL and our own software product developed by our team under my supervision at St. Petersburg University – *Knowledge.NET* [17], an extension of the C# language by knowledge management features, implemented as a plug-in to Visual Studio.

Software for information management is a set of office applications for document processing (e.g., Microsoft Office) and database management systems (e.g., Oracle DMBS, MySQL, Microsoft SQL Server).

Software for scientific computing is a set of software tools and packages that support the solving of scientific tasks, for example, MATHLAB.

1.2   CHARACTERISTIC FEATURES OF MODERN SOFTWARE

Now let us consider the most characteristic features inherent to most of the software systems, regardless of their problem domain and their implementation platform.

The most important feature of modern software systems is their *Web awareness*. The most popular kinds of modern platforms supporting this feature are .NET and Java.

A characteristic feature of modern software is *unification of models of programs and data*, which actually follows from their Web and net awareness. The *Unified Modeling Language (UML)* has been used for more than 30 years as a de facto standard for modeling software and the processes of its development. As for data representation, the de facto standard in this area is *XML,* which enables unified structured textual representation of data, used especially when transferring them via the network.

Trustworthy computing is a modern approach to software development proposed by Microsoft. Its main idea is to take into account the requirements and considerations of security and reliability of the software product under development from the early specification and design stages, to implement those requirements in the software product, and to apply specific kinds of software testing and verification.

An important principle of modern software is a *unified infrastructure* that integrates the tools, data, programs, and knowledge used to solve various application tasks.

Reusability of software code is very important for successful development of software, since it allows the developers to save resources and efforts in software development by using the same software modules in several software solutions.

Service-oriented architecture (*SOA*) of software reflects the trend toward explicit formulation of the concept of *software service* (preferably, Web service). Please see more details on SOA in Section 1.4.

Virtualization is widely used in software for modeling new hardware architectures, extending the features of data access, memory size, and so on.

Cloud computing is currently one of the most popular approaches to development and use of software, implementing the metaphor of the cloud – part of the Internet or intranet network through which the users have access to computing resources – applications, data, and knowledge. This approach is overviewed in the Introduction and covered in detail in the book.

Knowledge management plays an important part in modern software since, to solve many kinds of real world tasks, the use of purely algorithmic methods is not enough; what is required is *integration of methods of software engineering and knowledge* engineering. This important idea is implemented in our knowledge management toolkit referred to as Knowledge.NET [17].

1.3   BASIC CONCEPTS OF MODERN SOFTWARE ARCHITECTURE

Now let us consider the basic concepts of modern software architecture important for understanding cloud computing.

A *client* is the user and/or computer consuming some software service on the network. There are several categories of clients, depending on the kind of services they consume: *Web* clients, *email* clients, *database* clients, and so on. In relation to cloud computing, we mostly consider *Web* clients, since the cloud is controlled via Web interface enabled by a Web browser.

A *server* is a computer or datacenter, a related set of computers providing some software services. From the viewpoint of the above classification, a datacenter can be regarded as a big, structured, and complicated *Web server*.

A *thin client* is a client of a Web service (i.e., a *Web client*) with minimal user interface, *stateless* (without storing information on its state), unable to keep information on its *session*, without a full-fledged GUI comparable in its features to a typical non-Web client application. So a thin client is a Web client communicating to the Web service via basic features of the browser and via the HTTP protocol to send HTTP requests and to get HTML pages as response to them. From cloud computing view-point, the thin client scheme is surely non-suitable for cloud clients, although it is the simplest to implement. The cloud clients would expect from the cloud a comfortable user interface as they are accustomed to from most client applications, and without it they would consider the cloud non-suitable and non-trustworthy.

A *rich client* is a Web client having a rich user interface (windows, menus, scroll-bars, buttons, images, etc.), communicating to the Web service via the layer of inter-mediate software (currently referred to as *middleware*) that enables GUI functionality and network communications. This middleware is usually implemented as a *plug-in* to the Web browser that should be installed on the client computer above the browser before using the cloud. Examples of such plug-ins are *Microsoft Silverlight, Oracle JavaFX, and Macromedia Flash.*

A *layer* is a major independently implemented component of software (group of software modules) that communicates with the other layers that constitute a software product. To use simplified geometric analogies to represent the architecture of the software, there can be *horizontal layers* and *vertical layers (cuts).*

Abstraction layer (also known as *horizontal layer*) which, in classical scheme, has *number N* as a related set of software modules whose implementation can only use (call) modules of the previous layer $N-1$ only ($N>0$). Abstraction layer is the implementation of a related set of intermediary-level concepts (modules). Abstraction layer number 0 is implemented by the target platform hardware or by core software libraries (APIs) usually predefined in the implementation programming language, for example, by the package *java.lang* in Java language. The concept of abstraction layers was formulated by Professor E. Dijkstra in the late 1960s when developing the *"THE"* operating system at the Technical University of Eindhoven, Holland [13].

Vertical layer (cut), referred to in modern software paradigms as *aspect* [1], is a collection of scattered fragments of software code implementing some *cross-cutting* functionality, for example, a set of security checks, in some application. The authors of this concept are Professor A.L. Fouxman (USSR, Rostov University, 1979, in his monograph titled "Technological aspects of software systems development"; his approach was called *technology of vertical cuts*) and G. Kiczales, the father of aspect-oriented programming (Xerox PARC, now University of British Columbia; the scientific advisor of the AspectJ project) [1].

Middleware is a collection of software layers that lie between the clients and the server and enable their interaction via communication protocols.

A *tier* is part of a software solution implementing some independent functionality of the software solution architecture. For example, a *business tier* is the implemen-tation of the business logic of the solution; a *Web tier* is the implementation of the communication of the solution with the Web. A tier is a more complicated software concept than an abstraction layer. Abstraction layers can be represented, using geo-metric analogy, as vertically located segments of software relying bottom-up above each other, the layer N above the layer $N-1$. A tier, on the contrary, can be any part of the architecture of any software solution (or represent different parts of different software solutions), without any definite number, so the concept of the number for the tiers does not make sense. So a two-dimensional geometric analogy ("horizontal

Presentation tier

The top-most level of the application is the user interface. The main function of the interface is to translate tasks and results to something the user can understand

Logic tier

This tier coordinates the application, processes commands, makes logical decisions and evaluations, and performs calculations. It also moves and processes data between the two surrounding tiers

Data tier

Here information is stored and retrieved from a database or file system. The information is then passed back to the logic tier for processing, and then eventually back to the user

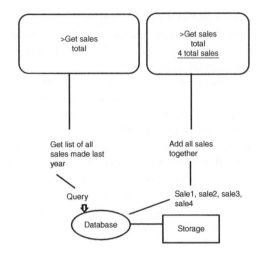

Figure 1.1   Multitiered architecture.

layer/vertical layer") does not work for modern software architectures whose more adequate representation could be imagined as a semantic net or a labeled graph.

Multitier architecture is a kind of software architecture based on the idea of implementing presentation of the results, data processing, and data control as separate processes. *Example:* using middleware to communicate with the server and using a database management system for communication with data.

An example of a multitiered architecture is depicted in Figure 1.1.

Multitenant architecture is a kind of architecture of client–server software based on the principle of the use of the same instance of a server solution, running on the server, by many *tenants* (clients). An example of multitenant software is a Web service.

From the viewpoint of the above approaches, cloud computing can be characterized as satisfying the principles of *multitiered* and *multitenant architecture.*

As for abstraction layers, for specifying modern software architectures this concept looks obsolete, since most of the modules in a software solution are reusable; so in different solutions the same tiers could have different numbers. Two-dimensional geometric models cannot adequately specify modern software architectures.

1.4   SERVICE-ORIENTED ARCHITECTURE (SOA)

SOA is one of the most up-to-date approaches to software development, based on the idea of representing software as an extensible set of *services* (typically, *Web* services).

Service is a software component available for the user for consuming, adding to the current workspace, and monitoring.

Simple example of a service: Getting the weather forecast via the Internet.

The *basic principle of SOA* is as follows. From the client viewpoint, a set of the software products to be consumed by the user is represented as a set of simple-to-use

Web services with comfortable graphical user interface. This working set of services is often referred to as *mash-up*.

A service-oriented model should be extensible: the client should be able to add new services or change the working set of available services.

The clients should be also able to call and consume services from different kinds of computing devices – desktop, laptop or tablet computers, or mobile devices.

The interface of a service is referred to as its *contract*. It is a set of *Web methods*. Each of the Web methods is specified by its name and types of its arguments. The contracts of each Web method should be explicitly specified and should be available for requests of SOA clients who are interested in the full set of the available Web methods.

The platform of implementation of services should be insignificant for the user. A service can be implemented on the .NET, or in Java, or any other suitable platform. The only important rule for the implementer of the service is to follow the *standards* of service development. Currently, there are two commonly used standards for developing services.

One of the service development standards is **WSDL (Web Service Description Language).** It is based on representing the contract of the service (its Web interface) in XML format in a specification language referred to as *WSDL*. A WSDL service works synchronously, so the client waits for one Web method call to finish before calling the other Web method. So this standard of consuming services works slower but is more reliable. In this standard, a service is *stateful* (remembers its state) and keeps information on the *session* of its consuming. The arguments of such service Web methods, objects of some types, are transferred via the network in *serialized* form – represented as a typed stream of bytes. One of the commonly used methods of serialization is XML; the other ones are offered by Java and .NET (on the .NET platform, the term *marshaling* is used as a synonym for the term *serialization*).

The other service development standard is **REST (Representational State Transfer)**. A common IT slang is to refer to such services as *RESTful*. With this standard, a Web method of the service is called *asynchronously* which is, generally speaking, faster, as compared to using a WSDL-based service. In addition, a RESTful service is *stateless*, so the information on its state, as well as the arguments of the Web method, is passed as parameters to the Web method call.

The developer of the services should have an opportunity to *publish* his or her Web services somewhere on the Web where the clients can find (*discover*) it.

Support of the SOA model is provided by a number of modern software tools and Web portals; for example,

- by *Microsoft SharePoint,* which is a simple-to-use toolkit to create extensible Web pages and Web services;
- by *UDDI* (*Universal Discovery, Description and Integration*) technology supported by Microsoft, available via the Web portal http://uddi.xml.org/ intended for publishing and discovering Web services.

From the viewpoint of the service-oriented model, cloud computing is the most up-to-date SOA model implementation. The cloud provides access to a set of its Web services via the client browser. Publication of the newly developed cloud services is quite possible via the cloud. For example, on the Microsoft Azure cloud platform, the cloud Web interface provides a simple way to create a new empty Web service and then to implement it using some integrated development environment (IDE, e.g., *Visual Studio*) and to *publish* the newly implemented Web service in the cloud.

1.5   SOFTWARE AS A SERVICE (SaaS)

Software as a Service (*SaaS*) is a model of software development based on the use of *licenses software services on demand* by the tenants who purchase their licenses from service providers. Sometimes the SaaS model is referred to as *software-on-demand*.

The term *SaaS* originated in the late 1990s.

The main idea of SaaS is to use software on demand at low price, instead of purchasing full license to the software for all platforms.

The main characteristics of the SaaS model are as follows:

- Access to commercial software via the network
- Remote control of the software by the tenants via the central Web site
- The use of the "one-to-many" (*multitenant application*) model, that is, the use of one instance of software service by many tenants
- Centralized control over new versions and patches of the software services (the tenants can download new versions via the network)
- Continuing integration of software services into the hybrid set of software consumed by the tenant, as *mash-up*, that is, hybrid Web applications.

From this viewpoint, cloud computing corresponds to the principles of SaaS, in the following respects.

On the one hand, the principle of SaaS was used by cloud providers as the main principle of consuming the cloud services. The cloud client should *subscribe* to a set of cloud services for some period of time (e.g., for a year) at a reasonable price. This is exactly the principle of SaaS, as stated in the late 1990s, before the cloud era. Surely, each cloud provider also presents to any cloud client a trial or a learning period of completely free use of the cloud – typically, 1 month. At the end of this trial period the tenant can make a justified decision on cloud subscription.

On the other hand, the term SaaS is used as one of the models for organizing cloud services, when the full capability of the cloud is not necessary and what is needed is to integrate into the current mash-up of the tenant some new cloud features, for example, a new kind of the Web search engine.

1.6   KEY IDEAS AND PRINCIPLES OF CLOUD COMPUTING

Cloud computing is one of the most popular, hottest, fashionable directions of information technology in progress. The concept of cloud has already been associated long ago with the metaphoric picture of the Internet that provides availability to a number of Web services. *Cloud computing* is a practical implementation of this idea, based on a structured collection of scalable and virtualized computing resources (software and data) available to the users via the Internet and implemented on the basis of powerful *data (processing) centers*. A cloud client entirely uses Web interface to the cloud enabled by a Web browser, and does not need any extra software to be installed on the client computing device for using the cloud.

Informally speaking, a cloud provided by some company is a good characteristic of this company. The cloud accumulates and expresses not only the technologies of the company but its spirit, trustworthiness, and its attitude also to the users "in one cloud cover."

The general structure of the cloud is depicted in Figure 1.2.

From the viewpoint of the users, there exist various kinds of clouds, as considered below.

Public cloud is a cloud model in which the cloud applications, cloud storage, and other cloud resources are available to any registered cloud user who pays for the cloud services. This model is the most prospective and the most convenient for users

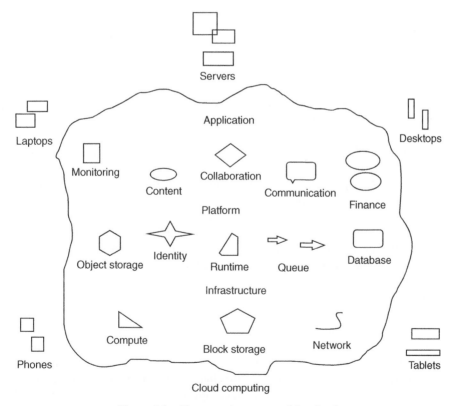

Figure 1.2 The general structure of the cloud.

but the most expensive to implement and the most resource consuming. Only a very large company can allow itself to develop and support such cloud model. The functioning of a public cloud is based on several big datacenters, each of which occupies a large building and consumes a lot of electric energy. An example of a public cloud is Microsoft Azure. Other examples are the Amazon Web Services cloud, Oracle cloud, and IBM Bluemix cloud.

Community cloud is a smaller cloud model in which the cloud infrastructure and services are available to some professional community. An example is the *Institute of Electrical and Electronics Engineers* (*IEEE*) community cloud. To use this cloud, the minimal requirement is to become an IEEE member.

Private cloud is a cloud model in which the cloud services are available only to the employees of some company. The development and maintenance of such a cloud is quite realistic for any company – even for a small one. I recommend the readers to start their own cloud development from creating a private cloud. Moreover, the providers of public clouds, such as Oracle, IBM, and Microsoft, provide support for the fast development of private clouds.

Hybrid cloud is a cloud model implementing a hybrid of several related public, community, or private clouds with the purpose of their joint use to solve some concrete tasks.

Clouds are offered by several companies (e.g., IBM, Oracle, Google, Microsoft, etc.) that serve as the *cloud (service) providers*. They provide, in the form of their clouds, structured collections of powerful computing resources, which the individual users typically do not have.

As a rule, the users must pay the cloud provider for the services of the cloud for a certain period of time (e.g., 1 year). There are also complimentary public cloud services, for example, those available on the Windows Live (http://www.live.com) portal.

Kinds of clouds in cloud computing (public, private and hybrid clouds) are illustrated in Figure 1.3.

No matter how prospective cloud computing is, there are some limitations and shortcomings of the cloud approach.

The first one is as follows. The user appears to be fully dependent on the cloud where the software and data consumed by the user are available and cannot directly control either the cloud computers in the datacenter, or even back up his or her data stored in the cloud. In this relation, there arise a lot of issues: security of cloud computing, keeping the privacy of the users' data, and so on. Some of those issues are far from their solution as yet.

The second group of serious problems of organizing cloud computing is related to managing the datacenters: their power consumption and their load balancing, since cloud computing with a public cloud inevitable leads to the need of serving many million users at each moment of time. For reasons of heavy power consumption, currently some companies, in spite of all the cloud computing perspectives, have even had to close their cloud datacenters, each occupying one or several big buildings of several thousand square feet.

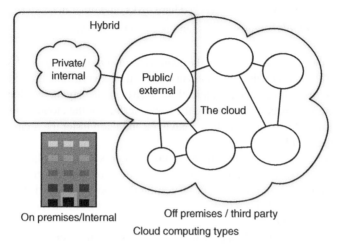

Figure 1.3 Kinds of clouds in cloud computing: public, private, and hybrid clouds.

1.7 COMPONENTS OF CLOUD PLATFORMS AND KINDS OF CLOUD SERVICING

Any cloud platform consists of the following main components:

- *applications* – the cloud software services available in the cloud;
- *runtimes* – the virtual and real machines available in the cloud that enable executing applications on some *platforms* (e.g., in Java or .NET runtime environments);
- *security and integration mechanisms*, including authentication, authorization, and encryption/decryption modules;
- *databases* – the databases available in the cloud that provide similar features as their non-cloud prototypes; for example, SQL Azure database management system available on the Microsoft Azure cloud platform, a cloud analog for Microsoft SQL Server;
- *servers* – computers with large volume of resources (memory, CPUs, and cores), controlled by server-side operating systems, for example, Windows Server or Linux; server hardware is usually clustered into tightly coupled groups;
- *virtualization tools* – software toolkits to support mechanisms of creating and using virtual machines, virtual networks, and other kinds of virtual resources; for example, Microsoft Hyper-V hypervisor and VMWare vSphere hypervisor; virtualization tools can be implemented in software and partly in hardware;
- *cloud user interface support* tools, in the form of *cloud management portal*; for example, Microsoft Silverlight plug-in for the Internet Explorer browser;

  – *storage* – memory racks, networked hard disks, and other mass storage devices;
  – *networking tools* – routers, hubs, and networking software.

Access to the cloud is enabled via the central *cloud management portal,* which first performs the cloud user authentication via login and password, and after the authentication, the user is redirected to the main cloud Web page displaying the cloud features available. The Web pages constituting the user interface of the cloud enable interactive help features for the users to better navigate and learn faster the architecture and features of the cloud.

For example, the cloud management portal on Microsoft Azure platform is http://manage.windowsazure.com. There is yet another Microsoft Azure portal, http://portal.azure.com, quite new at the moment of writing the book, at a preview stage. Both portals are linked together, so that it is possible to travel from the preview portal to the management portal.

This is just a general scheme of the cloud architecture; more details are given below. Different clouds may vary in their interface. User interfaces of the cloud portals tend to evolve and to change their appearance. For example, the cloud most familiar to me, Microsoft Azure (see Chapter 5), has changed the architecture and the appearance of its portal three times during the period 2011–2015.

What kinds of services are provided in the clouds? Let us consider their classification, which tends to evolve and to add the new "-as-a-Service" terms to the cloud terminology.

Based on the above scheme of cloud structure, from architectural viewpoint, clouds and the kinds of services can be classified as follows.

Private (On-Premises) cloud – a model of cloud servicing in which the cloud client (software developer) controls all of the cloud components outlined above.

Infrastructure-as-a-Service (IaaS) – in a cloud of this kind, the client (software developer) controls the applications, the runtimes, mechanisms of security and integration, and the databases. The rest of the components are controlled by the cloud provider. This is a model of cloud client servicing in which the cloud provider offers to the clients virtual machines and their resources: images of the disks, virtual networks, and so on. *Virtual cloud infrastructure* (at a small subscription payment, or just free) – this is what is the most valuable in cloud computing, one of the main reasons why so many clients started using the cloud.

Platform-as-a-Service (PaaS) – in a cloud of this kind, the client (software developer) controls only his or her own applications (cloud services of their own development); the rest of the cloud components are controlled by the cloud provider. This is a model of cloud client servicing in which the cloud provider offers to the clients the whole *computing platform*: an operating system, environment for running applications written in various programming languages, a database, and a Web server.

Software-as-a-Service (SaaS) – in a cloud of this kind, the client does not control any cloud components; everything in the cloud is controlled automatically by the cloud provider; the software components in the cloud are ready to use and there is no need to develop the client's own cloud services. This is a model of cloud client servicing in which the cloud provider publishes in the cloud a number of useful applications used by the cloud clients. A good example is the cloud approach by Google – *Google Cloud Apps*, a set of useful applications that can be easily integrated into the browsers of the cloud clients.

Network-as-a-Service (NaaS) is a relatively new kind of cloud servicing model. In this model, the cloud provider offers to the cloud clients some kinds of *network services*: transport of the network; virtual private networks (VPNs); cloud solutions to unite computing devices into a secure network. An example of such a solution is *Windows Intune*, a cloud solution in Microsoft Azure cloud to create a network of personal computers and smartphones. Another example of NaaS is cloud-based email service, such as hotmail.com.

Resource-as-a-Service (RaaS) is a new kind of cloud servicing and selling cloud computing resources. In this model, instead of offering whole virtual machines for long periods of time as in IaaS clouds, the cloud provider offers to the cloud clients individual resources (such as CPU, memory, and I/O resources) for brief periods of time. The idea of this approach is to help cloud users save their financial resources. In IaaS cloud, a full virtual machine is provided for the cloud user, but the user has to fully pay for it, although he actually uses only some working cycles of that machine. The RaaS approach helps calculate the cloud rental payment more exactly.

Recovery-as-a-Service (also abbreviated as **RaaS,** or **DRaaS**, for **Disaster Recovery as a Service**) is a new kind of cloud computing service to enable recovery of some application and data from disaster. The application or data suffering from disaster may run in some private datacenter. The cloud services in this case enable full recovery of the disrupted service or data in the cloud. An example of such a service is offered by VMWare as *vCloud* (http://vmware.com). The recovery service is available in a hybrid cloud. Generally speaking, there are three kinds of RaaS models:

- *To Cloud RaaS* – when the source to be recovered is in a private datacenter and the recovery services (backup or recovery target) are provided in the cloud;
- *In Cloud RaaS* – when both the resource to recover and the recovery services are in the cloud;
- *From Cloud RaaS* – when the source is in the cloud and the backup or recovery site is in the private datacenter.

Data-as-a-Service (DaaS) is a kind of cloud service in which the data files (texts, images, videos, sounds, etc.) are provided to the clients of the cloud on demand, regardless of their geographic locations. Examples of such cloud services are demonstrated by Oracle Cloud: http://cloud.oracle.com. Oracle provides the following kind of DaaS services:

  – *DaaS for Marketing*
  – *DaaS for Sales*
  – *DaaS for Social.*

In addition, Oracle cloud provides access to Oracle Cloud Database, a cloud analog of the widely used Oracle DBMS.

1.8   LAYERS OF THE CLOUD ARCHITECTURE

In the architecture of the cloud, the following layers exist.

The client layer is the client software used for accessing the cloud services, typically, *a Web browser*, for example, Internet Explorer or Google Chrome.

The services layer is formed of the cloud Web services used via the cloud model, that is, via a structured collection of Web sites with some kind of specific URL addresses. For example, in Microsoft Azure cloud platform, a typical structure of the URL address of any cloud service is http://username.cloudapp.net where *username* is the service name given by the cloud user, the developer of the service.

The applications layer is composed of the programs available via the cloud that does not require installation on the client computer (as already emphasized above, this layer is one of the main advantages of the cloud model). An example is the publicly available portal http://www.live.com implementing cloud mail (please try it to feel the advantages of the cloud).

The platform layer is a software platform that provides a full set of tools for deployment and the use of cloud computing on a client computer without any extra installations or purchase of new hardware. The platform layer consists of *software development platforms* used in the cloud platform implementation (e.g., *.NET* and *Node.js* for the Microsoft Azure cloud platform), *IDEs* (e.g., Visual Studio) that enable *development of cloud services* and their *publication* in the cloud, and *plug-ins for cloud client browsers* implementing rich client user interface for cloud users (e.g., *Microsoft Silverlight*).

The storage layer supports storing the cloud user's data in the cloud and accessing them via the cloud. In fact, cloud data, as well as cloud services, are available via the specific cloud Web sites they are stored on, with the specific URL addresses characteristic of the cloud used. For example, cloud storage objects on Microsoft Azure platform are stored on Web sites with URL addresses of the kind http://storageObjectName.core.windows.net where *storageObjectName* is the specific name of an object in cloud storage.

The infrastructure layer is the layer that provides full virtualized infrastructure via the cloud. An example is the cloud portal http://manage.windowsazure.com of Microsoft Azure cloud platform. A user that logs in to the cloud is provided by a full-fledged cloud platform infrastructure controlled by rich-client style cloud user interface. The cloud infrastructure supports ways of creating and using Web sites, virtual machines, cloud services, cloud databases, cloud mobile services, cloud multimedia services, and many other kinds of interesting cloud objects. This infrastructure is rapidly developing. Other cloud platforms, for example, Amazon Web Services cloud, provide similar opportunities.

1.9   SCHEME OF ARCHITECTURE OF THE CLOUD

A scheme of architecture of the cloud is illustrated in Figure 1.4.

The following components are depicted in the scheme:

- *Services* available via the cloud
- *Infrastructure* for their deployment and use
- *Platform* – a set of tools for using the cloud
- *Storage* – support of storing the users' data in the datacenter(s) implementing the cloud.

The components of the cloud are typically represented by Web services with their URL addresses. To continue the Microsoft Azure example, irrespective of whether the components of the cloud are cloud applications (services) or cloud data referenced by URL addresses of the kinds http://username.cloudapp.net (cloud application) or http://storageObjectName.core.windows.net (cloud storage), they all are implemented as specialized Web services providing access to cloud applications or cloud data, according to the Web services standards overviewed above. There are many other kinds of URL addresses for specific cloud objects in this scheme.

An example of cloud architecture is depicted in Figure 1.5.

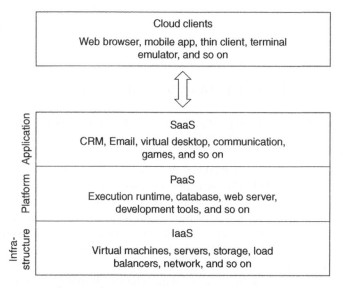

Figure 1.4   Scheme of architecture of the cloud.

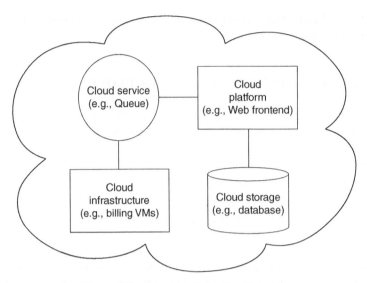

Figure 1.5   Example of cloud architecture.

In this example, the user may call some *cloud service*, for example, the one imple-menting the *Queue* concept. Tools to access this service are parts of the *cloud platform* that provides the *Web interface* (*Web frontend*) comfortable for accessing the service. Up-to-date cloud user interface, such as in Microsoft Azure or in other cloud plat-forms, is as comfortable as a typical user interface of local applications, so that the user will not feel any difference between cloud GUI and local application GUI. Via the cloud platform, the *cloud storage* is available (in Microsoft Azure, it is imple-mented by the *Storage* component), and also a *cloud database* (in Microsoft Azure represented by the *SQL Azure* component). Via cloud services, the whole cloud infras-tructure is available, for example, *virtual machines*.

1.10   ROLES OF PEOPLE IN CLOUD COMPUTING

With the advent of cloud computing, the *roles* of the specialists participating in its development and use have changed, as compared to traditional "developer/user" paradigm.

Cloud providers are the companies that own the *datacenters* supporting their clouds. According to NIST [18], the major activities of the cloud provider are *service deployment, service orchestration* (arrangement, coordination, and management of cloud services to enable their optimal use), *cloud service management, security,* and *privacy.* So the cloud provider is responsible to the cloud users for trustworthiness of the cloud services. The ISO/IEC Standards of cloud terminology [19] use the term *cloud service provider.*

Cloud users (clients) can be any users of the Internet who pay for the cloud services or use trial free subscription to the cloud, or use the private cloud of their company.

Hardware and software vendors for the cloud are the companies who develop hardware and basic software for datacenters. From this viewpoint, for example, Microsoft is the cloud provider for the Microsoft Azure cloud platform and is the major software vendor for this cloud platform. However, there are different hardware vendors and even different software vendors, since one of the server operating systems used in Microsoft Azure is *Linux,* which is not developed by Microsoft.

A *cloud architect* is the major developer of the cloud architecture.

A *cloud integrator* is a system administrator responsible for adding components to the cloud and updating them.

A *cloud auditor* [20] is a person or company who audits the cloud to examine the cloud *operations*, performance, and security against some criteria.

A *cloud service broker* [20] is an intermediary between cloud providers and cloud users, who negotiates the relationship between them.

A *cloud carrier* [18] is the intermediary that provides connectivity and transport of cloud services from cloud providers to cloud consumers.

Recently, a new role has emerged in cloud computing – *participant of a cloud community* of specialists who are interested in cloud computing, for example, *IEEE Cloud Computing Community.*

1.11 STANDARDS OF CLOUD COMPUTING

The cloud computing model and cloud implementation are based on the principles of following a whole set of standards.

Standards of cloud terminology, organization, and architecture are defined in [18–20]. I am trying to use the cloud terminology standards throughout the book; however, it does not appear to be stabilized yet.

There is a draft standard [21] for *InterCloud*, a "cloud of clouds," intended for the future integration of clouds provided by different companies. In this prospective role, the InterCloud standard is very important. However, currently the situation in cloud computing is far from the cloud integration stage. It can be characterized as active and aggressive development of many competitive cloud platforms.

For software components interaction in the cloud, the following standards are used, as explained subsequently.

HTTP – the hypertext transfer protocol, the basic networking protocol of the Web. The methods of HTTP have the format of *HTTP Method_Name URI_Address* and are as follows:

- *GET* – gets and displays in the client Web browser the requested HTML Web page (referenced by a URI address) from the Web server to the Web client
- *POST* – sends the filled out Web form from the Web client to the Web server
- *HEAD* – gets and displays in the client browser only the header of the requested Web page (without the body of the HTML page)
- *PUT* – uploads the content of the request to the URI address of the resource; if the resource with such URI is missing, it is created

- *PATCH* – updates a fragment of the resource, similar to *PUT*
- *DELETE* – deletes the given resource
- *TRACE* – traces the changes or additions of the intermediate servers (if any)
- *OPTIONS* – checks the functionality of the Web server by returning the HTTP methods the server supports
- *CONNECT* – converts the request connection to a transparent TCP/IP tunnel, to support SSL connection (*https*) via an unencrypted proxy.

At the end of any HTTP request, there can be a part starting with "?". After the "?" sign the Web client can provide parameters for the HTTP method performed by the Web server. For example, the request http://my/cloud/service?wsdl asks the given cloud service to return its Web methods if the service is implemented according to the WSDL standard.

The HTTP protocol is well suited for traditional non-grouped actions on the cloud, for example, for visualizing a cloud Web page. As for operations on *big data* (which are especially important now), the HTTP protocol is not fast enough and special; more efficient protocols should be used instead.

XML (extensible markup language) is used in cloud computing to represent Web configuration files (such as *Web.config* in .NET applications [14]), and to serialize data for their transfer via the network. One of the forms of networking data serialization in XML format is referred to as *SOAP (Simple Object Access Protocol)*. In SOAP standard, objects are represented and transferred via the network in the form of specific XML files referred to as *envelopes* (the *soap:envelope* XML tag is used to distinguish between SOAP and other files). XML is used also to specify the interface of Web services in the format referred to as *WSDL* (see Section 1.2). However, SOAP and WSDL are slower to use, as compared to REST [22]; so cloud providers prefer to use REST in their cloud access APIs. The calls of RESTful APIs do not require XML format and are almost as simple as the basic methods of the HTTP protocol.

XMPP (Jabber) is one of the widely used standards to send and receive *instant messages* from one computing device (typically a laptop, tablet or smartphone) to another. The standard is based on using the XML format to represent *instant messages*, which corresponds well to the spirit and standards of the Web. The XMPP protocol plays a central role in the InterCloud standard [21]: according to this draft standard, the clouds in the near future should communicate and configure their interaction using XMPP. However, to my mind XMPP-based style of cloud interaction may work slow (especially when processing big data) because of its verbosity caused by using XML.

SSL (Secure Socket Layer) is a standard of the secure use of sockets, which is especially important to securely transfer confidential information (such as people names, credit card numbers, mobile phone numbers, and so on) via the Web in encrypted form. The SSL standard is used in the *https* protocol.

AJAX (Asynchronous JavaScript and XML) is a standard to efficiently use Web browsers when the number of the Web pages and possible redirections from one to the other may be big. Cloud computing is based on very intensive use of Web browsers, so using AJAX on the client side can dramatically improve the Web connection performance. The AJAX standard and technology are based on the use of JavaScript and XML to reduce the amount of redirections between Web pages. AJAX implementation uses the idea for preliminary grouping of related sets of Web pages that are likely to be used together, and to transfer such a group via the Web by one GET command, instead of spending dozens of GETs for each individual page. The usability of AJAX for large Web applications can be confirmed by my own experience of developing commercial Web software products.

HTML 5 is the latest version of the hypertext markup language used on the Web, finally standardized in 2014. This new version is especially important for cloud computing, due to a number of new features of HTML 5: *offline clients* (including *offline databases*) used in cloud sessions; support of the use from *smartphones*; extended support to represent *multimedia information* (e.g., the new <video> and <audio> tags). These new features of HTML allow the users to refer to it as a special new version of HTML for cloud computing. HTML 5 is also considered as a potential candidate for cross-platform mobile applications. HTML 5 features were designed with considerations of being able to run on mobile devices (smartphones or PDAs) and on tablets. Also, the *Document Object Model* (*DOM*) that allows to represent documents as objects became an inherent part of HTML 5 specification (with previous versions of HTML, it was used just as some extension). So HTML 5 is suitable for use in cloud computing with mobile devices.

OMF (Open Media Framework) is a standard used in cloud computing for representing and transferring multimedia files, for example, video and audio.

OVF (Open Virtualization Format, or *Open Virtual Machine Format)* is an open standard for organization of *virtual machines* that play such a key role in cloud computing. The first version of the standard was developed by Microsoft, HP, Dell, IBM, and VMware in 2007, before the cloud era. The current version of the standard, OVF 2.0, accepted by the *Distributed Management Task Force* (*DMTF),* is targeted at cloud computing. The standard defines the structure of an *OVF package* that contains information on the packaged virtual machines. The OVF package contains an *OVF descriptor* – an XML file that describes the packaged virtual machine. The OVF package also contains *disk images* of the virtual machine, and may contain *certificate files* and other auxiliary files. The OVF format is approved by many software companies. For example, it is used in *Microsoft System Center Virtual Machine Manager*, in *IBM Smart Cloud*, and in *Oracle VM*.

Virtual Hard Disk (VHD) is a file format and standard used by Microsoft for representing virtual hard disks. The format was used since 2003 in *Microsoft Virtual PC* – the virtualization software product, a predecessor of *Microsoft Hyper-V (hypervisor)*. Currently the VHD format is used in Microsoft Azure cloud for representing virtual hard disks in Azure virtual machines, and for representing large multimedia files in Azure multimedia services.

REST (Representational State Transfer, see also Section 1.3 above) is a standard used in cloud computing to efficiently organize Web cloud services. As mentioned before, with such standard, information on the state of the Web service is passed via the arguments and results of a Web method. Also, Web methods are called asynchronously. So the REST standard is a good basis for efficient use of cloud services. The advantages of REST for cloud computing are as follows [22]:

- REST uses a standard HTTP protocol without additional messaging layers that would make it more "heavyweight."
- REST uses URI addresses to access Web (cloud) resources.
- REST uses the standard set of HTTP operations on Web resources: *GET, POST, PUT, DELETE, and HEAD.*
- RESTful Web services are fully *stateless*, that is, they do not explicitly keep information on their state. This can be tested by restarting the cloud server and checking its availability using REST APIs.
- RESTful Web services support *caching* infrastructure using HTTP GET method (for most servers). This can improve the performance if the data the RESTful Web service returns is not changed frequently and is not dynamic in nature. For example, RESTful services are well suitable to communicate to a cloud database, which is not too big and which is not at generation stage. For example, using RESTful services to get from the cloud or transfer to the cloud some *big data* may appear not so efficient. The issues of using the cloud with big data are discussed in Ref [23] and will be considered later in Chapter 4.
- The RESTful service producer and service consumer need to keep a common understanding of the context as well as the content being passed along, since there is no standard set of rules to describe the RESTful Web services interface.
- REST is especially useful for restricted-profile devices such as smartphones and PDAs, for which the overhead of additional parameters such as headers and other SOAP elements are less.
- RESTful services are easy to integrate with the existing Web sites and are exposed with XML so that the HTML pages can consume the same with ease. There is no need to refactor the existing Web site architecture. This increases the productivity of software developers, since they will not have to rewrite everything from scratch and just need to add the existing functionality.

REST-based implementation is simpler, as compared to SOAP and WSDL.

1.12   HOW THE CLOUDS COME TRUE: ORGANIZATION OF DATACENTERS AND CLOUD HARDWARE

Now let us try to understand the specifics of cloud datacenters organization – how the clouds come true and how a cloud datacenter is organized.

The concept of *datacenter*, as a special facility providing computing, storage, and networking services, appeared long ago, in the 1980s, since the needs of IT industry required aggregation of big computing resources. For example, Microsoft founded its first datacenter in 1989 in Redmond, Washington [24]. Very large datacenters are organized by many other big companies, for example, by Google and Facebook.

The question is how the *cloud* datacenters are different from the others, for example, from an IT enterprise-level datacenter belonging to some company? The distinction is in their *scale*. Cloud computing required a scalability that could hardly be imagined before. According to [24], an IT enterprise-level datacenter provides 10,000 seats (workplaces), whereas a cloud-level datacenter should provide 1,000,000 (a million) seats (workplaces) that can be geographically distributed worldwide. When you use, for example, the Microsoft Azure cloud, you can make your choice of placing your cloud service at any datacenter from the Washington state of the United States to Western Europe or Middle Asia. The order of magnitude of the number of computer servers in a typical public cloud datacenter can be one million. Similar is the situation with the public clouds provided by the other companies.

With such a giant number of computers, a different approach to availability and reliability of servers in a cloud datacenter should be used [24].

A classical approach to measuring reliability is the *Mean Time between Failures (MTBF)* – an average period of time between the subsequent failures of a hardware system (e.g., a server). However, with cloud-scale datacenters, this approach is impractical, since the sheer amount of hardware in cloud datacenters inevitably leads to possible hardware failures at each moment. So, the typical classical requirement of 99.9–100% availability of any server (with million servers running at a time) is not realistic. With the traditional approach of datacenter organization, it is not easy to quickly switch a software service to another, not faulty, hardware server.

So, yet another strategy is taken in cloud datacenters, based on another quantitative measure – *Mean Time to Recover (MTTR)*. This quantity characterizes the average time for a cloud datacenter to recover from a hardware failure. The responsibility of choosing another suitable server to switch a software service from a faulty server to an up-and-running one is taken by the specialized software. For example, in Microsoft Azure cloud, such operations are performed by *Fabric Controller*, a stateful software application that manages software services and distributes them between the hardware servers.

So, the principle of cloud datacenter organization, instead of enabling high *reliability*, is to enable high *resilience* – the ability to quickly recover from hardware failures.

Another common issue in cloud datacenters is their big power consumption. In this relation, the following quantitative measure is used to estimate the efficiency of power use – *Power Usage Effectiveness (PUE)*. It is calculated as the ratio of the *total facility power* to *IT equipment power*. The ideal value is 1.0, which is actually never reached. A typical datacenter in the United States has a PUE of 2.0 [24]. State-of-the-art datacenters now have PUEs of 1.12–1.2, with the industry average being 1.8 [25].

The following basic concepts are used to describe hardware in modern datacenters.

Rack is a group of related equipment (e.g., servers, telecommunication hardware) mounted in a single shelf. Rack is a typical way of organizing servers in large datacenters. A unit of rack height measurement is referred to as *U* (acronym for *Unit*). A 1 U rack is typically 19-inch (482.6 mm) or 23-inch (584.2 mm) high.

Blade server "is a stripped down server computer with a modular design optimized to minimize the use of physical space and energy. Whereas a standard rack-mount server can function with (at least) a power cord and network cable, blade servers have many components removed to minimize power consumption and other considerations, while still having all the functional components to be considered a computer" [26].

To mount racks together and to enable power supply and cooling for their hardware components, *chassis* are used. For example, in Microsoft cloud datacenters, 12 U-sized chassis are used, of original Microsoft design. Each of the 12 U chassis can accommodate up to 24 server blades – either *compute* or *storage*. The chassis enable efficient sharing of resources by multiple server nodes.

From higher level viewpoint, datacenters can be regarded as collections of hardware *clusters*. A cluster, generally speaking, is a group of tightly coupled computers working together as a single system. In a cloud datacenter, a cluster is a primary unit of hardware organization. In a Microsoft cloud datacenter, for example, each cluster consists of 20 racks, with a total of approximately 1000 rack-mounted blade servers (also called *nodes*). A cluster is a unit of fault isolation.

Each cluster is controlled by special software – *Fabric Controller*. For better availability, the Fabric Controller runs in five instances for each cluster. The role of the Fabric Controller is twofold: managing datacenter hardware and managing software cloud services. Actually, Fabric Controller is a kernel of the cloud operating system.

More details on Fabric Controller and its functions in Microsoft Azure cloud are provided in Chapter 5.

Detailed description of datacenter architectures is outside the scope of this book. Please see [24] for more details. The very good academic book [27] covers cloud datacenter hardware architecture in its Chapter 7.

1.13 SPECIFICS AND COMPONENTS OF SOFTWARE FOR CLOUD COMPUTING

As we have seen before, cloud computing is a new kind of client–server system. So, both client-side software and server-side software are used to implement cloud models. The client-side software components participating in cloud computing are as follows.

Cloud client operating systems. It is the operating system that controls the client hardware – a desktop, a tablet, a laptop computer, or a mobile device, such as a smartphone. There are some requirements and limitations for cloud client operating systems, although purely advertising texts on cloud computing are trying to persuade the users that "just an operating system is enough." Informally speaking, a client OS should be "novel enough." For example, it is not possible to use Microsoft Azure cloud with old client operating systems such as Windows XP. For accessing the cloud, it is necessary to use Windows 10, Windows 8/8.1, or Windows 7 with Service Pack 1 on the client computer.

Cloud client Web browsers and rich client support plug-ins. As well as the client operating systems, the client Web browsers used by cloud clients should be new enough. For example, to access Microsoft Azure cloud, the version of Internet Explorer should be 11 or newer (at the moment of writing the book, March 2015). Older versions of the browser do not support cloud communication. Moreover, the client browser should have a special plug-in installed to enable rich client Web interface. This requirement is suggested to the cloud client during the first attempt at accessing the cloud. For the Internet Explorer browser, the kind of plug-in to be installed is *Microsoft Silverlight*.

Developer clients' software tools and platforms for developing cloud services. Most cloud clients act purely as "end users" since they consume ready-to-use cloud services developed by cloud providers or third-party developer companies, already published in the cloud. But there are many active cloud users, especially students and researchers, who would like to extend the cloud by their own cloud services. Such users should take into account that the requirements of client computers, and the software to be used for cloud services *development* are much higher than just for ordinary cloud clients. The cloud stimulates creative activity of the users, due to the fact that it frees the users from mundane routine work. But to develop cloud services is a much more complicated work than to consume them. First, the client operating system must be novel enough to support cloud services. For example, Solaris 11, the new OS by Oracle, satisfies this requirement, since it is the first version of the Oracle OS to contain cloud computing support. As for Microsoft operating systems, only the latest OS – Windows 10, Windows 8 or Windows 8.1, or the enhanced version of the previous OS – Windows 7 with Service Pack 1 – are suitable for developing for the cloud. Second, to develop cloud services, there should be a suitable state-of-the-art *IDE* [7] based on a trustworthy underlying software platform. This IDE with the underlying software platform should support development of cloud Web services satisfying modern standards (such as REST or WSDL) and the principles of trustworthy computing [1]. A cloud service, as a server-side code, should be secure (resilient to attacks) and reliable (in particular, support type-safe data processing – the type of each object should be known and recognizable at runtime; there should be no memory leaks, etc.), and should guarantee the privacy of information processed. Not every software platform and programming language satisfies these requirements. For example, the C language is not suitable for cloud service development, since many of its inherent features, such as arbitrary casting from one type to another, contradict the principles of trustworthy computing and may cause hardly recognizable bugs and even potential security vulnerabilities. Actually, the most suitable software platforms for developing cloud services are Java and .NET. For example, .NET is the basic platform used for implementation of Microsoft Azure cloud. This platform should also be used for developing new cloud services for Microsoft Azure. The IDE most suitable for this purpose is Microsoft Visual Studio, more exactly, its latest version at the moment of writing the book – *Visual Studio 2013, update 3* [7]. This version supports special kinds of projects (solutions) for cloud services development – *Windows Azure Projects* – and for developing mobile services and mobile applications that can communicate to mobile services published in the cloud. Also, the *Windows Azure SDK* should be installed on your computer. Windows Azure SDK is not included into Visual Studio by default; it should be installed separately. This is just an example illustrating the amount of preliminary work that should be done to make your client computer a suitable tool not only for using the cloud but also for extending it by new cloud services. Examples of working cloud services for Microsoft Azure developed with Visual Studio are given in the Appendix.

Similarly, to develop cloud services for another company's cloud – Oracle Java Cloud – the Java language and platform should be used, with the corresponding IDE from Oracle – *NetBeans* [28]. A plug-in to NetBeans should be installed that supports special kinds of projects for cloud services development in Java. Similarly to Azure, the *Oracle Java Cloud Service SDK* should be installed and used together with NetBeans to develop cloud services for Java cloud.

The server-side software for cloud computing is even more complicated, as shown below.

***Cloud server-side operating system(s)*.** The operating systems used on the computers in a cloud datacenter. The server-side operating systems, as well as the server-side hardware, are provisioned by the cloud provider company. For example, in Microsoft cloud datacenters that support Microsoft Azure cloud, the latest server-side operating system used is *Windows Server 2012 Release 2* that supports large-scale computing and virtualization. Also, Microsoft uses some dialects of Linux as server-side OS, such as Ubuntu and SUSE. In Oracle datacenters supporting Oracle cloud, *Solaris 11* is used as server-side OS, positioned as the first Oracle operating system supporting the cloud. In IBM datacenters supporting IBM cloud, *z* operating system is used as the server-side OS.

***Host and guest operating systems*.** One of the most attractive features of cloud computing, in accordance to the IaaS cloud model, is an opportunity to create and use a *virtual machine* or a set of virtual machines. The virtual machine available in the cloud can have an operating system different from the server-side OS used in the datacenter. The following terms are used to refer to those operating systems. *Host operating system* is the operating system used on real machines of the datacenter. *Guest operating system* is the operating system running on the virtual machine. For example, in Microsoft Azure cloud, it is possible to create and use a virtual machine whose guest operating system can be Windows 2012 R2 (with some slight changes, as compared to Windows 2012 R2 host OS), Windows 8.x, Windows 7.x, Linux Ubuntu, Linux SUSE, Oracle Solaris 11, and a number of others.

***Hypervisors*.** To control virtual machines created and used in the cloud, a special software component is used, referred to as *hypervisor.* The term hypervisor (as hardware virtualization component) is being used from the 1970s when the first hypervisors were implemented in hardware. Now, different companies use different hypervisors in their cloud datacenters. For example, Microsoft uses *Hyper-V* hypervisor as part of their Windows Server 2012 R2 operating system. This hypervisor can also be installed on a machine running, for example, Windows 8. The predecessor of Hyper-V developed in 2007 was called *Microsoft Virtual* PC. Another widely used hypervisor is *vSphere* by VMWare. IBM uses in its cloud datacenters the *WebSphere* infrastructure solutions to support virtualization.

Cloud management middleware. Software of this special kind is used in cloud datacenters to fulfill the following functions:

- Provisioning and de-provisioning hardware and software components; replacing the faulty components in the total cloud datacenter configuration
- Monitoring hardware components and software services
- Load balancing, that is, distributing cloud services between the machines in the cloud datacenter or in different datacenters supporting the same cloud
- Metering cloud usage, tracking costs, and billing.

For example, in IBM cloud datacenters, the *Tivoli* system software [29] is used as cloud management middleware. Tivoli Systems was a company acquired by IBM who developed this software product. It includes a storage manager, workload scheduler, network endpoint manager, automation manager, and a configuration and change management database.

In Microsoft practice, several kinds of software products are used as cloud management middleware. The above-mentioned Fabric Controller is an internal cloud software component that controls hardware clusters and blades, and also manages software cloud services, enabling basic hardware and software availability, reliability, and resilience. Also, *Microsoft System Center* is used in various control functions, with the following components: *Configuration Manager, Virtual Machine Manager, Mobile Device Manager, Operations Manager, Capacity Planner, Data Protection Manager*.

1.14   CLOUD COMPUTING-RELATED TRENDS, ACTIVITIES, AND RESOURCES

There is a great, rapidly emerging interest among IT specialists in cloud computing. To meet this growing interest, lots of cloud computing communities and conferences are organized, and more and more cloud computing journals are founded each year.

The most popular cloud computing journal is the *IEEE Transactions on Cloud Computing* [30]. Its advantage over many other cloud publications is the deep scientific analysis of cloud issues in the papers of this journal. To understand the specifics of this journal and its scope, let us consider the current call for papers for the oncoming special issues of the journal:

- Many-task computing in the cloud
- Cloud security engineering
- Mobile clouds.

Another IEEE publication – *IEEE Computer Magazine* [31] – pays much attention to cloud computing in the section referred to as *Cloud Cover,* although it covers the more general scope of themes. It contains small papers on challenges and news of cloud computing. For example, the paper [23] poses a serious issue of efficiency of using big data with the current clouds.

Yet another interesting new journal on cloud computing is the *Journal of Cloud Computing: Advances, Systems and Applications (JOCCASA).* This is a *Springer Open Journal.* The site of the journal is available at [32]. The journal publishes research articles on cloud computing accessible at no cost.

One of the leading journals in the field is the *International Journal on Cloud Computing* [33]. The journal publishes extended versions of papers from prestigious conferences on cloud computing, for example, from IEEE CLOUD.

What also deserves the readers' attention is the SYS-CON company's *Cloud Computing Journal* [34]. This company already publishes a number of the other software developers' style journals – such as *Java Developer Journal* and *.NET Developer Journal* (the latter journal has published five of my articles on .NET development and teaching and on aspect-oriented programming). Now they have founded their own cloud computing journal, which looks very promising.

Cloud computing communities. The largest of them is probably the *IEEE Cloud Computing Community* [35]. Membership in this community is recommended to any IT professional with interest in cloud computing. The community provides a lot of information by email (cloud news). Membership in this community is free. The community has established the IEEE portal on cloud computing [36]. The portal is a rich collection of cloud computing information on the following topics:

- Cloud computing conferences
- Cloud computing education (courses) and careers
- Cloud computing publications (especially IEEE journals)
- Cloud computing standards, including two new IEEE standards related to *Intercloud* and *Cloud Profiles* (now existing in the form of working drafts)
- Special section on the *InterCloud TestBed* international project aimed at cloud interoperability.

There are also cloud computing communities organized by big industrial companies – cloud providers.

For example, the *IBM Cloud Computing Community* portal is available at [37]. It offers considerable information on IBM cloud – webinars, demonstrations, news feeds, and publications.

The *Oracle Cloud Computing Community* portal [38] offers interesting cloud forums, podcasts, and blogs.

The *Microsoft Azure in Education* [39] portal publishes many educational resources on cloud computing and Microsoft Azure. They offer a number of educational courses on Microsoft Azure on its features and parts, for example, virtual machines, mobile services, and cloud services. Also, they have launched the

Microsoft Azure Educator Grant program. As a result, any university educator who teaches Azure in his or her course can apply for free access to Microsoft Azure cloud for the duration of the course, typically, one semester, for him (her) in person and for the students taking the course. This is a great opportunity to try the Azure cloud in action, to organize hands-on labs on it, and to develop a term or graduate student project based on Microsoft Azure. I have been one of the grateful participants of this program since 2011. Thanks a lot to Microsoft Research for this opportunity!

Conferences on cloud computing. As for the conferences and exhibitions on cloud computing, hundreds of them are held worldwide every month, almost every week, in any region of the world. Most famous cloud conferences in scientific research style are organized by IEEE. The leading one is the annual *IEEE CLOUD* conference. The portal of the IEEE CLOUD 2014 is available at [40]. The 2014 IEEE seventh International Conference on Cloud Computing (CLOUD 2014) is the leading theme conference for modeling, developing, publishing, monitoring, managing, and delivering *XaaS* (everything as a service) in the context of various types of cloud environments. This is a traditional scientific research multitrack conference. Extended versions of the accepted papers are published in leading cloud computing journals such as *IEEE Transactions on Cloud Computing*.

The Microsoft TechEd (*technical education*) conferences attract special interest. They are organized annually in each major region, for example, TechEd Europe, TechEd America, and TechEd Asia. These conferences include many deep technical talks on various subjects related to Microsoft technologies, and other Microsoft partner companies – Intel, HP, and so on. Hundreds of talks at TechEd conferences are devoted to the Microsoft Azure cloud platform and the related software products – Windows System Center, Windows Intune, and Visual Studio with its support of developing cloud services. The materials of the latest of TechEd Europe 2014 are published in [41]. I participated in Microsoft TechEd Europe 2013 in Madrid, which was very impressive, because of its wide scope, number of talks, and number of participants. The number of participants was about 3,600 and there were several hundred talks. Among the lecturers at the conference were such famous cloud experts as Mark Russinovich and Mark Minasi from Microsoft. I consider the latest TechEd conferences, for the first turn, a great school of cloud computing, though many other subjects have been covered at those conferences. In general, the materials of TechEd conferences are well suited as a teaching resource at universities, for courses, seminars, and hand-on labs on cloud computing.

A very helpful series of conferences similar to TechEd is organized by Microsoft Russia [42]. Those conferences are held on the same high technical level as the TechEd conferences. Technical talks are given by young Microsoft evangelists, both from Russia and from other countries. The latest such event was called "The Cloud in Russia" [43] and was organized by Microsoft Russia with very good quality presentations made by Microsoft Russia evangelists. I was watching this conference online for several hours with great pleasure, and there was much information helpful to me as a cloud expert. The site [43] contains video materials of the conference. I highly recommend them not only for my students but also for every IT student and specialist interested in Microsoft Azure (English translation is available).

Educational resources on cloud computing. There are a lot of educational resources on cloud computing. Besides books such as [8–12] discussed in the introduction, there are hundreds of other cloud computing books, white papers, help and support Web pages, e-books, and other educational resources issued by academics and by public cloud provider companies.

Surely each of the companies teaches its own cloud approach, so it is hardly possible to use such material as "independent" on cloud computing. But they contain short general introductions about cloud computing, what it is, and what the basic SaaS, PaaS, and IaaS approaches to cloud services model are. One of the very good examples of such free e-books is the book [44] on Microsoft Azure Fundamentals published online in 2014 by Microsoft Press. Another good source of educational and reference information on Microsoft Azure is *Microsoft Developer's Network* (*MSDN*) Web pages. They are numerous and the user can find information on any aspect of the Azure cloud. MSDN pages are greatly suitable for quick reference but not so comfortable for learning, because of the scattering of pieces of the valuable material into hundreds of small pages, which is typical of the hypertext approach.

To compare Microsoft's approach on cloud educational resources to those by other companies, let us consider the approach by Oracle. The Oracle cloud e-books portal [45] contains dozens of small e-books on various aspects of Oracle cloud, for example, architecture of the cloud portal, running Java Enterprise applications in the cloud, and so on. Each of the e-books is about 12–15 pages, so they are more suitable to give general information and impression on the corresponding Oracle cloud aspect than for deep diving into details. Some of the e-books are written in purely advertising style. In comparison, Microsoft's Azure fundamentals book [44] has 246 pages, and its style is quite suitable both for self-education and for organizing hand-on labs.

However, there are very good introductory cloud books by Oracle [46–48] written by M. Wessler and published by John Wiley & Sons in "Oracle special edition" series. Those books cover the basics of Oracle cloud [46], Oracle enterprise cloud architectures [47], and Oracle approach to virtualization [48]. The books can be used as generals tutorial on cloud computing, and as overview of principles of Oracle cloud architecture in particular. Especially valuable are the section on cloud management in [46], and the description of Oracle virtualization tools in [48].

A good example of the right approach to technical education in the cloud area is demonstrated by IBM. The free e-book [49] has 146 pages, is published online in July 2014, and is a good introduction to general concepts of cloud computing and to IBM cloud approach.

Also freely downloadable are educational e-books on HP cloud. HP offers a rich collection of commercial books [50] on HP cloud published by HP press. One such HP cloud book is *HP ATP – Data Center and Cloud and HP ASE – Data Center and Cloud Architect Official Certification Study Guide*, HP Press, 2014, by Pluta Ch., 532 pp. This book provides material for certification exam on cloud computing and HP cloud. To my knowledge, such cloud computing books are unique.

As for educational resources on Google cloud, there is a good new book [51] on Google Compute Engine, the Google cloud platform. It is a tutorial and can be used for self-education on cloud computing and Google cloud platform.

Cloud computing universities. A helpful site on cloud computing is *Cloud Computing Wire* [52]. It publishes various kinds of information on cloud computing and surely deserves subscribing to their weekly newsletter. Especially interesting for IT students is the list of *cloud computing universities* [52]. It currently contains 44 American universities offering courses on cloud computing. Among them are Harvard, Stanford, Berkeley, Carnegie-Mellon, and some other leading universities in the United States. Hopefully there will appear similar European portals on "cloud computing universities." As for our St. Petersburg University, I think we deserve to be added to this list of cloud computing universities, due to my above-mentioned publications – Internet courses and books [3–7] on cloud computing, and due to our 5-year experience of teaching students cloud computing. I hope this book will increase the popularity of our school of cloud computing, both teaching and research in this area.

How to organize cloud computing education. Surely books, courses, and hand-on labs on cloud computing are very helpful and just necessary for any university. Cloud computing should be an important part of university education, both at bachelor and masters levels. However, I was a bit surprised when I found information on some European universities offering the MS degree in cloud computing. As an experienced university professor in IT area, I consider cloud computing to be a very important part of IT but not suitable for issuing MS diplomas in that area. Actually, cloud computing is just one of the possible approaches to organizing computing resources, quite popular at the current moment. But cloud computing-oriented education and diplomas is to my mind too narrow an approach. A university graduate in IT area should be more universally educated, and should also know many important other modern parts of IT, such as trustworthy computing, scientific computing, mobile computing, and so on. So I think MS in Informatics, Computer Science, Software Engineering, or Information Technologies are more suitable MS university degrees than, for example, an MS degree on cloud computing, as well as on compilers, operating systems, and databases.

I hope Chapter 2 will be helpful to get more educational and practical information on a number of popular cloud platforms.

EXERCISES TO CHAPTER 1

E1.1 Please list the modern kinds of software you know, and explain the meaning and role of each of them.

E1.2 What is the essence of the client–server paradigm and what kind of servers in local networks do you know?

E1.3 What software platforms are used for developing Web applications?

E1.4 What are the specific issues and features of mobile applications?

E1.5 What kind of software is middleware and for which purposes is it used?

E1.6 What are the main goals of software for virtualization?

E1.7 Why are software tools for knowledge management so popular now, and which knowledge management toolkits do you know?

E1.8   Please formulate the most characteristic features of modern software.

E1.9   Please provide a definition of client in the client–server paradigm.

E1.10   Please provide a definition of server in the client–server paradigm.

E1.11   What is a thin client and what kind of user interface does it consume?

E1.12   What is a rich client and what are its advantages over a thin client?

E1.13   What is a layer in software architecture?

E1.14   What is an abstraction layer in software architecture?

E1.15   What is a vertical cut (or aspect) in software architecture?

E1.16   What is a tier in software architecture? Please give some examples of typical tiers.

E1.17   What is multitier architecture?

E1.18   What is multitenant architecture?

E1.19   What are the main principles of SOAs?

E1.20   What is the contract of a service?

E1.21   What is a Web method of a service?

E1.22   Is the implementation platform of a service significant to its consumer in the SOA model?

E1.23   Please list the most popular standards for implementation of a software service.

E1.24   Please define the main principles of the WSDL standard.

E1.25   Please define the main principles of the REST standard. Why do you think cloud providers prefer to provision REST APIs for their cloud services, rather than WSDL APIs?

E1.26   Which popular Web site development tools and Web sites provide support for SOA?

E1.26   What is SaaS? What was the original meaning of this term and which meaning has it acquired now, due to cloud computing?

E1.27   Please give a definition of cloud computing and your own understanding of this term.

E1.28   What kind of user interface does a cloud client use?

E1.29   Are any software installations on a cloud client computer necessary to use the cloud? What are the minimal requirements to cloud client computers?

E1.30   What is a cloud datacenter?

E1.31   What kinds of clouds do you know?

E1.32   What is a public cloud?

E1.33   What is a private cloud?

E1.34   What is a hybrid cloud?

E1.35   What is a community cloud?

E1.36   Please give examples of free public cloud services and sites. Practice in their use (e.g., Windows Live).

E1.37 Please describe the major shortcomings and issues of the cloud model, in your own opinion.

E1.38 Please list the main components of the cloud.

E1.39 What is the cloud management portal? Please give examples of the URL addresses of cloud management portals you know and use.

E1.40 Please list all kinds of "-as-a-Service" cloud servicing models you remember, and explain their meanings and functionalities.

E1.41 What are architectural layers of the cloud? What are their meanings and roles?

E1.42 What kind of reference is used in cloud computing to address a cloud service?

E1.43 What are the main roles of people participating in cloud computing?

E1.44 Which organizations developed standards for cloud computing?

E1.45 What is InterCloud?

E1.46 Please define the main methods of the HTTP protocol used in cloud computing.

E1.47 Please explain how XML is used in cloud computing.

E1.48 What is XMPP protocol and how is it used (or planned to be used) in cloud computing?

E1.49 What is SSL and what is its meaning for Web in general and for cloud computing in particular?

E1.50 What is AJAX and how does it help optimize access to the cloud?

E1.51 What is HTML 5 and which of its features are well suitable for cloud computing?

E1.52 What is OMF and how is it used in cloud computing?

E1.53 What is Open OVF and how is it used in cloud computing?

E1.54 What is VHD format and how does Microsoft use it in its Azure cloud?

E1.55 What is REST and what are its advantages over the other standards (SOAP and WSDL) for use in cloud computing?

E1.56 What is a cloud datacenter and in which respects is it different from ordinary IT enterprise level datacenter?

E1.57 What is the classical approach (MTBF) to reliability of technical systems and its quantitative measurement?

E1.58 What kind of approach to reliability and resilience (MTTR) is used for cloud datacenters to take into account their specifics?

E1.59 What kind of measure of the efficiency of electric power consuming is used for datacenters?

E1.60 What is rack in datacenters and what units are used for its size measurement?

E1.61 What is blade server in datacenters and what is its difference from ordinary server?

E1.62 What is chassis and how is it used in datacenters?

E1.63 What is cluster and which role does it play in cloud datacenters?

E1.64 What is Fabric Controller and what kind of functions does it perform in Microsoft Azure cloud datacenters?

E1.65 What kind of requirements apply to cloud client operating systems?

E1.66 How should the cloud client browsers be enhanced to use rich client Web interface? Please give concrete examples.

E1.67 What kinds of software tools, including IDEs, should be used for developing cloud services?

E1.68 Which IDE and in which version is recommended to use for Microsoft Azure cloud services development? Which software platform is recommended for such kind of development?

E1.69 Is the Visual Studio itself enough for cloud services development or is any extra software tools installation needed for that purpose?

E1.70 Which language, software platform, and IDE are recommended for Oracle cloud services development?

E1.71 Is the C programming language recommended for cloud services development? Why not?

E1.72 Which server-side operating systems are used in cloud datacenters by major public cloud providers?

E1.73 Please provide definitions for host operating system and guest operating system.

E1.74 What is hypervisor, which role does it play in cloud datacenter, and which hypervisors are used by major cloud providers?

E1.75 What kinds of cloud management middleware are used in cloud datacenters and which functions do they perform?

E1.76 Please list the cloud computing journals you know.

E1.77 Please list the cloud computing communities you know.

E1.78 Please list the cloud computing conferences you know and describe your impressions of them if you have attended such conferences.

E1.79 Which educational resources on the cloud offer major cloud providers?

E1.80 Which universities are included in the list of cloud computing universities? Is your university on this list?

2

PLATFORMS OF CLOUD COMPUTING

2.1 A VARIETY OF CLOUD PLATFORMS: THE FIRST IMPRESSION

The leading cloud providers – Amazon, Microsoft, IBM, Oracle, Google, HP, and so on – enable a really overwhelming variety of cloud platforms and services. Let us consider some of them at a glance as "first impression," which is very important for a cloud user, since a good first impression is a major part of the trustworthiness intuition of a cloud platform.

Microsoft Azure cloud [53, 54] is quite familiar to me since 2011 and I have been tracking its progress for 4 years. Microsoft, as its cloud provider, offers a free 1 month cloud trial for everybody, and can provide as a grant a longer free cloud access – 1 year for a university course educator on cloud computing, and one semester for the course students. The Azure cloud offers a comfortable and reliable cloud management portal, which allows the user to create Web sites, virtual machines, cloud services, mobile services, virtual networks, active directories, cloud databases, and many other things using a unified-style self-evident user interface. A good-quality help is provided. The cloud user is authenticated using a single login and password for all kinds of cloud services. The cloud offers IaaS, PaaS, NaaS, and some other new kinds of cloud servicing, for example, machine learning in the cloud. The current version of the cloud works reliably, comfortably, and fast enough. More details of this are given in Chapter 5.

The first impressions of Amazon AWS (Amazon Web Services) cloud [55] are very positive. Amazon offers free access to its cloud for 1 year, which is probably the most comfortable free use condition for any public cloud available. On creating a free cloud account, a bit surprising is the phone call-based cloud user identification, wherein you enter your PIN code. Then, the cloud offers the initial set of user documentation in

Trustworthy Cloud Computing, First Edition. Vladimir O. Safonov.
© 2016 John Wiley & Sons, Inc. Published 2016 by John Wiley & Sons, Inc.

several formats. It is very easy to create a virtual machine from the proposed gallery (in IaaS style) and to choose and deploy a platform for your application (I tried Java GlassFish). The user interface is comfortable enough, though more guidance would be desirable at the initial usage period. The cloud user account is prepared quickly but not momentarily, so during a short initial period (about an hour) the user can receive warning messages that he/she is not fully registered. After that, you can feel the comfort of the Amazon AWS cloud. See Section 2.2.

The Oracle cloud [56] initially looks solid, with lots of choices for the cloud user – to use many kinds of clouds and cloud services. A free cloud user account is offered for 1 month. Not so comfortable for a user is the decentralization of cloud resources. Instead of using a single cloud management portal for everything, as in Microsoft Azure or in Amazon AWS, the user has to sign up to each cloud service separately – Java cloud, SaaS applications, cloud database, and so on. The process of preparing and registering a free cloud user account from Oracle takes about 2 days (as opposed to Microsoft Azure and Amazon AWS). Not quite comfortable is the concept of the identification domain name, which, in addition to user login and password, is required for authentication. The Oracle cloud actually requires two kinds of logging in – one to the user account and the other to the user-assigned cloud services. They require different credentials for authentication, and I (at the initial trial period) experienced problems with those different logins. Actually, to access any cloud service, the Oracle cloud user has to log in to it separately. Hopefully Oracle will change its cloud user authentication mechanism and will make it simpler, as well as implement a single cloud management portal accessible with a single login and password. See more details in Section 2.4.

As for using a cloud version of the Oracle DBMS, the initial video demo on the Oracle cloud site by Larry Ellison recommends importing to the cloud an on-premises (local) database. It is a good feature but I think it would be comfortable for many cloud consumers to use an interactive cloud constructor for relational databases, and a cloud version of SQL queries interpreter to quickly try the Oracle database in the cloud, similar to what is implemented in Microsoft Azure cloud as part of the SQL Azure cloud DBMS. This is just a recommendation for future versions of the Oracle cloud.

Yet another issue related to using Oracle cloud is that it does not like the latest version of Internet Explorer (11.0). The cloud complains that the browser is incompatible and you have to switch, for example, to the latest Google Chrome, which works well with Oracle cloud. It is just a tip for Oracle cloud beginners, non-documented by Oracle.

IBM Cloud [57] offers a free cloud trial in the form of provisioning a virtual cloud server from SoftLayer, an IBM company, for 1 month. The cloud user should make a choice of a datacenter and operating system for the server. The choice of operating systems is not so wide – only Linux Debian, CentOS, and Vyatta – as compared to Microsoft Azure and Amazon AWS, which provide much better choice of operating systems, including Windows and even Solaris OS for virtual machines. So the user might not accept this offer – his intent was just to try the full capability of IBM cloud for 1 month, but he cannot do that. More interesting is the IBM Cloud Marketplace portal [58]. It offers a number of cloud components and services – Cloud Orchestrator, Cloud Managed Services, Personalized Learning, and many others. However, the IBM Cloud Marketplace portal does not offer free trials and, instead, asks the user to contact the cloud provider, which is not so comfortable.

Another kind of IBM free cloud trial is IBM Bluemix, from IBM Ireland. Registration for a free trial takes 1 day, and the account activation email does not come in a moment. After registering, the IBM Bluemix cloud works well. First impression on Bluemix cloud is that it is a very interesting and well-documented cloud infrastructure. Documentation is provided online in the cloud. Very comfortable is a set of PaaS services that allows the cloud users to develop in the cloud and launch an application on one of the platforms offered, for example, Java, iOS, and Node.js. For example, a starter Web application in liberty for Java cloud toolkit is created and deployed at once. There are tools for pushing a Java application into the cloud. Everything is very attractive. Also, in IBM Bluemix cloud there is a virtual machines service in the beta stage (requiring a separate subscription). The cloud providers have promised to organize it shortly. More details in Section 2.3.

The Hewlett-Packard Helion public cloud is available for free for 3 months. There are some initial important details the user should know in advance. First, credit card information is required and checked. Second, HP checks the identity of the user and his data by a voice phone call during which they verify the user's address, email, and the four last digits of the credit card (everything by voice). It is a bit surprising. When the cloud account is activated, the user logs in to the public cloud (named Helion) in which no cloud services are started by default. The user has to explicitly choose which cloud services and in which datacenter to start. This is a little unexpected, comparing this style to Microsoft Azure cloud where such information is less explicit. I guess managing cloud services is implemented in such "minimalist" style to save the user's money, to avoid payment for unnecessary services. When activated, services appear to be reliable and fast. For example, it takes a couple of clicks to create a cloud MySQL database and a cloud private network. There is a very good collection of images for many kinds of operating systems. What is lacking is online help, which could be really useful, since the terminology is slightly different from the traditional. For example, creating a virtual machine action (one of the most popular cloud services) is not explicitly mentioned and the beginner user has to guess where to find it. An initial collection of cloud brochures or books, available directly from the cloud, would also be very helpful. The initial impression of the HP cloud is that it is an economically well-organized infrastructure.

There are two other widely known cloud platforms I tried – Kaavo IMOD cloud and Salesforce cloud.

The Kaavo IMOD cloud actually works as a container for accessing various clouds by *other* cloud providers – Amazon AWS and some others. Though it may appear useful in some cases, generally speaking, such kinds of cloud services are redundant. The clouds of each major cloud providers, for example, Amazon, are self-sufficient and do not require any third-party "plug-ins" to use their clouds. In addition, authentication services of the IMOD cloud do not look reliable enough. Sometimes (when logging in from a different machine) the cloud just silently "does not allow" the user who has entered the correct login name and password, without any message. Such cloud behavior is not trustworthy, so I decided not to use it any more, although I am eager to do that. I created two trial accounts for this cloud but none of them worked well.

The Salesforce cloud offers CRM solutions and is very helpful for organizing business. The first impression of this cloud is very positive. The Salesforce cloud is one of the first in cloud computing history. It is intended to support any company or individual business. But there is one initial issue related to the Salesforce cloud that you should keep in mind. The cloud requires a verification code when your login is created on one machine but you are trying to log in to the cloud from a different machine. The verification code is sent to you immediately by email on your request. To my mind, it does not correspond well enough to one of the principles of trustworthy cloud computing – availability of the cloud from any kind of computing devices. But, since the authentication procedure with the verification code should be performed once only for each new machine, this is acceptable. In my previous practice, very careful implementers of some major bank sites use similar verification code practice. As an initial tutorial, the Salesforce cloud offers a guided tour to their cloud. The tour is personalized by the role of the cloud user in his or her company using the cloud – the company owner, the sales representative, and so on. This provides a necessary initial atmosphere of trustworthiness for Salesforce cloud users. A spectacular part of the demo of Salesforce cloud is a tool to import your contacts from Outlook to the cloud, though the importer is loaded to your machine too slowly. It should be more in "cloud style." A nice feature of the Salesforce cloud is the "Company Performance Dashboard," which provides various forms of diagrams to demonstrate the progress of the company.

Hope, at the end of this short "first-impression" introduction into some of the cloud platforms, some helpful practical information was provided for cloud users on the possible initial surprises or advantages the users may feel when using those clouds.

2.2 AMAZON AWS CLOUD PLATFORM – A PIONEER OF CLOUD COMPUTING

As well known, Amazon is one of the world's largest Internet stores, the company that sells over the Internet everything and everywhere. We scientists and educators use Amazon mostly for purchasing other authors' books and selling our own ones. So it is quite understandable that this big online company initiated cloud computing. Another very helpful Amazon product is Kindle e-books reader. Both my Wiley books have been published in Amazon Kindle versions, as well as in paper versions.

Amazon provides free access to their public cloud, referred to as *Amazon AWS* for 1 year, which is perfect – this is the longest trial cloud period I have ever used. Before me, my doctoral students used Amazon cloud for their dissertation projects for a few years and were very satisfied.

The Amazon cloud portal is available at [55]. The structure of the Amazon cloud portal is shown in Figure 2.1.

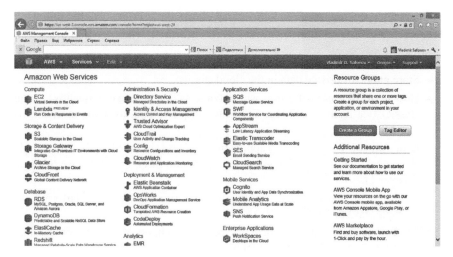

Figure 2.1   The structure of the Amazon Cloud portal.

From the very beginning, from the first impression on Amazon cloud, you feel a comfortable infrastructure, very simple to use. The portal gets access to all cloud features. The first recommended "stop" in Amazon cloud is its documentation, available at [59–64], that should be read before using the cloud. From the typical set of starting documentation, the Amazon Big Data e-book should be emphasized. It demonstrates that Amazon pays a lot of attention to the important problem of efficiently handling big data in the cloud. More details are given subsequently. Please note that big data processing functionality was implemented in major public clouds recently, in the latest versions (e.g., in Microsoft Azure cloud).

Just one example of Amazon cloud comfort is the creation of a virtual machine (also known as *Amazon EC2 instance*). Everything for creating the virtual server is provided by default, so creating a virtual machine really takes a couple of clicks. Comment on the acronyms: *EC2* is the first historical name of the Amazon cloud, the abbreviation for *Amazon Elastic Compute Cloud*.

Especially comfortable is the *Review* functionality: it makes smart suggestions on the user's current cloud configuration. For example, the Review advisor suggested to me that I should enhance the security of my cloud resources.

The user can create a *group* of cloud resources for each project, for his or her convenience.

From any cloud page, the user can return to the main AWS portal page (displaying the list of all services) by pressing the yellow 3D cube image located in the left upper corner of the portal.

The history of AWS cloud [65] started since the early 2000s. In 2003, Amazon started developing its retail cloud infrastructure. The first AWS started in 2004, and in 2006 the first 180,000 users signed up to Amazon cloud. See more details in [65].

Generally speaking, Amazon AWS cloud allows the user to solve the following tasks:

- Create and use cloud virtual machines.
- Store public or private data in the cloud storage.
- Host *static Web sites* (the sites whose contents don't change frequently), using classic-style features: HTML, CSS, JavaScript, without dynamic mechanisms like ASP.NET.
- Host *dynamic Web sites* (Web applications). These sites are based on the classic *three-tier* scheme, including *Web tier, application tier,* and *database tier* (see Chapter 1).
- Develop and launch in the cloud applications running on some platforms, for example, Java or Node.js.
- Process business and scientific data, including support of *big data* processing, considered especially important now.

Amazon Machine Images

The basis of constructing new virtual objects in Amazon cloud is the *Amazon Machine Image (AMI)* [60]. AMI is a template for creating a virtual machine. It contains the operating system, the application server, applications, and the sizes of the computing resources (memory, CPUs, etc.). An AMI should be used to create an *instance* that is running as a virtual server on an Amazon datacenter. This functionality is available in the EC2 cloud, which is accessible from the Amazon AWS portal (see Figure 2.1) in the upper left corner. By clicking EC2, the user enters the starting EC2 page shown in Figure 2.2.

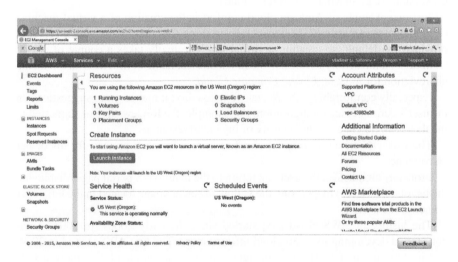

Figure 2.2   The Amazon EC2 starting page.

Virtual Private Clouds

The EC2 page displays the cloud resources of the user. In the upper right corner, the *Supported Platforms* are shown as *VPC*. When the user creates an account in AWS and logs in, a virtual network is created, which is associated with the account, referred to as the *Virtual Private Cloud (VPC)*. The VPC is isolated from the other VPCs. Actually the VPC works as a "cloud sandbox" for the user, which is quite a reasonable decision from cloud security viewpoint. The EC2 page displays the identifier of the VPC created for you.

Creating an Instance

The EC2 cloud offers to launch an instance of a virtual server by pressing the *Launch Instance* blue button. On doing this, the user is switched to the page to choose an AMI. This page is shown in Figure 2.3.

Plenty of AMI configurations are offered, with different kinds of Linux OS and Windows 2012 or Windows 2008 OS versions. Let us choose *Windows 2012 Base*, and on the next page, press *Review and Launch* for the configuration marked by default.

Here, we feel the good cloud trustworthiness approach of the Amazon cloud. The *Review* functionality suggests that our security group is open to the world (see Figure 2.4).

The cloud suggested to me to create a security key pair. I followed this advice (the page is not shown), downloaded the key pair file to our client machine, and launched my selected virtual server configuration by pressing *Launch Instances*. So, in a few clicks, I created and launched a new instance of a virtual server. A very comfortable

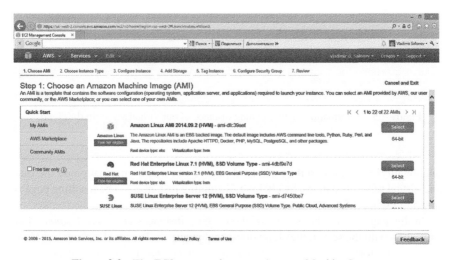

Figure 2.3   The EC2 page to choose an Amazon Machine Image.

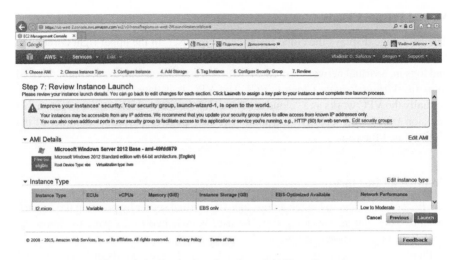

Figure 2.4   Reviewing the selected AMI configuration.

Figure 2.5   Information on the running instance of our virtual server in the cloud.

functionality! Returning to the main EC2 page, I can watch information on the running virtual server instances, by clicking "1 running instances." The resulting page is shown in Figure 2.5.

On this page, I can choose one of the running instances and click *Connect*. For connection with the server, the cloud offers to download a Remote Desktop file. Connection is performed by the *Remote Desktop Connection* mechanism standard for Windows.

Each of the virtual server instances created in your AWS session is assigned a public Domain Name Services (DNS) domain name. For example, my virtual server, as seen from Figure 2.5, was assigned the following domain name:

`ec2-54-69-121-116.us-west-2.compute.amazonaws.com`

where

- **ec2-54-69-121-116** – the first syllable denotes a unique name of the instance;
- part of the name **54.69.121.116** corresponds to a public IP address of the instance;
- **us-west-2** – code of the *region* – US-West (Oregon);
- **compute.amazonaws.com** – the standard suffix for all Amazon AWS domain names.

All in all, there are the following regions in Amazon cloud:

- Asia Pacific (Tokyo)
- Asia Pacific (Singapore)
- Asia Pacific (Sydney)
- EU (Frankfurt)
- EU (Ireland)
- South America (Sao Paulo)
- US East (North Virginia)
- US West (North California)
- US West (North Oregon).

Each of the regions has its own region code, used as part of DNS names of the servers located in that region. Each region has several locations referred to as *Availability Zones*. Availability zone is a unit of fault isolation. The cloud resources are not replicated in other availability zones.

Please note that the IP addresses provided by the cloud to the users are *real* public IP addresses available to everybody by default. If necessary, they can be protected by a firewall. It requires multiple explicit actions of creating a security group, getting a key pair for encryption, and encrypting the password. Without these actions connection to the virtual server is not possible. I think it would be more comfortable for the cloud user if he does not have to go into these details, and be able to access the virtual server through a *Virtual IP (VIP) address*. A mechanism of VIP is currently implemented in Microsoft Azure cloud (see Chapter 5).

Let us consider the steps of creating my virtual server in Amazon EC2, and connecting to it. I will use the *Launch Instance* functionality provided by the cloud. On pressing *Launch Instance* on the page shown in Figure 2.5, I am prompted to choose an AMI of the instance from the gallery. I choose the basic Windows Server 2012

R2 configuration. The virtual server is started and displayed on the running instances page. Then, to connect to my VM instance, I choose the *Connect* command available when the virtual server is launched. The full DNS name of our server is displayed. I will use it for remote desktop connection. Next, I am prompted to download the RDP file for remote desktop connection and store it on our machine. To create an encrypted password, I am prompted to create a *key pair (public key, private key)* using the classic RSA encryption scheme by default. I let the cloud know the location of our key pair on our client machine. Next, I get the public part of the encrypted password for logging in to our server. I am notified that the login name should be *Administrator*, and the public part of the password is displayed to us. On attempting to connect to my server, I am advised by the Review functionality that I should create a security group to enable private access to our server from our machine's IP address only. This is very simple to do.

Finally, I log in to the server. A simple way to do this on my Windows 8.1 computer is to launch the Remote Desktop Connection client by typing the *mstcs* command from the Command Prompt console. Another way is to find the application *Remote Desktop Connection* and launch it. The Remote Desktop Connection window is opened. I type *Administrator* as the login name, and the public part of the password is suggested to me by the cloud. After ignoring some usual warnings on security certificate, I have finally performed a remote log in to our virtual server running Windows 2012 Server R2 operating system. The result is shown in Figure 2.6. Please note that the upper line displaying the DNS name of the server (typical when using Windows Remote Desktop Connection) is *not* displayed on the screenshot.

The parameters of the virtual server (name, IP address, configuration, etc.) are displayed.

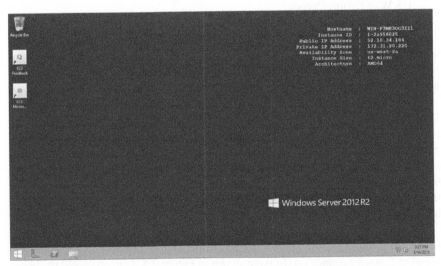

Figure 2.6   Remote login to the virtual server in Amazon AWS cloud.

The first thing I did on our virtual server is to provide my positive feedback on my first experience of using Amazon EC2.

Some useful applications are available on the virtual server, for example, *Server Manager,* which is helpful for configuring the server, for example, for adding new users.

I highly recommend you, the readers, to perform the same actions to better feel the spirit and service of Amazon cloud. Please perform by yourself all the actions I described, as a useful micro hands-on lab on cloud computing.

Databases in Amazon Cloud

Amazon AWS provides comfortable features to work with relational and other kinds of databases in the cloud. The user can create a *DB instance* in the cloud using *Amazon Relational Database Service* (RDS) [66]. DB instances may contain one or more databases. The following database engines are available: MySQL, PostgreSQL, Oracle, and Microsoft SQL Server. Each DB instance can use from 5 GB till 3 TB of storage in the cloud. DB instances are accessible using Amazon AWS console, Amazon AWS command line interface, and programmatic APIs. Libraries for accessing Amazon RDS databases are available for the following platforms: Java, PHP, Python, Ruby, and .NET.

Now let us create a database in the cloud. We should specify the DB instance name (*safdb* in our example), the master username (*saf* in the example), and the database engine (*MySQL* in the example), and reasonable settings for creating a DB instance will be taken by default. Information on the created DB instance is shown in Figure 2.7.

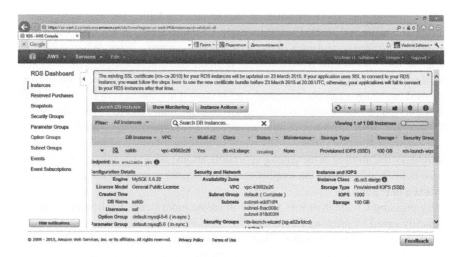

Figure 2.7   Information on the database instance created in Amazon cloud.

Now what is next? After creating a DB instance, I find out that MySQL database engine is not directly supported in Amazon cloud. To use MySQL, I should download and install on my client machine a MySQL client application, and use command line interface to connect to it. A similar situation exists with the support of Oracle and Microsoft SQL Server database engines: the user has to download the appropriate third-party SQL clients for those database engines, and use their custom command-line features to connect to the cloud DB instance. I should note that it is not quite comfortable and somewhat contradicts the spirit of cloud computing. We expect that everything for use of our DB instance should be implemented in the cloud. Actually Amazon cloud provides support for hosting, creating, managing, and monitoring a database in the cloud, and a secure connection to access it. But the functionality for creating, modifying, and accessing the database should be implemented programmatically or taken from the corresponding database machine by another company. I guess this is a typical situation when the cloud provider and the database machine provider are different companies. Documentation on Amazon RDS [66] mentions a new database product by Amazon – *Aurora* relational database; however, the Amazon RDS service does not yet offer Aurora as one of the database machines. Hopefully that may be implemented in near future.

Please compare this situation with what is available in Microsoft Azure cloud. Microsoft provides a cloud analog of its SQL Server, referred to as *SQL Azure*. In SQL Azure, the relational database scheme can be created using the interactive database constructor provided in Microsoft cloud, and the content of the cloud database itself can be created using an SQL interpreter built into SQL Azure. More details are given in Chapter 5.

However, Amazon provides a good, simpler alternative to relational databases – *Amazon DynamoDB non-RDS* [67]. It allows the cloud users to create *NoSQL* databases in the form of tables and enables fast performance, reliability, and scalability. The DynamoDB cloud service page is shown in Figure 2.8.

The starting page of DynamoDB invites to create a table. The user can create a table that consists of *items*. Each item corresponds to a row in the table. The item has several *attributes*, and each of them should be assigned a *value*. When creating a table, the user chooses the table name, the attribute that can be used as a *primary key*, and the list of the other attributes to be added. The user interface is very simple and self-evident. In my example, I created a table named *my_lab* (a simplified list of my laboratory). The primary key is the *Employee_Id* attribute, and its type is defined as *Number*. The other attributes of an item are *Name* (of type *String*) – the full name of the employee; *Position* (*String*) – the name of the employee's position; *Publications* (*Number*) – the number of the employee's publications; *Books* (*Number*) – the number of the published books by the employee. The result, the content of the created table, is shown in Figure 2.9.

By pressing *Create item* it is possible to create more items. Each item should be explicitly saved by pressing *Put item*.

The *List Tables* functionality allows us to visualize all the tables we created in DynamoDB. The page displaying this general view is shown in Figure 2.10. Below the list of the tables, monitoring information is displayed – the statistics of operations

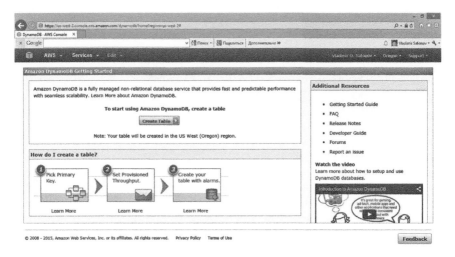

Figure 2.8   DynamoDB cloud database service page.

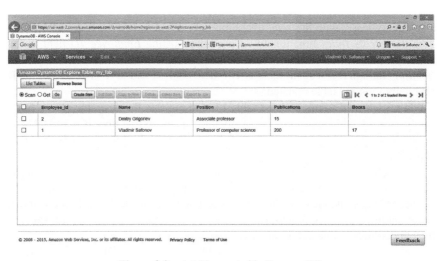

Figure 2.9   A table created in DynamoDB.

on the tables during the last hour, the average times to perform the operations, and so on. There is a special cloud service *CloudWatch* responsible for monitoring the use of cloud resources in terms of a set of *metrics*.

There is also the *Trusted Cloud Advisor* service recommended to get advice on optimizing the use of the cloud resources.

Documentation on DynamoDB is available at [68].

If the user needs to perform queries on the table created, it is necessary to create an *index* to the table. Initially, I forgot to create an index to my table, so my table appeared

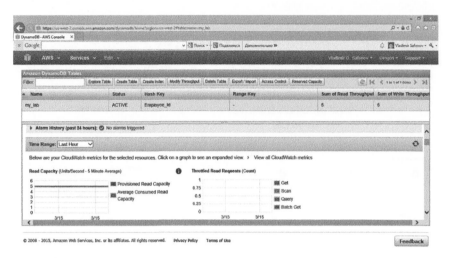

Figure 2.10   General view of the created DynamoDB tables with monitoring information.

to be "query-less," with the *scan* operation only. I had to add the index afterwards using the *Create Index* functionality. I used the existing *Employee_ID* field as the hash key. Next, I had to wait for a few minutes while the status of my table was still *Updating*, though it is a small table of two items only. I had to re-enter DynamoDB and finally I got my table updated.

When I returned to my updated table I found out that the desirable *Query* functionality for my table appeared. I performed the query to find myself in the table as the employee whose *Employee_Id* is equal to 1. The result of the query is shown in Figure 2.11.

So the Query functionality is comfortable and logical enough. Not quite comfortable are two things: first, DynamoDB should explicitly advise beforehand that the user has to create an index; second, DynamoDB should update the table status information on time; the user should not be misguided with incorrect status information when updating the table is actually done.

I only explored the simplest actions on tables with DynamoDB and should agree that this functionality is quite helpful. Any action with the table is performed in the cloud using self-sufficient cloud GUI, without using any extra code or third-party product.

Other data handling services in Amazon cloud are as follows:

- *ElastiCache* – a Web service to launch, manage, and scale a distributed in-memory cache in the cloud. The user can create a cache cluster, then connect to it, and manage the ElastiCache environment desirable.
- *RedShift* – a fast petabyte-scale data warehouse in the cloud. This functionality is very helpful to handle big data.

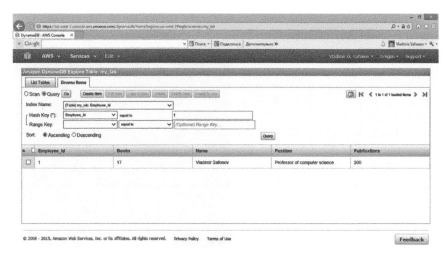

Figure 2.11   The result of DynamoDB Query to a table with the index added.

Elastic BeansTalk – Deploying, Monitoring, and Scaling Applications in the Cloud

This service is a typical PaaS cloud service that allows the users to run in the cloud their applications on several platforms:

- PHP
- Ruby
- Python
- (Java) GlassFish
- Node.js
- Tomcat
- Python
- Ruby.

As an example, I launched a sample Node.js Web application in the default environment provided by the cloud. Node.js is a modern extended JavaScript-based software platform for developing Web applications. Elastic BeansTalk deployed and launched the sample application on Amazon Linux. The URL of the Node.js Web application is http://default-environment-ucqidnmgwz.elasticbeanstalk.com/ . The result of running is shown in Figure 2.12.

Amazon cloud provides some other ways and PaaS services tools to deploy and run applications in the cloud:

- *AWS OpsWorks* – application management service

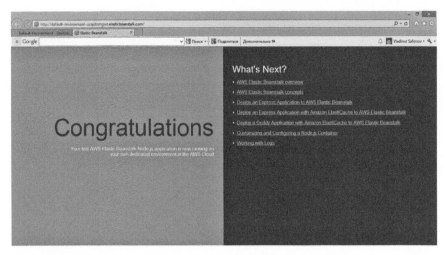

Figure 2.12   Running a sample Node.js Web application using Elastic BeansTalk.

– *AWS CloudFormation* – service to deploy the user's infrastructure resources and applications in AWS
– *AWS CodeDeploy* – service to deploy the user's applications in Amazon EC2 instances.

I am not going to review all the Amazon cloud functionality. It is well documented. This is just a list of sections of the Amazon AWS cloud services (see Figure 2.1):

– Compute
– Storage and Content Delivery
– Database
– Networking
– Administration and Security
– Deployment and Management
– Analytics
– Application Services
– Mobile Services
– Enterprise Applications.

In general, Amazon AWS is a modern trustworthy cloud with comfortable user interface and advanced IaaS, SaaS, and PaaS features. I highly recommend the readers to get access to Amazon cloud and to make experiments with it to learn it better.

Figure 2.13   The login page of the Bluemix cloud.

2.3   IBM CLOUD

As mentioned before in Section 2.1, IBM offers several kinds of clouds that actually originate from different providers – *SoftLayer Smart Cloud* and *Bluemix* cloud. In this section I consider the Bluemix cloud. The login page of Bluemix is presented in Figure 2.13.

On logging in to Bluemix portal, the user can overview the main features of Bluemix:

- *Applications (CF Apps)* – PaaS servicing to support running the user's applications in the cloud (*CF* stands for *Cloud Foundry*, see below)
- *Services* – SaaS servicing on managing the user's cloud services in the cloud
- *Containers* – IaaS servicing on creating containers in the cloud
- *Virtual Machines* – IaaS servicing on creating and managing virtual machines in the cloud.

The starting page of the IBM Bluemix portal is shown in Figure 2.14.

Online documentation on Bluemix cloud is available at page [69], via the main menu item *Docs*.

Some of the main features of the cloud – Virtual Machines and Containers – appeared at the beta stage, and I was added to the waiting lists for beta trial subscription to them (later on, I was invited to create a virtual machine in IBM Bluemix). So, at first impression, PaaS servicing is yet more developed in this cloud rather than IaaS features. To my mind, as stated above, virtual machines are one of the most important features of modern clouds. The Virtual Machines page with notification on the beta subscription to them is shown in Figure 2.15.

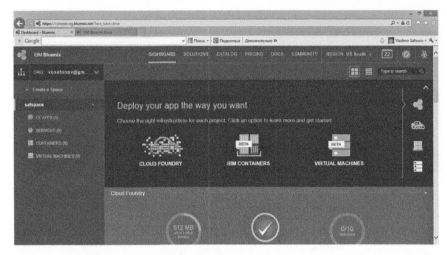

Figure 2.14   The starting page of the Bluemix cloud portal.

Figure 2.15   The Virtual Machines page of the Bluemix cloud portal.

As I noticed, IBM is positioning its Bluemix cloud as primarily PaaS oriented, paying most attention to running user applications in the cloud on various platforms. IBM was one of the initiators of creating the non-commercial association referred to as *Cloud Foundry* [70]. The purpose of the Cloud Foundry is positioned as *Open PaaS*, an open source technology for implementing Platform-as-a-Service functionality in the clouds. The Cloud Foundry association was created in December 2014. The corporate contributor's license agreement on creating Cloud Foundry was signed by 54 organizations. Among them, some of the most famous are IBM, HP, Intel,

Cisco, Fujitsu, SAP, and Symantec. On its portal [70] Cloud Foundry published much documentation on designing cloud applications, pushing them to Cloud Foundry, managing Cloud Foundry deployment, and Cloud Foundry concepts.

So the PaaS functionality of the Bluemix cloud is implemented according to the Cloud Foundry association principles.

Bluemix provides the following features [70]:

- A range of services that enable the users to build and extend web and mobile applications fast
- Processing power for the user to deliver application changes continuously
- Fit-for-purpose programming models and services
- Manageability of services and applications
- Optimized and elastic workloads
- Continuous availability.

Bluemix is currently located in two *regions*:

- United States South region; the URI address of the GUI console located in this region is https://console.ng.bluemix.net
- Europe United Kingdom Region; the URI address of the GUI console of that region is https://console.eu-gb.bluemix.net.

Similar to many other clouds, Bluemix operations are available using not only cloud GUI but also a command-line interface called *cf* (for Cloud Foundry), which can be downloaded, installed, and used on the client machine.

In the Bluemix architecture, there are three ways of deploying, running, and managing user applications (as shown on the page in Figure 2.14):

- via *Cloud Foundry* infrastructure;
- via *IBM Containers*: the application can be placed to a container that contains everything needed for the application to run, and then the container can be made available to Bluemix;
- via *Virtual Machines*; the application can run on a virtual machine available in Bluemix.

Both containers and virtual machines are currently implemented in beta stage and require trial subscriptions on separate requests.

There are two kinds of developer *applications* hosted by Bluemix:

- *Web applications*, whose code should be uploaded to Bluemix for hosting. For example, for Java application, only the binary code (*Java bytecode*) has to be uploaded to Bluemix. The user can develop Web applications in languages such as PHP, Node.js, Ruby, Python, and Java.

- *Mobile applications* that are run outside Bluemix, but they can use Bluemix *mobile services* that represent cloud back-end for those mobile applications. Mobile applications can be developed on iOS and Android platforms, and HTML with JavaScript. For mobile applications, the Bluemix cloud provides a new kind of cloud servicing – *Mobile Backend as a Service (MBaaS)*. It means that the delivery of the mobile application is simplified, due to a set of ready-to-use services and hosting capabilities.

In Bluemix, *cloud services* are understood as *cloud extensions* that are hosted by Bluemix. Cloud services can be predefined and can be developed by the cloud users. The predefined services in Bluemix include *database, messaging, push notifications for mobile applications*, and *elastic caching for Web applications*.

The full list of prebuilt Bluemix cloud services is available via the *Solutions* main menu item on the dashboard:

- *iOS* – ready-to-use iOS applications to integrate with new mobile applications
- *Hybrid cloud* – features to use for constructing hybrid clouds
- *DevOps* – tools for fast cloud services development
- *Data Management* – a wide spectrum of database services, including *Analytics Warehouse, Cloudant NoSQL database, Mobile Data, SQL Database, Time Series Database*
- *Security* – a unique cloud services toolkit developed "in the spirit of trustworthy computing" that includes tools for quickly adding authentication modules into applications, scanning applications for vulnerabilities, generating reports, and making recommended security fixes
- *Internet of Things* – services for extending applications by features of data processing and analytics from the connected devices and sensors
- *Open Architecture* – services for using Cloud Foundry – its runtimes, containers and virtual machines
- *Web and Application* – services for rapid development of Web and other applications in the cloud
- *Big Data* – cloud services for processing big data – *IBM Analytics for Hadoop; Time Series Database; dashDB* – data warehousing and analytics solution
- *Watson* – cognitive (intelligent) services, for example, speech recognition
- *Integration* – services for integrating data and APIs for application development
- *Mobile* – a set of tools to quickly create mobile applications
- *Business Analytics* – APIs for adding business analytics features into Bluemix applications.

This is a really spectacular list, deserving very careful learning and describing in several special books.

Especially comfortable is a catalog of *starters* – packages of sample code and services for developing various kinds of applications, available via the *Catalog* main menu item. The starters are provided in the form of *boilerplates* – samples of code for solving specific tasks, for example, a sample code for *Java Cloudant Web starter*, a sample code to demonstrate how to use a NoSQL database in Java using the *Liberty for Java* runtime on IBM cloud. Also available are *runtimes* for various languages – Java, Node.js, Python, Ruby, Go, PHP. The *Watson* section provides sample codes for intelligent cognitive applications. The *Mobile* section offers code templates for typical kinds of mobile applications, and so on. Fragment of the catalog is shown in Figure 2.16.

Now let us practice in creating and running applications in IBM Bluemix. I created a sample Java Web application named *safapp* using IBM Liberty for Java. After some time for preparing the environment and deploying the application, it started. Figure 2.17 illustrates the cloud features for monitoring and managing my Java application.

The URI address of my application is http://safapp.mybluemix.net. Now let us see the Web page displayed by the application by clicking the address. The result is shown in Figure 2.18.

Now let us see how the process of application development is integrated to the cloud services for monitoring my cloud application. Press "Add a service or API" to the page in Figure 2.19. Then, a list of all predefined services is visualized, for me to select one. I chose the *Message Resonance* service from the Watson section whose functionality was explained by the cloud: "Communicate with people with the style and words that suits them." As a result, the plan of adding the service to my application was visualized, and I was recommended to restage my application to add this service. The restaging of my application was performed automatically and the service became available with my application. The result of calling the Message Resonance service is shown in Figure 2.19.

Figure 2.16   The catalog of starters for application development in Bluemix.

Figure 2.17   Starting sample Java application in Liberty for Java.

Figure 2.18   The Web page displayed by the sample Java application.

Now, to delete the service from my application, it is enough to use the appropriate contextual menu at the right upper corner of the started service image. The service was deleted without my intervention.

I am greatly impressed by the degree of integration of various kinds of cloud services to IBM Bluemix cloud, especially intelligent services from the Watson section. This is an excellent idea with excellent implementation.

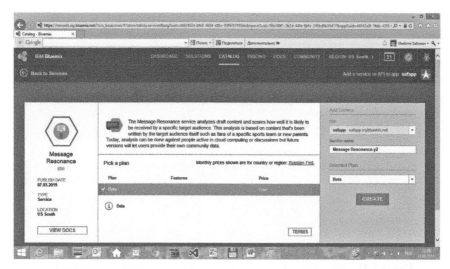

Figure 2.19   Adding a service or API to the application: Call Message Resonance.

Figure 2.20   A sample Python Web application *safpython* in IBM Bluemix cloud.

Now let us create yet another sample Web application, in Python. Its name is *safpython*. The application was created and started in a few minutes. Information in the cloud on my Python application is shown in Figure 2.20.

The URI address of my Python application is http://safpython.mybluemix.net/. By clicking the address, I visualize the Web page that the application implements (see Figure 2.21).

Now let us pay more attention to the implementation of the working environment for managing the application. In the overview page for the *safpython* application (see

Figure 2.21 Visualizing the Web page the *safpython* application implements.

Figure 2.20), on the left hand side, there is a menu for manipulating the application. The *Files and Logs* menu item allows the user to see the source code of the application and the related configuration files. The *Environment Variables* menu item allows the user to visualize the environment variables predefined for the application. Of them, the *VCAP_Services* environment variable refers to the cloud services associated with the application (if any). Also, the user can define his or her own environment variables in this item. The *Start Coding* menu item allows the user to update the code of the application in several ways. Figure 2.22 shows the *Files and Logs* page for the application.

The page displays the cloud directory structure representing the code of the application. Let us click the *app* subdirectory in which the *server.py* is the main source code file in Python. Clicking on the name of the source code file visualizes it on the Web page. The Python server code is shown in Figure 2.23.

The Python code looks elegant, brief and reliable, in spirit of trustworthy computing. Exception handling is in place for server import operations. The starting HTML page *index.html* of the application can be found on the *static* subdirectory. In the root directory of the source code, there are starting scripts (such as *.bashrc*) typical for UNIX/Linux scripting languages.

In summary, with a few clicks I created a starter application in Python, and studied its source code, configuration, and HTML files. Everything is available in the cloud, without any extra installations on my computer and without programming any lines of source code. Again, as an experienced software developer, I would like to emphasize the comfortable cloud working environment created by IBM cloud engineers. I appreciate that very much.

For further updating and development of the starter application, IBM Bluemix offers the following ways. First alternative is to use the Cloud Foundry command-line

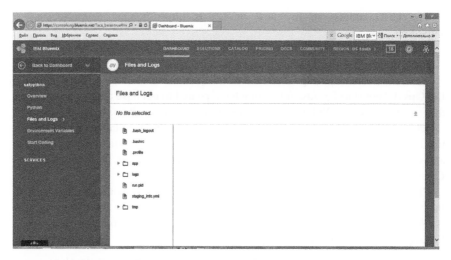

Figure 2.22 The *Files and Logs* page for *safpython* application: Way to source code.

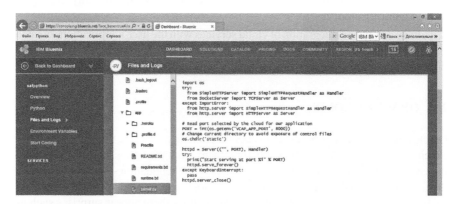

Figure 2.23 The server source code in Python for *safpython* application.

interface. In this case, the user should download and install it on the client machine. The second alternative is to use the *Git* toolkit to deploy the source code. *Git* is a widely used source code control system with good and comfortable Web interface, used in many large open source software projects. I leave both variants of updating the source code of the application to the readers as a good exercise in modern programming.

To continue my experiment with PaaS in IBM Bluemix, I created a *Git* repository for updating the source code of my starter Python application. The cloud required me to choose an alias (*safgit*) for using the Git repository together with my IBM credentials. Then, the IBM DevOps cloud toolkit called. So I created a new project in IBM DevOps.

The URL address of my new project is https://hub.jazz.net/project/safgit/safpython.

The URL address of my Git repository is https://hub.jazz.net/git/safgit/safpython. I was notified by email on my project and Git repository names.

Next, on the DevOps page, I clicked *EDIT CODE*. But the Orion editor built into DevOps did not start because my computer appeared to not have the latest version of the Internet Explorer. With Internet Explorer 11, the users will be able to use DevOps editor for their applications in the cloud without any extra installations on their computer. It is notable that IBM DevOps services can be used from the browser, or from any other appropriate client, for example, from a Git client or from *Eclipse Team Concert*.

Please continue this hand-on lab by yourselves, since I do not intend to overload the book with lots of screenshots and other details.

Now let us summarize the advantages of the IBM Bluemix cloud for users, which I checked and tested in practical experience:

- Advanced and comfortable PaaS implementation; support of developing and updating applications in many languages and running them in the cloud
- A variety of very interesting ready-to-use cloud services, especially intelligent (cognitive) services
- Easy automated integration of cloud services with the user's applications created in the cloud
- For future use: containers and virtual machines (still in beta stage).

2.4 ORACLE CLOUD

Oracle cloud offers PaaS, SaaS, and DaaS functionality. The free trial period for Oracle cloud is 1 month. As mentioned before, there are some issues when logging in to the Oracle cloud, since Oracle uses two kinds of authentication – one for managing the user account and the other for managing cloud services. Also, when requesting trials for different kinds of cloud services, sometimes there appear surprises such as purging trial services or waiting periods for several days when attempting to try new kinds of services. These issues do not help feel the trustworthiness of Oracle cloud and to stay in friendly atmosphere. Nevertheless, Oracle offers many kinds of interesting cloud services. Let us consider some of the Oracle cloud opportunities in more detail. I list only the most interesting Oracle cloud services that can be tried for free.

Applications (SaaS/DaaS):
- *Sales cloud* – cloud services for marketing, sales, and advertising.
- *Global human resources cloud* – cloud services providing information on human resources and workforce distribution.
- *Talent management cloud* – cloud services for seeking talents in various areas of human activity.
- *Social network cloud* – secure enterprise social network in the cloud.

- *DaaS for sales* – cloud data for overviewing customers and contacts when doing sales activity.

Platform (PaaS/IaaS):

- *Java* – cloud services for deploying, running, and managing Java applications in the cloud.
- *Developer* – cloud services for Java development in the cloud, supporting the software lifecycle and related collaboration and deployment.
- *Database* – Oracle database cloud services, cloud analog of the world famous Oracle database, which allow to create a schema of the database in the cloud, to port a ready-to-use on-premises database from client machine to the cloud, and to use a database in the cloud with direct network connections.
- *Database backups* – a set of cloud services for database backup to the cloud.
- *Storage* – cloud storage services that allow Java application developers to use cloud storage programmatically to store application's data in the cloud via RESTful services.
- *Marketplace* – an online store to find and immediately start cloud services available in the Oracle cloud.

Surely this is a spectacular choice of cloud services, oriented both to software developers and to non-programmers (commercial agents, businessmen, etc.).

As for PaaS services, in Oracle cloud they do not have such universal integrated support as in IBM cloud. Application developers should use for developing their cloud applications one of the integrated development environments by Oracle – *Oracle JDeveloper* (also known in the past as Borland JBuilder) and *NetBeans* – one of the most world popular IDEs for developing applications in Java, C, and C++.

Now, to feel and understand the style of Oracle cloud, let us consider the cloud portal and its related pages. Figure 2.24 shows the Oracle cloud portal [56].

The portal gives access to all other features in Oracle cloud, and to e-books that advertise and explain them. The next step is to log in to Oracle cloud. When clicking *Sign in*, the user of Oracle cloud, unlike all other clouds I ever tried, does not immediately enter his or her login and password, but, instead, is redirected to the other page [71] – *the login page to the user account or to cloud services*. That page is shown in Figure 2.25.

The *My Account* section of the login page (on the right) is intended for logging in to the Oracle user account only. The *My Services* section (on the left) of the login page is intended for logging in to the cloud services available to the user (e.g., whose trial use is active). Using *My Services* section, the user has to remember and explicitly indicate in which Oracle datacenter the available services are located (US commercial 1, US commercial 2, etc.). Moreover, the login and password for logging in to the cloud services are different from the general Oracle user's login and password used to log in to Oracle account. To my mind, this approach is not quite comfortable for the cloud user. Please compare these specifics of Oracle cloud to similar functionalities of the other clouds (Microsoft Azure, IBM Bluemix, Amazon AWS). The user of

Figure 2.24   The Oracle cloud portal.

Figure 2.25   The Oracle cloud page to log in to the user account and to cloud services.

those clouds does not have to remember explicitly in which datacenter the available services are located, or to seek the service among all datacenters. Instead, the cloud user just logs in to the single cloud portal – that is much more comfortable than the Oracle approach. Because of the above-mentioned Oracle cloud specifics, the user permanently has a feeling of discomfort, since the available services are split from each other, and require separate logins. I hope in near future Oracle will correct it, following the requests of probably many users.

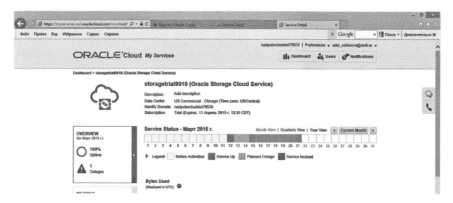

Figure 2.26 The cloud page related to the Oracle Storage service.

So, on logging in to *My Services*, the user finally gets access to the service he or she requested for trial. Figure 2.26 shows one of the examples of the pages displaying information on the available cloud service – *Oracle storage*.

The Storage page provides detailed information for monitoring the available service – on its status, statistics of use, the trial period, and so on. However, two things are lacking on the page (as compared to similar pages of Microsoft Azure, Amazon, or IBM clouds): first, *online help* for immediately getting brief explanations and overview of the service features, and, second, *tools to access the service online*. Similar is the situation with Java cloud service, and so on. The user has to dig into separate documentation to get this information, and to find out that the Storage service is available programmatically only (e.g., from a Java application). Unfortunately, such implementation cannot be considered trustworthy and user friendly. My viewpoint is that the implementation of a cloud service, in any cloud platform, should be "cloud service oriented," in the sense that everything related to the service (overview, set of possible actions, help, etc.) should be available "close" to the service, on the same page or tightly related pages. Such approach is demonstrated by Amazon, IBM, and Microsoft clouds. The Oracle approach can be referred to as *decentralized* and *scattered*. Surely it is fixable in future versions of the Oracle cloud.

A very comfortable feature of the Oracle cloud is its *Try It* page [72]. This page accumulates all information on the cloud services that can be tried for free. I recommend the users to start your Oracle cloud use from this page. For each service that can be tried, click on *Try it* initiates an order for free trial of the service. The *Try It* page of the Oracle cloud is shown in Figure 2.27.

Also, a very interesting page in the Oracle cloud is the *Oracle Cloud Marketplace* [73]. This is a typical SaaS page in the best sense of this word. It contains a wide extensible collection of references to cloud services by Oracle and its partners, ready to use. Many of these services relate to social cloud, talent management cloud, financial cloud, and so on. The Oracle cloud marketplace page is shown in Figure 2.28.

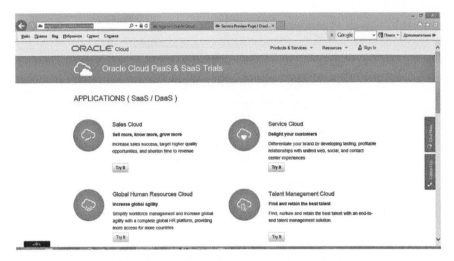

Figure 2.27   The Try It page in the Oracle cloud.

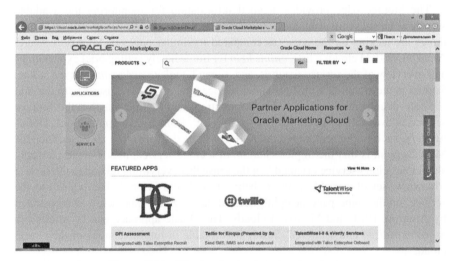

Figure 2.28   The Oracle cloud marketplace page.

Oracle Cloud Marketplace is available without logging in to the cloud. Each of the company and service names and icons of the cloud services represented in the Marketplace (e.g., a social advertising service by *Brand Network Platform*) leads to the appropriate page with brief information on the service and the *Get App* button for paying for the service and getting it from the Web. The Marketplace portal applications surely are not free.

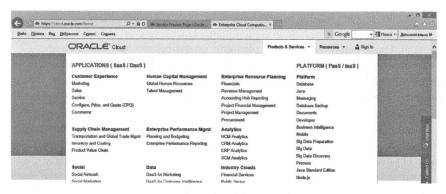

Figure 2.29 The Oracle cloud marketplace page.

Products and Services Menu of the Oracle Cloud

On the Oracle cloud portal [56], there is a pop-up menu item *Products and Services*. Via this item, all kinds of products and services of the Oracle cloud are available. Most of them are not available as trials and should be paid for. The Products and Services pop-up menu is shown in Figure 2.29.

For example, the following items are *not* available as trials:

- *Business intelligence* – business data analytics services.
- *Messaging.*
- *Java Standard Edition* – this item is for future use; it is marked as *Coming Soon*. It will allow the users to deploy and run in the cloud any Java Standard edition (Java 7 or Java 8) application. In IBM cloud, this kind of PaaS functionality is already implemented (see Section 2.3).
- *Big Data* – services for managing big data in Oracle cloud on the basis of Apache Hadoop. This item is marked as *Coming Soon*, so managing big data is just in the implementation stage in Oracle cloud. Please compare with Microsoft Azure and IBM Bluemix where big data cloud services are already implemented (see Section 2.3).
- *Node.js* – cloud services for deploying and running a Node.js application in the cloud. This item is marked as *Coming Soon*. So, in this respect IBM cloud is also ahead of Oracle; similar functionality is implemented in Bluemix (see Section 2.3).
- *Integration* – cloud services for integration in the cloud of SaaS and on-premises applications. This item is also marked as *Coming Soon*.
- *Compute* – this IaaS functionality implements cloud services for running virtual machines in the cloud, and associate block storage with them.
- *Storage* – services for handling object storage in the cloud. The cloud storage is available from Java applications via REST APIs.

There are plenty of cloud services for customer experience, logistics, social networks, industry solutions, human capital management, enterprise performance management, DaaS, enterprise resource planning, analytics, and financial services.

To conclude this section on Oracle cloud, let us take a look at a fragment of the cloud dashboard displaying all available cloud services and those whose trial is yet to be initialized, related to my Oracle account. The dashboard is presented in Figure 2.30.

To summarize, Oracle cloud offers to users, as SaaS servicing, many commercially oriented cloud services for analytics, sales, marketing, and so on. In this respect, the value of Oracle cloud can be highly appreciated. PaaS functionality in Oracle cloud is growing fast, and many important features are at the implementation stage. IaaS features are implemented in the form of virtual machines and object storage. What disappoints a little is a decentralized system of organizing cloud services, without a single-login integration portal. In near perspective, Oracle cloud may be competitive to IBM Bluemix and Microsoft Azure clouds.

2.5   GOOGLE CLOUD PLATFORM

Google cloud platform [74] from the first minutes of its use is attractive with its simplicity, ease of use, high speed, and maximal possible services, even for trial use. On filling out a simple questionnaire, the user gets a free trial for 60 days in a moment (after checking the credit card), without any waiting period. The Google cloud platform portal is shown in Figure 2.31.

Google offers to create a project for deploying the cloud services you are going to use. The main page on which the user works in the Google cloud is the Google developer's console [75].

At first glance, Google provides any kind of cloud services for trial: Hosting and Compute services, App Engine and Compute Engine, Cloud Storage, Cloud Datastore, Cloud SQL, Big Data processing (by Hadoop), and a host of other cloud services.

Figure 2.30   A dashboard of all my available cloud services in Oracle cloud.

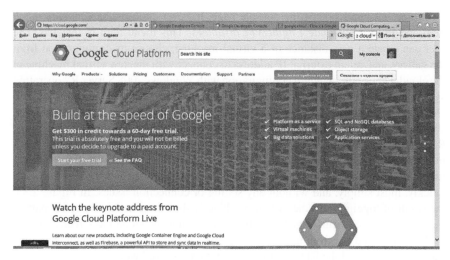

Figure 2.31 The Google cloud platform portal.

The main principle of the Google cloud is that it provides services as building blocks from which the user can easily compose a new application – from simple site to complex applications. So it appears that SaaS servicing is the key principle of Google cloud. However, IaaS services (such as Compute engine) are also on board.

First, I managed to create a virtual machine in the Google cloud and connected to it using the external IP address Google provided – everything in 5 minutes. In Figure 2.32, the Google Developer Console is shown, on which my cloud activities are presented.

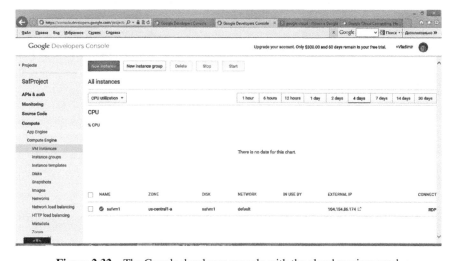

Figure 2.32 The Google developer console with the cloud services used.

On the left hand side of the console page, the user chooses the *Compute* menu item and from it *Compute Engine/VM instances*. This menu item is selected. The user can create a new instance of a virtual machine, choose its configuration from the gallery, and get an external IP address to connect with the new virtual machine in the cloud. I chose the standard configuration with Windows 2008 Server R2 operating system, changed the Google proposed login and password to mine, then used Remote Desktop Connection window, the external IP address, and my login and password to connect to the virtual machine, without any kind of explicit settings for endpoints, RDP protocols, downloadable RDP files, and so on. Everything was very quick – in 5 minutes – and I was working on my Google cloud virtual machine. Of all the clouds I used, the Google cloud allowed me to create a virtual machine and connect to it most quickly, most simply, and without any setting or connection issues. In Figure 2.33, the result of logging in to the virtual machine is shown (as usual, the upper part of the screen with the virtual machine's IP address is not shown on the screenshot).

Then, I logged out from the virtual machine, and logged on to it again, using the same IP address and the RDP protocol. Everything worked well.

Now let us try the *App Engine* – PaaS functionality to develop and run applications in the cloud. When choosing "Explore the starter code" in different languages – Java, Python, Flask, Django, Bottle, and so on the user can feel the simplicity of the Google PaaS approach. The result – the starter Python application, its source code, and the result of its run in the cloud are shown in Figure 2.34.

So, with Google PaaS, deploying applications in the cloud works even simpler, faster, and more comfortably than with IBM Bluemix PaaS features.

The convenience of the Google cloud also lies in the fact that Google does not require explicit logging in to its cloud. Instead, it allows me to use the

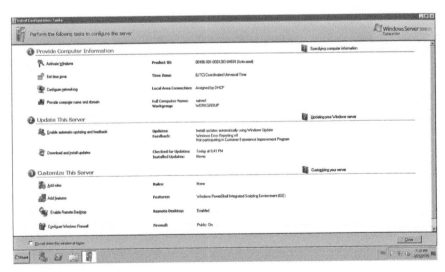

Figure 2.33 Logging in to a Windows 2008 R2 virtual machine in the Google cloud.

Figure 2.34 Google App Engine: running the starter Python application and exploring its source code.

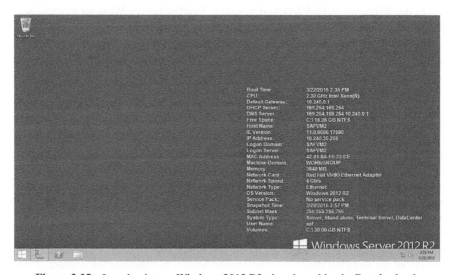

Figure 2.35 Logging in to a Windows 2012 R2 virtual machine in Google cloud.

ordinary account I use for my Google mail and other Google services (vosafonov @gmail.com).

Now let us try to create a Windows 2012 R2 virtual machine in the Google cloud and connect to it. I use the same method as with Windows 2008 R2 virtual machine – remote desktop connection by the IP address of the virtual machine. The result is shown in Figure 2.35.

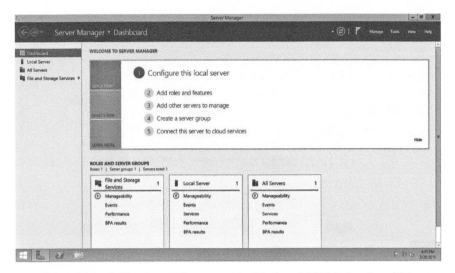

Figure 2.36   Calling Server Manager on the Windows 2012 R2 virtual machine.

On the Windows 2012 R2 virtual machine, I called Server Manager to make settings on my virtual server. The result is presented in Figure 2.36.

One of the possible actions of the Server Manager is *"Connect the Server to cloud services."* Using this choice, the user is directed to Microsoft Azure Web pages and can set up a trial use of Microsoft Azure from the Google cloud!

Let us create a Linux virtual machine in the Google cloud. Using a scenario as that I used for working with Windows virtual machines, I created a Linux Debian virtual machine of the standard configuration. The protocol recommended to connect to this virtual machine is SSH. I clicked the name of the protocol in the dashboard and in a moment I logged in to my Linux virtual machine. My credentials were passed to my Linux virtual server with an SSH file. The result is shown in Figure 2.37.

The Linux shell console started in Internet explorer. The default Linux shell is *bash*. Please note the address string of the browser that refers to my Linux machine (*saflinux1*). It also contains the name of the datacenter.

On the Linux virtual machine, I performed several Bash shell commands: *whoami* – to identify my login name on the Linux machine, *ls* – to visualize the content of the working directory, and *cat/etc/hosts* – to visualize the content of my network hosts. The results are shown in Figure 2.37.

During the Linux session, it is possible to visualize information on my virtual machine instance and perform a couple of other simple actions such as Copy/Paste.

One of the most interesting of the Google cloud services is Big Data. It allows the users to create tables of big data (e.g., the results of some experiment), to compose queries to these data, and to save the result as a table. The service outputs the statistics of the query run – the time to perform the query and the size of the big data processed.

In Figure 2.38, a query to one of the big data samples and the results of running the query are shown. The big table *publicdata:samples.shakespeare* stores the

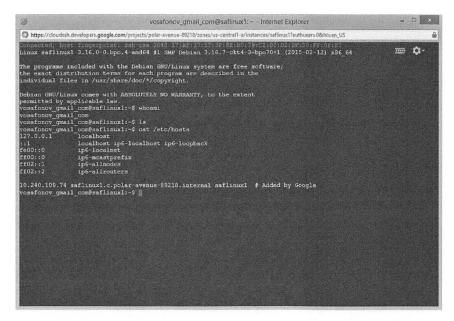

Figure 2.37 Logging in to Linux Debian virtual machine in the Google cloud.

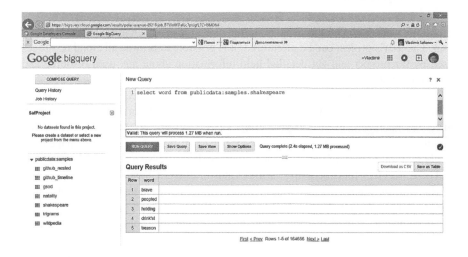

Figure 2.38 Using Big Data in the Google cloud: results of a request to a sample big table.

usage of words in Shakespeare's masterpieces. The query *select word from public-data:samples.shakespeare* selects the first column (*word*) from the table and displays the result – a new table of just one column. The total number of rows in the table is 164656. It is possible to browse the result – the big table – from the first row to the last one.

Here is a list of the most important Google cloud features available:

– *APIs & auth* – references to all available API to work with the Google cloud.
– *Monitoring* – features to monitor the use of the Google cloud; in particular, it is possible to view all the logs of the actions the user has performed in the cloud (e.g., creation and deletion of virtual machines).
– *Source code* – tools to browse and update source codes for the projects the user created in the cloud. In particular, this section contains references for downloading the *Google Cloud SDK, Android Studio,* and other tools for development Google cloud applications.
– *Compute* – cloud services to manage applications, virtual machines, disks, networks, cloud zones, and containers to store and run applications, and so on.
– *Networking* – cloud services to create *virtual private networks (VPN)* and *DNS* in the cloud.
– *Storage* – cloud services to manage several kinds of storage in the Google cloud: *Cloud Storage* – creating and updating *buckets* of cloud data using RESTful APIs in various languages; *Cloud Datastore* – creating and managing NoSQL databases; *Cloud SQL* – creating SQL databases in the cloud.
– *Big Data* – creating big tables of data and performing queries to these tables (see Figure 2.38).

All the work with Google cloud is started using the project name(s) created by the user. The user's project can be monitored; it is possible to browse all cloud resources used by the project and get detailed help information about any used resource and service in the Google cloud.

Monitoring the user's project in the Google cloud is depicted in Figure 2.39.

In general, I have a very good impression on Google IaaS (in particular, on virtual machines management in Google cloud), PaaS (tools for creating, deploying, and running applications in the cloud), and SaaS (ready-to-use cloud services that can be easily built into the user's applications). Especially impressive are the big data tools and other services for processing various kinds of cloud data and storage.

Some of the important cloud services are yet in alpha stage – for example, containers and cloud monitoring tools.

As compared to IBM Bluemix cloud, Google cloud does not have such intelligent (cognitive) cloud services as IBM.

In spite of that, Google cloud is very attractive because of the simple user-friendly interface and simple authentication, registration, and trial settings.

2.6   HP HELION CLOUD PLATFORM

The HP public cloud platform is named Helion. The cloud portal is available at [76] and shown in Figure 2.40.

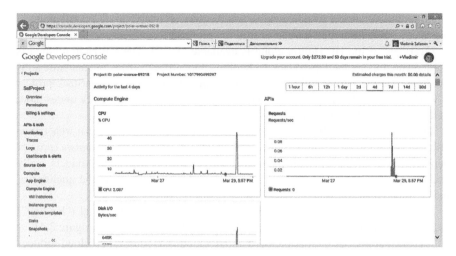

Figure 2.39 Monitoring the user's project in the Google cloud.

Figure 2.40 HP Helion public cloud portal.

To learn HP cloud in detail, a good choice is a rich collection of HP cloud books [50]. However, those are commercial books not available for free.

HP offers a 3-month free trial. For getting the trial, I have passed a kind of phone mini-interview, a little unexpected but nice and friendly. During the interview the HP contact person asked me to confirm my contact information by voice and was interested in why I needed a trial use of HP cloud. My answer was quite understandable: I would like to learn the HP cloud, to compare its features to public clouds by other cloud providers, to feel its advantages, and to make an overview of the HP cloud in my Wiley book. So in this section I fulfill my promise.

Overview of the HP Helion cloud is available at [77]. The HP Helion cloud is implemented using the OpenStack technology. OpenStack [78] is open source software for creating public and private clouds. The purpose of the OpenStack project is worldwide collaboration of cloud technologists. Currently OpenStack unites more than 20,000 people from more than 150 countries.

The qualities of the HP cloud highlighted in the overview are its *open style* (since HP believes in the great future of the open cloud community); its *dynamism* (prompt deployment of cloud services, payment only for the services and products really used); and its *high reliability*. Now let us take a look and estimate the qualities of the HP cloud advertised in the overview.

Finally, I am in the HP Helion cloud. The starting HP cloud portal ("landing") page, shown after logging in to it, is available at [79] and depicted in Figure 2.41.

As stated above, the first impression on HP cloud is as follows: no cloud services activated, and everything should be launched explicitly, unlike many other cloud platforms. This may seem surprising but, to analyze it for a moment, it looks like a good way of taking care of the cloud users. There are many "counter-examples" of servicing: sometimes in real life providers of electronic services (e.g., of cell phone communications) impose their free services for a short period of time, for example, for a month, and after that, they start billing the users without explicit warning, which is surely a non-trustworthy approach. On the contrary, the HP approach to offering their cloud services is based on taking care of the user's expenses: the user should carefully investigate which cloud services are really necessary, and after that should activate only the necessary cloud services. In Figure 2.41 I intentionally did not show the "initial" picture after the first log in to the cloud. Near the information on each

Figure 2.41   HP Helion public cloud portal "landing" page.

kind of cloud service on the portal (either a global service or a service available in concrete regions), the HP cloud has the "Activate" button. Some services shown in Figure 2.41 are marked as "Activated" – this is the result of my initial explicit actions of activating them.

As can be shown from the portal and from Figure 2.41, there are some *global* cloud services – of them, only the *DNS* is displayed. There are two regions – *US East* and *US West.* In the *US East* region, the *Compute, Monitoring,* and *Object Storage* services are available. In the *US West* region, the *Compute, Monitoring, Object Storage,* and *Relational Database MySQL* are available. The *Compute* set of services in both regions consists of *Networking, Block Storage,* and *Image Management.* The *Load Balancer* cloud services in both regions are in beta stage, so for using them an explicit request for beta access is needed.

The main menu of the HP cloud portal, located in the upper left corner, contains four items: *Manage Services* (actions to activate the services); *Identity* – get information on the cloud use's *domains, projects, users, groups,* and *roles*; *Project* – the main item whose sections cover all possible actions of the user in the cloud; *Metering* – the user's billing information.

The *Project* menu item's contents are very similar to what the other public clouds (Amazon, IBM, Google, etc.) offer – access to cloud virtual machines, cloud disk volumes, network, object storage, database, DNS, access and security. I think this is a very positive fact – on diving to a new cloud, the user finds a familiar set of terms and services, similar to other clouds. This is a positive consequence of de facto standardization of clouds, their functionality, architecture, and sets of services. This makes the clouds predictable, friendly and trustworthy for cloud users.

Of the *Compute* services functionalities, one of the most spectacular is a uniquely wide collection of virtual machine *images* – total 91 (!) items. *Images* in HP cloud, as in the other clouds, are templates for creating *instances* of virtual machines in the cloud: the operating system and the memory size. Example of image: *SUSE Linux Enterprise 12, size of memory – 493.1 MB.* The family of the available operating systems and the related cloud products includes *CoreOS* – a version of Linux for massive server deployment; *HP LoadRunner (HP LR-PC); Linux Ubuntu; Linux SUSE; Linux Fedora; Linux Debian; CohesiveFT; ActiveState Stackato; Windows 20008 Server* and others. So most operating systems available for HP cloud virtual machines are dialects of Linux. Only one question arises: why is Windows 2012 Server image lacking in this very rich set?

During trial generation and launch of a virtual machine image, an issue occurred: the HP cloud required explicit generation of the public/private key pair using the *SSH* protocol commands. This is not quite comfortable for a cloud user, since it throws the user down to networking protocol details, which he (she) prefers not to know at all: the user's only purpose is to quickly create a virtual machine and connect to it. The HP cloud does not provide enough information for the user to make the task of creating a key pair easier. The best option would be to implicitly create a key pair and implicitly pass it to the virtual server (this option is implemented in the Google cloud). The SSH protocol and the *ssh* command are typical for UNIX-like operating systems; on Windows machines this command does not exist at all. So it looks like the HP cloud implementers silently assume that most cloud client machines are Linux machines, whereas it is well known that the most widely spread client OS family is Windows.

Now let us analyze what is easy to do in the HP cloud. An easy action to do in the HP cloud is to create a MySQL cloud database. The cloud provides hosting, backup, and securing the database. But the only way to connect to the database is to use command line and a third party MySQL client that should be downloaded and installed on the user's client machine. This approach to implement a cloud database is typical for most public cloud providers. A good exception is Microsoft who implemented an interactive database constructor and SQL interpreter in their Azure cloud.

A cloud database *safdb* in the HP cloud is depicted in Figure 2.42.

Another comfortable feature of the HP cloud is *containers*. The user can create a container for storing any kind of objects, in particular, an image, but any other object is OK, for example, a multimedia file. To create a container, let us choose the *Project/Object Store/Containers* menu item. Then, a page is opened with the *Create container* button. When creating a container, we must specify its *name*, *access* to the container (private or public), and the *content* of the container (empty or VM image). Let us create the empty public container **safcontainer**. The page with the resulting information on the created container is shown in Figure 2.43.

Unlike databases, handling containers is supported by the cloud GUI well enough. Clicking *Upload object*, we open a browsing window for choosing a file from my computer to upload to the container. Let us choose my picture in JPEG format and upload it to the container. The result is depicted in Figure 2.44.

As shown in Figure 2.44, it is possible to download the object from the container, to upload more objects to the container, and to create a pseudo-folder in the container to enable a better structuring of information. So, a cloud container is acting as a kind

Figure 2.42   A MySQL database created in the HP cloud.

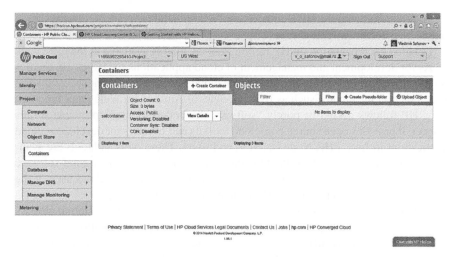

Figure 2.43 A container created the HP cloud.

Figure 2.44 A file from the client computer uploaded to the container in the cloud.

of cloud disk with some emulation of a directory structure. Since the container is public, it is available via a public URL, as follows:

https://horizon.hpcloud.com/project/containers/safcontainer/

To manage security permissions, the concept of a *security group* is used as in many other clouds.

To get started with the HP Helion cloud, I recommend the readers to use the good online help document available at [80].

Detailed documentation on HP Helion Public Cloud is available at [81].

As for development and management of cloud applications for HP cloud, there is no direct support of PaaS in the HP Helion cloud portal. It looks unexpected, since most other public clouds, such as IBM, Google, or Amazon, provide PaaS functionality. HP follows a kind of purely "software developer-oriented" principle in this respect. It provides open source non-cloud toolkits and libraries for developing cloud applications in Java, PHP, Node.js, .NET, and so on. These APIs and tools are available within the framework of the OpenStack project [78]. This is a good software development practice but I think it would be highly desirable for cloud users if the PaaS functionality is added to the HP Helion cloud portal.

Now let us try to create an instance of a virtual server in the HP Helion cloud. I chose a Windows 2008 R2 virtual machine with minimal configuration. The name of my virtual server is *safvm.* I have created a new security group *safsecgroup* and added to the security group a rule for connection by RDP (remote desktop connection) protocol. However, the Compute cloud service ultimately required the generation of a pair of SSH keys (public and private key) for connecting to my virtual machine. Since the SSH commands (unlike Linux) are lacking on my Windows client machine, I had to download and use the free *Putty* toolkit emulating SSH commands on the Windows platform. Finally (after some unsuccessful attempts) I managed to generate a pair of SSH keys and to rename the key pair file appropriately. Then, I clicked on "Import key pair," and my key pair was successfully imported. I clicked on "Launch" to launch an instance. In the Instances dashboard, I clicked on "Console" and logged in to the console of my Windows 2008 R2 virtual server. The resulting virtual server console is shown in Figure 2.45.

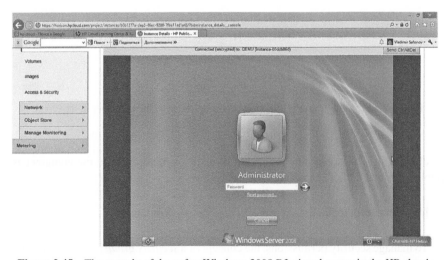

Figure 2.45   The console of the *safvm* Windows 2008 R2 virtual server in the HP cloud.

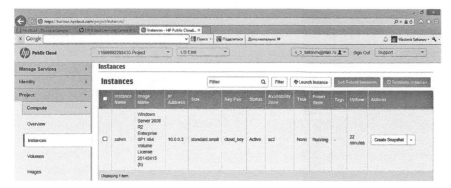

Figure 2.46 Information on the running virtual server instance in the HP cloud.

To view the running virtual server instance, I clicked on the Compute/Instances dashboard. The result – virtual server configuration, state, and other information on it – is depicted in Figure 2.46.

The URL address of the virtual server instance in the HP cloud is as follows:

https://horizon.hpcloud.com/project/instances/b0b1377a-dea5-46ec-9280-7fba11ad1a43/

This address can be also used for visualizing information on the virtual server and for logging into its console.

Since for logging in to a Windows machine, a CTRL-ALT-DEL key combination is required, the console of the virtual server provides a special button "Send Ctrl-Alt-Del" for this purpose.

Of possible actions on the running VM instance (see the Actions) menu item on the right), it is allowed to log in to its console, to create a *snapshot* of the disk state of the instance, to associate a floating IP address with the instance, to edit the instance (its name and its security group), to reboot the instance, and to terminate it.

In spite of some experience I already have in working with various clouds, I should honestly say that creating, running, and connecting an instance of a virtual server in the HP cloud took me the longest time, as compared to similar action in other public clouds. The main reason for that is the very uncomfortable and non-friendly implementation of security actions related to VM launch. Hopefully the HP cloud team will correct this issue in the nearest cloud versions and enable fast and simple security settings related to creation of a virtual server. Everything or most of those actions should be done by default. The user should be provided with high-level tools to create a key pair.

After successful creation of the first virtual server *safvm1*, now let us try to create yet another virtual server *safvm2* running under Linux Debian. Fortunately, the security key pair created for the previous virtual server fits for yet another one, so I did not experience any issues to run the virtual server in a moment. So, to conclude on

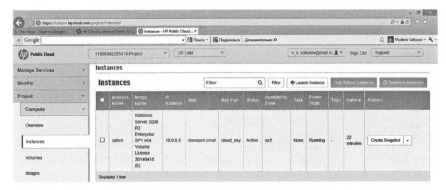

Figure 2.47   The console of the *safvm2* Linux Debian virtual server in the HP cloud.

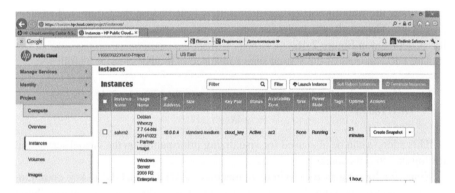

Figure 2.48   Information on the two (Windows and Linux) virtual servers in the cloud.

this matter, the user of the HP public cloud may experience issues when creating and importing the first security key pair, but can use the same key pair for any number of other virtual servers. The result – console of the Linux Debian virtual machine – is depicted in Figure 2.47.

Information on the two running VM instances in the cloud is shown in Figure 2.48.

Creating bigger size virtual servers in the HP cloud (like *medium size*) takes substantially longer, about 10–15 minutes. Also, some types of VM images appear to demonstrate unstable behavior, for example, CentOS server: booting this version of Linux on the VM causes a hang-up. I do not recommend using images such as HP Cloud Development Platform Loader: they do not demonstrate trustworthy behavior either. The most reliable platforms for cloud server are Windows 2008 versions. In addition, their support for the instance console includes the *Send Ctrl-Alt-Del* button to initiate a log in to a Windows machine.

Sometimes the virtual server does not react to the keyboard input. In this case, the cloud developers recommend the user to click the status bar in the console window.

What is lacking for virtual servers in the HP cloud is a simple way to create a password for logging in to the created virtual machine. The best option would be to allow the users to avoid using an encrypted key pair and, instead, to create an ordinary password, as in most Web applications, simple for logging in. On the contrary, the HP cloud offers the user to retrieve an encrypted password for a Windows virtual server by pasting the private key for subsequent password decryption. This feature is available only for a few minutes after the actual start of the VM, whereas, to my mind, the password should be available on request anytime; otherwise the cloud behavior regarding interaction to virtual server should be considered non-trustworthy.

So, in a word, a simple action of authenticating the user for log in to the created virtual server should not look like an unnecessary exercise in RSA encryption.

Of the other features of HP cloud, it is possible to create in the cloud a network with subnets. Surely there is a default network created for any user, and it fits the user's requirements for most cases. As for virtual servers, in this section I demonstrated only creation of a VM from an image. It is also possible to use another method: to create a *volume* (cloud disk), to save the selected image in the volume, and to use the volume for booting the virtual server.

Another feature of the HP cloud is *monitoring* the health of the cloud services used. To use monitoring, the cloud user should create a monitoring *endpoint* and to choose a set of *metrics* to be used in the monitoring process.

In general, the HP cloud works in very economic style but its behavior, even in simple situations, sometimes can be non-trustworthy. Hopefully the situation will be corrected in the oncoming versions of the cloud.

2.7   SALESFORCE CLOUD PLATFORM

As stated below, Salesforce is a cloud platform to support any company's and personal business. This cloud platform is one of the oldest but it is rapidly progressing.

The Salesforce cloud login page is available at [82] and depicted in Figure 2.49.

The process of getting a free trial to Salesforce is fast and simple. The trial period is 1 month. On logging in to Salesforce, the user finds a very friendly starting atmosphere: lot of information, ready-to-use tours and video demos, and so on. The starting page of the Salesforce cloud is available at [83] and is shown in Figure 2.50.

As seen from the first minutes of using the Salesforce cloud, it is oriented quite differently from the other cloud platforms I consider in this section (by Microsoft, Google, HP, etc.). Those clouds are more suitable for software developers and other kinds of IT specialists, whereas the Salesforce cloud is oriented to business managers.

For each cloud page and functionality, there is a detailed help.

Instead of virtual machines, security groups, and so on. favored by IT persons, the features of the Salesforce cloud offered in the main menu are as follows:

– *Getting Started* – the starting page [83] offering videos and tours to get started.
– *Contacts* – contact information necessary for the business manager user who can start looking for possible contacts from the Outlook.

Figure 2.49   The Salesforce cloud platform login page.

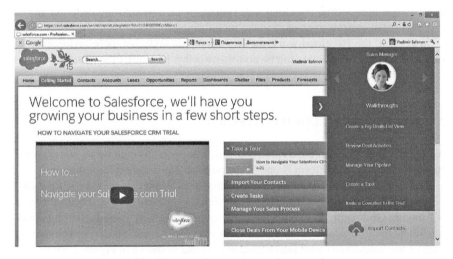

Figure 2.50   The Salesforce cloud platform starting page.

- *Accounts* – user accounts of employees of the business organization who use Salesforce.
- *Leads* – people who can potentially lead some campaign managed by the cloud user.
- *Opportunities* – list of financial and other kinds of business opportunities, tied to *financial quarters (FQs)* and *financial years (FYs)*.
- *Reports and Dashboards* – list of the reports and dashboards of the user. The most interesting is the *Company Performance Dashboard* shown in Figure 2.51.

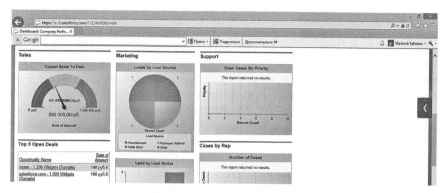

Figure 2.51   The Company Performance Dashboard in the Salesforce cloud.

- *Chatter* – a service to organize chat with potentially interesting people (e.g., the chatter proposed me to organize a chat with my university people).
- *Files* – a cloud storage for uploading, sharing, and downloading files.
- *Products* – the list and different kind of views to the products participating in the sales process by the user.
- *Forecasts* – list of business forecasts for near future.

Similar to other cloud platforms, Salesforce has its applications marketplace named *Salesforce AppExchange*. It is available at [84] and depicted in Figure 2.52. AppExchange is a marketplace for exchanging SaaS ready-to-use business-related cloud services. Some of them are developed by Google, for example, Gmail, Google Apps, and Google Calendar for Salesforce.

Salesforce is a non-traditional cloud organized in an unusual way. It does not have explicit IaaS servicing in the traditional sense, though the cloud has some business-oriented infrastructure and the related services. Most of its services are

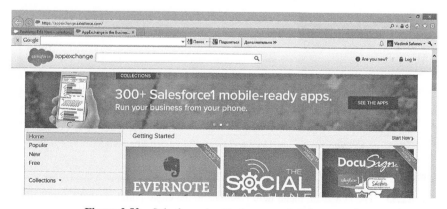

Figure 2.52   Salesforce AppExchange marketplace portal.

SaaS. As for PaaS, the Salesforce cloud does not have support for developing applications in a variety of languages and platforms directly in the cloud (unlike Amazon or IBM). Instead, it provides REST API for accessing the cloud from mobile and other applications. Also, Salesforce has a built-in mechanism for creating business-related applications without explicit programming in *APEX* – an environment initially developed by Oracle for fast development of Web applications related to the use of Oracle DBMS. The APEX toolkit enables to quickly create a schema of a database and related Web pages that get integrated into the structure of the Salesforce cloud Web portal.

For example, following the recommendations of the Salesforce cloud, I created an APEX application (named **safapp**) to handle information on positions in my orga-nization. The schema of the positions database was created by a couple of mouse clicks and got seamlessly integrated to my Salesforce cloud portal. The item *Posi-tions* became a new item in the main menu. The structure of the updated cloud portal, with a new menu item, is shown in Figure 2.53. The *Positions* menu item is a new one, created for my *safapp* application.

The new menu item *Positions* is handled similarly to the previous menu items. I clicked the Positions item and created a new position of professor of computer sci-ence. The resulting page with the newly added position is shown in Figure 2.54. Please note that my custom application name **safapp** is displayed in the upper right corner as the current action item.

The Salesforce cloud recommended me to make a post on this new position, to share information on the position with the cloud colleagues, and to create a new task related to the new position.

This simple example shows a high degree or integration of the extensions to the Salesforce cloud structure, and the trustworthiness of this cloud for business purposes.

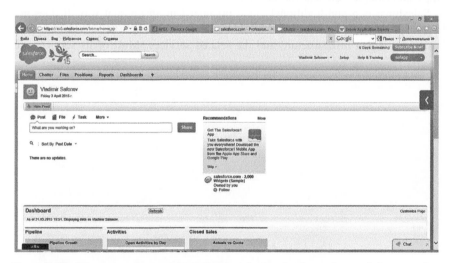

Figure 2.53 The new main menu item *Positions* in the cloud portal created for my *safapp* Web application.

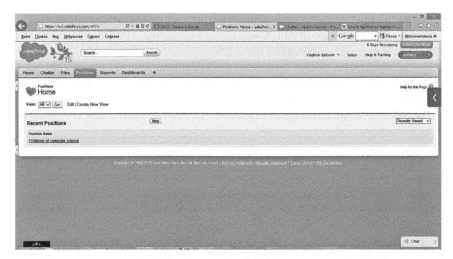

Figure 2.54 The use of the new Positions item: creating a position of a professor of computer science.

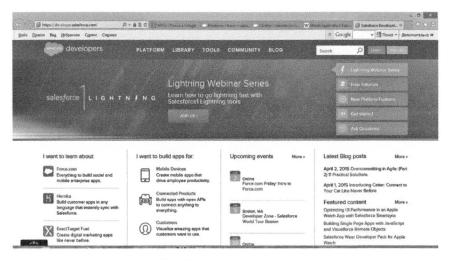

Figure 2.55 The Salesforce developers portal.

The Salesforce cloud provides access to the *Salesforce 1 lightning platform*, which allows software developers to quickly create social and mobile enterprise applications. The Salesforce developers portal is available at [85] and is depicted in Figure 2.55.

The main toolkit used by the Salesforce developers community is *Force.com IDE* [86]. This IDE allows the developers to create and test applications in APEX. Force.com IDE is based on the Eclipse platform. It is a client-side application so it should be installed on the client computer for further application development. The Force.com IDE has a built-in APEX Test Runner for testing APEX applications. The Force.com IDE portal is shown in Figure 2.56.

For the convenience of the cloud users, the Salesforce cloud has the *All Tabs* page. It allows the user to feel all the power and features of the Salesforce cloud. The page is available at [87] and is shown in Figure 2.57.

The Salesforce All Tabs page is extensible. The user can add a new tab for his or her convenience.

Figure 2.56　　The Force.com IDE portal.

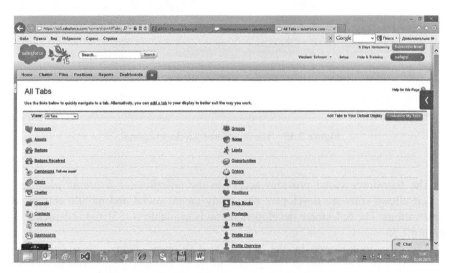

Figure 2.57　　The Salesforce cloud All Tabs page.

To demonstrate the ease of creating a new APEX application in Salesforce cloud, let us add a new application to handle information on my students. By clicking *Setup* and then *Build App* in the main menus, I opened the *App Quick Start* window. A new application in APEX handles a tab or a group of tabs. Let us create a new application and call it *safstudents*. The application designer recommends adding the name of the application, the name of the tab as *single* and its *plural* version. Let us call the single tab *Student* and the plural tab *Students*. The *App Quick Start window* with the above information for the *safstudents* application is depicted in Figure 2.58.

The *Students* table that will be processed by the new application is visualized in the lower part of the window.

Next, I click *Create* with the hope of creating my new application. However, I get a message from the cloud that I have exceeded the maximal number of the applications I can create during my free trial. I already have created one application *safapp*, so the maximal number of the applications that can be created during the trial of the Salesforce cloud is 1.

The cloud provides the way to delete my application. So, I deleted the *safapp* application and, because of that, could create the new application *safstudents* as shown in Figure 2.58. As a result, my new application gets integrated into the cloud portal structure, similar to my deleted application *safapp*. The result – the updated cloud portal with the new application *safstudents* – is shown in Figure 2.59.

A very nice feature! I created an application in APEX without writing a line of code by a few clicks, and the application automatically got integrated into the cloud structure. I should acknowledge this is the fastest and most comfortable way of cloud extension I have ever seen in any cloud. Congratulations to the Salesforce team!

Now let us consider one more opportunity provided by the Salesforce cloud. There is a *developer console* for creating new APEX applications. The console is available

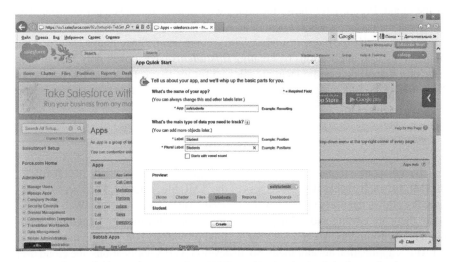

Figure 2.58 Quick start of an APEX application in the Salesforce cloud.

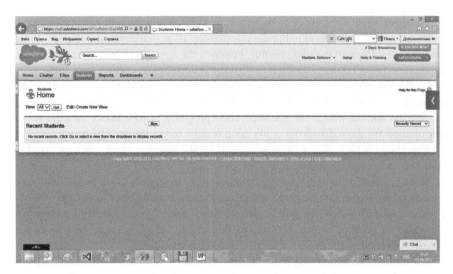

Figure 2.59   The new APEX application *safstudents* integrated into the cloud portal.

in the contextual menu related to my account (located in the upper right part of the main portal window). By clicking on my account name and then *Developer Console*, I get access to the Force.com APEX developer console in the cloud. Yet another great functionality! So one way to create an APEX application was just demonstrated – a quick start of an application. Yet another way to create an APEX application in the cloud is the developer console. The developer console is available at the URL address [88] in the cloud, and depicted in Figure 2.60.

The APEX developer console looks like a traditional IDE but is available as part of the cloud. Figure 2.60 shows the *New* menu item of the developer console. The developer may create a new element of an APEX language – an *APEX class*, an *APEX trigger*, a *VisualForce page,* or a *VisualForce component*. Since I have exceeded the limits of my trial applications by creating **safstudents** (see above), only VisualForce page or a VisualForce component are allowed for me to create. An APEX page is an XML file of the following structure:

```
<apex:page>
</apex:page>
```

and the *.vfp* name extension (for *Visual Force Page*). So, there is a built-in constructor of XML pages. It checks the correctness of the XML file structure. The *Preview* functionality allows the users to preview the created Visual Force page in a Web browser. Also, there are editing and debugging features, typical for modern integrated development environments. So, the Salesforce cloud provides a comfortable modern IDE for APEX application development. So, to develop APEX applications, the cloud user can develop them completely in the cloud, without using any client-side installations.

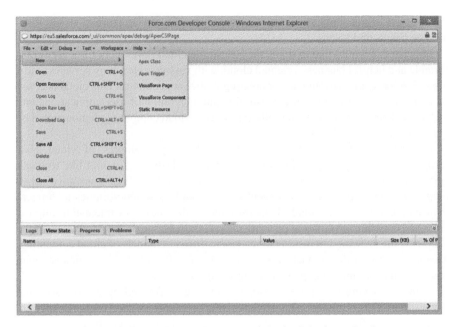

Figure 2.60 APEX developer console in the Salesforce cloud.

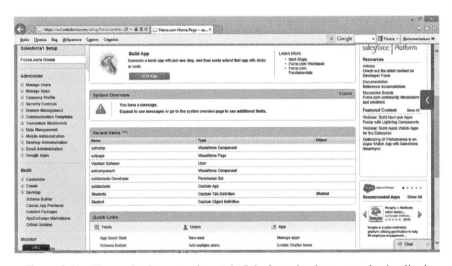

Figure 2.61 The result of my experiments in Salesforce developer console visualized.

To overview the results of my experiments in the Salesforce cloud – APEX applications, VisualForce pages, VisualForce components, and so on – I click the *Setup* item and go to the Salesforce1 Setup platform page shown in Figure 2.61. All my created items are displayed as hypertext items, and can be viewed by clicking – including the structure of my application, the structure of its tabs, the structure of all my VisualForce pages, and so on.

In general, I would like to thank the Salesforce cloud developers for a very comfortable and helpful business-oriented cloud, with very good teaching services, and a great development environment for creating APEX applications. This cloud is based on contemporary principles of extensibility and integration of user applications into the cloud. This is an example of really trustworthy cloud computing demonstrated by Salesforce cloud developers.

In summary, in this chapter I considered many examples of cloud platforms – Amazon, IBM, Oracle, Google, HP and Salesforce. I would like to thank very much the developers of all the clouds considered for their innovative ideas, trustworthy implementations, excellent services, and great opportunities to "finger" their clouds for about a month. Hopefully the readers have got interesting impressions and concrete information on using these clouds. I hope the main outcome of the chapter is the growing interest in the readers to different models of cloud computing. Thanks also to all the contact persons from IBM, HP, and Oracle companies who contacted me by email. I appreciate their attention.

I am also asking the cloud developers not to get offended by my remarks and suggestions. This is an understandable reaction of an experienced user and software developer. Hopefully the critique I included into this chapter will be beneficial for the progress of trustworthy cloud computing.

EXERCISES TO CHAPTER 2

E2.1 What company is the pioneer of cloud computing and how is its public cloud called?

E2.2 What does the acronym EC2 mean in cloud computing?

E2.3 What kind of features does the Review functionality in Amazon cloud provide?

E2.4 Please list the main features of the Amazon cloud.

E2.5 What is an AMI?

E2.6 What is a VPC in Amazon cloud platform?

E2.7 What is an instance of a virtual machine and how is it created in the cloud?

E2.8 What kind of networking protocols are used for connecting with a virtual machine?

E2.8 What kind of support does the Amazon cloud provide for databases in the cloud? Which database platforms are supported?

E2.9 What is Amazon DynamoDB and what kind of databases (tables) does it support?

E2.10 What is Elastic BeansTalk in Amazon cloud, what kind of PaaS functionality and which application platforms does it support?

E2.11 Which two public cloud platforms does IBM support and what are the specifics of each of them?

E2.12 What are the main features of the IBM Bluemix cloud platform?

E2.13 Please compare IaaS functionalities in Amazon and IBM Bluemix clouds.

E2.14 What is Cloud Foundry and what is the role of this organization in developing of IBM cloud and other public clouds?

E2.15 What kind of SaaS cloud services, in your opinion, are especially innovative and important in IBM cloud?

E2.16 Please overview the PaaS features of the IBM Bluemix cloud platform.

E2.17 What kind of social public clouds does Oracle provide?

E2.18 What are the specifics of the architecture of the Oracle cloud portal? Which of them are not quite comfortable and why?

E2.19 What kind of cloud servicing is DaaS and how is it supported in Oracle cloud?

E2.20 Please overview the PaaS and SaaS features of the Oracle cloud.

E2.21 Please overview the Oracle cloud marketplace portal.

E2.22 What kind of cloud servicing is characteristic of the Google cloud?

E2.23 Which cloud console is used for working with the Google cloud?

E2.24 Please characterize Google services (including cloud services) approach to user authentication.

E2.25 Please overview the specifics and features of Google cloud approach to IaaS and virtual machines.

E2.26 What is the Google App Engine and what kind of features does it provide?

E2.27 Please overview Google cloud Big Data processing features.

E2.28 What are the specifics of HP Helion public cloud architecture regarding cloud services activation?

E2.29 Please analyze the HP's economical approach to cloud services and to the related user expenses.

E2.30 What kind of approach does HP cloud follow regarding database support? Why is it so, in your opinion?

E2.31 Which operating systems families for cloud virtual machines does HP support? Compare it to Amazon, IBM, and Google cloud's IaaS features.

E2.32 What is a container in HP Helion cloud and what kind of features does it provide?

E2.33 What kind of cloud services does the Salesforce cloud provide and to what kind of users is it oriented?

E2.34 What is APEX and how is it supported in the Salesforce cloud?

E2.35 How can an APEX Web application be developed and added to the Salesforce cloud portal?

E2.36 What is the Force.com IDE and for which language is it used by Salesforce developers?

E2.37 What is the Salesforce developer's console and what kind of cloud application development does it provide in the Salesforce cloud?

E2.38 Please list all kinds of APEX language entities available for development by the Salesforce developer's console in the Salesforce cloud.

E2.39 Please get trial access to all the clouds covered in this chapter – Amazon, Oracle, HP, IBM, Google and Salesforce. Please repeat all the hand-on labs with those clouds included into this chapter. Describe your impressions and issues (if any) you experienced.

3

PRINCIPLES AND PILLARS OF TRUSTWORTHY COMPUTING

3.1 VITAL ISSUES OF TRUSTWORTHY COMPUTING

The needs and vital issues of trustworthy computing [89, 90] surround us and penetrate all our everyday life. Most of our activities are tightly related to the use of computing technologies – seeking any important information, purchasing goods in a store, calling on a smartphone, watching a Smart TV, and so on – everything is now related to the use of computing and computing devices. So we depend so much on the trustworthiness of computers and software that the need of trustworthy computing became vital. Software bugs can be used as *vulnerabilities* to attack software products. Confidential information that we have to trust to computers – personal data, credit card numbers, PIN codes, and so on – becomes the subject of attacks with the purpose of stealing it and using for malicious purposes. Naive emotional reaction of computer users to fake warnings on danger for personal bank accounts forces people to unreasonable actions that lead to passing personal secrets to hackers by clicking Web references one should never click (*phishing*). Any computer user should keep in mind that at any moment he or she is on the Internet, there is a great risk of being attacked. How can this be avoided? The first rule is always to behave reasonably: do not trust traps such as panic style emails or Web pages; do not pass on confidential information by yourselves to unknown people or sites. The second rule is to always use trustworthy software.

So, there is evidently a growing need for trustworthy computing, since "cyber-attacks" may happen every day, hour, or minute, and can lead to fatal consequences, from the crush of some data or the whole computer system to a fault in some company or even the death of a live organism controlled to some extent by a computer.

Trustworthy Cloud Computing, First Edition. Vladimir O. Safonov.
© 2016 John Wiley & Sons, Inc. Published 2016 by John Wiley & Sons, Inc.

The book "Trust in Cyberspace" [91] considered to be a classical book on trustworthy computing defines this term as follows: "Trustworthiness is assurance that a system deserves to be trusted – that it will perform as expected despite environmental disruptions, human and operator error, hostile attacks, and design and implementation errors. Trustworthy systems reinforce the belief that they will continue to produce expected behavior and will not be susceptible to subversion."

The concept of trustworthy computing is wide and based on a number of scientific, engineering, business, and human factors.

In most cases, however, trustworthy or non-trustworthy computing starts with the user interface of the software you are using. Sometimes non-friendly user interface can undermine the user's trust in a useful tool. This is especially important for cloud GUI, since cloud specifics and tools are not so well known to the majority of users as, say, Microsoft Office. To be really trustworthy, the cloud GUI should easily provide explanation and help to the user who is not so accustomed to it.

Let us consider briefly the history of trustworthy computing issues.

The first computers appeared in the 1940s and their software was inherently non-trustworthy because of the poor user interface, such as using punched tape or punched cards to code and input a program written directly in binary machine instructions, and using operator control panel with manual switches and LEDs to input and visualize each bit of memory. However, those computers were "monopolized" by single users, in their turn, for some definite periods of time, so the main danger of user-to-user intervention just could not occur. So, the first computers were non-trustworthy by their low level interface.

A common point on trustworthy computing is that it originated in the 1960s, with the appearance of multiuser and multitasking systems.

One of the first approaches to trustworthy computing (as stated in Wikipedia) was formulated by Allen-Babcock computer company in 1967 in very similar terms as later Microsoft's trustworthy computing approach in 2002: "An ironclad operating system [reliability]; use of trustworthy personnel [business integrity]; effective access control [security]; user requested optional privacy [privacy]."

Later, in the 1960s and the 1970s, computer networking started, which brought many other issues of computing trustworthiness, related to increasing probability of network attacks, and the corresponding need to mitigate them.

Typical kinds of attacks are *viruses, Trojan programs, and network worms* – malicious software aimed at making harm to computer systems; *distributed denial of service* – a network attack based on generating several requests to the server causing its faults; *phishing* – stealing user logins and passwords by frightening and deceiving users with false threats (e.g., threat of deleting their bank accounts) with malicious email messages and Web sites; *pharming* – redirecting users to malicious Web sites to steal their confidential data; *elevation of privilege* – achieving administrator's permissions to modify system files and directories.

Another source of attack is the use of security vulnerabilities in ordinary software. A classical attack is referred to as *buffer overrun* and uses the following vulnerability. The standard C library function for copying strings – *strcpy (dest, source)* – is often used to copy a null-terminated string *source* to another memory location *dest*. However, the size of *source* is not explicitly indicated, so it may happen that the result of such copying (either mistakenly or intentionally) will lead to corrupting the memory of another process or task. A simple recipe to preventing such attack is the use of a more secure version of the C function – *strncpy (dest, source, length)* – where the maximal length of the source string to be copied is indicated explicitly. The book [92] provides a host of such security recipes.

3.2 THE TRUSTWORTHY COMPUTING INITIATIVE BY MICROSOFT

The trustworthy computing (TWC) Initiative started in 2002 with the historical email from Bill Gates, the founder and at those times the head of Microsoft, to all company's employees on the *trustworthy computing initiative*. This event was really the starting point of the modern approach to trustworthy computing – its principles, discipline, tools, and software development lifecycle to support development of trustworthy software products. The immediate reason for that was the need to make an urgent security refurbishment of Windows 2000 after its first official customer shipment, known in Microsoft history as *security push* [92], fixing a big number of security vulnerabilities found by Windows 2000 operating system users. Now, 13 years later, we can summarize that Microsoft has been applying these principles in practice to all its software products, including its cloud computing platform Microsoft Azure (see Chapter 5). Also, due to appearance of cloud computing, the trustworthy computing principles were renovated, as applicable to cloud, and now we all experience the "second life" of trustworthy computing. More details on this are given in Chapter 4.

The principles of trustworthy computing were clearly formulated in Craig Mundie's white paper [93]. Trustworthy computing should be based on four "pillars": *security* – the ability of software to be resilient to attacks; *reliability* – the ability of software to perform its required functions under certain conditions for a certain time period; *privacy* – preserving personal and company's confidential information; and *business integrity* – prompt ways of running software maintenance business to fix security, privacy, and reliability bugs on the one hand and correctness of software business on the other, paying much attention to its legal aspects. So Microsoft's approach to the problems of trustworthy computing is wide and based not only on purely software development principles but also on business, legal, and human factors.

Of the four TWC pillars formulated by Microsoft, security and reliability are the most "traditional." For many people, the motto of TWC is first associated with *security* – encrypting programs and data, struggling with viruses and worms, mitigating network attacks, and so on. *Reliability* is another area equally important for TWC, since non-reliable software is vulnerable to attacks, based on its known bugs and issues, and may cause insecure and unsafe situations during its use.

The remaining two TWC pillars, *privacy* and *business integrity*, are the most dependent on people's activity and behavior, since they not only need to keep the software business correct and legal (as far as private and confidential information is concerned) but also recommend to follow software process disciplines aimed at making software products trustworthy. So the "human factors" still remain an important part of TWC. What software technologies can do to make the human factors more trustworthy is to implement and offer appropriate suggestions and software process disciplines for the users.

In my opinion, all the four pillars of TWC are very important, but I think a fifth, equally important one, should be added to them – *usability: ease of use and user-friendly interface*. This quality of any software product is so important from the user's viewpoint, when assessing whether a product is trustworthy, that the user will not take the product into his or her hands any more as non-trustworthy after a short trial experience, in case the product is not attractive for some reason, and its appearance and operating interface is awkward and uncomfortable. I already described earlier the non-trustworthy interface of the first computers, based on triggers and LED on the control panel. That "shortcoming of growth" was overcome long ago. But, from time to time, there appear software products that force the users to do a lot of redundant actions. They impose on the users some non-flexible disciplines of operation that most users do not agree with, but are unable to customize. Their output consists of incomplete, unclear, or silly messages. Therefore, they have users wasting their time and, as a result, push them away not only from using these products but also from using computing technologies for a long time. No usability – no trust. So I think usability features are as equally important from TWC viewpoint as security, reliability, and privacy. In the TWC white paper [93], usability is defined as one of the *means* to achieve the four main goals, but, in my opinion, it should be one of the TWC pillars, as a crucial product quality for users. This is especially important for clouds and their user interface. In Chapter 2, I made a detailed and sincere analysis of the comfortable and uncomfortable features of several popular cloud platforms.

3.3   THE SECURITY PILLAR

According to many papers [1], computer security is a field of computer science concerned with control of risks related to computer use. In more common sense, security (including computer security) is the ability to be resilient to attacks. In the security paradigm, there are three parties: the *system* to be secured, the *user* willing the security of the system, and the *attackers* trying to break the system. So the main task of the security subsystem in any computer hardware should be to undertake *systematic security measures* to preserve the security of the system, for example, checking any Web site to be browsed for potential phishing threats; asking the permission of the user to download any kind of document or code (no implicit downloads). Such security actions are likely to make the software running slightly slower, but this is the necessary security overhead – it is not recommended to switch off any security checks because of high risk of attacks.

The following major tasks can be formulated in relation to computer security.

The first one is *classification and analysis* of systems and their kinds of security, categories of users (from security and allowed actions viewpoint), known and imaginable kinds of attacks and attackers, and possible security measures to be taken. There are a number of very interesting papers in this area, in particular, [92] – one of the best on the subject I know.

The second task is to find ways of *quantitative assessment* of security. This task is one of the most complicated, an intellectual challenge to be solved. As far as I can judge, we are now only on our way to solving it. Using mathematical formulas in terms of probability theory and statistics would probably be not the most suitable approach, due to the polymorphic and complicated nature of security and a lot of "human factors" participating. But, clearly, any scientific approach to such complicated problem as computer security should include its quantitative evaluation.

The third task, more practical and traditional for software engineering up to now, is to develop *security technologies and tools*. A lot of progress has been made in this direction, especially in cloud computing (see Chapter 4). Actually each of the operating systems and software development platforms paid a lot of attention to security technologies involved, and this tendency is growing more and more.

In a more practical and ubiquitous sense, for *home users*, security means everyday struggle with viruses and worms penetrating into the user's computer from flash memory devices or from the Internet (mostly by email). Their attacks may crush the system or at least are likely to have the user waste a lot of working time on cleaning the computer of viruses. Another important aspect is the user's understanding of how to properly configure security on his or her computer – for example, when using an Internet browser whose new more secure versions may require explicit selection and setting of a suitable layer of security.

For *office users,* there are a lot of security aspects to be remembered, including protection of confidential information from malicious actions or from colleagues, securing LANs and WANs, installing and using security patches of the operating systems and software tools of everyday use, and so on.

For *cloud users,* as explained in Chapter 2, there are a number of security specifics related to securing IP addresses of virtual servers and authentication protocols used to log in to them.

For *software developers*, security should be an inherent part of the software process and discipline. A developer should think about the security of his or her product every day, at every milestone and stage of the project development. At product maintenance stage, *security patches* should be issued when needed, to protect the product and its users from newly invented attacks and malicious software.

The following security principles are followed and recommended for software developers by Microsoft's trustworthy computing approach. They form the basis of the Microsoft approach to secure software development used in all new products by Microsoft, including Microsoft Azure cloud – *security development life cycle* (*SDLC*) – covered in [94]. This approach is pursued by Microsoft in developing its own software products since 2002 and recommended to other software developers.

Implementation of the SDLC scheme should enable three facets of developing secure software pointed out by Microsoft – *repeatable process; engineers' education*; *metrics and accountability*. As for repeatable process, it has been implemented and pursued by Microsoft for over 13 years. It includes regular engineers' education performed by extra class security experts. However, even the latest publications on software metrics recommend sets of metrics that *post-assert* security qualities of the product version already developed, whereas the most valuable approach could be to develop and use *predictive security metrics* that could be helpful to make an assessment of the efforts required to secure software development – but the latter task is much more complicated.

SDLC is based on the following formula: *SD3+C: secure by design, secure by default, secure in deployment,* and *communication.*

Secure by Design principle means that the software product should be, starting from the early stages of its development, designed to enable protection of itself and its data from attacks. In particular, it may use some data encryption algorithm, and may also support extra checks for data integrity, especially when the data are received via Internet or Intranet. As for resistance to attacks, the software product should be intelligent enough to recognize typical attacks and to "learn" how to mitigate more and more of them. The latter quality means that *knowledge bases, data mining,* and *machine learning* techniques should be used by products for processing network traffic (e.g., firewalls) and large data streams. Especially important is the *least privilege* design principle: secure software should run correctly when launched by the ordinary user without administrator's permissions. When developing and testing software, developer engineers often log on to their workstations under login names with administrator's privileges, so they are likely to miss the fact that the software may not run when the ordinary user launches it.

Secure by Default means that the security checks should be turned on by default when using the product, according to the heuristic that the other software in general is assumed to be insecure by default. For example, when using the latest Internet Explorer versions, the users may be surprised that, with the default security layer, it requires the user to explicitly select the set of trusted Web sites, unlike some earlier versions of the browser. However, this security functionality is quite reasonable and easy to use, to avoid malicious redirections. To investigate whether your .NET application is secure by default or not, please pass it to Microsoft *FxCop* utility [95] for checking against its security rules. You will be surprised at the big number of security violations FxCop detects. In more allegoric terms, such software quality as security by default may be associated to a battlefield, with troops of knights and dragons struggling against each other, in such a way that every knight puts his helmet on and holds his sword by default, since he assumes a dragon can attack at every moment. Although in some cases that will not be quite comfortable for the knight, he can save his life and health, by pursuing this security principle. What to do – whether to carry a heavy helmet and sword or die of an occasional dragon's attack – is up to the knight to decide.

Secure in Deployment means that the product and its documentation should help ordinary users and system administrators to use it securely, and to easily install and deploy security updates of the product. For example, on booting the latest versions of Windows, a number of security alerts are issued, for example, a warning that antivirus software is not installed, or is off, if so. Also, as well known, Windows notifies its users on any security updates, downloads, and installs them automatically, unless the user has explicitly refused to do that. In cloud computing, I considered in Chapter 2 some examples of *security analysis and recommendations* by the cloud to the cloud user on how to make his cloud resources more secure (e.g., this functionality is implemented in IBM Bluemix cloud).

Communications, in the context of the above security formula, means that the developers of the software product should be responsive to end users' and system administrators' requests on product vulnerabilities discovered and on the urgent help (advice) needed by the users on appropriate security settings for the product. The developers should promptly make patches to fix new security vulnerabilities and make them available for download, installation, and use. Microsoft demonstrates pursuing this policy every day – a lot of security patches for all Microsoft products promptly appear on their Web sites.

The security development lifecycle, in addition to the classical waterfall software development scheme, should enable a number of extra actions during the whole process of software product development: at the requirements stage – formulating security requirements; at the design stage – making security risk analysis; at the test planning stage – developing risk-based security tests; at the code implementation stage – using code static analysis tools to verify the security of the code developed. A typical example of a static analysis tool is *FxCop* [95] – a tool to check the binary code of .NET assemblies against the extensible set of security and other trustworthy computing requirements and rules. Using FxCop is mandatory at some Russian software companies that develop .NET code.

Requirements. At the requirements phase, the product team interacts with the central security team that assigns from its staff the *product security advisor (buddy)*. The product team works with the security advisor to develop security plans, to integrate them into the product schedule, and to clarify security requirements based on user's recommendations, previous experience, and industry standards.

Design. The design phase should be targeted at security. The main principle that should be followed is to use a *trusted computing base*. Microsoft recommends, for the first turn, using secure design techniques such as *layering* and *strong typing*. I can also add principles of *modularity* and *abstract data types* – encapsulating representation of complicated data structures. All these design principles have proved their practical applicability and importance since the 1970s, long before the "TWC era." In addition, Microsoft formulates three closely related security design principles: *minimal attack surface, least privilege,* and *threat modeling. Minimal attack surface* means that the default configuration of the software should minimize chances of successful security attack, since the software is supposed to be used in non-secure environments. *Least privilege* principle recommends designing, developing, and testing software so that it is launched and used by ordinary non-privileged users, rather than by system administrators, in case system administrator's privileges are really not necessary for running the software – this is the case for most software products. It helps avoid the stealing of extra privileges and their malicious usage by the attackers. *Threat modeling* should be performed, starting from the software design stage, to determine possible kinds of attacks and the ability of the software to resist them. Microsoft also emphasizes the importance of defining *supplemental (security related) shipping criteria* at the design stage – in particular, the criteria for the product to be free from externally reported security vulnerabilities before shipping its new version. When the product is shipped with a list of known security bugs (or probably some others not yet discovered), instead of fixing these bugs prior to release, it may widen the attack surface for hackers.

Implementation. This stage is the most decisive from security viewpoint, since the developer's team should avoid security vulnerabilities in the product code resulting from this phase. The following principles are recommended by Microsoft as part of SDL at the implementation stage:

- Apply coding and testing standards
- Apply security testing tools, including fuzzing tools
- Apply static analysis code scanning tools
- Conduct *code reviews* by security experts.

Coding standards should include security recommendations – how to avoid typical security flaws such as buffer overrun and to insert proper security checks into the code.

To enable proper level and quality of the security subsystem for a software product, *security experts (buddies)* should be included into the software product development team and should participate in all stages of the product discussions, planning, design, development, testing, shipment to users, and analyzing users' feedback on the product.

At the *verification (testing) phase*, Microsoft recommends the developers to make a *security push* – additional security code reviews, and focused *security testing*, including *fuzz testing (fuzzing)*. Fuzzing is a technique for automated boundary values testing using "semi-correct" data. For example, all the input data for the test are taken to be correct, except for an integer input value taken less by 1 than the minimal correct value, or greater by 1 than the maximal correct value. The boundary values testing principle was formulated by Myers in the 1970s, but now, in the era of TWC, the principle became especially important. Fuzzing technique is applied not only to integer input data but also to IP addresses when testing network protocol implementations, which is of high importance, since it is well known that generating sequential IP addresses is a popular technique used by hackers to find a security breach and the networking software product should be resistant to such attacks.

As for the latest security initiatives, Microsoft has organized a Security Response Center. Its progress report is available at [96]. Since 2003, it supported many security-related projects. One of them is the *Enhanced Mitigation Experience Toolkit (EMET)* – a toolkit to help various organizations improve their security. EMET attracted the attention of many organizations, including the US Department of Defense. The latest version of EMET at the moment of writing the book is 5.1. EMET is targeted at securing any kind of software from threats and attacks.

3.4   THE RELIABILITY PILLAR

Reliability is the ability of a software product to enable its expected functionality under certain conditions during a certain period of time. According to the IEEE's definition, reliability is *the ability of a system or component to perform its required functions under stated conditions for a specified period of time*. From the viewpoint of reliability theory for technical systems, the most commonly used quantitative assessment of software product reliability is its *mean time between failures* (*MTBFs*) – the average time between system failures during some large period of time. Informally speaking, a reliable software product is a software product the customers can rely on. Intuitively, a piece of software is reliable if it checks its environment (e.g., the arguments of procedures or methods) for correctness, and behaves reasonably if an incorrect input condition is found, by issuing an understandable error message.

As explained in Section 1.12, for cloud computing, the MTBF principle is often replaced by the *Mean Time to Recover* (*MTTR*) principle, since cloud hardware may demonstrate failures because of very large numbers of (many million) users of the public cloud.

Also, to measure software reliability, software *complexity* metrics are often used, such as the number of source code lines; or Halstead's metrics, the number of operands and operators in a program; or cyclomatic complexity (McCabe's metrics – the number of control branches in the program) [97]. The latter approach is based on the heuristic suggestion that the more complicated the system is, the less reliable it is likely to be, which is surely not always true. Even the authors of the thorough software reliability measurement paper [97] recognize that measuring software and software reliability in particular is actually almost at the initial stage.

So, as applicable to software, practitioners, including Microsoft experts, usually understand reliability in a more intuitive meaning close to the IEEE definition: reliable software is the software the customers can rely on, in the sense that it fulfills its expected functions when required.

Actually it is a very complicated task to develop an appropriate, precise, and complete quantitative theoretical estimate of software reliability, for the following reasons:

- Each software module requires separate reliability assessment, and the ways the modules communicate also require reliability assessment.
- Software is evolving much more rapidly than hardware, due to bug fixes and functionality enhancements in the course of software maintenance.
- The environment in which the software runs shall also be taken in account, and that environment may vary on different machines. Each update of environment settings can change the reliability of a software system: for example, manual update of the Windows registry by *regedit* may cause crush of some software tool considered 100% reliable, since the tool implementation is based on the assumption that some information is located in the registry.

Under these circumstances, such simple quantitative assessment as one MTBF or one cyclomatic complexity figure for the whole system is not appropriate but is a little helpful, since it can reflect statistics of the system use or provide general understanding whether the system, taken in whole, can be considered reliable or not. A more general theoretical quantitative assessment model taking into account the environment, all software components, and any software updates, is likely to be too awkward and hardly usable. So, in this book I will use the term "reliability" in the intuitive sense just explained.

Currently, the following techniques are used to improve software reliability:

- *Reliable design and implementation methods*: modularity; abstract data types; structured programming; object-oriented analysis and design; design-by-contract; aspect-oriented programming, and so on. The goal of all those technological approaches is to decompose software into reliable components – easy to specify, design, integrate, reuse, test, document, and maintain. In particular, to improve reliability of a software module, according to classical papers by Myers, the module should check its input information (arguments) to be consistent and complete, and, if not, should terminate with clear notification of the abnormal condition detected (throw an exception, speaking in modern terms).

- *Software testing*: unit testing, system testing, black box testing, white box testing, measuring and increasing test coverage, boundary values testing, equivalence class partitioning, fuzzing, and so on. Testing techniques and tools are numerous. Most valuable, from reliability viewpoint, are those tools to measure the completeness of testing and to recommend the user ways to make the process of testing more complete.

- *Formal specification and verification methods*: Floyd–Hoare program calculus (Hoare's triples); algebraic specification (particularly, using SDL or OBJ specification languages); set theoretic specification (in particular, Z notation); denotational semantics; the latest approach – model checking, and so on. Formal methods seem to produce "100% reliable" code, since they formally prove that the code corresponds to the given set of specifications. But it should be taken into account that the software specifications and software correctness proofs themselves can be buggy. In addition, formal methods may be difficult for practitioners to apply, for the very simple reason that software developers just forget mathematics from years of working hard on commercial software projects. A more deep reason why most formal methods are still not suitable to apply to software practice is as follows [1]: the paradigm of thinking and the basic concepts of computer science are fundamentally different from those of mathematics, the basis of formal methods. In particular, a variable is treated in computer science as a changeable "cell," but in mathematics, a variable (say, x) usually denotes some magnitude whose value is supposed to be *constant* during mathematical speculations, in particular, in a theorem proof. This contradicts the dynamic nature of programming and may cause difficulties in attempts to describe changeable behavior of a program by mathematical concepts. However, I do think that suitable formal methods can (and will) be worked out to be really helpful to software reliability improvement. Two positive examples are SDL – algebraic specification language used as de facto standard in telecommunication software development; and Spec# – an extension of C# and Visual Studio.NET by formal specification and verification features, designed and implemented by Microsoft Research. Formal methods are evolving since the 1960s and are still mostly used in theoretical papers. Currently there are practically usable languages and tools to support them. For example, Microsoft Research developed and implemented the Spec# language – an extension of C# by formal specifications in design-by-contract style. This allows software developers to make object-oriented software more reliable by checking (at verification time if possible, or at runtime) the *contract* for any class developed – the appropriate pre-conditions and post-conditions for its methods, and the class invariant.

All of those techniques of reliable software development have proved their practical importance for 60-odd years of computer programming. However, software is getting more and more complicated (e.g., cloud platforms), so these techniques need to evolve.

The most important task in software reliability theory is its adequate *quantitative assessment*. Although the discipline of quantitative assessment of trustworthy computing has only recently started, in the books [98, 99] the theoretical basis is proposed for such kinds of quantitative assessments.

3.5 THE PRIVACY PILLAR

Privacy is the ability of the software product to keep private all confidential data by the users. The product should explicitly ask the users for permission to collect and use any kind of data on the user and its computer system. All sensitive information (such as private addresses or credit card numbers) should be used in *encrypted* form, especially when transferring over the network. The software product should prevent the users from privacy-related attacks through anti-phishing filters (for the Web sites used), and by anti-spam filters (when using email messages). In addition, the user himself or herself should be smart enough not to trust too much to messages on his or her bank account, unexpected lottery prize, and so on, since, in most cases, they are deceptive and targeted at phishing.

For example, imagine that a CD with a computer database of full names, addresses, and contact phones of the people living in some country or city appears to be publicly on sale in the underground or in newspaper kiosks. Such a situation is a serious threat not only to information security and privacy of the people but to their lives, safety, and health, since this information can be maliciously used by criminals for kidnapping and blackmail – and this actually happens, fortunately not often. How can we fight against this? In my opinion, the appropriate laws, obligations for the people to obey them, and punishment for their violation should be wise and fair, including punishment not only for malicious use of such CDs but, equally severe, also for their sales. This is just one example to demonstrate that using only IT methods and tools, whatever high level they are, is not enough to keep privacy. What also matters is law enforcement and positively evolving the consciousness of people. All people and families must be sure that everything is being done to prevent the situations described. Also, some software developers of Web applications do not always realize what kind of information they should not make publicly available on the Internet. I have sometimes prevented such Web publications (made mistakenly in student projects) of real full names of the members of whole families.

Another common example is a *phishing* attempt – such issues are experienced by almost everyone, while using email. Imagine you get an email that your bank account is in danger and you need just to click a Web link and *enter your name and bank account number* to save it. This is a typical attempt to steal your private data with an obvious goal. No doubt, clicking the Web link will cause *pharming* you to a malicious Web site set up by a criminal group. They even try to use such design and colors that their trap email reminds you of the site of your favorite bank. How do we prevent it? At first, please put your mouse cursor onto the Web reference and try to read the URL in the pop-up window, without clicking it. You will most likely find out that the reference is *not* to the bank Web site. Looking at this situation from a more general viewpoint, let us try to analyze how to counter such situations. Using ordinary spam filters does not 100% help, as we have already noted. In my own experience, such spam filters often filter out important emails but leave all the email "traps" in your inbox. It should be mentioned in this context that Microsoft's SmartScreen technology built into Microsoft Outlook combats spam by using probability-based weighting to analyze an email message, and find and close Web beacons that can be used by spammers to determine active email addresses. In some cases, the *Human Interface Proofs* (*HIPs*) technique is helpful in preventing automated registration and creation of new Web and email accounts by spammer malware (rather than by humans). The idea of the HIP technique is to use decorated exotic text labels readable and understandable by humans only but non-recognizable by spammer programs. As for the "human factor" side, special laws and social measures are necessary to struggle with spam and phishing – such measures are now introduced in many countries.

Equally important, if a software product you are using occasionally asks you to enter any kind of private information, either for activation purpose, or for registration, or during everyday use, you should be able to know how this private information will be used by the product. This is a very important privacy principle followed by Microsoft in all latest versions of all its software products. The same principle is followed if a Microsoft software product implicitly collects private information. Keeping the users fully informed on the private data collected by the software and the purpose of such collecting benefits greatly in guaranteeing the users' trust.

To enhance privacy and security features, Microsoft implemented and shipped in all latest operating systems and service packs to earlier OS the privacy protecting measures which include the following:

- *Internet Explorer InfoBar*, to prevent malicious dialog screens;
- built-in pop-up blocker turned on by default, especially valuable to get rid of lots of advertisements imposed on anyone each moment of using a browser;
- download blocker, to suppress unsolicited downloads;

- redesigned version of *AuthentiCode based dialog box* to double check the down-loaded code identity and integrity before its installation;
- the *Never Install* option that allows the user to avoid unsolicited and undesirable downloaded code installations.

All the above functionality is easy to use and intended to guard the user from many kinds of common attempts to bring to his or her machine and install malicious code. Surely the process of checked downloading now takes a little longer because of the need to explicitly handle new related GUI, but it is quite justified. As for pop-up advertisements appearing in browsers, they do not violate the normal functioning of your system, but can lead to waste of your working time in struggling with them, and can even be harmful to your health because of the negative emotions they cause by their rough nature (I am sharing my own impressions with you). So, in practical use of operating systems starting with such early product as Windows XP Service Pack 2, Microsoft now saves our time, health, and privacy, by blocking those pop-ups.

An important part of privacy is *encryption* of data, programs, emails, instant messages, banking information, and any other kinds of communications via the Internet. This topic is already thoroughly investigated and widely discussed in scientific literature. In particular, email encryption is a common practice of many IT companies trying to keep their technical information private and confidential. Worth mentioning are the new types of file systems with automatic data encryption, such as ZFS in Oracle's Solaris operating system. Traditionally, encryption is one of the favorite topics for students. However, I will only mention this subject in my book, since its main goal is different.

3.6 THE BUSINESS INTEGRITY PILLAR

The *business integrity* pillar is twofold. On the one hand, it means prompt reaction of the software product team to users' questions and the bugs found, especially those related to security, privacy, and reliability issues. On the other hand, it means correctness of business principles of the software product developer company. So, unlike security, privacy, and reliability, this pillar of trustworthy computing is more related to human, legal, and business factors. "Trustworthy" in the context of business integrity means keeping the trust of the product customers. From my own practice of software product maintenance, I can recommend the following principles of business integrity by the product team [1]: deep knowledge of the product source code and all its details; the ability of the product technical leader (based on the source code knowledge) to promptly answer customers' questions and evaluate bugs; the ability to quickly handle bug duplicates (that often happen since customers from different regions can face the same kind of software product issues); never ignoring and closing bugs for the reason of lacking human resources; testing the bug fixes very carefully.

Recognizing Microsoft's continuous efforts in keeping business integrity, I would like to share with you my own experience of software customer communications. I acquired a lot of software product maintenance experience in the 1990s when I was the project lead of the Sun Pascal compiler. I realized pretty well that quick response by the software maintenance team is extremely important for the customers. Due to our maintenance work at Sun Pascal in 1992–1993 when we fixed several hundred open "legacy" bugs (inherited from the previous maintenance team) and issued two bug fix releases (3.0.2 and 3.0.3) of Sun Pascal for 1 year, Sun Microsystems, as was acknowledged by their managers, succeeded in keeping such big customers as Siemens whose office was located in Vienna, Austria, and whose 400 software engineers intensively used the compiler I was responsible for. Our work received a press release in "Business Week." Siemens was a kind of "P1" customer, in the sense that each bug or request for enhancement (RFE) they submitted was priority 1 or 2 (extremely urgent). If you are the project lead, it means that you should forget about days-off and any other work until you fix the bug. Another high priority customer of Sun Pascal was Fannie Mae government company located in Washington, D.C. One special case was the customer from Germany who very scrupulously tested our compiler against the items of Pascal ISO standard (many thanks to him for that, though, surely, we did use a test suite for Pascal standard compatibility testing). Some of the customers persisted in not switching to (at those times) new version of Sun Pascal (4.0) whose front-end we refurbished to speed it up 2–4 times, as compared to the previous version. But some customers were scared that their Pascal applications would stop working on the new compiler version, and I spent a lot of time in convincing them to start using the new version.

To summarize my Sun Pascal maintenance experience, I formulate the following recommendations to software maintenance teams on how to organize their work to enable business integrity:

- *Learn the source code of the product by heart.* I am quite serious. Thorough knowledge of the product sources and design (no matter you are not the person who originally developed that code) is the basis for successful maintenance and, accordingly, for business integrity. I used to teach my students to print out the sources of the product they maintain, to make it their desktop book, to read it every night before sleeping as their favorite novel, in order to learn the sources and feel their behavior as if it were your own creation (though, actually, the product can be the result of the efforts by many years of work of several companies, with different design and coding styles applied). This takes time, but this is useful time spent.

- *The project lead should be the person to answer any customer's question or to evaluate any bug without spending days or weeks to dig into the sources and documentation* – in a short period of time, from five minutes to a few hours. This business integrity quality should be based on deep knowledge of the product sources.

- *Take special care of bug duplicates.* One or two months after the product is shipped, the product development and maintenance team receives a bunch of emails from customers with bug reports. But actually many of them report similar or the same bug found simultaneously by quite different people in different countries, different environments and locales, when using different customer applications (some of them may be proprietary), reported with different bug ids. The task of the project lead is to recognize these duplicates, to answer the customers promptly, to fix the bug if it hasn't yet been done, to explicitly indicate which bug ids actually refer to the found duplicates of the same bug, and to promptly issue a product patch, with the bug fixed. The task of recognizing bug duplicates can hardly be automated by any software tool or technology, and its successful and quick solving can only rely on the project lead's experience and deep knowledge of the product design and source. I was in the role of such project lead for 5 years, while working on Sun Pascal compiler.

– *Never close the bug as "will not fix."* The trust of the customer falls if he receives an update of his bug report, with the bug closed for the reason that the maintenance team manager decided not to spend human resources to its fixing (official explanation is "no resources"). The customer's bug report should always be the first priority. The customer should feel "the breath" of the maintenance team working on the bug he found, and should soon receive their results – the bug evaluation, and, finally, in a few days, the product patch with the bug fix – rather than a refusal from the product team to fix the bug; there is nothing worse. Similarly, the practice of decreasing the priority of the bug before a new product release, with the only goal to avoid fixing it in reasonable time, should be avoided. This also undermines the customer trust and business integrity principles.

– *Don't rush too much in fixing the bug and testing the fix – please check the fix very carefully.* Many software engineers, especially the young, are very ambitious to very quickly fix the bug, report their fix to their bosses, and next, very soon, to the customers. They think they are right and are very proud of how promptly they managed to solve a complicated problem. But, instead, they are likely to create new problems for the product team, for their management, and for their customers because of integrating a not properly tested bug fix. Developing new tests, complete enough to check the new bug fixes, and running all the existing test suites against the patched version of the product, takes time, and, intuitively and emotionally speaking, the maintenance engineer is sometimes reluctant to do everything to ensure that his or her fix is correct. This is a common software process organization bug to be avoided. There should be (and actually there is) a systematic software process discipline used to test any new bug fix. The customers can wait for a few days to receive a correct and complete fix. But they can stop trusting you and your company if, from time to time, they very quickly receive untested and erroneous bug fixes from you.

– *Do not zero out the product bug count in the bug tracking database, to leave the product alive.* This principle may sound funny and paradoxical. Nevertheless, it does make sense, as our Sun Pascal practice shows. When we fixed *all* the Sun Pascal bugs and zeroed out the product bug count, Sun management soon decided to "end-of-life" (EOL) Sun Pascal and put it into pure maintenance mode. Now it is no longer supported for years. And it is well known that when the software product is not supported by the developer company, it dies.

3.7 TOOLS AND SOFTWARE LIFECYCLE MODELS TO SUPPORT TRUSTWORTHY COMPUTING

Currently there are the two software platforms, .NET and Java, that support trustworthy computing principles most adequately.

The .NET platform, developed in 2000, enables full type checking (either at compile time or at runtime) for any program written in any language implemented for .NET. All compilers for the .NET platform translate source codes to the same kind of binary code – *Common Intermediate Language* (*CIL*), a postfix notation for the program, the same intermediate language for all source languages. Also, the .NET compilers generate *metadata* – a standardized format of the information on the types defined and used in the compilation unit. Both the CIL code and metadata form the binary *assembly* structure – platform-independent portable executable file. The metadata contains *attributes* (annotations) indicating security permissions and other specifics of the assembly. At runtime, assemblies are processed by the *Common Language Runtime* (*CLR*) that enables the special *managed execution* mode of executing programs, with full type checking and security restrictions checking, based on the availability of metadata at runtime. The mechanism of exception handling is common for all .NET languages. All of that enables .NET software security and reliability. The .NET platform provides enhanced security mechanisms to prevent different kinds of attacks: *code access security* – checking the whole chain of methods called on the stack for the appropriate security permissions, to prevent elevation of privilege attack; *role-based security* – attaching sets of security permissions to user *roles* (like *manager* or *engineer*); *evidence-based security* – a set of security checks for an assembly based on its author, time zone, digital signature, and other trust evidences collected on it by the runtime. So, based on the above, .NET should be mentioned as the most secure and reliable software platform right now. However, it should be kept in mind that all security checks and type checking require extra time during the program run and can slow down the program execution.

The Java platform that originated in 1995 follows similar principles of software security and reliability – type checking and security checking on the basis of *Java bytecode*, a binary intermediate code based on postfix notation and binary platform-independent *class files* containing the bytecode and the type-related information on the source code program. Java provides modern security mechanisms based on the concepts of security manager and configurable security policy. However, there are some reliability issues in Java: its integer arithmetic does not check overflow; there is no *unsigned* arithmetic in Java, so the Java programmers have to model it using signed arithmetic and logical masks, which is not reliable. Also, *generics* (parametrized types) in Java are not 100% trustworthy in the following sense. When different instantiations of generic classes are used in a Java application (e.g., *Stack* <*int*> or *Stack*<*string*>), at runtime those instantiations are undistinguishable from each other. There is no way in Java to check at runtime to which specific instantiation of a generic class an object belongs. This issue is referred to as *type erasure*. It does contradict the modern principles of type-safe execution and trustworthy computing at all. Surely in modern software languages and platforms *any* type of an object should be recognizable at runtime. Please compare this situation to .NET: in C#, it is quite possible to check the instantiation of a generic class at runtime. So, in this respect, the .NET platform and the C# language are more trustworthy than Java. Please see my book [100] on more details of parametrized data types in different languages and platforms.

Now let us go into more detail regarding .NET security principles. They are based on the following cornerstones: *code access security, role-based security, evidence-based security,* and *configurable security policies.* The main .NET security principle is as follows: unlike earlier security models, for example, UNIX, which bind security features and permissions to the *user* and *user group,* .NET, for the first turn, ties security permissions to the *code (assembly)* and *user executing the code.* Actually, .NET security approach combines and enhances former security approaches – code-centric and user-centric. Code-centric approach is based on the concepts of *code access security* and *evidence-based security.* User-centric approach is relied upon the concept of *role-based security,* which is a generalization of UNIX-style user group model.

During code execution, .NET CLR loads each assembly "by need" – first time the assembly is called. During assembly load, CLR collects *evidences* (information) about the assembly that helps CLR to determine whether the assembly is trusted and secure, and what kind of security permissions it should be granted. The following types of evidences are collected: information on the *location where the assembly code is loaded from* (*site, URL, zone,* and *application directory*); information on the *code developer* (*strong name* and *publisher*); and the *hash* value of the assembly.

The evidences of the assembly are checked by the CLR against the *security policy,* which can be defined at different levels – for *user, machine, enterprise,* and *application domain.* Security policy should be configured by system administrators and is typically specified in special XML configuration files. Based on the assembly's evidence, CLR checks whether the security policy permits is to be executed.

Generally speaking, at runtime, .NET security checks are enabled, due to its *managed, type-safe execution mode.* The metadata (types) of any assembly are available to CLR, so it can check at runtime any security related type or attribute of the code. If it were not for managed code and metadata, it would not be possible to make the necessary security checks.

Code access security can be expressed in terms of *permissions* granted to some code. This set can be described either in *declarative style* – by *security attributes* annotating the pieces of code – or in *imperative style* – by *objects and API calls* representing the security permissions and their demands by the code. The difference between those styles is as follows. Security attributes are activated once, at *assembly load time,* so using declarative approach is more efficient, secure, and reliable, since the CLR is guaranteed to check the security permissions expressed by attributes, and code checking utilities can easily detect them. However, attribute-based approach does not provide an opportunity of exception handling. The other approach – imperative style of checking permissions – is surely more flexible. The code can check for a permission (e.g., whether it is possible to write to some file) when actually needed, handle any possible security exceptions, and issue appropriate messages to the user when necessary. However, without using attributes that "stick" security permissions to the code, there is a risk of forgetting to make imperative security checks, and as a result the code terminates with the security exception.

A very important mechanism used in .NET security is referred to as *security stack walk*. To enforce CLR to check if some security permission is granted, the currently running method calls the *Demand* method of the corresponding security permission object. Then, the CLR performs security stack walk: it checks whether *each* method on the stack is granted the same permission. If not, *SecurityException* is thrown. Though, obviously, this mechanism is expensive, it guarantees that a partially trusted malicious assembly cannot call a fully trusted assembly's method to elevate privileges and perform an action it is not allowed to perform.

User-centric security in .NET is based on the following concepts of role-based security that enhance the traditional framework of users and user groups. The user in .NET is described by the concept of *principal* – in more common sense terminology, the main person to make the business decisions related to his application. A principal can have one or more *roles* – similarly to the old UNIX approach where a user can belong to one or more user groups. Examples of roles are "*sysadmin*," "*manager*," and "*engineer*." The set of roles expressed by strings is user defined. The *IsInRole* method of the *IPrincipal* interface allows software developers to find out if the given principal belongs to a given role. *PrincipalPermission* object ties a principal to his role. The reference to the current principal can be extracted from the current Web request; it reflects the Web-aware nature of .NET. The principal object contains a reference to its *identity* – the *user name, authentication type,* and the flag whether the principal has been authenticated. One of the possible authentication types is *Windows authentication* based on traditional Windows login name and password. The other authentication type is *passport authentication* based on *.NET Passport*. There are some other types of authentication, such as *Kerberos authentication*.

In general, the concepts of user-centric security – principal and identity in .NET are flexible enough, though they do not bring anything novel to the security field: they are based on similar concepts as in earlier versions of Windows and in UNIX.

Now some words regarding .NET's support of the reliability concepts – .NET is designed for developing reliable software. The following core features of .NET support reliable programming: *managed execution, attributes, properties, exception handling,* and *reflection.* Due to these features that work for single-language or multi-language applications, .NET enables much more reliability than traditional programming systems with weaker typing models, especially C and C++.

Managed execution mode guarantees that for each object p its actual type can be determined at runtime using metadata. In managed execution mode, for each operation $A \ op \ B$, it is checked that the types of A and B operands comply to the operation op; otherwise, an exception is thrown. In particular, especially important for reliability, as well as for security, is the fact that, in managed execution mode, address arithmetic (adding an integer to a pointer) or arbitrary casts of a pointer to any type are now allowed and attempts to do that immediately cause exceptions, as well as an attempt to address via a null pointer. It eliminates a lot of bugs and security threats.

Managed execution mode ensures that no array limits are exceeded by any index (otherwise an exception is generated by the CLR). In this relation, .NET's managed execution mode resembles the old principles of tagged hardware architecture first formulated and hardware implemented in the 1960s, though managed execution is implemented programmatically, via metadata and runtime type checking performed when the native code is executed. Surely such dynamic typing approach requires substantial overhead, but it is much more reliable than just ignoring actual data types at runtime (such as in C language).

Attributes in .NET are the way to annotate any named entity (class, method, field, etc.) by any useful information that can help preserve and make runtime available any specification-time and design-time decisions in the code – formal specification, input and output conditions, contracts, aspects that the code defines, and so on. At runtime, CLR and any utilities that process the code of the assembly (debuggers, verifiers, profilers, etc.) can check its attributes via *reflection* mechanism to control the runtime behavior of the code, check it for correctness (compliance to the specifications the code is annotated by), transform, and enhance it (e.g., weave some aspects into the code). So, if properly used, attributes are very helpful to increase software reliability.

Property is a concept that allows software developers to define a "virtual" information item in a class, with two basic operations: *get* – access (or calculate) the value of the item – and *set* – assign a new value to the item. In C#, "syntactic sugar" is provided, so that the developer can write: $p \cdot X = V$, where p is an object and X is its property name. Actually the concept of property in .NET is another incarnation of an old idea of *procedural representation of data* originated in the 1970s. Instead of defining the data (by a field), the software developer provides operations (methods) to access it and to assign it. The implementations of *get* and *set* may contain arbitrary code. If properly used, this technique may improve code reliability, since any kind of value, environment, or security (permission) check can be added to *get* or *set*. .NET security guideline books and documents recommend software developers to use in any class *public* properties (with necessary checks included) but *private* fields.

Exception handling, though it is surely not invented by .NET authors, became an inherent part of the .NET execution model and contributes to software reliability. A typical example is related to checking the arguments by a method. Suppose there is a condition (contract) expressed by a predicate $P(x)$ that should hold for an argument x of the method m. The method's code should check it and if the contract does not hold, generate an exception. The exception should be specified in the method's header and can be caught and processed by any caller method. There are hundreds of predefined exception types, such as *NullReferenceException*, to identify typical bugs in the code. The advantage of .NET, as compared to all previous programming platforms with built-in exceptions, is that the exception thrown from a module written in one language can be caught by another module written in another .NET language, in case the implementations of both languages are CLS compliant.

Reflection is the way to determine and analyze at runtime the type of any object and its components. It is very important to implement any kind of runtime type checks and analysis, in addition to those made by CLR. Reflection also provides access to attributes whose role has already been considered. If properly used, reflection can enable any kind of type checking not performed by .NET compilers and the CLR. Unfortunately, if improperly (or maliciously) used, reflection enables software developers to ignore the access restrictions provided by the *private* and *protected* access modifiers.

In this chapter, general concepts, principles, lifecycle models, and tools of trustworthy computing are overviewed. In Chapter 4, specifics of trustworthy computing, as applicable to cloud models, are considered. In Chapter 5, the Microsoft Azure cloud model is covered in detail, as an example of trustworthy cloud computing.

EXERCISES TO CHAPTER 3

E3.1 Why, in your opinion, are trustworthy computing issues so vital?

E3.2 What is trustworthy computing and which parts (or pillars) does it consist of?

E3.3 Please overview the security pillar.

E3.4 Please overview the reliability pillar.

E3.5 Please overview the privacy pillar.

E3.6 Please overview the business integrity pillar.

E3.7 What is vulnerability? Please describe some kinds of vulnerabilities you know.

E3.8 Which kinds of attacks do you know?

E3.9 What is phishing?

E3.10 What is pharming?

E3.11 What is distributed denial of service and to what kind of servers is it applicable?

E3.12 What kind of trustworthy computing issues appeared in the first computers?

E3.13 What is buffer overrun and why is this vulnerability so dangerous for organizing attacks?

E3.14 When, by whom, and in relation to what kind of situation with Microsoft software was the TWC Initiative announced?

E3.15 What is usability and why is it so important, in addition to trustworthy computing pillars?

E3.16 What kind of tasks are related to security pillar?

E3.16 Please describe what security means and what kind of tasks it requires to solve for different categories of users – home users, office users, and software developers?

E3.17 What is security development lifecycle (SDL)? How does it relate to the traditional waterfall software lifecycle model?

E3.18 Please describe the main principles of SDL: secure by default, secure in design, secure in deployment and communications.

E3.19 Which security tools do you know? Please describe each of them and their functionality.

E3.20   How should security be taken into account in various phases of software life-cycle – requirements and goals, specification, design, implementation, testing (verification), support and servicing, according to SDL principles?

E3.21   What is threat modeling and why is it important for secure software development?

E3.22   Please explain the essence of the least privilege principle and the minimal attach surface principle in SDL.

E3.23   What kind of specific security tests are used in SDL?

E3.24   Please overview different approaches to software and hardware reliability. What is MTBF and MTTR?

E3.25   Please overview the methods you know to increase software reliability.

E3.26   Why, in your opinion, are formal methods still not so widely used in software development?

E3.27   Please overview the privacy techniques and tools you know. Describe SmartScreen, HIP, and other techniques to achieve privacy.

E3.27   What kind of issues are addressed to the business integrity pillar in trustworthy computing?

E3.28   Please overview the principles of prompt software maintenance recommended in the book. What is your opinion on this matter? Describe your own experience and principles of software maintenance.

E3.29   Please overview the .NET platform features to support trustworthy computing.

E3.30   Please describe the principles of .NET security system and explain their importance in increasing software security.

E3.31   What is EMET? Please describe its goals and its importance in improving software security.

E3.32   Please explain why the principles of type-safe (managed) execution in Java and .NET are so important for trustworthy computing. Compare these features to those of earlier languages such as C.

E3.33   What is your opinion of Java technology, in relation to trustworthy computing? Which features of Java are especially substantial for trustworthy computing support? Which features of Java are not so trustworthy?

E3.34   Please compare generics (parametrized types) in Java and in C#. In which of the two languages, in your opinion, are generics trustworthy and in which are they not? Please explain your position. In general, please overview the importance of generics for trustworthy computing.

4

MAKING CLOUD COMPUTING TRUSTWORTHY

4.1 PSYCHOLOGICAL BARRIERS BETWEEN THE CUSTOMERS AND THE CLOUD, AND THE WAYS TO OVERCOME THEM

One of the first problems that arise when applying some new innovative technology is a serious psychological barrier between the technology and the users. Users are somewhat conservative, and sometimes are just scared of new technologies as of something too novel, have a lot of concerns related to complicated architecture, to uncomfortable and unclear user interface, to security, reliability, privacy, and so on. The farther the users are from IT and programming, the higher those barriers are.

In the 1980s and even in the 1990s, a similar situation took place in relation to the use of computers in general in the everyday activity of experts in some fields other than IT. For example, my own experience in the early 1990s of communicating to medical staff in our country, in relation to the use of computers and expert systems for their activity, has shown some aspects of psychological barrier: medical experts were afraid to pass their data knowledge to computer, scared that computers can replace them and their work would become redundant, did not understand the specifics of computer–user interface, and so on. Fortunately, as a result of many years of hard work by IT specialists on improving user interface and training users, that barrier has been overcome, and now doctors or specialists in chemistry or even in philosophy sometimes know and can handle computers better than some IT experts.

Currently such psychological barriers exist between millions of potential users of cloud technologies and the cloud. Let us consider and analyze them in more detail, to better understand how to make cloud computing more trustworthy.

There are the following psychological issues that can initially prevent users from understanding and using the cloud.

Trustworthy Cloud Computing, First Edition. Vladimir O. Safonov.
© 2016 John Wiley & Sons, Inc. Published 2016 by John Wiley & Sons, Inc.

The Cloud and Its Resources are Distant from the User and Do Not Exist on the Client Machine

For decades, the users have been accustomed to the "local" style of using computers (in spite of networking). In the traditional manner, the user should install all necessary software and data on his or her client computer. The user knows that some of the software can be downloaded from the Internet, some other parts of software taken from DVDs, and so on. Finally, the user has done all the installation work and feels and sees all the software and data on his machine. He knows its size, directory structure, can "finger" or reorganize those local resources for his own convenience, and enable back-ups when he is comfortable to do so, and this situation looks traditional and trustworthy for him. On the contrary, the cloud computing paradigm is quite different and radically changes the viewpoint on the style and the paradigm of computations. Computing without the use of locally available software and data is still too unusual to be understood by most users. My friend who actively uses his personal computer every day, when he first learned the term "cloud computing" from me, considered it a joke and was sure that I was kidding. So, it is really necessary to make a kind of "revolution" in the consciousness and subconsciousness of users to have them fully understand the specifics of cloud computing and realize its perspectives. This can be achieved by years of users' education and practice of cloud computing, starting from high school or even from the kindergarten. It cannot happen in a moment but it should be done.

The Architecture of the Cloud Is Very Complicated and Geographically Distributed

Up to now, most users have been concentrating on the use of their personal computers, office local networks, and on regularly "diving" into the Internet. They have understood the computing architectures they are using, know their machine names and ways of contacting their colleagues and providers, and trust them. When starting to use the cloud, the users are faced with the situation of logging in to yet another unknown complicated computing world, with many datacenters distributed over the world regions, and the computing resources belonging to just one cloud user distributed over several continents. So the users have to think about nontraditional issues they did not have to pay attention to by now: where their cloud services, virtual machines, and databases are located, what should be their optimal distribution and location, how and when to activate or deactivate their cloud resources, and so on. It is very interesting for the users, but may also be somewhat scary and troubling. Thinking in terms of geographical regions for the purpose of optimal organization of computing is nontraditional for most users. It was not required for organizing computations before, with previous computing paradigms. Moreover, when attempting to learn the internal architecture of the cloud to better understand its functionality, the users have come across the degree of architectural complexity they have not even met before. Organization of datacenter hardware is nontrivial and requires deep learning and understanding. Cloud software services, layers and tiers, multitenancy, and specific security features of the cloud are complicated to learn, but it is worth doing so to understand modern software features.

The User Is Concerned of the Security of His or Her Data in the Cloud

This is one of the most serious issues of cloud computing use, quite natural, and corresponding to the common way of thinking. In spite of all advantages of cloud computing, the user may have doubts and concerns related to the way of data processing in the cloud. The user can have intuitive objections to the situation when he has to pass his data (probably including confidential information) on to the cloud where they are stored and processed remotely in various regions of the world, rather than on the user's machine. The user can ask, "Why should I trust my secrets to the cloud datacenters located many thousand miles from my home? Why should I consider it trustworthy?" This issue can be overcome when the user gets more experience in really secure data processing in the cloud.

The User Is Not Yet Accustomed to the Style of Regular Payment for Cloud Resources

When using the cloud, in the initial period, the user does not have to very carefully and regularly check his cloud resources and delete them on time when they are not needed any more, to avoid extra payments. In the cloud trial period, the user can perform many experiments on creating various kinds of resources in the cloud – virtual machines, databases, containers, working cloud applications (services), and so on. But the user has not yet acquired a habit to track and check his cloud resources. Unfortunately, the cloud does not always warn him that, in his experiments, he has exceeded the limits of free trial use (although such warnings are just necessary to keep the cloud behavior trustworthy). As a result, the user can easily forget to delete unnecessary cloud resources on time, and finally get an unexpected bill from the cloud providers. This is a helpful but severe school of using paid computing resources. Such issues can for some time deepen the gap between the user and the cloud, but everything can be overcome by practical experience.

Cloud and Cloud Computing May Seem too Slow for the Users

On realizing that he uses Web browser interface for each action in the cloud, the user may think that it works too slow. In my practice, it happened before I switched to using 4G modems and routers. On the cloud side (I mean Microsoft Azure cloud), there has been great progress on making the cloud faster and more reliable, so now even when the speed of connection is not fast enough, the user does not feel that, due to good organization of caching and buffering data and services in the cloud. So I hope the period of "slow cloud" has gone, due to the progress of communication hardware and software and to enhancement of cloud architecture.

For the Beginners of Cloud Software Development, the Way of Addressing Cloud Resources Is too Unusual

For many years, software developers have been taught to operate in their applications by variables, arrays, and then databases. Those resources are named and addressed in traditional ways – by variable names, component variables, and database names in traditional database management systems (*on premises*, in cloud slang). When switching to cloud software development, a programmer does not always realize that each cloud resource, from cloud application viewpoint, exists and is addressed as a Web site (Web page), with the corresponding URL address. In Chapter 2, many examples of such cloud resources organization are provided. So, when porting a useful application to the cloud, the software developer should radically change the way of addressing and processing resources. URL address becomes an elementary unit of resource addressing. There is only one way to get accustomed to it – practice of cloud services development.

4.2   USER INTERFACE FOR CLOUD COMPUTING, ITS CONVENIENCE, USABILITY, AND FUNCTIONALITY FOR TRUSTWORTHY CLOUD COMPUTING

User interface for cloud computing is especially important, since cloud architecture is complicated. User interface should help the user to better understand the architecture of the cloud and to navigate in cloud features and components. As already stated above, user interface to the cloud is an important part of its trustworthiness, the trust to the cloud by the users.

Based on my experience of using different cloud models (see Chapter 2), the following requirements to trustworthiness of user interface of the cloud can be formulated.

Integration to a Single Portal

User interface of the cloud should be based on the single integrated cloud portal that provides access to all cloud features. User interface that provides access to each of the cloud services separately is not comfortable for cloud users. User interface should emphasize the integrated spirit and style of the cloud, rather than separate cloud services from each other.

Using a Single Authentication Mechanism for All the Cloud

User interface should have a single and simple authentication mechanism for logging in to the cloud. The situation when the cloud user has to remember and use different logins and passwords for different parts and functionalities of the cloud is not comfortable for cloud users at all.

More Guidance, Help, and Navigation

User interface should provide the necessary degree of guidance and navigation for the cloud users, since the cloud architecture is very complicated to acquire.

Clear and Detailed Picture of the Cloud Resources Used

User interface should provide a clear picture for the cloud user on what kind and how many cloud resources the user is consuming, with categories of cloud entities (virtual machines, storage, databases, containers, etc.) and with the "weight" of each cloud item for the user, in terms of the space and time used, and in terms of the oncoming payment of the user for the corresponding cloud feature.

Default Warnings on Payment and Billing

User interface should explicitly warn the cloud user on the big cloud resources used and the corresponding payment for these resources. User interface should clearly separate the free cloud resources (used without payment) for the user from other kind of cloud resources that will require payment. This option should be switched on by default. This is especially important during the cloud trial period when the user does not have experience of cloud use at all, and can easily make a mistake, for example, creating a big database whose size is beyond the free trial limits, just for a proof-of-concept experiment. In such a case, a clear and understandable warning should be issued by the cloud–user interface, which will prevent the user from such inaccurate actions. There should not appear a situation when a big cloud resource "silently" hangs in the cloud, nonusable for a long time. The user should not "guess" (often afterwards, on getting a bill) that he or she has not turned on the billing warnings. Instead, the user should always have a default suggestion from the cloud that he probably forgot to delete a big cloud resource, and have time to react and make appropriate deletion actions to avoid unnecessary surprisingly big bills. Otherwise, the cloud will be considered nontrustworthy for the user, which may lead to cancelling the cloud account by the user. In my opinion, an ideal situation would be if, at least on each log in to the cloud, the user immediately gets a warning that a big cloud resource is unusable for a long time, and the exact reference to this resource is provided. In case the user has not logged in to the cloud for a long time but has big cloud resources that are unusable, a reasonable measure, from the cloud side, would be to send to the user a warning email with advice to log in to the cloud and to delete the unused big resource.

Reviewing the Cloud Resources and Providing Security Recommendations

The user interface should review by default the cloud resource settings made by the user, in terms of security, and provide reasonable suggestions to the user on how to improve them (e.g., to make IP addresses of virtual cloud servers private).

Monitoring the Cloud Resources

The user interface should provide functionality for monitoring the cloud resources used, in terms of usage times, space, and the money spent.

Help in Structuring the Cloud Resources to Projects

The user interface should help the user to structure the cloud resources used and to bind them to the user's cloud projects, tasks, virtual servers, and applications.

Samples, Patterns and Galleries to Make the Cloud Resource Creation Easier

The user interface should provide samples, patterns, and galleries for creating and using each kind of the cloud resources, since it may be initially complicated for the user to understand. It may be difficult for the user to make an appropriate choice of, say, a virtual machine with appropriate operating system and a set of resources, so the cloud interface should help the user to do that.

Avoid Overloading the User with too Much Detail, Make Important Things by Default

The user interface should not "overload" the cloud user with too much of details needed to set up access to cloud resources, especially to virtual machines. A reasonable style would be for the cloud–user interface to make most of such settings by default. For example, if, to access a cloud virtual machine, a key pair (*public key*, *private key*) is needed, the cloud interface should provide a comfortable way for the user to create such a key pair directly in the cloud and then store the created key pair on the user's machine, without using a third-party utility outside the cloud, which is necessary to seek on the Web and install on the client machine. Some of the cloud platforms provide such a service, while some others do not. Please see Chapter 2 for details.

Enable the Way to Do All the Work with the Resources in the Cloud

In general, user interface should enable to do most or all of the work with the cloud resource in the cloud, without using programmatic APIs when unnecessary. For example, when creating a cloud database, the user should be able to fill the database with the content directly in the cloud, using some form of database scheme constructor and database content (table) constructor available in the cloud. It would be much less comfortable if, instead, the user has to install and use a third-party database management system outside the cloud to fill the cloud database with its content. So DBMS should be integrated to the cloud, and that would be a right choice for cloud–user interface developers.

Enable Ways and Tools to Do All Application Development in the Cloud

The user interface should provide cloud tools to create and update the user's cloud application (service) directly in the cloud, using some form of cloud integrated development environment as the most comfortable form of PaaS support. It would be less comfortable if the user has to seek and install a third-party IDE outside the cloud to create an application, and then to publish it in the cloud. In my opinion, the cloud–user interface should be enhanced in such a way that the necessary IDEs should be integrated to the cloud, and cloud developers are on the way to do that. Positive examples are *Visual Studio Online* in the Microsoft Azure cloud and PaaS features (mini-IDEs) in Google, IBM, and Salesforce clouds. In general, the cloud users are ready to consider the cloud to be a universal remedy to solve all their current problems, so, the more services available directly in the cloud without the need to install local software, the better. In this case, the users will consider the cloud more trustworthy.

Trustworthy Organization of Cloud Free Trial, Related Checks, and User Information Gathering

User interface of the cloud should be friendly and should not frighten the cloud users at the initial period of their free trial use of the cloud. The cloud should ask the user to fill out the initial questionnaire with the user's contact information for free trial use (a month is enough); it is quite understandable. But the first thing that can push the user away from the cloud is the need to enter the credit card information, in case the user only intents to try the cloud for free. The user can understand this need as a possibility of unexpected bills and payments during the free trial period. According to a known proverb, if a gun is hanging on a nail on the stage during the theater performance, it will inevitably shoot later on, as part of the performance. So my opinion and recommendation for the cloud providers: please do not hang this "gun" of credit card number on the stage of their cloud platform, and you will get much more cloud users for your platform, so the cloud "performances" will always be a success. However, of the cloud platforms I have ever tried, only Microsoft, Oracle, Salesforce, and Kaavo clouds do not require credit card numbers for free trial use. I would recommend the following trustworthy scenario of free trial period. Please do not take from the trial user the number of his credit card. Let the user make any experiments with creating and using cloud resources in the trial period, but with some reasonable limitations. If the cloud resources the user is trying to create are excessive, just do not allow the user to do that; issue an understandable explanation message that contains the amount of money to be paid for this feature in case it is used (without actually taking this money), and that will be the best and the most trustworthy lesson for the cloud user that he will remember forever and will continue using this cloud platform, as friendly and trustworthy. Yet another unexpected way of checking the user before the cloud trial period is a phone interview during which the user has to provide explanations why he decided to try the cloud, and should confirm his postal address by voice. I think this is not appropriate. Instead, automated sending of an SMS message with a testing code is I think quite enough to check the correctness of the user's phone number; sending to the user an email is the best way to check the email address of the user, and all those simple checks are I think quite enough for cloud trial. In my opinion, the current moment for most of potential cloud users should be a turning point to feel the advantages of the cloud, and at this moment it is especially important to make the cloud as attractive as possible, to get the trust of the user to the cloud, and his or her desire to use the cloud for a long time.

4.3   THREATS AND ATTACKS TO CLOUDS

Since, as shown before, the cloud is a very complicated structure, there are many potential threats and attacks dangerous for the cloud. All kinds of attacks I describe in Chapter 3 are applicable to the cloud: distributed denial of service, phishing and pharming (in case the cloud Web page is replaced by some malicious one by the hackers), elevation of privilege (in case the attacker has stolen the permissions of the cloud user), and so on.

The rest of this section is organized as follows. I will cite a very good paper [101] that explains cloud threats and attacks in a clear way. Instead of retelling the story, I would like to cite the whole fragment of the paper, since it looks very self-explanatory and understandable (thanks to the author). After the cited fragments of the paper [101], I will provide my comments and additions.

The following cloud vulnerabilities should be taken into account when migrating to the cloud:

Session Riding: Session riding happens when an attacker steals a user's cookie to use the application in the name of the user. An attacker might also use CSRF attacks in order to trick the user into sending authenticated requests to arbitrary web sites to achieve various things.

In the subsequent fragments, the term CSP stands for Cloud Service Provider. The term *CSRF* stands for *Cross-Site Request Forgery*. This kind of attack is also known as *session riding*. Its goal is to send unauthorized commands to the Web site that is considered trusted by the browser.

Virtual Machine Escape: In virtualized environments, the physical servers run multiple virtual machines on top of hypervisors. An attacker can exploit a hypervisor remotely by using a vulnerability present in the hypervisor itself – such vulnerabilities are quite rare, but they do exist. Additionally, a virtual machine can escape from the virtualized sandbox environment and gain access to the hypervisor and consequently all the virtual machines running on it.

Reliability and Availability of Service: We expect our cloud services and applications to always be available when we need them, which is one of the reasons for moving to the cloud. But this isn't always the case, especially in bad weather with a lot of lightning where power outages are common. The CSPs have uninterrupted power supplies, but even those can sometimes fail, so we can't rely on cloud services to be up and running 100% of the time. We have to take a little downtime into consideration, but that's the same when running our own private cloud.

Insecure Cryptography: Cryptography algorithms usually require random number generators, which use unpredictable sources of information to generate actual random numbers, which is required to obtain a large entropy pool. If the random number generators are providing only a small entropy pool, the numbers can be brute forced. In client computers, the primary source of randomization is user mouse movement and key presses, but servers are mostly running without user interaction, which consequentially means lower number of randomization sources. Therefore the virtual machines must rely on the sources they have available, which could result in easily guessable numbers that don't provide much entropy in cryptographic algorithms.

Data Protection and Portability: When choosing to switch the cloud service provider for a cheaper one, we have to address the problem of data movement and deletion. The old CSP has to delete all the data we stored in its data center to not leave the data lying around.

Alternatively, the CSP that goes out of the business needs to provide the data to the customers, so they can move to an alternate CSP after which the data needs to be deleted. What if the CSP goes out of business without providing the data? In such cases, it's better to use a widely used CSP which has been around for a while, but in any case data backup is still in order.

CSP Lock-in: We have to choose a cloud provider that will allow us to easily move to another provider when needed. We don't want to choose a CSP that will force us to use his own services, because sometimes we would like to use one CSP for one thing and the other CSP for something else.

In my own experience, cloud providers sometimes behave according to the principle: "Don't let him go." They extend the period of trial use of the cloud, though the user is willing to finish up with the cloud provider and to switch to another one. Such practice does not add trustworthiness to the cloud, from the user viewpoint. I quite agree that different clouds can be helpful for different purposes. In some of them, PaaS functionality is the best, in some others IaaS is the most comfortable, and so on. Please see Chapter 2 for the examples.

Internet Dependency: By using the cloud services, we're dependent upon the Internet connection, so if the Internet temporarily fails due to a lightning strike or ISP maintenance, the clients won't be able to connect to the cloud services. Therefore, the business will slowly lose money, because the users won't be able to use the service that's required for the business operation. Not to mention the services that need to be available 24/7, like applications in a hospital, where human lives are at stake.

Cloud computing threats

Before deciding to migrate to the cloud, we have to look at the cloud security vulnerabilities and threats to determine whether the cloud service is worth the risk due to the many advantages it provides. The following are the top security threats in a cloud environment:

Ease of Use: The cloud services can easily be used by malicious attackers, since a registration process is very simple, because we only have to have a valid credit card. In some cases we can even pay for the cloud service by using PayPal, Western Union, Payza, Bitcoin, or Litecoin, in which cases we can stay totally anonymous. The cloud can be used maliciously for various purposes like spamming, malware distribution, botnet C&C servers, DDoS, password and hash cracking.

The acronym DDoS stands for *Distributed Denial of Service* – the kind of attack I considered in Chapter 3. I quite agree that it is very simple to organize an attack to the cloud. If the cloud does not properly check the size of the resource created and does not prevent from creating very big cloud resources and hold them for a long time, it may lead to denial of service.

Secure Data Transmission: When transferring the data from clients to the cloud, the data needs to be transferred by using an encrypted secure communication channel like SSL/TLS. This prevents different attacks like MITM attacks, where the data could be stolen by an attacker intercepting our communication.

The term *MITM* is an acronym for *Man-in-the-Middle*. This is a kind of attack when the attacker "inserts" himself between two communicating parties, for example, when the attacker inserts himself, by virtue of being within reception range of an unencrypted Wi-Fi access point.

Insecure APIs: Various cloud services on the Internet are exposed by application programming interfaces. Since the APIs are accessible from anywhere on the Internet, malicious attackers can use them to compromise the confidentiality and integrity of the enterprise customers. An attacker gaining a token used by a customer to access the service through service API can use the same token to manipulate the customer's data. Therefore it's imperative that cloud services provide a secure API, rendering such attacks worthless.

I quite agree that cloud services should provide a secure API. A good example is APIs for the Microsoft Azure cloud, since they are based on the secure .NET platform with full type-checking and managed execution. APIs based on less secure platforms and languages, such as C or C++, which have many insecure features (related to arbitrary changing types by cast constructs) should not be used at all, since they can lead to hardly detectable bugs, and their effect is unpredictable.

Malicious Insiders: Employees working at cloud service provider could have complete access to the company resources. Therefore cloud service providers must have proper security measures in place to track employee actions like viewing a customer's data. Since cloud service providers often don't follow the best security guidelines and don't implement a security policy, employees can gather confidential information from arbitrary customers without being detected.

Shared Technology Issues: The cloud service SaaS/PasS/IaaS providers use scalable infrastructure to support multiple tenants which share the underlying infrastructure. Directly on the hardware layer, there are hypervisors running multiple virtual machines, themselves running multiple applications.

On the highest layer, there are various attacks on the SaaS where an attacker is able to get access to the data of another application running in the same virtual machine. The same is true for the lowest layers, where hypervisors can be exploited from virtual machines to gain access to all VMs on the same server (example of such an attack is Red/Blue Pill). All layers of shared technology can be attacked to gain unauthorized access to data, like: CPU, RAM, hypervisors, applications, and so on.

Data Loss: The data stored in the cloud could be lost due to the hard drive failure. A CSP could accidentally delete the data, an attacker might modify the data, and so on. Therefore, the best way to protect against data loss is by having a proper data backup, which solves the data loss problems. Data loss can have catastrophic consequences to the business, which may result in a business bankruptcy, which is why keeping the data backed-up is always the best option.

Data Breach: When a virtual machine is able to access the data from another virtual machine on the same physical host, a data breach occurs – the problem is much more prevalent when the tenants of the two virtual machines are different customers. The side-channel attacks are valid attack vectors and need to be addressed in everyday situations. A side-channel attack occurs when a virtual machine can use a shared component like processor's cache to access the data of another virtual machine running on the same physical host.

Account/Service Hijacking: It's often the case that only a password is required to access our account in the cloud and manipulate the data, which is why the usage of two-factor authentication is preferred. Nevertheless, an attacker gaining access to our account can manipulate and change the data and therefore make the data untrustworthy. An attacker having access to the cloud virtual machine hosting our business website can include a malicious code into the web page to attack users visiting our web page – this is known as the watering hole attack. An attacker can also disrupt the service by turning off the web server serving our website, rendering it inaccessible.

Unknown Risk Profile: We have to take all security implications into account when moving to the cloud, including constant software security updates, monitoring networks with IDS/IPS systems, log monitoring, integrating SIEM into the network, and so on. There might be multiple attacks that haven't even been discovered yet, but they might prove to be highly threatening in the years to come.

SIEM stands for *Security Information and Event Management. IDS/IPS* stands for *Intrusion Detection (Protection) Systems.*

Denial of Service: An attacker can issue a denial of service attack against the cloud service to render it inaccessible, therefore disrupting the service. There are a number of ways an attacker can disrupt the service in a virtualized cloud environment: by using all its CPU, RAM, disk space or network bandwidth.

Lack of Understanding: Enterprises are adopting the cloud services in every day operations, but it's often the case they don't really understand what they are getting into. When moving to the cloud there are different aspects we need to address, like understanding how the CSP operates, how the application is working, how to debug the application when something goes wrong, whether the data backups are already in place in case the hard drive dies, and so on. If the CSP doesn't provide additional backup of the data, but the customer expects it, who will be responsible when the hard drive fails? The customer will blame the CSP, but in reality it's the customer's fault, since they didn't familiarize themselves enough with the cloud service operations – the result of which will be lost data.

User Awareness: The users of the cloud services should be educated regarding different attacks, because the weakest link is often the user itself. There are multiple social engineering attack vectors that an attacker might use to lure the victim into visiting a malicious web site, after which he can get access to the user's computer. From there, he can observe user actions and view the same data the user is viewing, not to mention that he can steal user's credentials to authenticate to the cloud service itself. Security awareness is an often overlooked security concern.

The above description shows a variety of kinds of attacks to the cloud and cloud users. In the following sections of this chapter, security countermeasures are considered on how to mitigate or exclude those kinds of attacks.

4.4   TRUSTWORTHY CLOUD COMPUTING FROM HARDWARE SIDE: DATACENTER ARCHITECTURE, SERVERS, CLUSTERS, HYPERVISORS

As already stated in Section 1.12, cloud data centers are built for their trustworthiness as the main goal. The following principles are pursued to achieve the goal of trustworthiness of data centers, in the wide sense of this term: security, reliability, optimal resource usage, and minimal negative influence on the environment.

All data center hardware described in Section 1.12 – racks, blade servers, chassis, and so on – is duplicated, or multiplied to the appropriate number of times, for possible replacement of any hardware component by another one similar to it.

The viewpoint on the data center hardware is as follows: it is not considered 100% reliable. So the principle of minimizing *Mean Time To Recovery* (*MTTR*) is pursued, rather than the principle of minimizing *Mean Time Between Failures* (*MTBF*), which is impractical for cloud data centers, keeping in mind the big number of cloud users (several million at a time). So the main principle for cloud datacenters, as stated in Section 1.12, is to enable *high resilience* – the ability to quickly recover from hardware failures that are inevitable, rather than to enable high reliability. To speak in these terms, the principle of *minimizing MTTR* is one of the key principles of cloud datacenter hardware.

The trustworthiness of cloud datacenters is violated if they consume too much electrical power. In this respect, as stated in Section 1.12, the following metric is used – *Power Usage Effectiveness* (*PUE*) – the ratio of *total facility power* to *IT equipment power*. The ideal amount of PUE = 1.0 cannot be reached in practice. Best known PUE amounts in real cloud datacenters now reach 1.12–1.2. So, *minimizing PUE* is yet another key principle of trustworthy cloud datacenter. Another version of formulating this principle is for a cloud datacenter is *to be lean* [25].

To be green is another important principle for trustworthy cloud datacenter [25]. Being green means to use *renewable energy sources* to power cloud datacenters, instead of carbon energy. Microsoft has a special collaboration program with other companies to seek and use renewable energy sources [25].

Using *virtualization* to improve server utilization and increase operational efficiency [25] is very important. A known problem of big datacenters is *underutilized servers*. Server utilization levels are often about 11–15% only. To avoid it, Microsoft is using the Hyper-V technology to migrate applications from physical to virtual machines. So each of the physical servers can run several virtual machines. This approach enables consolidating multiple workloads per server, while maintaining isolation of each workload. It increases server utilization from a typical 11–15% up to 50%. The result is significant energy savings and reduced carbon output.

Multitenancy: As stated above in Chapter 1, this principle means that each cloud service is used by multiple cloud clients (tenants). Using this principle allows cloud providers to reduce total energy usage and carbon emissions. Moreover, due to reasonable load balancing, it is possible to balance capacity among tenants with offsetting demands, and to make resource usage more optimal.

Datacenter design: Microsoft started the use of free-air cooling and ultraefficient water utilization in its latest modular datacenter designs, and uses recyclable materials for their construction. As a result, latest Microsoft modular datacenters take 50% less energy than their previous designs of a few years ago. In addition, renewable energy sources started to be used in cloud datacenters.

Hardened Workstation for Management

This is another very important innovative idea for making cloud datacenters and access to the cloud from the client trustworthy [102]. The goal of the idea of *hardening* a workstation is to eliminate all but the most critical functions required for its operation, thus making the potential attack service as small as possible. The hardened workstation is recommended to be used for managing the communication to the cloud platform, for example, Microsoft Azure. This way many types of attacks can be eliminated or prevented. Hardening a workstation includes minimizing the number of the services and applications installed on the workstation, limiting applications execution, restricting network access to the minimum needed, and always keeping the system up to date. Using a hardened workstation for cloud management separates administrative tasks from other kinds of activities. Using the least privilege minimized software on the hardened workstation for cloud management and cloud application development will help the cloud users to reduce the risk of security incidents by standardizing the remote management and development environments. The hardened workstation configuration can help prevent hijacking the accounts responsible for managing critical cloud resources. In particular, it is possible to use the *Windows AppLocker* and *Hyper-V* technology to control and isolate client system behavior and mitigate threats rooted from using email or Web browser. On a hardened workstation the administrator works as *standard user* (with no administrative-level execution allowed), and all associated applications are controlled by a special allow list. The basic elements of a hardened workstation specifics and behavior are as follows:

- *Active scanning and patching*: Deploying antimalware, do regular vulnerability scanning, applying the latest security updates to the hardened workstation.
- *Limited functionality*: All unnecessary applications are uninstalled, to disable unnecessary services.
- *Network hardening*: Use the Windows firewall to allow only valid IP addresses, ports, and URLs related to communicating to the cloud platform (e.g., Microsoft Azure). Block all possible inbound remote desktop connections to the hardened workstation.
- *Execution restriction*: Allow to execute on the hardened workstation only a predefined set of the executable files necessary for management of the cloud

platform. If an application is not in this allow list, permission of its execution should be denied by default.

– *Least privilege*: The users of the hardened workstation should not have any administrator's privilege on the local machine. This way, they will not be able to change the configuration of the system, either occasionally or intentionally.

In the standalone hardened workstation scenario, the local instance of the firewall should be configured to block all inbound connections such as remote desktop protocol (RDP). The administrator can log in to the hardened workstation and initiate an RDP session to connect to the cloud platform. But it is not allowed to log in to a corporate personal computer and use remote desktop connection to log in to the hardened workstation itself. In case a separate hardened workstation is too costly or uncomfortable, the hardened workstation can host a virtual machine to perform nonadministrative tasks.

To centralize all administrative access and simplify monitoring and logging, it is possible to deploy a dedicated *Remote Desktop Gateway* (*RD Gateway*) server in the local network of the cloud client organization, connected to the cloud environment. Access to the RD Gateway should be protected by the cloud platform management certificate, and by the appropriate Windows network domain rules.

Thus, different kinds of approaches and ideas help to make cloud datacenters hardware really trustworthy in many respects.

4.5 TRUSTWORTHY CLOUD COMPUTING FROM OPERATING SYSTEM SIDE: DESIRABLE OS FEATURES TO IMPLEMENT CLOUDS AND DATACENTERS

Keeping in mind the cloud architectures and the need to support IaaS, SaaS, and PaaS features, let us now consider the appropriate trustworthy features in operating systems to be used in cloud datacenters.

As stated in Section 1.13, there are two kinds of operating systems, in relation to cloud architectures: *host operating system* and *guest operating system*. Host operating system is the operating system used on real machines of the cloud datacenter. Guest operating system is the operating system used on virtual machines created in the cloud.

Running virtual machines in the cloud is one of the most important IaaS functionalities of the cloud. So the most important trustworthy feature for host operating systems in the cloud is to support cloud virtual machines.

The latest and the most novel OS used in cloud datacenters as the host operating system is *Microsoft Windows Server 2012 R2* [103]. This operating system is also used as one of the guest operating systems for virtual machines in public clouds by many companies – for example, Google, IBM, and HP. Examples of the use of Windows 2012 Server R2 as the guest OS are provided in Chapter 2.

In the book [103] Microsoft characterizes Windows Server 2012 R2 as the heart of its cloud platform Microsoft Azure. Microsoft is developing and implementing the general idea of the *Cloud OS* that consists of the following three platforms:

- *Windows Server* (currently represented by Windows Server 2012 R2) – enterprise-class platform, the foundation for developing and deploying cloud solutions
- *Windows System Center* (currently represented by Windows System Center 2012 R2) – an integrated platform for managing public and private clouds and administering cloud networks
- *Microsoft Azure* – the Microsoft public cloud platform (see Chapter 5).

In the concept and implementation of the Cloud OS, the Windows Server forms its foundation, Windows System Center provides management features, and Microsoft Azure provides cloud solutions. Now let us consider the new trustworthy cloud computing support features in Windows Server 2012 R2 in more detail.

Hyper-V Enhancements

The first and most important trustworthy cloud computing feature available in Windows Server 2012 R2 is the *Hyper-V (hypervisor)* technology. Hyper-V is the foundation for cloud virtualization infrastructure. The following major features are available in Hyper-V:

- *Increased scalability and resiliency*: Windows Server 2012 Hyper-V technology supports up to 320 logical processors and 4 terabytes of memory. Cloud virtual machines running on these hosts can be configured with 64 virtual processors and 1 terabyte of memory.
- *Storage migration:* Hyper-V in Windows Server 2012 allows the users to move the virtual hard disks used by a cloud virtual machine to different physical storage without interrupting the run of the virtual machine.
- *VHDX format:* With Windows Server 2012 R2, it is possible to use the new virtual disk format that supports 64 terabyte of storage. In addition, this new format provides built-in protection from power failures.
- *Windows PowerShell module:* Windows PowerShell is a new command scripting language used since Windows 2008. In Windows 2012 Server, Hyper-V includes a PowerShell module for Hyper-V that provides more than 160 *cmdlets* (scripts) for Hyper-V managing tasks.
- *Improved virtual machine support:* The improvement features in Windows Server 2012 Hyper-V include the opportunity to import a virtual machine by copying its files manually, instead of having to export the virtual machine first.
- *Hyper-V replica:* In Windows Server 2012, Hyper-V allows to replicate virtual machines between storage systems, clusters, and datacenters. This is the key feature that is very important for trustworthiness of the cloud, since it allows the users to continue running their business and to recover from disasters.

– *Secure boot based on UEFI*: It is very important for cloud trustworthiness to be able to securely boot or reboot a virtual machine in the cloud. Starting from Windows Server 2012 R2, Windows now supports a new mechanism of secure boot, based on *Unified Extensible Firmware Interface (UEFI)*. It replaces the old BIOS firmware used in the previous versions of Windows. Since Windows 2012 Server R2, the *second generation* virtual machines are able to use Secure Boot based on UEFI.

– *SCSI boot*: In generation 2 virtual machines, starting with Windows Server 2012 R2, it is possible to boot directly from SCSI disks – virtual disks attached to the virtual machine using the SCSI controller. Generation 2 virtual machines can also boot from an SCSI virtual DVD.

– *Faster deployment:* Network-based installation of a guest operating system is now much faster than the previous generation of virtual machines for the following reasons. First, the legacy network adapter device is no longer required for generation 2 virtual machines. Instead, it is possible to do PXE-boot a generation 2 virtual machine using a standard network adapter. Second, the SCSI controller used for Hyper-V virtual machines in Windows Server 2012 R2 works much faster than the previous IDE controller used for a similar purpose. As a result, installing a guest operating system on a generation 2 virtual machine now works twice faster than installing the guest operating system on a previous generation virtual machine.

Virtual machines created by Windows 2012 Server R2 are referred to as generation 2 virtual machines. I am citing the book [103] on the benefits of generation 2 virtual machines. "The key benefits of using Generation 2 virtual machines, as opposed to Generation 1 virtual machines, are twofold. First, as mentioned previously, new Generation 2 virtual machines can be quickly provisioned because they can boot from a SCSI device or a standard network adapter. This can be useful in scenarios where you need to quickly deploy new virtual machines in order to scale out a cloud-based application to meet rapidly increasing demand" [103].

"The second main benefit of Generation 2 virtual machines is in the area of security. Because Generation 2 virtual machines are UEFI-based and support Secure Boot, unauthorized operating systems, drivers, and firmware can be prevented from running when the virtual machine starts. In order for this to apply, however, Secure Boot must be enabled for the virtual machine. As Figure 2.3 (in [103]) shows, you can enable or disable Secure Boot on a Generation 2 virtual machine by opening the Settings of the virtual machine, selecting Firmware under Hardware, and selecting or clearing the Enable Secure Boot check box. By default, Secure Boot is enabled when you create a new Generation 2 virtual machine" [103].

Storage

Two new trustworthy storage technologies for cloud infrastructure support are implemented in Windows Server 2012 R2: *storage spaces* and *scale-out file server (SoFS)*. Storage spaces provide storage virtualization capabilities. They allow the users to group disks such as Serial ATS and Serial Attached SCSI disks into *storage pools*. Then, it is possible to create virtual disks called *storage spaces* and thus provide resilient storage volumes of the required sizes. This technology is comfortable for creating virtual machines of different disk storage capacities. In Windows Server 2012, the new *Resilient File System (ReFS)* was introduced. ReFS supports volume sizes up to 18 exabytes and could be especially useful on file servers storing large amounts of data or running disk-intensive applications that require high levels of performance.

Network

Several networking technologies in Windows Server 2012 are especially useful for trustworthy cloud computing.

IP Address Management (IPAM) is a new built-in framework introduced in Windows Server 2012 for discovering, monitoring, auditing, and managing the IP address space used on a corporate network. IPAM provided a central and integrated experience for managing IP addresses that could replace manual, work-intensive tools such as spreadsheets and custom scripts that can be tedious, unreliable, and scale poorly [103].

Network virtualization was introduced in Windows Server 2012 as a way for organizations to keep their own internal IP addresses when moving their servers into a host's cloud. It works by allowing the users to assign two different IP addresses to each virtual machine running on a Windows Server 2012 Hyper-V host: the *customer* address, which is the IP address that the server had when it resided on the customer's premises before it was migrated into the cloud; and the *provider* address, which is the IP address assigned by the cloud provider to the server once the server has been migrated to the provider's datacenter. Network virtualization lets the cloud provider run multiple virtual networks on top of a single physical network in much the same way as server virtualization lets you run multiple virtual servers on a single physical server. Network virtualization also isolates each virtual network from every other virtual network, with the result that each virtual network has the illusion that it is a separate physical network. This means that two or more virtual networks can have the exact same addressing scheme, yet the networks will be fully isolated from one another and each will function as if it is the only network with that scheme [103].

4.6   USING ASPECT-ORIENTED PROGRAMMING FOR REFACTORING CLOUD SERVICES AND MAKING THEM TRUSTWORTHY: THE CONTRIBUTION OF ST. PETERSBURG UNIVERSITY

Cloud computing with Microsoft Azure [3, 4] is a rapidly evolving, state-of-the-art collection of software technologies. The architecture of cloud applications is very complicated. It consists of cloud Web services that should be developed, keeping in mind their trustworthiness, configurability, and elasticity.

Another very important approach to software development is trustworthy computing [1, 2], which unites software security, reliability, and privacy of confidential information.

The main goal of this section is to present a method of refactoring and configuring cloud application projects and solutions for Microsoft Azure cloud platform with application blocks of implementations of *cross-cutting concerns* (caching, cryptography, data access, exception handling, logging, security, validation) provided by Microsoft Enterprise Library Integration Pack for Microsoft Azure [104]. Refactoring and configuring is implemented using aspect-oriented programming (AOP) and our Aspect.NET [1, 105] AOP toolkit for the .NET platform currently used for research and teaching in 26 countries. The latest version of Aspect.NET compatible to Visual Studio 2013 [106] contains a novel feature of replacing the base class of the target application and the calls of all its methods, which is a powerful mechanism for *aspect-oriented refactoring* of cloud applications.

The Enterprise Library Integration Pack for Microsoft Azure is a solution by Microsoft for separation of cross-cutting concern in developing cloud applications. Using this library implies modification of the source code of the target application. In practice, there appear situations when the source code of the target application is just unavailable for confidentiality or any other reasons, so AOP tools relying on the source code are inapplicable. Our basic idea [106] is a method of seamless integration of aspects and the target project with Aspect.NET that allows us to avoid changing the source code of the target application.

AOP [1] is a relatively new (invented in the 1990s) software development and modification paradigm intended to support modularization of cross-cutting concerns. Typical examples of such concerns are security, privacy, logging, error handling, and configuring. In general, most of the tasks to be solved with AOP are those of *trustworthy computing* [1]. Also, AOP is well suited for solving the tasks of software configuration, since it deals with multiple automated code injections and replacements. *Aspect* in AOP is an implementation of a cross-cutting concern specified as a new kind of module. Aspect specification, in our terms [1], consists of a set of *actions* and their *weaving conditions*. *Weaving* is the way to use aspects – injecting the code of aspect actions into the *join points* of the target application code, selected as satisfying the corresponding aspect's weaving conditions. Weaving is performed automatically, based on the aspect specification, by an AOP toolkit, namely, by its component referred to as *weaver*. The aspect action may catch and process the context of the join point. So AOP is a powerful mechanism to make systematic changes and enhancements of software. In particular, AOP is well suited for configuring and securing Web services in the cloud; however, the use of AOP in cloud computing is still at the starting point, so we hope our project will help to leverage it.

Overview of the Aspect.NET Project

Our Aspect.NET [1, 105–113] is an AOP toolkit for the .NET platform. Its ideas were first presented in 2003 in [107]. The main goal of the project is to support AOP for Visual Studio.NET as one of the ubiquitous technologies available with Visual Studio, as a Visual Studio add-in.

We are grateful to Microsoft Research for their research grant support of the Aspect.NET project in 2002, 2004, and 2006. We have presented Aspect.NET in a number of conferences [109, 110, 112].

In 2005, the first working version Aspect.NET 1.0 was developed and published on Microsoft Faculty Connection Web site [114]. Since then to date, we have developed four more versions of Aspect.NET: Aspect.NET 1.1 [115], Aspect.NET 2.0 [116], Aspect.NET 2.1 [117], and Aspect.NET 2.2 [118] published on Microsoft Faculty Connection Web site, and an experimental version of the weaver to be published on our project site [105] yet.

Aspect.NET is based on a number of novel principles of its architecture and implementation (at least, those principles were novel when Aspect.NET appeared): multilanguage AOP (currently Aspect.NET allows to combine aspects and target applications written in C# or VB); use of very simple language-agnostic AOP meta-language Aspect.NET.ML to specify aspects with *AOP annotations*; use of custom attributes to implement aspects; integration to Visual Studio; user-controlled weaving [105–112].

All versions of Aspect.NET – from Aspect.NET 1.0 to Aspect.NET 2.2 – have the following architecture:

- *Aspect.NET Framework* – GUI for aspect visualization, weaving, and calling the updated target applications after weaving, implemented as Visual Studio add-in.
- *Converters* from Aspect.NET.ML AOP annotations to source code in C# (VB) that defines our specific AOP custom attributes used by the Aspect.NET weaver – *AspectAction* and *AspectDescription*.
- *Weaver* that performs, as the first stage, search of potential join points in the target application, and, as the second stage, actual weaving of the selected aspects into the selected join points, after the user's approval (the user can deselect some undesirable join points). Weaving is performed at CIL (*Common Intermediate* Language, also known as *MSIL – Microsoft Intermediate Language*) binary intermediate code level.

Aspect.NET does not have any specific extended language compiler, unlike the classical AOP tool AspectJ, since the scheme we use to process aspects is different: first, convert Aspect.NET.ML annotations to the aspect implementation source code, with the AOP custom attributes injected, and, next, use the appropriate common Visual Studio compiler to generate the binary CIL code of the aspect. So the binary code of the aspect is just a normal .NET assembly, and our AOP attributes do not prevent the normal processing of .NET assemblies by commonly used tools – compilers, debuggers, profilers, and so on. No specific XML configuration files, and so on. are needed with our approach.

Our latest results on the project are *Aspect.NET 3.0*, still at the experimental stage, compatible to Visual Studio.NET 2013 to be published on the Aspect.NET project site yet [105], and our new *Aspect4Cloud* aspect library [105] for refactoring Microsoft

Azure cloud applications with the help of Microsoft Enterprise Library Integration Pack for Microsoft Azure.

Since Aspect.NET 3.0 is an experimental version, it only contains a weaver and a set of scripts to integrate aspect weaving into the Visual Studio assembly build process. The version of Aspect.NET Framework GUI compatible to Visual Studio 2013 is still under development and testing.

Here is an example of Aspect.NET aspect:

```
%aspect CloudServiceSecurity
 public class CloudServiceSecurity
    %rules
    %before %call MyCloudService*  %action
    public static void SecurityCheck() { … }
}
```

This aspect injects a call of the *SecurityCheck* method before each call of any cloud service whose name starts with *MyCloudService*, that is, makes the use of the service more secure. So, using AOP, there is no need to perform such code modifications manually, which would be unsafe. All code updates (weaving) will be performed by the weaver and controlled by the user via GUI. The advantage of AOP in this respect is as follows: automated modification of the code controlled by aspects and by AOP toolkit will be made safely, regardless of the size of the code that may be very large, and regardless of the required (probably big) number of aspect action injections. It is allowed for a developer to avoid using Aspect.NET.ML meta-language and instead use the AOP custom attribute *AspectAction* to specify the weaving rule for an aspect action. For example, the above aspect's action code written "in attributes" would look like this:

```
["AspectAction" %before %call MyCloudService*" ]
public static void SecurityCheck() { … }
```

Refactoring Microsoft Azure Cloud Applications with Aspect.NET

Now let us consider the feature of Aspect.NET that helps to refactor cross-cutting functionality provided by Enterprise Library Integration Pack for Microsoft Azure. A simple example is «Hands-on Lab 1: Using the Logging Application Block with Microsoft Azure Storage» [119], where by adding a reference to Enterprise Library assemblies a logging application block is used in the project, and its method is called for passing a message into the WAD cloud repository of diagnostics information. It enables to tune the parameters of collecting and keeping debug messages via the graphics interface of the Logging Application Block or via its configuration files:

Example 1 Web role with the use of Logging Application Block

```
//Web role on whose page the Logging Application Block is being tested:
  public partial class Default : System.Web.UI.Page {
```

```
// The message is sent in the handler of the mouse click
// on the page button
    protected void LogButton_Click(object sender, EventArgs e) {
  Microsoft.Practices.EnterpriseLibrary.Logging.
    Logger.Write
    ("Message from the Logging Application Block");
  }
}
```

Our task with this example is to move all the dependencies from Enterprise Library and logging method calls to a separate project implemented by the aspect. Then, on applying by Aspect.NET the given aspect to the original project, we obtain its seamless integration with the Logging Application Block.

Traditionally, in Aspect.NET and other AOP tools, similar tasks are solved by placing the logging code into the aspect as aspect actions, and injecting the calls of those actions before, after, or instead of the call of the target method in the original project. In our case, the target method is the handler of the button click event *LogButton_Click()* of the *Default* Web page class. The object of that class is created and the events are passed to it by the ASP.NET and the IIS. It means that the code of the call of the target method is located outside of the assembly of the original project, and is not available to Aspect.NET. So, in our opinion, intercepting the external events handling method calls can be implemented via the inheritance of classes. If, in the aspect project, we define a class that inherits from the base class, and then to replace by that aspect class the original base project class, the desirable interception can be implemented in the overridden virtual method:

Example 2 The replacing aspect descendant

```
//The project with the replacing aspect descendant
[AspectDotNet.ReplaceBaseClass]
    public class AspectClass : Default {
        protected void LogButton_Click
        (object sender, EventArgs e) {
            Microsoft.Practices.EnterpriseLibrary.Logging.
            Logger.Write
            ("Message from the Logging Application Block");
            base.LogButton_Click(sender, e);
        }
    }
}
//The original project, after eliminating
// the dependence from Logging Application Block
public partial class Default : System.Web.UI.Page {
protected void LogButton_Click(object sender, EventArgs e) {}
}
```

The special custom attribute *[ReplaceBaseClass]* forces the Aspect.NET weaver to replace the target class by its aspect replacement descendant. More exactly, the weaver performs the following actions:

- Replace in the original assembly all calls of the methods of the base target class (including the constructors) by the appropriate calls of methods from its aspect replacing descendant.
- Make virtual all methods of the target class that are overridden in its replacing aspect descendant. If they are private, make them protected.
- If the calls of those methods in the original assembly are implemented by MSIL instructions of *call* or *ldftn*, replace them by *callvirt* and *ldvirtftn*, accordingly.
- Unite by the *ILRepack* tool (from the project Mono.Cecil [120]) the assemblies with the aspect and the original assembly.
- Assign some service name to the original base class, and assign its original name to the replacing aspect descendant.

Please note that the AOP refactoring features described above, to our knowledge, are not implemented in any other AOP toolkit for .NET.

Now let us consider "Hands-on Lab 6: Implementing Throttling Behavior," which illustrates limitation of functionality under some workload with the use of services of the functional block Autoscaling Application Block. The separate component *Autoscaler* performs monitoring of diagnostic information and, depending on the current workload to the cloud, sets up the property *ThrottlingMode* in the configuration file of the initial project. Depending on the value of this property, some of the methods of the Web page class may change their behavior (see Example 3).

Example 3

```
// The Web role on whose page
// the Autoscaling Application Block is being tested
public partial class Default : System.Web.UI.Page {
protected override void OnPreRenderComplete(EventArgs e) {
   base.OnPreRenderComplete(e);
string throttlingMode =
   RoleEnvironment.GetConfigurationSettingValue("ThrottlingMode");
      switch (throttlingMode)
      {
          case "HighActivity":
              this.ThrottlingLabel.Text =
                "Working with high activity…";
            break;
        default:
            this.ThrottlingLabel.Text =
                "Working with normal activity…";
    this.DoSomeUsualWork();
                break;
          }
    }
 private void DoSomeUsualWork() {/*…*/}
}
```

This method can be moved to the aspect and therefore the target class will be concentrated on solving its own problem only, whereas the *Autoscaler* component and seamless integration with the aspect will enable the reaction on the extended workload. The problem could be solved similarly to the previous example, but here exists an issue with the private method in the target class – *DoSomeUsualWork()*. To make it available to the replacing aspect descendant, the aspect weaver could convert this method to a *protected* one. However, it will violate the encapsulation of the target class, so the only way to keep it is to use .NET reflection. The private members of the target class will become the fields of its aspect descendant that will be initialized in the constructor. Also, suppose that in the replacing aspect descendant of the target class we will need to call the method *OnPreRenderComplete* of the next (according to the class hierarchy) base class *System.Web.UI.Page*. The protected and the public methods of the target class are used in its replacing aspect descendant without any limitations. The resulting aspect is represented in Example 4 below.

The next example of seamless integration is based on the example "Hands-on Lab 11: Transient Fault Handling." Here, the task is to add to the target code dealing with the database some strategy of exception handling. The strategy is separated from the code working with the database and is configured by means of the Enterprise Library. For example, for any query to the database, the following strategy is possible: to attempt to make four sequential queries, in case any of the previous ones ends with failure. Between the second and the third queries, there should be a pause of five seconds. The source code of the target class is given in the Example 5.

The query to the database is made by calling the method *SqlCommand.Execute Reader()*, which can throw an exception in case the connection to the database fails. To apply the strategy of exception handling, it is necessary to execute this block within the method *ExecuteAction()* of the class *Microsoft.Practices.TransientFaultHandling. RetryPolicy<T>*, where *T* is the class implementing the strategy. The object of this class is available via the special manager *TransientFaultHandling.RetryManager,* which should be initialized by the Enterprise Library and passed to us in the constructor of the target class. To do that, it is required to create an object of our replacing aspect descendant by means of the Enterprise Library (see Example 6). Features of AOP, including those of Aspect.NET, provide mechanisms of replacing the call of the target method by the aspect action. We did that to replace the class of the aspect descendant; however, in this case the situation is more complicated, since the "target" block is the whole *using* block. It is for such situations that we implemented our mechanism of replacing the target class by replacing aspect descendant. The resulting code of the aspect is given in the Example 7.

Example 4

```
using System.Reflection;
[AspectDotNet.ReplaceBaseClass]
public class AspectClass : _Default {
MethodInfo DoSomeUsualWork;
     public AspectClass() {
       Type BaseType = this.GetType().BaseType;
  //Getting a reference to the private method
         // of the _Default base class
```

```
        DoSomeUsualWork = BaseType.GetMethod("DoSomeUsualWork",
BindingFlags.NonPublic | BindingFlags.Instance);
  // Reference to the method of the base class
          // System.Web.UI.Page
PageOnPreRenderComplete =
  base.GetType().BaseType.
GetMethod("OnPreRenderComplete",
BindingFlags.NonPublic | BindingFlags.Instance);
      }
    protected override void OnPreRenderComplete(EventArgs e) {
   //Call the method of the base class System.Web.UI.Page
        PageOnPreRenderComplete.Invoke(this, new object[] { e });
        string throttlingMode = RoleEnvironment.
   GetConfigurationSettingValue("ThrottlingMode");
        switch (throttlingMode) {
              case "HighActivity":
   // Using in the aspect the member
              // of the target class _Default
                this.ThrottlingLabel.Text =
                 "Working with high activity…";
                break;
              default:
                this.ThrottlingLabel.Text =
                 "Working with usual activity…";
     // Call of the private member of
              // the target class _Default
  DoSomeUsualWork.Invoke(this, null);
                break;
      }
    }
}
```

Now let us consider some engineering problems of adaptation of Aspect.NET for implementing methods of seamless integration. We are sure that getting acquainted with them will allow the readers to better understand the process of creating such tools that transform target assemblies at MSIL binary code level.

Modern development of Microsoft Azure services implies the use of the latest Microsoft Visual Studio 2013, which radically simplifies the deployment of cloud applications. It is enough for a software developer to make a few mouse clicks to publish his or her application on the cloud. The latest stable version of Aspect.NET, version 2.2, is only compatible to Microsoft Visual Studio 2008, since its COM library for debugging information handling (*msdia90.dll*) is used in Microsoft Phoenix toolkit [2] for compiler development, which we have been using in Aspect.NET project for a long time. Installing and using Microsoft Visual Studio of a later version leads to the situation when Microsoft Phoenix automatically tries to use the new version of the *msdia90.dll* library and terminates with an error. Unfortunately, since 2008 the development of the cross-platform environment for building optimizing compilers Microsoft Phoenix has stopped. But, nevertheless, wide spectrum features of Phoenix are still used by my academic researchers, so incompatibility with the latest versions of Visual Studio puts a serious barrier for such research projects. Our solution of this problem is as follows. The needed version of the library is placed in the Aspect.NET weaver directory, together with its manifest *msdia90.manifest* (see Example 8).

Example 5

```
public class Main : Form {
    private void ExecuteQueryButton_Click(object sender, EventArgs e) {
        //…
            try {
                using (var connection =
                  new
                    SqlConnection(ConfigurationManager.ConnectionStrings
["Northwind"].ConnectionString)) {
                    connection.Open();
                    var command =
                      new SqlCommand("dbo.GetProductDetails",
                                        connection)
  {CommandType =
   CommandType.StoredProcedure};
                        // …Filling out the parameters of the command…
                        using (var reader = command.ExecuteReader()) {
                            while (reader.Read()) {
// Processing the result
// of the successful query
                            }
                        }
                }
            } catch (Exception ex) {
                //…
            }
        }
}
```

Example 6

```
//All aspect classes in Aspect.NET should inherit from the Aspect class
class ChangeRunAspect : AspectDotNet.Aspect {
        [AspectDotNet.AspectAction("%instead %call *.Application.Run")]
        static public void ReplaceAction() {
Application.Run(EnterpriseLibraryContainer.Current.
        GetInstance<AspectMain>());
        }
}
```

Example 7

```
[AspectDotNet.ReplaceBaseClass]
public partial class AspectMain : Main {
private RetryManager retryManager;
     public AspectMain(RetryManager retryManager) {
```

```
        this.retryManager = retryManager;
    }
    private void ExecuteQueryButton_Click(object sender, EventArgs e)
    {
//…
    try {
             using (var connection = new
               SqlConnection(ConfigurationManager.ConnectionStrings
["Northwind"].ConnectionString)) {
               connection.Open();
               var command = new SqlCommand("dbo.GetProductDetails",
  connection){CommandType =
      CommandType.StoredProcedure};
                  // …Filling out the command parameters
                  var policy = this.retryManager.GetRetryPolicy
   <HolSqlTransientErrorDetectionStrategy>
    ("HOL Strategy");
                  policy.Retrying += (s, a) =>
                     Log.Invoke(this,new object[]
                        {"Attempt of the new connection …"});
                  policy.ExecuteAction(() => {
                   using (var reader = command.ExecuteReader()) {
    while (reader.Read()) {
      //… Processing the result
            // of the successful query
                    }
                  }
                  });
          }
        } catch (Exception ex) {
  //…
        }
    }
}
```

Example 8

```xml
<?xml version="1.0" encoding="utf-8"?>
<asmv1:assembly manifestVersion="1.0"
 xmlns="urn:schemas-microsoft-com:asm.v1"
 xmlns:asmv1="urn:schemas-microsoft-com:asm.v1" >
<assemblyIdentity type="win32" name="msdia90" version="9.0.30729.4947"
  language="neutral" processorArchitecture="x86"/>
<file name="msdia90.dll">
        <comClass clsid="{B86AE24D-BF2F-4ac9-B5A2-34B14E4CE11D}"
    threadingModel="both"/>
</file>
</asmv1:assembly>
```

The next issue is to publish by means of Visual Studio the resulting assembly, with the aspects woven, on Microsoft Azure cloud. For cloud Web application, after choosing in the contextual menu of the project properties the *Publish* item, the process of publication is implemented as compilation of the project, packing its assembly with the used libraries and the other supplementary files into a special archive, and then passing it to Microsoft Azure services (see Chapter 5). The weaver of Aspect.NET, in its turn, is a console application that takes as command line arguments the paths to the assemblies: aspect assembly, target assembly, and the resulting assembly:

```
weaver -aspects MyAspect.dll -in HelloWorld.exe -out AspectHelloWorld.exe
```

So if we manage to execute this command directly after the stage of compilation and to replace the target assembly by the resulting assembly, Visual Studio will send to publishing in the cloud the resulting application with the aspects woven. Moreover, now starting of the project execution will result in starting the projects with the aspects woven, which will make easier the aspect-oriented program development. As a result, the following algorithm of development and seamless integration of aspects by Aspect.NET in Visual Studio was implemented:

Input: The project with the sources of the target application to apply the aspects.

1. Create a separate project for the aspect (of the kind Class Library) and unite it with the target project within the common solution.
2. To enable integration of the aspect with the target assembly, in the project properties, in the Build Events tab, add the script shown in Example 9.

Example 9

```
:: Set the folder with the build of the target project
set TargetAssemblyDir=C:\HelloWorld\HelloWorld\bin\Debug\
:: The name of its assembly
set TargetAssembly=HelloWorld
:: The name extension for the target assembly
set TargetAssemblyExt=.exe
:: For each new aspect or the target project, it is necessary
:: to change the above environment variables only
:: Set the path to the Aspect.NET directory
set AspectDotNetDir=C:\AspectDotNet
set TargetAssemblyPath=%TargetAssemblyDir%%TargetAssembly%%TargetAssembly
Ext%
set TargetAssemblyName=%TargetAssembly%%TargetAssemblyExt%
cd %AspectDotNetDir%
weaver -aspects $(TargetPath) -in %TargetAssemblyPath%
    -out  %TargetAssemblyName%
:: Replacing the assembly in the target project by the resulting one
move /Y %TargetAssemblyName% %TargetAssemblyPath%
```

3. Switch off the process of weaving the aspects in case the target assembly compilation fails by choosing "When the build updates the project output" in the option "Run the post-build event."

4. Change the order of building the aspects (*Project Build Order* in the contextual menu of the aspect project) so that the first project to build would be the target one, then, the aspect one.

5. Set up the target project for running (in its context menu "Set as StartUp Point")

Output: The solution with the aspect and non-modified target project. When compiling the aspect project, aspect weaving will be performed, and when running in Visual Studio – running the resulting assembly will be performed. In its turn, compiling and running the target project will run the target project, with no aspects woven.

In seamless integration of the aspects with the target assembly, it is desirable to apply the Visual Studio debugger for testing the resulting assembly. All information on the relationships of the source code and the breakpoint in the executable code is contained in the .pdb files generated by the Visual Studio compiler. On applying the weaver, the executable file with the aspects woven is created, but the .pdb files with the debugging information for the aspect and the target project do not correspond to it. This makes impossible setting the breakpoint in aspects and step-by-step debugging of the resulting assembly.

So our final task is to create a .pdb file with the debugging information corresponding to the resulting assembly. During its work, the weaver injects into the target assembly some extra MSIL instructions for calling the actions of the aspect and for passing to them the context of the join point. Those operations are implemented with Microsoft Phoenix, and Mono.Cecil is responsible for the steps 2, 4, and 5 in the above algorithm for substituting the replacing aspect descendant. The Microsoft Phoenix as well as the Mono.Cecil tools, when transforming the target assembly, automatically supports the correspondence with the debugging information. In other words, with the corresponding parameters of those tools, the .pdb file will be created automatically. All that we need now is to add by means of Microsoft Phoenix the debugging information for the new MSIL instructions. Taking into account that their adding does not influence the source code of the target project, it is only necessary to copy to the new MSIL instructions the debugging information from their preceding instructions in the target assembly. It is implemented by copying the value of the property *DebugTag* of the class *Phx.IR.Instruction* – high-level representation of instructions in Microsoft Phoenix [2, Chapter 10]. So the debugger will be now able by one step to execute the new instructions and step into the aspect action. Then, the debugging information of the aspect assembly will be used, which is already created by the .NET compiler.

Seamless integration of aspects into target cloud applications makes it possible to efficiently solve the problems of project maintenance when it is necessary to add a new functionality without updating the source code. The presented approach allows software developers to apply third party libraries to delete (refactor) cross-cutting concerns, with the goal to avoid dependences on them in the source code of the target project. During further research and development, it is quite possible to quit using the selected third party library or to change this library to another one. So the risk is minimized of an undesirable situation when the failure to select an appropriate

AOP solution or library would cause substantial refurbishment of the target project. Implementation of the presented method by Aspect.NET allows the developers to use commonly used development environment of Microsoft Visual Studio and a simple process of creating aspects that enable the use of cloud services of third party libraries. All the aspects presented in this section are available on the Web site of the Aspect.NET project [105].

Related Work

The most commonly used AOP toolkit for .NET is PostSharp [121]. Aspects are defined in PostSharp by custom attributes. PostSharp provides the following kinds of join points: method calls, accessing and updating properties, fields of a class, and generation of an event or an exception. To weave aspects, it is necessary to add to the target project some references to PostSharp service assemblies, to add the source code of the aspects to the target project, and to mark by special attributes the join points in the code of the target project. All of that requires storing aspect definitions and weaving rules together with the source files of the target project, so too high coupling is created between them. If the AOP tool is to be changed from PostSharp to some other tool, it would be difficult to do. To our knowledge, there is no documented way of seamless integration of aspects with PostSharp.

A technique somewhat similar to our *ReplaceBaseClass* functionality is provided in CaesarJ [122] – virtual classes that solve similar task of giving more flexibility to object-oriented scheme. However, CaesarJ is implemented for the Java platform, and its specifics are to use a special extra keyword *cclass* (for CaesarJ class). We provide our replace base class functionality for .NET, without introducing any extra keywords, driven by a specific AOP custom attribute.

As already noted, using AOP for cloud computing in general is now in the starting stage yet. The Enterprise Library Integration Pack for Microsoft Azure [104] itself contains a feature named Unity Application Block to enable limited weaving of the Enterprise Library's cross-cutting functionality into target applications. But weaving in Unity is implemented by a type of interceptors controlled by special Unity containers, which is not so comfortable and does not allow the developers to perform seamless integration of the code. The advantages of our approach are, first, enabling of the powerful mechanism of aspect-oriented refactoring using the replacing aspect descendant, and, second, enabling of the seamless integration of the cross-cutting code and the basic cloud application functionality.

Perspectives of the Proposed Approach

As stated above, the section is actually a summary of already published results on the Aspect.NET project. The results till now have been already published mostly in Russian journals, so one of the goals of the section is to widen the scope of the results we consider important for the IT community.

Using the method proposed above, we developed the *Aspect4Cloud* aspect library for Aspect.NET to support refactoring and configuring cloud applications for

Microsoft Azure using Enterprise Library Integration Pack. The code of the library is published on the Aspect.NET project site [105].

Seamless integration of aspects into target applications enables the developers to efficiently solve the problems of maintaining software projects without modification of the target source code. The proposed method allows us to use service libraries to implement cross-cutting functionality but to avoid explicit dependences on those libraries in the source code of the target project. In further project development, it is possible to drop using the library or to replace the library by another one. So we decrease the risk that a mistaken AOP decision would cause substantial updates of the target project. Implementing the proposed method with Aspect.NET allows the developers to use the common Visual Studio IDE, and to follow our simple code patterns implemented in Aspect4Cloud library to create aspects that implement access to library services.

Possible future research directions can be targeted to development of more aspect libraries to make it easier to refactor Microsoft Azure cloud applications by adding service libraries functionality with the help of aspects and Aspect.NET.

So in this chapter, different kinds of cloud trustworthiness issues, approaches, solutions, and tools are considered. The progress of trustworthy cloud computing is huge and rapidly progressing.

EXERCISES TO CHAPTER 4

E4.1 What kinds of psychological barriers arise between the cloud users and the cloud and why?

E4.2 What is the principal difference between the cloud approach to managing resources and applications from more traditional approaches used for decades? Why can the remote character of cloud computing create psychological problems for cloud users?

E4.3 Why can geographical distribution of cloud resources between regions and datacenters create problems for the cloud users? Please overview the problem of thinking in terms of geographical regions for cloud users.

E4.4 What is the main security issue of cloud computing for most cloud users? Why are they so concerned about security of their data in the cloud?

E4.5 What kind of problems do cloud users experience when tracking and understanding regular payments for the cloud resources consumed?

E4.6 Please overview the problem of slow connection to the cloud and its possible consequences.

E4.7 What kind of understanding issues do cloud users experience when referring to cloud resources?

E4.8 Please overview the requirements to cloud–user interface, its usability, and trustworthiness.

E4.9 Please overview the requirement of integration to a single portal for cloud–user interface.

E4.10 Please overview the requirement of using a single authentication mechanism for cloud–user interface.

E4.11 Please formulate the requirement of clear and detailed picture of the cloud resources used for cloud–user interface.

E4.12 Please overview the issue of default warnings on possible payment and billing for the cloud–user interface. Why is it so uncomfortable if a big cloud resource silently "hangs" in the cloud for a long time?

E4.13 Please formulate the requirement of monitoring the cloud resources for the cloud–user interface.

E4.14 What is your opinion on the convenience of galleries and samples that make it easier to create complicated cloud resources? What are your recommendations to cloud service providers in this respect?

E4.15 What is your opinion on the convenience of connecting to virtual machines in different cloud platforms? What kinds of details are redundant for most cloud users in this respect? Which cloud platforms, in your opinion, provide the most comfortable way of connection to virtual machines?

E4.16 Why, in your opinion, is it comfortable to do all the work with cloud resources, applications, databases, and so on. directly in the cloud, without using programmatic APIs and extra "on-premises" third party products?

E4.17 Please overview the cloud PaaS features to handle cloud applications in the cloud. What are your impressions on PaaS functionalities of different cloud platforms?

E4.18 What are your personal impressions of organization of cloud free trials on different cloud platforms? Which cloud platforms in this respect do you like best? What kind of recommendations can you give to cloud service providers to improve the process of cloud free trial?

E4.19 Please overview possible attacks and threats to clouds and cloud resources.

E4.20 What kind of attack is session riding (cross-site request forgery)? Why is it so dangerous?

E4.21 What kind of attack is virtual machine escape? How can it be organized using the specifics of the hypervisor?

E4.22 What can you say on reliability and availability of cloud services as a potential threat, based on your personal experience?

E4.23 What can you say on insecure cryptography in the cloud as a potential threat, based on your personal experience?

E4.24 What kind of problems related to handling cloud data arise when the cloud user has to move from one cloud provider to another? What can you say on the approach "Don't let him go" from cloud service providers side?

E4.25 How can you characterize the dependency on the Internet connection for cloud users? In which cases can it be undesirable or dangerous?

E4.26 What is the danger of ease of use of cloud services and how can it be exploited by cloud attackers?

E4.27 Why is it so important for cloud service provider to enable secure data transmission in the cloud and from the cloud to the user? What kind of attack is "man in the middle" and how is it organized?

E4.28 What kind of security issues, in your experience, arise because of insecure APIs? Which programming languages and platforms, in your opinion, are most suitable for using cloud services programmatically, and why? Which languages are insecure?

E4.29 What can you say on the danger of malicious insiders in the cloud? Have you faced malicious behavior of some representatives of cloud service provider company?

E4.30 How are the specifics of the hypervisors used for attacks to virtual machines? Have you experienced such kinds of attacks?

E4.31 Please overview the threat of data loss in the cloud, why is it so dangerous, and for which reasons it may happen?

E4.32 Please overview the threat of data breach in the cloud. How can it happen when using cloud virtual machines?

E4.34 What kind of attacks to the cloud and cloud resources can happen as the result of account (service) hijacking? Why are hijacking of accounts that give access to virtual machines especially dangerous?

E4.35 How can the denial of service attack be organized for cloud services?

E4.36 Please overview the threat related to lack of understanding for individual and enterprise cloud users.

E4.37 Why, in your opinion, is cloud user education and informing users of different kinds of attacks so important? In your personal experience, have your cloud service providers organized this?

E4.38 Please overview the principles of trustworthiness and trustworthy organization of hardware in cloud datacenters.

E4.39 What are MTBF and MTTR? Which of these principles, in your opinion, is most suitable for cloud datacenters, and why?

E4.40 What is PUE as a trustworthiness metric of cloud datacenter? Which values of PUE are reached in state-of-the-art datacenters?

E4.41 Why is it so important for cloud datacenters *to be green*? Please explain.

E4.42 How does the use of virtualization in cloud datacenters help to increase the percentage of server utilization in cloud datacenters?

E4.43 How can the use of multitenancy help to save power consuming of a cloud datacenter?

E4.44 Please overview the principles of modern datacenter design by Microsoft, and their positive effect on the trustworthiness of cloud datacenters.

E4.45 Please overview the concept of *hardened workstation* and its importance as a secure way to connect to the cloud and to minimize the attack surface.

E4.46 Please overview the requirements to host operating systems used in the cloud.

E4.47 Please overview the innovations implemented in Windows Server 2012 and Windows Server 2012 R2 to support cloud datacenters.

E4.48 Please overview the concept of Cloud OS by Microsoft and its three components – Windows Server, Windows System Center, and Microsoft Azure.

E4.49 Please overview the enhancements of the Hyper-V hypervisor by Microsoft in the latest server-side operating systems.

E4.50 What is Generation 2 virtual machine in Windows Server 2012 R2 and what are its advantages over the previous generation?

E4.51 What is AOP? How can it be used to make the cloud software more trustworthy?

E4.52 Please overview the principles and evolution of the Aspect.NET AOP toolkit.

E4.53 Please overview the basic concepts of Aspect.NET. What are aspect, weaving, weaver, weaving rules, aspect actions?

E4.54 Please overview the principles of the use of Aspect.NET for refactoring cloud applications.

E4.55 What is Enterprise Library Integration Pack for Microsoft Azure? Please overview its features.

E4.56 Please explain the innovative idea of replacing aspect descendant implemented in Aspect.NET. Why is this mechanism helpful in refactoring cloud applications?

E4.57 How is the Aspect.NET weaver and aspect weaving implemented in the new version of Aspect.NET (3.0)? What is the role of Visual Studio in Aspect.NET?

E4.58 Which software tools are used in Aspect.NET for implementing aspect weaving? What is Microsoft Phoenix and Mono.Cecil?

E4.59 Please explain by the given examples the relationships between Visual Studio with its build processes, and Aspect.NET.

E4.60 Please overview the perspective of using AOP and Aspect.NET for refactoring cloud applications.

5

EXAMPLE OF A TRUSTWORTHY CLOUD COMPUTING PLATFORM IN DETAIL: MICROSOFT AZURE

5.1 OVERVIEW OF MICROSOFT AZURE ARCHITECTURE AND ITS EVOLUTION

Microsoft Azure (also known as *Windows Azure* until 2014) is the cloud Internet platform developed by Microsoft Corporation. Actually it is one of the foundations of the Cloud OS (see Chapter 4) and a unique cloud toolkit. Microsoft Azure enables storing, using, and updating data (including big data) and running applications on server computers located in Microsoft datacenters worldwide. No extra software besides a Web browser is required on client computers for using Microsoft Azure.

Figure 5.1 illustrates the architecture of Microsoft Azure.

Interaction of a cloud user to Azure components is accomplished by the Azure *management portal* [53]. The interface of the Azure management portal is depicted in Figure 5.2.

The Azure management portal is actually a new version of the Azure user interface, designed in the style close to that of Windows 8.x operating system.

Yet another latest version is Microsoft Azure portal (currently at the preview stage) available at [54]. The style of the interface of the new Azure preview portal is shown in Figure 5.3.

To my knowledge, this is the third version of the Azure portal since 2011. This fact confirms rapid evolution of the Microsoft Azure platform.

The user interface of the Azure management portal and the Azure preview portal, as compared to the previous versions, has become more explicit, clear, comfortable, and close to modern user interfaces for desktop computers, laptops, and tablets, with simple self-explanatory pictograms that denote the most important actions for the cloud users to perform: creation of a new site, new storage account, new database,

Trustworthy Cloud Computing, First Edition. Vladimir O. Safonov.
© 2016 John Wiley & Sons, Inc. Published 2016 by John Wiley & Sons, Inc.

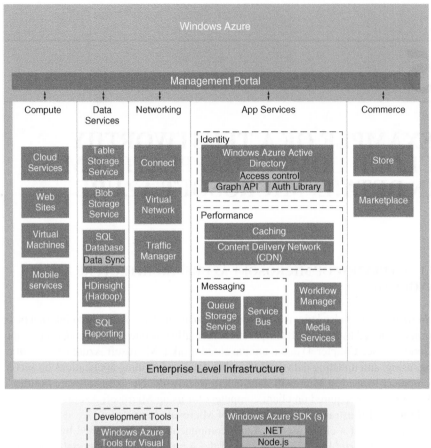

Figure 5.1   Architecture of Microsoft Azure.

new virtual machine in the cloud, and so on. See the next section on more details on the Azure user interface.

In the new version of the Azure platform, as shown in Figure 5.1, the following major components are available.

Compute – management of all kinds of computing in the cloud: cloud services, Web sites, virtual machines, and mobile services.

Data Services – managing cloud data and databases.

Figure 5.2 Microsoft Azure management portal.

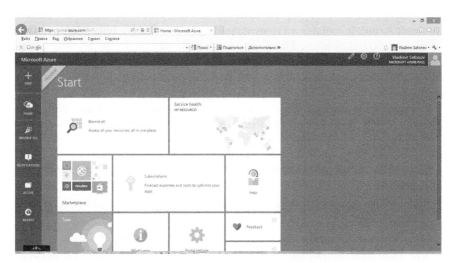

Figure 5.3 Microsoft Azure preview portal.

Networking – management of network connections (*Connect*) between the local area network of the client and the cloud applications, virtual private networks (*Virtual Network*), and load balancing of the cloud (*Traffic Manager*).

App Services – managing applications in the cloud.

Commerce – selling (*Store*) and distributing (*Marketplace*) of cloud applications.

The Compute Component

This component allows the users to execute applications in Microsoft Azure using the following features:

Web Sites – tools for quick creation of Web sites controlled by any OS using such tools as ASP.NET, PHP, or Node.js.

Cloud Services – quick deployment of multi-tiered applications and managing them. The Microsoft Azure platform enables service provisioning, load balancing, monitoring, and checking for availability.

Virtual Machines – getting full control over the virtual cloud server, according to the needs of the cloud user's task. It is possible to choose an operating system from the gallery of Windows and Linux OS's with different sets of pre-installed applications.

Mobile Services – tools for development of mobile applications that use Microsoft Azure features.

The Data Services Component

This component enables storing and updating data and generating reports for them in Microsoft Azure. It contains services supporting tables (*Table*), binary large objects (*Blob*), and *SQL databases*. These services provide storage for binary and textual data, messages, structured data, and relational data. Their advantages are manageability, availability, and scalability, using a development model comfortable with the developers.

It is possible to use *SQL Data Sync* for synchronizing relational data with other instances of SQL databases or with local (on-premises) SQL Server databases.

The following major features are available for Data Services component:

Blobs allow the users to store nonstructured text or binary data (video, audio, and images).

Tables allow the users to store large volumes of nonstructured and nonrelational data (NoSQL).

SQL Database allows the users to store large volumes of relational data.

SQL Data Sync allows the users to organize regular synchronization between SQL database and local (on-premises) SQL servers or other instances of SQL database.

SQL Reporting is a cloud service for report generation, implemented on the basis of technologies for report generation for SQL Server. It allows the users to build features for report generation into Microsoft Azure applications. The reports are generated on the desktop; it allows the developers to avoid implementation of their own infrastructure for generating reports.

HDInsight is a cloud service based on the *Apache Hadoop* toolkit for parallel processing of big data. It simplifies processing big data because of the tools like Microsoft Office and System Center.

The Networking Component

Networking services of Microsoft Azure provide features for network connections and routing at TCP/IP level (transportation protocols of the Internet) and DNS level (mapping domain names to IP addresses).

The *Microsoft Azure Connect* service enables configuring of secure IP connections between the computers or virtual machines of the client's company and the instances of the applications running in Microsoft Azure.

The *Microsoft Azure Virtual Network* component enables the setting up of virtual private networks (VPNs) in Microsoft Azure for their secure connection to the local infrastructure of the client. It allows the users to use Microsoft Azure as a protected network in the cloud.

The *Traffic Manager* service performs load balancing of the incoming traffic between various services available via the Internet, using the policies based on DNS.

Services for Application Management (App Services)

The set of services for application management in Microsoft Azure includes the following:

- Services for access management and user identification
- Services to control the application performance
- Services to control messaging between applications in Microsoft Azure
- Services for application workflow
- Services to handle multimedia information (media services).

Services for Access Management and User Identification

The *Microsoft Azure Active Directory,* the cloud version of the widely known Microsoft component Active Directory, provides the following services for controlling the identification of users in cloud applications:

- *Access Control Service (ACS)* – the cloud service for simple authentication and authorization of users for getting them access to cloud applications and services, allowing the developers to move the authentication and authorization checks from the application code.
- *The graph control library (Graph API)* – enables programmatic access to Microsoft Azure Active Directory (AD) by calling REST-based methods.
- *The Authentication Library* (AAL) – provides functionality for the developers of client applications to authenticate the users via the Microsoft Azure Active Directory or via other authentication providers, and then to get access tokens for secure method calls. The AAL also enables the developers of cloud services to protect their resources by checking the input tokens.

Services to Control the Performance of the Applications

This group of services allows the developers to cache big data.

The Microsoft Azure Caching services allow the developers to set up caching in the cloud for the use by applications and services to improve their performance. In particular, the commonly used scenario is supported for caching the session state and the output from ASP.NET. Caching allows us to improve the performance of applications because of the temporary storing of information from other server sources.

The content delivery network (CDN) services cache binary large objects of Microsoft Azure into the static output content of the compute objects in strategically allocated points to enable maximal speed of the content output for the users.

Services for Controlling Messages between Cloud Applications

Messages are stored in different kinds of queues, as follows:

Storage Queues enable reliable exchange of the stored messages between the tiers of applications executed in Microsoft Azure. The message queues are parts of the Microsoft Azure Storage component, which also provides services for handling binary large objects (Blob) and tables (Table).

Service Bus enables secure and highly available infrastructure for services communication, distribution of events between them, as well as their naming and publishing. The Service Bus, by means of connection by Windows Communication Foundation (WCF) and other ways of communication, includes method calls according to REST standard (see Chapter 1). There are examples of integration of the Service Bus into applications in which *bridges*, *transforms*, and B2B messages are implemented on the base of Azure Service Bus.

5.2 USER INTERFACE AND THE MANAGEMENT PORTAL OF MICROSOFT AZURE

To get acquainted to Microsoft Azure, let us start with the Azure management portal [53]. It is depicted in Figure 5.2. The URL address of the Azure management portal is https://manage.windowsazure.com.

The previous version of the Azure portal, developed in 2011, is https://windows.azure.com. It was available from the new portal for a few years.

It is possible for everyone to get free trial access to Microsoft Azure for 1 month. To get free access, first it is necessary to register as the user on the **Windows Live** (www.live.com) Web site, or on some other sites supported by Microsoft, for example, www.outlook.com. Then, it is necessary to log in to the appropriate Azure Web page for getting trial access, wait for a few days to get the access, and you can start your practical work with Microsoft Azure.

Figure 5.4 depicts the login page of the management portal of Microsoft Azure.

Figure 5.4   Login page of the Microsoft Azure management portal.

You should enter your login name and your password you registered on the Windows Live or the www.outlook.com Web site. The cloud finds your login automatically if you have already used it; all you need to do is to enter the password.

Figure 5.2 shows the starting page of the Microsoft Azure management portal.

The user interface of the portal is characteristic for modern principles and tools for supporting GUI, in particular for *Microsoft Silverlight*, which lays the foundation of the Microsoft Azure GUI.

Unlike the previous versions of the Azure portal, the style of the user interface is more explicit and self-evident and very close to the style of GUI of Windows 8.x operating systems.

On the starting page of the Azure portal, all the items are visualized that we have already created in the cloud. These items can be of following kinds:

- *Web sites*. It is possible to create Web sites in the Azure cloud, either an empty Web site (quick create), or from gallery of ready Web sites, or with an SQL database attached to the Web site.
- *Virtual Machines*. New virtual machines (VMs) can be created from the gallery of VMs or on individual choice of parameters. VMs are the main feature of Microsoft Azure IaaS. The three main principles of managing VMs in Microsoft Azure are *communication* – creating *endpoints* to connect to virtual machine outside the Microsoft Azure; *availability* – load balancing virtual machines to be always available; and *connectivity* – enable connection of the virtual machine to resources such as Active Directory Domain Services or SQL database.
- *Mobile services*. It is a set of services that enable the back-end for mobile applications. Mobile services allow the developers of mobile applications to use cloud tables, to send push notifications to mobile applications, and to

communicate with other cloud services. Mobile services can be developed on the Node.js platform in JavaScript language, or on .NET platform using Visual Studio, for example, in C#.

- *Cloud services*. Cloud service is any kind of application running on Microsoft Azure. Cloud services can implement *multi-tier* applications (see Chapter 1). They can be a combination of *Web roles* (dedicated Internet Information Services Web server) or *worker roles* (long-running computing processes), and also the connected *virtual machines*.

- *SQL databases*. The cloud users can create and use cloud SQL databases with the help of *SQL Azure* – a cloud analog to SQL Server. The database can be constructed and filled by the data either by a built-in constructor or programmatically.

- *Storage* in Azure can be used in the forms of *Blobs*, *tables*, or *messages*.

- *HDinsight*. This kind of Azure services provide an opportunity to manage big data of any size – process the data using *Apache Hadoop*, perform complex data analysis, or connect to the data using Microsoft business intelligence tools.

- *Media Services*. The users can store media content in the cloud. For this purpose, it is necessary to create a Media Services account. The account should be associated with some region and a storage account. The media content is stored in the form of a Blob. There is a cloud media player for playback the media data in the cloud.

- *Service Bus*. It is possible to create a *service namespace*. This is a container for Service Bus messaging entities. The service namespace is structured as a set of URI subdomains. Each of the URI addresses has the following form: [scheme]://[service-namespace].service.windows.net/[name1]/[name2] …

- *Visual Studio Online*. This is the cloud version of the Team Foundation Server (TFS) of Microsoft Visual Studio. In the latest version of Microsoft Azure, it is possible to create and manage team Visual Studio projects, collaborate with the project team, add members to project, watch project events like builds, and so on. To accomplish all of this, a Visual Studio Online account should be created. So, from now on, Visual Studio is integrated with the Microsoft Azure cloud.

- *Cache*. Azure Cache is a distributed, in-memory, scalable solution that enables the developers to use superfast access to data.

- *BizTalk services*. Microsoft Azure provides integration with Microsoft BizTalk product. A set of BizTalk services can be created and deployed in the cloud, and managed using this menu item.

- *Recovery services*. In the latest version of Microsoft Azure, disaster recovery features are implemented. They are referred to as *vaults*. Vaults are based on Azure Backup and Azure Site Recovery functionality. They can be used to protect the cloud user's data and provide continuous availability for applications and workloads.

- *CDN*. The Azure CDN caches Azure Blobs and static content to enable maximum bandwidth for delivering content to users. It is possible to create a CDN endpoint which is associated with a unique URL for accessing the cached content.
- *Automation*. An automation account that can be created in the Azure cloud is a container for automation resources – *runbooks, jobs*, and *assets*. An automation account is related to one Azure region. It is possible to create *affinity* between this region and the regions where the other resources by the user (e.g., VMs) are located.
- *Scheduler*. This new feature (existing on the Azure portal but not yet covered in Azure help) allows the users to declaratively describe actions to run in the cloud – either recurring application actions (e.g., periodically read the news from some site) or daily maintenance actions (e.g., daily backups). For this purpose, the Azure scheduler allows the users to create and use *job collections*.
- *API management*. This is a new feature in Azure to design, test, and publish APIs used in cloud services development.
- *Machine learning*. This is an innovative cloud service referred to as *Azure Machine Learning (ML) Studio*, the cloud service that combined new analytics tools, powerful algorithms, and the latest results of Microsoft Research in machine learning into one easy-to-use cloud service. It gives the cloud users the ability to develop and deploy predictive analytics solutions that operate on the user's data.
- *Stream analytics*. This cloud service provides an opportunity to set up a streaming job to analyze a stream of data.
- *Operational insight*. This service allows the cloud users to create *operational insight workspaces*. Each of them is actually a container that includes account information and simple configuration information for the account. Operational insight workspaces reflect information on the IT infrastructure of the cloud user company.
- *Networks*. The Microsoft Azure platform allows the users to create *virtual networks* that can include the VMs and cloud services available to the user. When creating a virtual network, the following elements should be indicated: the region and the affinity group for the network, the address space of the virtual network, the subnets in the virtual network for the cloud services, virtual machines, and the DNS servers that will be used for name resolution of the virtual network (optional).
- *Traffic manager*. Microsoft Azure Traffic Manager can be used to control the distribution of user traffic between similar cloud services or Web sites running in different data centers across the world. Load balancing of the user traffic can be done on the basis of different criteria – performance, business continuity, price, compliance, or other purposes. The work of Traffic Manager is based on intelligent DNS queries on the user's domain names.

- **RemoteApp**. Microsoft Azure RemoteApp allows the users to access their corporate applications running in Azure from anywhere and a variety of devices on different platforms – Windows, MacOS, iOS, Android. The user can access his cloud applications remotely from a remote laptop, tablet, or mobile device.
- **Management services**. This item can be used for managing *alert rules* according to some metrics, and visualizing the status of these alerts. There can be up to 10 alert rules for different kinds of services – VMs, cloud services, mobile services, and so on.
- **Active Directory**. Similar to classic Microsoft Active Directory, Azure Active Directory provides an identity service to manage organizations, users, and their cloud IT infrastructure.
- **Marketplace**. This item provides the functionality to browse the *Azure Store* and get *add-ons* – extra cloud services that add power to the cloud infrastructure of the cloud user. The add-ons in the Store are characterized by their *names* and *types*.
- **Storsimple**. This is a manager for storage devices. When creating a StorSimple storage device service, the geographical region and a friendly name should be given. The user can have multiple StorSimple device services.
- **Settings**. This item provides functionality to make different kinds of settings in the cloud, related to the cloud subscriptions, management certificates, administrators, affinity groups, usage, and RemoteApp.

All Azure dashboard items existing at the moment were shortly commented on above. The most important of them will be explained later in this chapter.

In the Azure main page, on the left there is a panel visualizing all these item names and the number of the already created items of each kind. There is a vertical scrollbar for this panel.

In the central part of the page, the items themselves are visualized, in the form of a table with their names and brief information about them: the type, status, subscription, location (the region in the Azure cloud where the item is actually located).

The lower part of the page is the menu of the actions that can be performed with the selected item. For example, the NEW action is denoted by "+" and located under the vertical list of items. The menu of the actions is changed depending on the session state and the items selected.

To create a new item, it is necessary to click on "+" (NEW) and the cloud will propose to a menu for choosing an item for creation.

In my opinion, this GUI style is very explicit and comfortable, and corresponds to modern principles of GUI design.

The globe symbol in the right upper part of the main page can be used to switch on the desirable language to display the Azure interface. Independent of the locale you use in your operation system, you can choose a language for communicating to Azure. For example, I had to explicitly switch on the English language using this globe, since my version of Windows 8.1 is Russian.

The User Contextual Menu

The upper part of the main page, on the left, contains the "V" symbol for visualizing the main menu of Microsoft Azure. In the upper part of the main page, our login name is visualized. Clicking on login, we can visualize the user menu of Azure – see Figure 5.5.

The contextual menu of the user is located in the right upper part of the main page (for its visualization, the user login name should be clicked). In contains a number of useful actions:

- Sign out
- Change password
- View my bill
- Contact Microsoft Support
- Give feedback
- Privacy & cookies (Microsoft Online Services Privacy Statement)
- Legal (Service Agreement and Terms)
- Switch to Azure Preview portal.

I would like to emphasize the *Give Feedback* menu item. Feedback is one of the most desirable information for Microsoft, as well as for any cloud developer and provider company, since the cloud is very complicated and innovative software product.

The menu item *Switch to Azure Preview portal* is a link between the existing stable Azure management portal and the new one – the Azure preview portal. I think this is

Figure 5.5 User contextual menu of Microsoft Azure.

Figure 5.6   Main menu of Microsoft Azure.

one of the main principles of Microsoft in general, namely provide a bridge from the existing to the new.

The Main Menu of Microsoft Azure

Clicking on the "V" symbol in the upper part of the main page, we visualize the main menu of Microsoft Azure (see Figure 5.6).

The menu contains the following items: *Home, Pricing, Documentation, Downloads, Community*, and *Support*. To hide the main menu, the "^" symbol should be clicked.

By choosing the *Home* item in the main menu, we are redirected to the main informational and advertising page of Azure – http://azure.microsoft.com/en-us/. It contains brief information on components of Azure, as well as its tools and resources, and, which is most important, contains a reference to the page for getting free trial access to Azure for 1 month (Figure 5.7).

I'd like to emphasize that, besides this opportunity, teachers and students of universities can get, as a Microsoft Research grant, free academic access to Microsoft Azure for a longer term, for example, for teaching and attending some university course involving Azure material. To do that, it is necessary to log in to the Web site www.WindowsAzurePass.com/AzureU (Azure for universities) and fill out the required information about the university teacher, his university course, and students. It is that way that I managed to receive from Microsoft Research several times since 2011 free academic access to Microsoft Azure for a semester or for a year, and free academic access for my course students for a whole semester of taking my course. I am deeply grateful to Microsoft Research for such a great opportunity to learn and use Microsoft Azure.

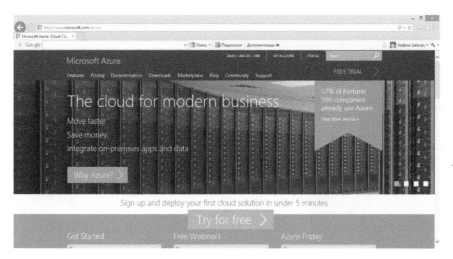

Figure 5.7   Home page of Microsoft Azure with free trial offer.

To compare with other companies, not every public cloud provider offers really free trial access to their public cloud. See Chapters 2 and 4 for the related discussions. Some of the companies do provide free trial access but they require information on credit card numbers, which may cause charging an unexpected bill. Microsoft, on providing free academic access to Azure, since earlier versions of Azure 4–5 years ago, never requires credit card information for trial cloud access, which is especially important for teachers and students; so, in this respect, I can refer to Microsoft as, in my personal opinion, the most comfortable and trustworthy cloud provider all over the world.

Help on the Azure Portal

In the right lower corner of the Azure portal page, the question mark "?," denotes contextual help which can be clicked at any moment of work and available at any Azure portal page. The main part of the help information is a short summary in your native language. In some cases, the help summary refers to detailed information in English on the appropriate Microsoft Developer Network (MSDN) page. It should be kept in mind that some of the documentation on Azure is not yet translated into your native language, since the user interface of Azure and the platform itself are brand new and are in the process of rapid evolution.

The Documentation Item of the Main Azure Menu

By choosing in the main menu of Azure the item *Documentation*, we are redirected to the main documentation page on Azure (see Figure 5.8).

On the documentation page, there is a large choice of documents and video materials on the Azure platform. The majority of them are in English. If you happen to

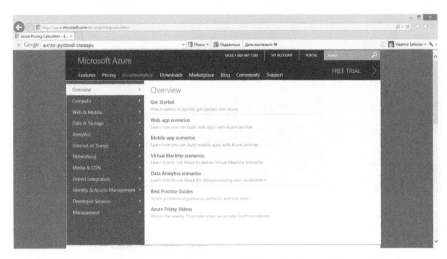

Figure 5.8   Documentation page of Microsoft Azure main menu.

need training information on Azure in Russian, for learning Microsoft Azure, I recommend my books [3, 4] and my online courses [5–7]. The MSDN library contains a lot of documentation on Azure.

The Downloads Page of the Azure Main Menu

By choosing the item *Downloads* in the main menu of Microsoft Azure, we are redirected to the main downloads page of the Microsoft Azure platform (see Figure 5.9).

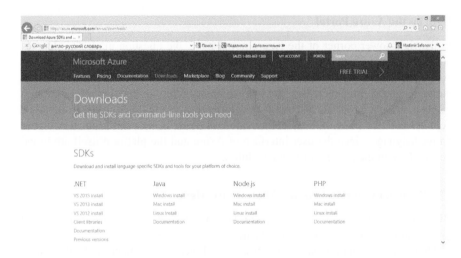

Figure 5.9   Downloads page of Microsoft Azure main menu.

From that page, it is possible to download and install on your computer a toolkit for developing cloud applications for Microsoft Azure – a software development kit (SDK) for any commonly used language (platform), for example, for Java or PHP. It is evident that the Azure platform itself, because of the principles of cloud computing, does not need any download – for a cloud client, it is enough to use a Web browser and an Internet connection.

The Azure Marketplace

The Microsoft Azure Marketplace is a new, modern component providing the opportunity to use new cloud services of Azure. Principles of the Azure Marketplace are similar to those of Windows Store. The Azure Marketplace enables the users to publish and freely distribute (or sell) useful cloud services for Azure.

To reach the Azure Marketplace page, it is enough to choose the Azure main item menu *Marketplace* (see Figure 5.10).

Among the 3,200 proposed items in the Azure Marketplace are VMs, application services, API applications, Azure Active Directory applications, Web applications, Microsoft Dynamics solutions, and Data Services.

5.3   THE COMPUTE COMPONENT: MANAGING AND OPERATING CLOUD SERVICES

Microsoft Azure Compute is the component to manage computations in Microsoft Azure.

The Microsoft Azure Compute provides for the developers a platform for deploying and managing cloud applications executing in Microsoft cloud datacenters.

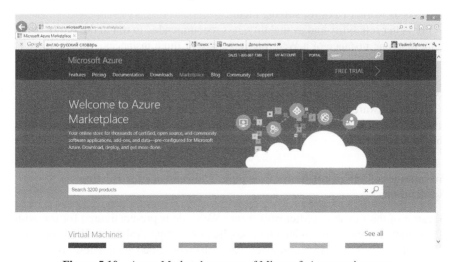

Figure 5.10   Azure Marketplace page of Microsoft Azure main menu.

The main features of Microsoft Azure Compute:

- Managing Web sites
- Managing cloud services
- Managing virtual machines
- Managing mobile services.

These features will be practically demonstrated in this section.

Roles

Applications in Microsoft Azure are built from one or more components referred to as *roles*. Form the very beginning, let us make it clear that the term *role* on the .NET platform (one of the basics of Azure implementation) has quite a different meaning – a group of users with some definite permissions. It may cause some confusion during the initial learning the Azure platform. So, let us repeat it again: in the Azure platform (as opposed to .NET platform) a *role* is a *software component of a cloud application*. Roles in Azure can be of three kinds: *Web role, worker role*, and *VM role*. Such classification adequately reflects different kinds of software architectures. *Web role* is a *Web application* (typically, *ASP.NET application*); *worker role* is an independent process (typically performing some computing work); *VM role* is an application (task) executing in its separate VM.

A Web role in Microsoft Azure is used for hosting Web applications that use Internet Information Services (IISs). A worker role can execute any kind of application but is typically used for hosting background processes for a Web role. In Microsoft Azure, Web roles and worker roles offer for developers opportunities for deploying and managing cloud services to be executed in the same VM. For any kind of applications, the common interaction method is the interaction via Web role and distributing the tasks as worker roles for solving them.

For better reliability and availability, it is recommended to run in the Azure cloud more than one instance of a Web role (e.g., two or three instances). Surely, there is a difference between the *role* and an *instance* of the role: the role is the application code, and an instance of the role is just one launch of that code. The number of Web role instances is indicated in the configuration file of the Web service.

Cloud software developers are free in their decision to use the .NET Framework or other kind of software platform in the Windows environment to implement a Web role or a worker role.

Advantages of Microsoft Azure Compute: Convenience for Hosting Applications

Because of the fact that a Microsoft Azure Web role is pre-configured for use with IIS, it makes it easier to create cloud applications using ASP.NET, WCF or other Web technologies. Software developers can also create cloud applications using such languages as PHP or Java.

Advantages of Microsoft Azure Compute: Accent on Processing the Application rather than on Functionality Limitations.

Automated service management gives the following advantages to Microsoft Azure users:

- *Administration*: Microsoft Azure automatically performs a number of functionalities such as load balancing and fault handling, thus decreasing the effort and cost of administration for the environment for launching applications;
- *Availability*: Microsoft Azure implemented for the goal of providing to the users the available applications *always, at each moment,* even in case of software upgrades or hardware faults;
- *Scalability*: Microsoft Azure gives the users an opportunity to develop *scalable* applications to be executed at Microsoft datacenters. The Azure platform also lets the users decrease the use of resources, if necessary, by providing exactly only the resources that are necessary.

Using Compute to Create and Manage Web Sites

It is very easy to create a Web site using Microsoft Azure. In Figure 5.2, the Azure management portal is depicted. Let us log in to the portal and click *Web Apps* in the *All items* dashboard. The portal allows us to create a Web app (i.e., a Web site) – see Figure 5.11.

Now take a look at the offerings by Compute in the *New item* creation menu. The following kinds of new items are possible to create using Compute – a *Web site (Web app),* a *VM,* a *mobile service,* or a *cloud service.*

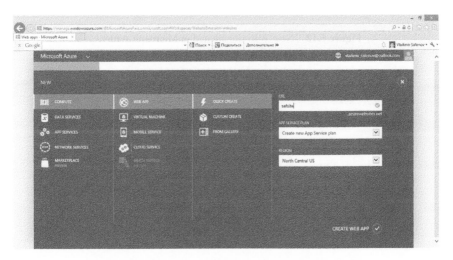

Figure 5.11   Creating a new Web site in Microsoft Azure.

Let us choose to create a new site. We enter the name of the site – *safsite*. The other components of the new site's URL address are already provided. The full URL address of the new site looks as follows:

safsite.azurewebsites.net

By default, we perform the *Quick create* action, so a new "empty" Web site is created. Clicking the URL address of the site, we visualize it in our browser – see Figure 5.12.

The main page of the new site provides recommendations of how to fill out the new site by the content. As possible options to do that, the following ways are recommended: *Git, FTP, Visual Studio, Visual Studio Online,* or *WebMatrix.*

The site can be managed in Azure as follows. By clicking *Web Apps*, we visualize the information on all the Web sites we created (just one yet). See Figure 5.13.

We see the name of the site – *safsite*, its status – *running*, the name of my academic subscription, location of the site – *North Central US* (by default, proposed by the

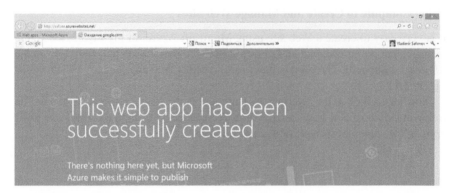

Figure 5.12   New Web site created in Microsoft Azure.

Figure 5.13   Visualizing information an all-cloud Web site we created.

cloud), pricing – *free* (since my subscription is academic), and the URL of the site we already used for browsing it.

The lower line of the page shows possible actions on the site: *browse* – launch the browser to see the site, *stop*, *restart, delete*, or use *WebMatrix* to fill out the site with the content.

Now, by clicking the name of the site and then clicking *Monitor,* we can monitor our new site (see Figure 5.14).

On the site monitor panel, we see information on the CPU time used, data in and data out, http server errors, and requests to the site.

Next, we can configure the site by clicking *Configure* – choose the version number of .NET Framework, PHP, Java, and Python to be used with the site (see Figure 5.15).

The following functionality is also available for the site: *Dashboard* – summary information on the site; *Webjobs* – adding Web jobs related to the site; *Scaling* – the plan of scaling the site; *Linked Resources* – information on the resources linked to the site; *Backup* – backing up the site.

Using Compute to Manage Virtual Machines

The new version of Microsoft Azure Compute provides very comfortable features for creating VMs in the cloud and managing them. On VMs created by the cloud user, it is possible to execute different kinds of applications (roles). It is possible to create virtual machines working under Windows 2012 R2 OS, or under Linux. By default, a Windows 2012 virtual machine will be created.

For creating a virtual machine, let us click the item *Virtual Machines* in the *All items* dashboard. We get information that there are no VMs yet, and an invitation to create a virtual machine (see Figure 5.16).

Figure 5.14 Monitoring the site.

Figure 5.15   Configuring the site – choosing the versions of .NET, Java, Python.

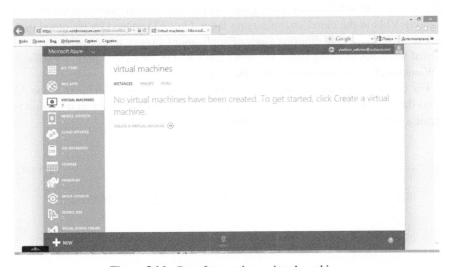

Figure 5.16   Page for creating a virtual machine.

To create a VM, we choose the option of quick create. We define the name of the virtual machine – *safVM* (the full domain name of the VM will be *safVM.cloudapp.net*); choose the default image of the virtual machine with its parameters: operating system – *Windows 2012 R2*, size – 768 MB memory; the user name for logging in to the virtual machine; the password for authentication, and the region for creating a virtual machine – datacenter in West US. Looking at other alternatives of new virtual machine parameters, we find a big gallery of possible

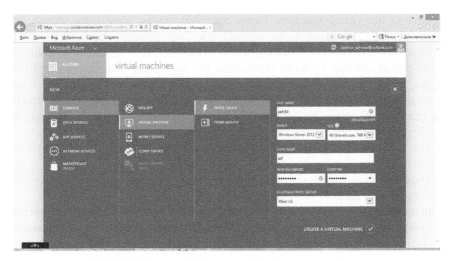

Figure 5.17   Parameters of the virtual machine to be created.

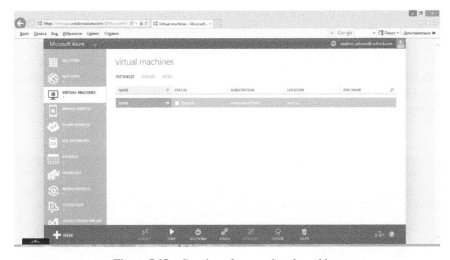

Figure 5.18   Creation of a new virtual machine.

operating systems for new VM – Windows 2012 R2, Windows 2008 R2, and a big choice of Linux versions. See Figure 5.17.

Now let us create our virtual machine. The cloud requires that the password be complex enough. Let us choose a complex password and create a virtual machine. The new virtual machine is created in *Stopped* state (see Figure 5.18). Then it starts running.

On creating the virtual machine, let us connect to it. By clicking *Connect*, we get a message that the cloud is downloading a Remote Desktop Protocol (RDP) file to connect to the virtual machine. Please note that, unlike some other clouds, in Microsoft Azure the user is not puzzled with any nontrivial network protocol settings. The endpoint is created by default. Then we get an invitation to connect to the virtual machine by RDP. We provide the login name and the password for logging in, and then we are on the virtual machine! It takes some time for the cloud to prepare the machine and the Windows OS, and finally we are on the virtual machine with Windows 2012 R2 and the Server Manager is running to configure it (see Figure 5.19).

The result of calling the Server Manager on the virtual machine is shown in Figure 5.20.

Then we choose by pressing the Start button on our virtual machine. The result is shown in Figure 5.21.

In the Start menu, we choose calling the Windows PowerShell – a new powerful scripting language by Microsoft. In the PowerShell console, we execute the command *ls* – listing the contents of the current directory. The result is shown in Figure 5.22.

Using Compute to Manage Cloud Services

The Microsoft Azure platform allows the users to create cloud services and to manage them. It should be kept in mind that the implementation of the cloud service should be done programmatically, using Visual Studio or any other suitable toolkit (which will be considered later on in this chapter). In this section, some basic features related to cloud service are considered (actually, creation of an "empty" cloud service) – choosing the name of the cloud service and the region to allocate it, and starting the work on its implementation.

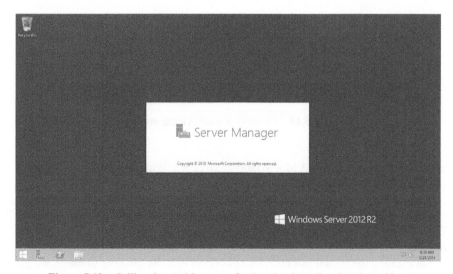

Figure 5.19   Calling Server Manager after logging in to the virtual machine.

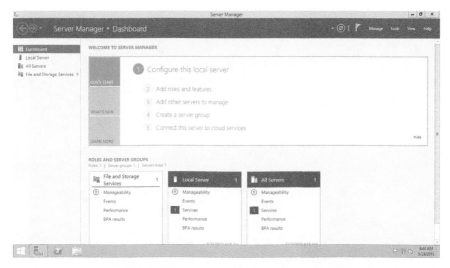

Figure 5.20   Server Manager is called on the virtual machine.

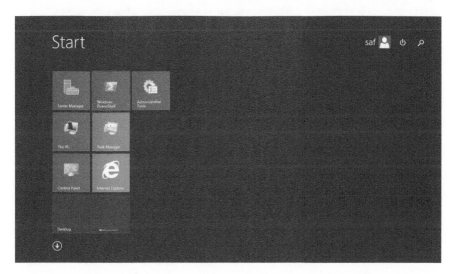

Figure 5.21   Pressing the Start button on the virtual machine.

By clicking *Cloud* services on the all items on the dashboard, we get information about all our cloud services. Currently, no cloud services are created yet, so the cloud issues an appropriate message and offers to create a new cloud service (see Figure 5.23).

Let us click *Create cloud service*. The new cloud page is opened for defining and choosing the parameters of the new cloud service (see Figure 5.24).

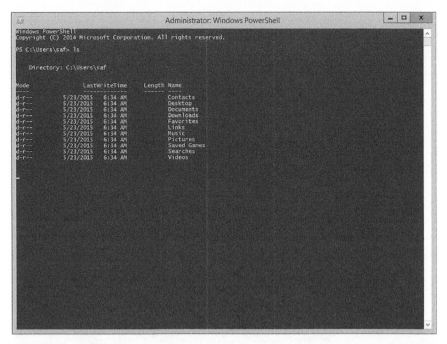

Figure 5.22   Executing the PowerShell *ls* command on the virtual machine.

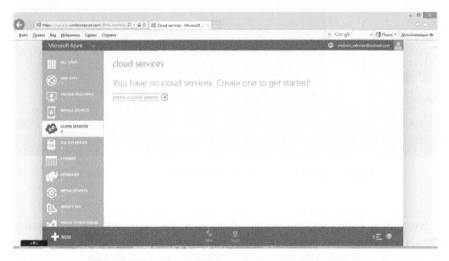

Figure 5.23   Cloud before creating a new cloud service.

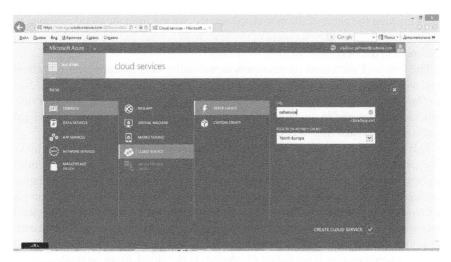

Figure 5.24 Cloud page with the parameters of the new cloud service.

We choose the name of the new cloud service – *safservice*. The full domain name of the new cloud service is *safservice.cloudapp.net*. Then, we choose an appropriate cloud *region* for our service – *North Europe*. A possible alternative could be to create a special *affinity group* for allocating the service.

Next, we click *Create cloud service*, and in a few moments the new cloud service is created (see Figure 5.25).

So the new "empty" cloud service is created. Information on its name, status (created), subscription, and domain name is visualized. However if we attempt to click on the domain name of the service, we get a message from our browser that the Web page with such URL address does not exist yet. To implement the new cloud service, we should first develop the implementation using some toolkit (e.g., Visual Studio) and then *publish* the new service by means of Visual Studio.

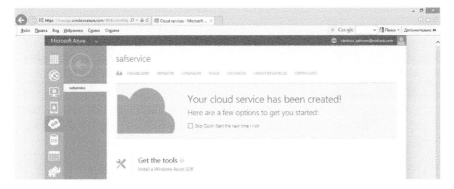

Figure 5.25 New cloud service created, and information on it visualized on the dashboard.

By clicking the name of the new cloud service, we get from the cloud recommendations on starting the development of the new cloud service and the appropriate Web references to the development tools to install.

The first tool the cloud recommends downloading and installing on our client machine is *Microsoft Azure SDK*. It is used together with *Visual Studio* or *Visual Studio Online* (the cloud version of Visual Studio). On implementing the cloud service, it should be *deployed* in the cloud. The deployment can be done either with Visual Studio or with Visual Studio Online.

This explicit approach to cloud service development in Microsoft Azure looks appropriate and trustworthy. The cloud developers could implement some form of implicit "dummy" cloud service creation (similar to the dummy Web site creation considered above), but the more appropriate way implemented in Microsoft Azure is as follows: the cloud service developers should feel the difference between the cloud service domain name and its implementation. The domain name cannot be used until the work on developing the implementation of the cloud service is done and the cloud service implementation is published (deployed) in the cloud. More on implementing cloud services is given later in this chapter.

Using Compute to Create and Manage Mobile Services

A *mobile service* is a cloud service specially created in the cloud for interaction with mobile applications working on some mobile platform – *iOS*, *Android* or *Windows Phone*. A mobile service should have a connected *cloud database* for communicating with the mobile application. The user from the mobile device can fill out or edit the content of the database, and then the cloud user will be able to browse or update cloud database.

Now let us try to create a new mobile service. By clicking *Mobile services*, we are redirected to the page that offers to create a mobile service. Next, click *Create a mobile service* and we are redirected to the page on which we need to provide the *parameters* of the new mobile service (see Figure 5.26).

Figure 5.26 Page for setting the parameters of the new mobile service.

The parameters of the mobile service are as follows:

– The *name* of the mobile service. We choose the name *safmobile*. So the full domain name of the mobile service is *safmobile.azure-mobile.net.*

– The *database* for communicating the mobile service with the connected mobile applications. The cloud offers the following choice: create a new free 20 MB database, or use the existing database. We choose the first option, since there are no databases among our cloud resources yet. If we happen to choose the existing database, it should be located in the *same region* of the cloud as the mobile service itself. If such restriction cannot be satisfied, the user should re-create a database for the mobile service in the same region as where the mobile service located. Also, there can be problems with this step if you happen to have an academic subscription (I've had such an experience myself). Such subscription allows the users only to create one database per account. So if you already have a database and are going to create a mobile service (and hence its related database), you will have to delete your existing database if it is located in a different region than that where the mobile service should be located

– The *region* where the new mobile service will be located. We choose the option offered: *West US*;

– The mobile service's *backend* platform. There are two alternatives: *JavaScript backend* and *.NET* backend. We choose the latter one.

Then, we click the tab with the number 1 – this is only the first step of creating the mobile service. The second step will be to create a database for the mobile service. We are redirected to yet another cloud page for specifying the parameters of the new database (see Figure 5.27).

Figure 5.27 Page for choosing the parameters of the database for the mobile service.

The first parameter of the mobile service's database is the *database name*. The cloud offers the name of the database derived from the name of the mobile service – *safmobile_db*. The second database parameter is the *server* for the database. The cloud offers two options – create a new SQL database server, or choose an existing database server. Since we have not yet created database servers, we have to follow the first advice – *create a new SQL database server*. We are now redirected to the cloud page to specify the parameters of the database server (see Figure 5.28).

The name of the new database server will be offered by the cloud. We specify the login name and the password, confirm the password again, and choose the region where the new database server will be located. Please note that the cloud by default offers the creation of the database server in the same region as the mobile service – this is an important restriction of the cloud, as already mentioned.

Finally, we click the sign to create the database server and the mobile service itself. The creation process is started. In a few moments, the mobile service and the related database (with the new SQL database server) are ready. In the cloud, it is displayed by a standard way for any other item (see Figure 5.29).

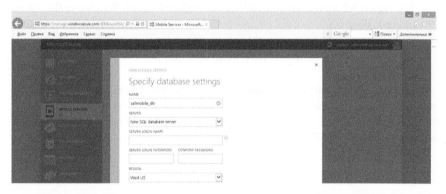

Figure 5.28   Page for setting the parameters of the new SQL database server.

Figure 5.29   New mobile service (with the related database) is created in the cloud.

For the new mobile service, the following parameters are shown in the cloud dashboard: the *name (safmobile)*, the *status (ready)*, the subscription id within which the new mobile service is created, the *backend* for creating connected mobile applications for the mobile service (.*NET*), the *location (West US)*, and the *URL address* – https://safmobile.azure-mobile.net. The new mobile service is ready to use and ready for creation of connected mobile applications with the given back-end (.NET).

Now let us click on the URL address of our new mobile service. As the result, in our browser we see the Web page of our mobile service created by Azure (see Figure 5.30).

Now we need to create a connected mobile application for the mobile service (it will be discussed later on in this chapter).

Now let us take a look at the new SQL database created for our mobile service. To do that, let us find in the cloud dashboard the item *SQL databases* and click this item. The result is shown in Figure 5.31.

The following database parameters are displayed by the cloud: *name (safmobile_db)*, *status (online)*, *replication (none* – it means that the new database is not

Figure 5.30   Launching the new mobile service.

Figure 5.31   SQL database created for the mobile service.

replicated), *location* (*West US* – located in the same region as the mobile service), our *subscription ID*, the *name* of the new SQL database server offered by the cloud, *edition* (*Web* – this is one of the kinds of database editions in Azure), *max size* – 20 MB (*free*). Please pay attention to the fact that the Azure cloud, as for other kinds of the newly created cloud items, explicitly mentions that the new database is *free*. This is really a trustworthy approach to creating cloud resources demonstrated by the Azure platform: the cloud user is explicitly notified whether his newly created cloud resource is free or not. If not (i.e., if the cloud user has to pay for the new database), the cloud user can immediately delete the database to avoid unexpected bills. As my own experience with some other clouds shows, the cloud provider will charge for the non-free database the amount depending on its size and on its time of use.

Now let us try to manage our new SQL cloud database. To do that, click *Manage* (below) as one of the possible actions on the database. The cloud updates the *set of firewall rules* to manage the IP address of the new database (it is performed without extra troubles for cloud users – no explicit actions are required from the user's side). In a few moments, we are redirected to the login cloud page for the new database (see Figure 5.32).

On the database login page, the following attributes should be specified:

- the domain *name of the* database *server* – *servername.database.windows.net*, where *servername* is the name of the database server offered by the cloud; please note the general format of URL addresses for cloud databases in Azure;
- the *name* of the *database* – *safmobile_db*;
- the user name and the password for logging in to the database.

Let us specify all these attributes and log in to the database.

In a few moments, we have logged in to our database. We are redirected to the cloud page for managing the database (see Figure 5.33).

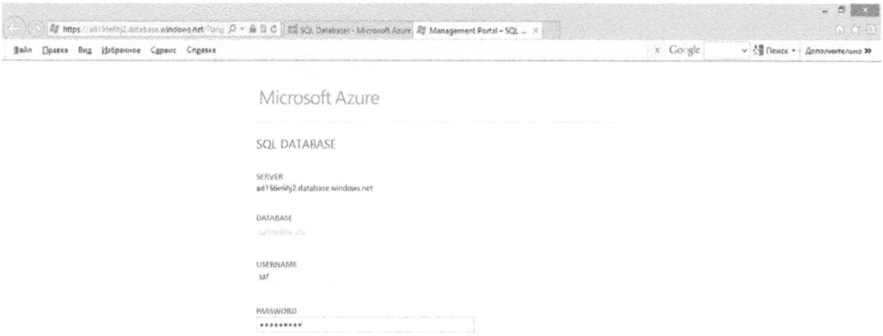

Figure 5.32   Managing the new SQL database: logging in to the database server.

Figure 5.33   Managing the new SQL database: the management page.

In the top part of the database management page, we see the domain name of the database. Next, we see possible actions on the database. In particular, the cloud allows us to type and execute an *SQL query* to the database. This is a very comfortable feature of the Azure cloud, unlike many other cloud platforms lacking such a feature. The *SQL Azure* database management system has a built-in *SQL interpreter* which can parse and execute SQL queries. As we have seen from the previous chapters, in most cloud database management systems on other cloud platforms, it is not possible to execute SQL queries directly in the cloud. Instead, it is offered to download and install some third-party DBMS, which is not always acceptable for cloud users. So the Microsoft Azure platform demonstrates yet another aspect of trustworthiness and friendly behavior to the users by offering such a comfortable feature.

For our cloud database, the following information is provided by the cloud DBMS: *date created, active users, maximum size, space actually used, free space,* and so on.

In the left lower part of the cloud database management window, there are some actions offered to do with the database:

- *Overview* – information on all databases we created in the cloud;
- *Administration* – opening, refreshing the database, and executing SQL queries on it;
- *Design* – yet another comfortable feature of SQL Azure – the *built-in database designer*. Using it, it is possible to create a new database scheme, a new table following this scheme, and then, using SQL queries, to fill out the database by content. To my knowledge, no other SQL cloud database management system provides such features, which are surely desirable and comfortable for any cloud user.

We will avoid execution of SQL requests and doing other actions on the database right now and will do it later on in this chapter to demonstrate the features of SQL Azure. Surely the database related to a mobile service will be mostly filled in and updated programmatically, by connected mobile applications. So, clicking *Log off* in the upper right corner of the database management page, we log out from managing the database.

Returning to the cloud dashboard page with our database, we can click on the name of the database server and perform some management work on this server if necessary.

5.4   THE STORAGE COMPONENT: MANAGING AND OPERATING CLOUD STORAGE

This section covers cloud storage in Microsoft Azure.

Microsoft Azure Storage is the component to manage storage in the Microsoft Azure platform.

The Microsoft Azure Storage services component enables stable and reliable storing information in the cloud.

To access the Storage services, it is necessary to create a storage account via the Microsoft Azure Platform Management Portal.

The major services of Storage include the following:

- The **Blob** service to store text or binary data, including multimedia information
- The **Queue** service to enable reliable messaging between the cloud services
- The **Table** service to work with structured storage available for requests.

The Microsoft Azure SDK provides *REST API* (**REST,** *Representational State Transfer*, as explained above, is one of the standards of developing Web services based on passing the state information via the arguments and the results of methods) and *managed API* for working with the Storage services (*managed API* means that it is possible to access Storage from .NET applications). Access to Storage services is possible from a service executing in Microsoft Azure, or immediately via the Internet from any application that can send or receive data using the HTTP/HTTPS protocols.

Detailed information on the REST API for Storage services is given in the document Windows Azure Storage Services REST API Reference [123].

In the latest version of Microsoft Azure, there is a comfortable library Storage Azure Client Library [124] with high-level API, in particular, for accessing the Storage component.

Major features of Microsoft Azure **Storage:**
- **The Blob** Service – the simplest way of storing binary data in Microsoft Azure
- **Table** Service – support of working with tables
- **Queue** Service – support of reliable exchange of messages between the instances of Web roles and worker roles
- Windows Azure Drive – enables applications for Microsoft Azure to mount a *Page Blob* onto a separate volume of the NTFS VHD file system.

Advantages of Microsoft Azure Storage:

Fault tolerance and the built-in CDN network. All user information stored in Microsoft Azure is duplicated *three* times. Independent of when kind of Storage the cloud client is using, his data are duplicated in several *fault domains*, which means better fault tolerance. The Microsoft Azure *CDN* enables one-click integration with Storage services. The CDN improves the performance by allocating the user's information closer to the point where the information is more often used.

REST and Managed API. In addition to the Storage services for user applications executed in Microsoft Azure, the Azure Storage can work with the on-premises applications running on the local machine or on some other cloud platform. Using the Azure SDK, it is possible to use REST API or managed API to work with the Storage services. REST API is covered in more detail in MSDN documentation [123].

Microsoft Azure Client Library. In the latest version of Azure, since 2013, the new Azure Client Library is available with more friendly interface for creating and processing items of Azure Storage [124].

Details of the provision of cloud services of Microsoft Azure Storage. The size of the used Storage in Microsoft Azure is calculated on the basis of the average actual use within some paid period of some binary large object, table, or queue. For example, if the Azure user consumed 10 GB of Storage in the first half of the month and did not consume Storage in the second half of the month, the user will be billed for using (in average) of 5 GB of Storage.

In the new version of Azure, three Storage services are provided: *tables*, *queues* and *blobs*.

Each Storage service has programmatic .NET managed API and HTTP REST API. The REST nodes of the network have the following format of domain names:

.[storage,blob,queue].core.windows.net.

There are also *commandlets* (in Microsoft PowerShell scripting language) for developing and maintaining the Storage data at their development and maintenance stages.

Tables. Tables are structured, schemeless, scalable data storages. They can store billions of objects and terabytes of data. Tables are a more efficient alternative of storing and processing information than SQL Azure databases.

Entity model of a table. Each table object has the *table name* and a set of properties of the kind: *key/value*. Explicit representation of the scheme of the data is not required. The limitations on the objects are as follows: maximal size is 1 MB, and maximal number of properties is 255.

The following kinds of properties are supported:

- string
- binary object
- int
- long
- bool
- double
- guid (global universal identifier used in COM model).

There are three special kinds of properties: *partition key, row key*, and *version*.

The partition key identifies a partition, that is, a group of objects that should be stored together. Each partition can be stored in a separate virtual machine. The row key identifies an object in a partition. The combination (partition key, row key) is a *primary key* for an object. The partition key and the row key are strings of the size up to 64 KByte.

Organization of tables in Microsoft Azure is depicted in Figure 5.34.

Queues to Tables

Besides standard table operations, tables in Microsoft Azure support some limited form of queues. In the previous version of Azure, only equality relation was supported for keys with one or several properties. The result is calculated in lexicographic order, according to the (*partition, row*) key. In the new version, user-defined secondary indexes are supported for sorting.

Programmatic API used for queries is based on *LINQ (Language Integrated Query)*, the same as in .NET languages. LINQ is similar to GQL query language implemented in Google App Engine (see Chapter 2). The HTTP REST API uses the *Astoria API* based on using URL addresses for calling ADO.NET services.

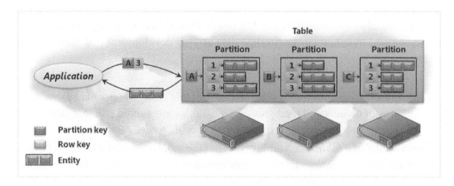

Figure 5.34   Organization of tables in Microsoft Azure.

Integrity and Transactions

The Microsoft Azure tables support full integrity. Accesses to any objects are strictly synchronized. There are no "dirty reads" (race conditions). For handling of any object, the *Asynchronous, Consistent, Isolated, Durable* (*ACID*) style transactions are used.

Implementation of Tables

Tables in Microsoft Azure are designed similar to the data stores of *Bigtable* and the *App Engine* in Google cloud platform. Partitions are similar to *tablets* of *Bigtable*. All objects are stored on the same data server. Transactions are implemented similar to *App Engine datastore*. For objects, version control is used.

Queries to Tables

Queues to tables are similar to *Amazon SQS* (see Chapter 2). They allow the users to put a message into a queue and process it later on, in a loosely coupled form.

Operations defined on queues are as follows: *enqueue* (to put a message into a queue); *dequeue* (to delete a message from a queue), *delete* (delete all messages from a queue). The messages are typed. Their size is limited to 8 KByte.

The *dequeue* operation uses *lease* – a synchronization primitive that allows the developers to keep for some time interval a message in the state invisible to all other clients of the queue. By default, the delay time is up to 30 s.

Binary Large Objects

The *Blob* service is used for storing "opaque" objects. They are similar to Amazon S3 (see Chapter 2). Binary objects can be created and processed programmatically. Binary objects are identified by unique paths in the following form of URL addresses of the kind:

<account>.blob.core.windows.net

The organization of binary large objects in Microsoft Azure is depicted in Figure 5.35.

Binary large objects can be *blocks* or *pages*. Blocks up to size of 64 MBytes can be processed immediately; blocks of larger size should be separated to smaller blocks. Each block is uploaded to the cloud separately. On finishing the operation, it is checked if all the blocks are uploaded.

It is possible to use paged binary objects of the size up to 1 TB. They are intended for random access to memory.

The name space used for binary objects is a hierarchy of URL addresses of the following kind:

<account>.blob. core.windows.net

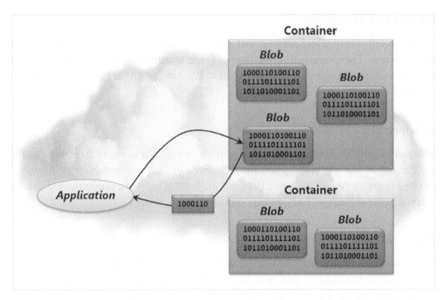

Figure 5.35   Organization of binary large objects (blobs) in Microsoft Azure.

Binary objects can be updated or cloned, but they are not immutable.

Queues

The Microsoft Azure Queue is a cloud service to store big amounts of messages. Access to it is possible via the Web by authenticated calls using HTTP or HTTPS protocols.

Each of the messages in a queue can have the size of up to 64 KB.

The queue can consist of several million messages. The maximum size of an account is 100 TB.

Major ways of using queues are as follows:

– Creating a working set for asynchronous processing

– Passing messages from a Web role to a worker role of Microsoft Azure.

An example of organizing queues within some storage account is shown in Figure 5.36.

Queues are addressed using the following URL format:

http://<storage account>.queue.core.windows.net/<queue>

In the example in Figure 5.36, the following URL address is referred to one of the queues in the diagram:

http://myaccount.queue.core.windows.net/imagesToDownload

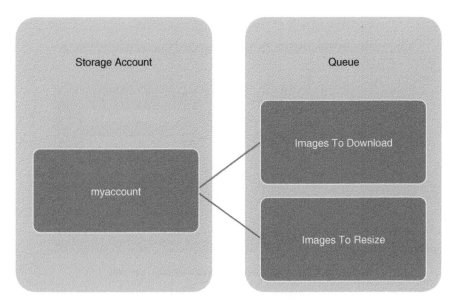

Figure 5.36   Example of organizing queues within a Storage account.

Hand-on Lab with Microsoft Azure Storage

Now let us illustrate the above theoretical material on Microsoft Azure Storage with a kind of hand-on lab.

Let us log in to the Microsoft Azure management portal. In the dashboard, click "Storage." The cloud invites us to create a storage account (see Figure 5.37).

Figure 5.37   Creating a Storage account.

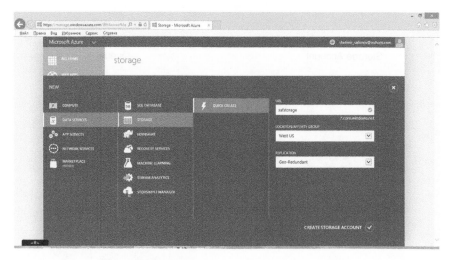

Figure 5.38   Parameters of the new Storage account.

On clicking *Create a Storage account*, we are redirected to the page where we should choose the parameters of our new storage account (see Figure 5.38).

We choose the *Quick create* mode. The name of our storage account is ***safstorage***. So the full URL address of the storage account will be ***safstorage.core.windows.net***. Next, we should choose the region or the affinity group where to create a Storage account. We accept the offer of the cloud providers and create the new account in the region *West US*. Then, we make our Storage account *geo-redundant*. Geo-redundancy means that our Storage account is replicated in a secondary Storage region, for better availability and reliability.

In a few moments, our new Storage account is created (see Figure 5.39).

The following information is issued on the new Storage account: its *name, status (online), location (West US),* and *our Azure subscription ID*.

On clicking on the name of the Storage account, we are switched to the starting page of the new Storage account (see Figure 5.40).

On this page, there are references to the tools suggested by the cloud providers to handle the new Storage account: *Storage explorer* and *Microsoft Azure SDK*, that should be downloaded to our client computer and installed. Also, the starting page provides references to learning resources on Azure Storage.

By clicking *Dashboard*, we can visualize the *endpoints* to work with the new Storage accounts:

– the endpoint for the *blob* – https://safstorage.blob.core.windows.net
– the endpoint for the table – https://safstorage.table.core.windows.net
– the endpoint for the queue – https://safstorage.queue.core.windows.net

See Figure 5.41, where those endpoints are depicted.

Figure 5.39   Creation of a new Storage account.

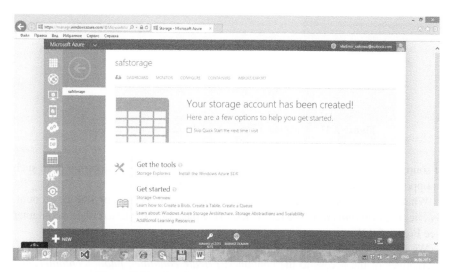

Figure 5.40   Starting page of the new Storage account.

These endpoints should be created programmatically. This is not already done. For an experiment, let us try to use one of the above URL addresses for reference. Let us copy the first URL address, paste it to the browser, and try to access it. We surely will get the error 404, since the appropriate resource does not exist yet.

What else we can do directly in the cloud with the new Storage account, without any programmatic access? My opinion is that the most comfortable option for the cloud user would be an opportunity to create a blob, queue, or table without any lines

Figure 5.41   Endpoints for a blob, table, and queue in the new Storage account.

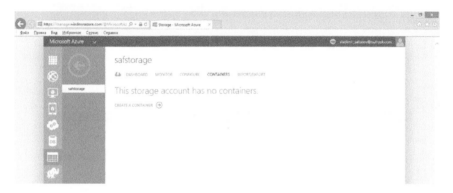

Figure 5.42   Creating a container in the new Storage account.

of source code, directly in the cloud. However, the Azure cloud does not have such an opportunity. Neither does any other cloud platform.

What we can do in the cloud is to create a *container* related to our Storage account. By clicking *Containers*, we are redirected to the page offering us to create a container (see Figure 5.42).

We choose the name *safcontainer* for our container. The cloud offers us three alternatives of the access to the container: *private container, public container*, and *public blob*. We are choosing the latter variant, since our container is intended to store a blob.

Now our public blob container is created (see Figure 5.43).

Please note the URL address of the blob container:

https://safstorage.blob.core.windows.net/safcontainer

When clicking on the URL address, we get error 404 in the browser.

When clicking on the name of the container, we get a message from the cloud that the container has no blobs.

Figure 5.43   Public blob container created.

As noted above, a new blob should be created programmatically using REST API, or by using Azure Client library. I leave this task to the readers as an exercise.

The new Storage account in the cloud can be monitored, its geo-replication mode can be tuned, and its access keys can be created. Please explore these features by yourself.

To summarize, in the new version of Azure, great progress has been achieved. The Storage became reliable and comfortable and has a very good user interface.

For cloud users, especially beginners, it is very important to understand that actually all elements of cloud Storage in the Azure platform are implemented as *Web sites*, with their appropriate URL addresses.

5.5   THE SQL AZURE COMPONENT: THE CLOUD DATABASE

This section covers cloud databases in Microsoft Azure.

Microsoft SQL Azure is a highly available and scalable database cloud server built according to the SQL Server technology. Because of using SQL Azure, the cloud users do not need to install or tune any kind of cloud database software. High availability and fault tolerance are built into SQL Azure, and no specific administration is needed to use this component. Besides that, the developers can improve their performance when using SQL Azure because of the use for cloud DBMS the same relational model based on T-SQL and the same tools for development and management, which are also used for local (on-premises) databases.

Besides database management services, there are some extra services such as **SQL Azure Database**, **SQL Azure Reporting**, and **SQL Azure Data Sync**.

Major features of SQL Azure:

- Support of building enterprise and Web applications using databases.
- Relational Database Management Systems (RDBMS) let the users manipulate, by tables, ways of visualization, indexes, roles, stored procedures, triggers, and

functions, and provide functionality to define and execute complex queries to databases, including those with multiple tables.

– Access to the data via ADO.NET – a managed .NET component to handle databases, via more traditional ODBC API, and via PHP and JDBC (Java Data Base Connectivity – Java API for handling DMBS).

Advantages of SQL Azure:

– No special administration is needed to work with SQL Azure. The developers can fully devote their time to design, optimization, and use of software solutions.
– Since SQL Azure is a managed cloud service, no installation or upgrade is needed on the client machine. All necessary tools for high availability, managing virtual machines, and error handling are already built into the cloud platform.

In the latest version of Microsoft Azure (since 2013), the SQL Azure component works very reliably. Unlike other cloud platforms, the user of Azure can create a database server, choose its location, then log in to it, create a database using the built-in table constructor and SQL queries, fill out the database with the content, and execute SQL queries on it without writing any line of code in C# or VB. All these features are considered in this section by examples. Please compare them with typical features of other cloud platforms, which support only creation and storing of the cloud database but require installation on the client machine some third-party DBMS client to fill out and handle the database.

As an alternative, a cloud database can be created using a special kind of Visual Studio project with SQL Server Data Tools installed over it. But to get acquainted to SQL Azure, graphical user interface for constructing databases and executing queries is much more comfortable.

In addition, from the previous sections of this chapter, you already know that, in Microsoft Azure, cloud databases are used as a way for communication between mobile applications and mobile cloud services.

Now let us start with creating a cloud database server and a cloud database.

On logging in to the Microsoft Azure management portal, we choose in the dashboard the item *SQL Databases*. The cloud offers us to create a new SQL database (see Figure 5.44).

By clicking *Create a SQL database*, we are redirected to the page for choosing the database parameters (see Figure 5.45).

The parameters of the database include the following:

– The name of the database – in our example, *safdatabase*;
– the Azure subscription ID;
– *Service tiers* – the scale to specify the size of the database. There can be the following service tiers: *Basic* – maximum size of 2 GB; *Standard* – maximum size of 250 GB, and *Premium* – maximum size of 500 GB. For our example, we choose the Basic service tier. The old names of the service tiers – *Web and Business* – are provided on the right for information only, and will be retired;

Figure 5.44 Creating a new SQL database.

Figure 5.45 Specifying parameters of the new SQL database.

– *Performance level* – this is the measure of the resources allocated for a new database. In the latest version of Azure, the performance level is measured in *Database Throughput Units* (*DTUs*). We choose basic level of performance – 5 DTUs;

– *Max size* – the size of the database is determined by its service tier and performance level. In our example, the size of the database is 2 GB;

– *Collation* – determine the rules that sort and compare data. The collation, once selected, cannot be changed after creating the database. This parameter is used for searching and indexing the database;

– *Server* – determines the name of the cloud database server where the new database will be created. In our case, we have not yet created a database server, so the only option offered to us is *New SQL database server*. The actual name of the server will be told to us by the cloud.

On clicking *Create SQL database*, we are switched to the next page where we are asked to specify the parameters of the database server when the database will be allocated (see Figure 5.46).

The following parameters should be specified for the database server:

– *Login name* – the login name to be used for logging in to the database server;

– *Password* – the password to be used for logging in to the database server. The rules to create a reliable password are suggested by the cloud;

– *Region* – the region where the database server will be created. We chose the region *West US*.

Now let us click the "V" sign and create the database server.

The database and the database server are created. The result is depicted in Figure 5.47.

The following information is issued by the cloud on the new SQL database:

– name – *safdatabase*

– status – online

Figure 5.46   Specifying parameters of the SQL database server.

Figure 5.47   Creation of new SQL database.

- replication – None; it means that the database in the basic level is not replicated (typical approach is to replicate cloud databases for better reliability)
- location – West US
- subscription – our Azure subscription ID
- server – the name of the database server allocated by the cloud for our database
- edition – Basic
- max size – 2 GB.

The cloud offers several ways to start working with the new database. They are visualized when clicking on the name of the database. One of them is to download and install the SQL Server Data Tools over the Visual Studio. However, we will avoid programmatic ways of handling the database. We click the *Manage* action in the bottom of the page. Because of that, we are switched to the database server management page (see Figure 5.48).

In the SQL database management page of Microsoft Azure, the name of the database server is shown. It has the format *<servername>.database.windows.net*. Next, our database name is provided – *safdatabase*, and the fields to enter the login and the password. We enter them and click *Log on*.

On logging on, we enter a page for cloud database management (see Figure 5.49).

In the central part of the page, summary information on our database is depicted – creation date, the number of users, maximum size, space used, and so on.

In the upper part, there are actions related to queries to the database. In particular, the following actions are most important:

- *New Query* – an opportunity to create and execute a Transact-SQL query to the database;
- *Open* – open a new Transact-SQL query to execute.

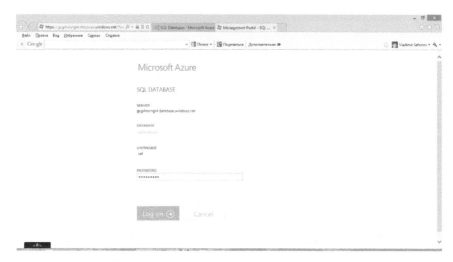

Figure 5.48   Database server management page.

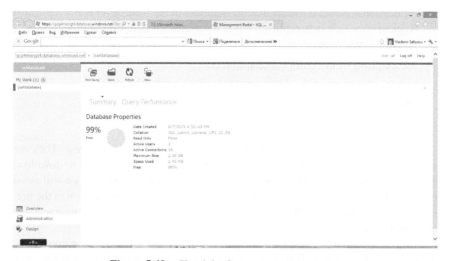

Figure 5.49   Cloud database management page.

In the left lower corner, there are possible kinds of actions with the database:

- *Overview* – the starting page to manage the database (see Figure 5.50);
- *Administration* – switch to the page depicted in Figure 5.49;
- *Design* – designing s schema of a table, or a new table (this item is of special interest to us).

In the *Design* item, let us construct a new table. We select *New table* with a simplified list of my laboratory employees (see Figure 5.51).

Figure 5.50 Overview of the new database and quick start page.

Figure 5.51 Creating a new table in the database.

The name of the table is **MyLab.** The built-in constructor of tables by default offers us a table with three columns – *ID* (integer number) and two strings of variable length. We accept this offer and rename the three columns into *ID*, *Name*, and *Surname*. The *ID* field is by default the primary key (see Figure 5.52).

Next, we are to fill out the table by content. The cloud GUI does not provide any comfortable ways for inputting the field values (hopefully such functionality will appear in further versions of Azure). Instead, the cloud suggests the following scheme of work: The user can enter and execute Transact-SQL queries, which allow them

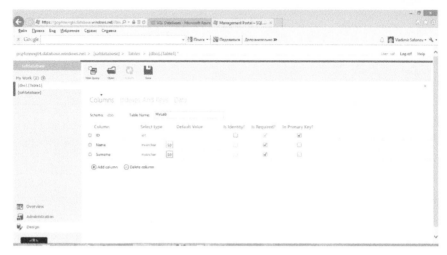

Figure 5.52   Designing the structure of the table.

to fill out the table by data. Let us enter one row (record) consisting of the fields: ID = 1, Name = "Vladimir", Surname = "Safonov". To insert such row, let us enter and execute the following SQL statement:

```
INSERT INTO MyLab VALUES (1, 'Vladimir', 'Safonov')
```

We enter this statement on clicking *New Query*, and then click *Run*.

The SQL statement is successfully executed – to error messages issued (see Figure 5.53).

Now let us continue using SQL to check the content of the table. Let us execute the SQL query to issue the row entered:

```
SELECT * FROM MyLab WHERE ID = 1
```

The query is executed successfully, and as the result the row entered is visualized (see Figure 5.54).

So we have made sure that the full cycle of working with a cloud database – creation of a database server, creation of a database, creation a new table in the database, and filling out and visualizing the table by means of Transact – SQL interpreter is quite possible to do in the Azure cloud without any third-party on-premises products installed. I think this is a very comfortable, self-evident functionality.

After using SQL queries, the cloud offers to save the SQL statements in separate files on our local machine.

On finishing our database session and on saving all information needed, we log out from the database server management page.

So, as we have seen from the examples, SQL Azure provides a simple-to-use and comfortable GUI for communicating with cloud database servers and with cloud

Figure 5.53 The INSERT SQL statement is executed on the table.

Figure 5.54 The SELECT SQL statement executed on the table.

databases itself. There is an interactive table designer as well as an SQL interpreter in the cloud. Besides database management, there is also a functionality to generate reports for databases – SQL Azure Reporting.

Now, on exiting from the cloud database, we can monitor it. To do that, we should click on the name of the database in the Azure dashboard, and click *Monitor*. The result is shown in Figure 5.55.

The monitoring diagram shows the actual use of storage, successful and failed connections, and DTU percentage. The set of metrics to monitor can be extended.

Figure 5.55   Result of monitoring the use of the cloud database.

It is also possible to monitor the database server.

5.6   NETWORKING IN THE AZURE CLOUD: NETWORK-AS-A-SERVICE (NAAS), CONTENT DELIVERY NETWORK (CDN), VIRTUAL NETWORK, TRAFFIC MANAGER

The content of this section is networking in the Azure cloud. We have already considered features of networking in other cloud platforms (Google, Amazon, etc.) in Chapter 2. Now let us compare those features to networking services in Azure.

NaaS

Generally speaking, *Network-as-a-Service* (*NaaS*) is a relatively new kind of cloud servicing. For example, in previous versions of the Azure cloud (e.g., in 2011), the term NaaS was not used although actually NaaS servicing was implemented.

Virtual Network

The main networking feature in the Azure cloud is an opportunity to create a *virtual network* address space that the cloud user wants to use with his or her cloud services and virtual machines.

When creating a virtual network in the Azure cloud, the following settings should be used:

– the *region* and the *affinity group* to be used with the virtual network;
– the virtual network *address space*;

- the *subnets* within that address space to be used for our cloud services and virtual machines;
- the *DNS servers* that will be used for the name resolution in the virtual network;
- the *VPN devices* – routers, static routing VPN gateways, and so on.

Virtual network settings are reflected in the *netcfg* file in XML format, where all the above elements are defined as XML tags.

In the Azure dashboard, the features to create and manage a virtual network are grouped in the *Networks* item. Now let us login to the Azure management portal and create a virtual network. To do that, click on *Create a virtual network* (see Figure 5.56).

As we see from the dashboard, a virtual network is created in three stages. As the first stage, we define the virtual network *name* – **safnetwork** in our example, and the *region* – we choose *East US* as proposed by the cloud. Our network preview is depicted in the left bottom part of the page.

The second stage of defining a virtual network is *DNS servers and VPN connectivity* (see Figure 5.57).

This setting is optional. If necessary, we can add new DNS servers for name resolution in our virtual network. On this page, we can add a name and an IP address for the new DNS server. Otherwise, the existing DNS servers will be used for this purpose. We choose the option of not adding new DNS servers.

The third stage of creating a virtual network is to specify our virtual network address spaces and subnets (see Figure 5.58).

We choose to create one subnet for our virtual network – **safsubnet**, with no extra address spaces.

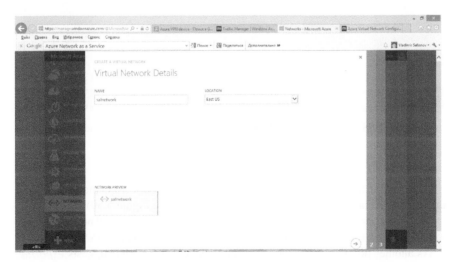

Figure 5.56   Creating a virtual network: name and region.

Figure 5.57 Creating a virtual network: DNS servers and VPN connectivity.

Figure 5.58 Creating a virtual network: specifying address spaces and subnets.

Now we finish the third stage of creating our virtual network, and the new network *safnetwork* becomes visible on the Azure dashboard (see Figure 5.59).

The cloud provides the following opportunities for our new virtual network: create a *local network* related to the virtual network, and to create a new *DNS server*.

As another possible action on the virtual network, the cloud suggests *exporting* our network settings to a network configuration XML file.

Figure 5.59   New virtual network created.

Content Delivery Network (CDN)

Azure CDN is used to optimize the use of Azure blobs or cloud services across the cloud, to enable maximum bandwidth for cloud users. The idea of the CDN is to deliver each piece of cloud content to the cloud user in the optimal way. Azure CDN is related to a storage account referring to a blob, and allows the cloud users to cache the blob across the Azure cloud infrastructure. To cache a piece of content (either a blob or a static content of a Web site), it is necessary to create a *CDN endpoint*. The Azure cloud links to the cached content a unique URL to access this item of the content. When creating a CDN endpoint, it can take time (up to 60 min) to propagate worldwide the information of that newly created CDN endpoint.

Now let us try the above in practice. Let us create a storage account and a CDN endpoint to deliver its content. In the *Storage* section of the Azure dashboard, let us click *Create a Storage account*. The name of the new account will be **safcontent**, and the full URL address safcontent.core.windows.net (see Figure 5.60).

The new storage account is created.

Now let us create a CDN endpoint for this storage account. In the *CDN* section of the Azure dashboard, click *Create a new CDN endpoint*. The cloud suggests the blob URL for the content in the new storage account – http://safcontent.blob.core .windows.net (see Figure 5.61).

When we fill out the storage account with the real blob (e.g., programmatically by calling a RESTful method), this reference will work.

The Azure CDN creates a URL address for caching the content – http://az780047 .vo.msecnd.net/. This reference will work when we actually create a blob content.

The new CDN endpoint can be disabled: the *Disable endpoint* operation is available. Disabling actually means that this CDN endpoint stops working, so the blob content can be accessed only via the original URL, and will not be cached.

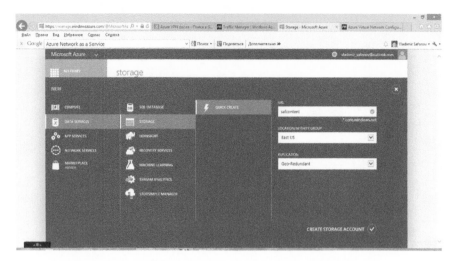

Figure 5.60   Creating a storage account to be cached by the CDN.

Figure 5.61   Creating a CDN endpoint for the new storage account.

A disabled CDN endpoint can be enabled again. Also, a CDN endpoint can be permanently deleted, and in this case caching by this endpoint will stop forever.

Traffic Manager

The Microsoft Azure Traffic Manager can be used to control the distribution of user traffic to similar cloud services running in the same datacenter or in different datacenters across the world. The cloud user may send the traffic to the best cloud service or the best Web site for performance, or for some other criteria. Traffic Manager works by applying an intelligent policy engine to the DNS queries on the cloud user's domain names. Traffic Manager can help

- to improve availability of critical applications;
- to improve responsiveness for high performing applications;
- to upgrade and perform service maintenance without downtime;
- to improve traffic distribution for large complex deployments.

For practical use, Traffic Manager is available via the *Traffic Manager* section of the Azure dashboard.

In Figure 5.62, creation of a Traffic Manager profile is depicted. The URL address of our Traffic Manager profile is saftm.trafficmanager.net. When creating a Traffic Manager profile, it is necessary to choose its load balancing method. There are three methods of load balancing available in Traffic Manager: *Round Robin, Performance,* and *Failover*. The result of creating our new Traffic Manager profile is shown in Figure 5.63.

The new Traffic Manager profile is created in the *inactive* state. To make it active, it is required to use RESTful Web methods. For example, to add a new definition to some traffic manager profile, it is necessary to perform a request in the following form:

https://management.core.windows.net/<subscription-id>/services/WATM/
    profiles/<profile-name>/definitions

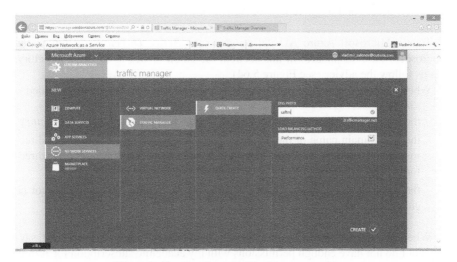

Figure 5.62   Creating a Traffic Manager profile.

Figure 5.63   New Traffic Manager profile created.

5.7   ACTIVE DIRECTORY IN THE CLOUD: A WAY OF STRUCTURING USER ACCOUNTS

Active Directory is a widely known product by Microsoft used for structuring information on user accounts. The users belong to some organization and have access to some resources. Microsoft Azure Active Directory (AD) is its cloud version.

Microsoft Azure AD can be used for the following purposes:

– securing identity data of an organization in the cloud for local and remote access using multi-factor authentication (see more details a little later);
– change and reset passwords of the users from any device and at any location by the administrator;
– create and edit users of Active Directory;
– view access and usage reports of Active Directory.

To use Microsoft Azure AD, let us go to the *Active Directory* section of the Microsoft Azure dashboard. In this section, the cloud invites us to add a directory. Let us follow the advice (see Figure 5.64).

When creating a new Azure AD, the following information should be provided:

– the name of the directory to be created, in our example – *saf_active_directory*
– the full domain name of the directory: *safactivedirectory* – my personal directory name; *onmicrosoft.com* – the standard base name for all Azure active directories. The full domain name is: *safactivedirectory.onmicrosoft.com*
– the name of the country where the directory is created (this name cannot be changed).

When creating the new active directory, the cloud did not allow me to create it, saying that I do not have enough permissions with my academic subscription for Azure. The process of creating an AD hanged. So let us terminate this attempt, keeping this

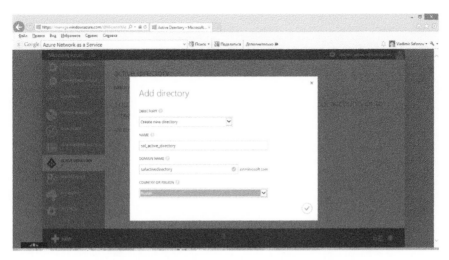

Figure 5.64   Adding a new Active Directory.

Figure 5.65   New Azure Active Directory created.

fact in mind. On freeing all my other cloud resources, logging out, and logging in to the Azure cloud again, I finally got my Azure AD up and running in the cloud, with an *Active* status. The result is shown in Figure 5.65.

However, when I switch to the rights management tab, my right management status is indicated as *Inactive*. Nevertheless, I managed to add a new user – Adel Safonova – to our active directory. The result of adding the new user is shown in Figure 5.66.

Figure 5.66   New user added to our Azure Active Directory.

I, as a user of Azure AD, am indicated by my Microsoft Account, and Adel is indicated as the Azure AD user by her ***onmicrosoft.com*** domain account.

Of other important features of the Azure AD, the following should be especially noted:

– entering and visualizing information on the organization to which the users belong, and on the working position of any Azure AD user in the organization;
– opportunity to add a group to which the users belong;
– reference to the Web application available to us by default: Office 365 Management APIs.

Here is the full list of possible actions on the Active Directory (the list is available when we click on the name of our Active Directory in the Azure dashboard):

Users – the list of all the users of our AD; as we have seen before, for our example it contains two users: Vladimir Safonov and Adel Safonova. Possible actions on the AD users are to add a new user, to reset the user's password, to manage multi-factor authentication (the latter option is available only for the users licensed to use Microsoft Online Services), and to delete the user. Multi-factor authentication is a method of authentication that requires the use of more than one user identity verification method to enable higher level of security. Possible methods of multi-factor authentication are password, a trusted device not easy to duplicate (e.g., a phone), and biometric information on a person.

Groups – adding a group of users from the AD. In our example, we are adding a new group *SPBU* for the users from St. Petersburg University (see Figure 5.67):

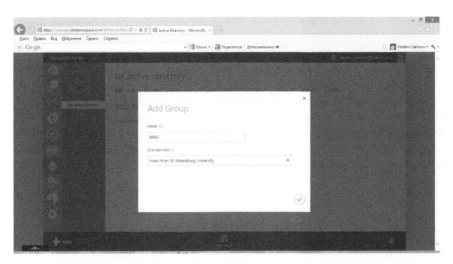

Figure 5.67   Adding a new group of users to our Azure Active Directory.

Into the new group SPBU, we added two members – Vladimir Safonov and Adel Safonova. Also, we added the owner Vladimir Safonov to the new group using the *Add Owners* functionality. Please do it yourself as simple exercise.

Add application – allows the users to add applications to the AD, either applications the user's company uses or applications the user's company owns. Applications can be added from the gallery. Default application suggested by Microsoft to use is Microsoft Office 365

Domains – allows the users to create a custom domain for better structuring, in addition to the default domain already created (in our example – *safactivedirectory.onmicrosoft.com*).

Directory integration – provides an opportunity to integrate our cloud AD to a local Active Directory, with automatic synchronization of both directories.

Configure – Setting some properties of the AD: the directory *name*; the language for email *notifications* related to the AD (Russian or English); settings for *multi-factor authentications*; the number of *joined devices* per user, and the ways to join devices; *integrated applications* – an opportunity for the AD to have integrated applications, and an opportunity for the AD users to give the integrated applications permissions to access their data; *invitations* – a new feature allowing the users of AD to invite guests and to limit those invitations.

Reports – a very important item from trustworthy cloud computing viewpoint. It allows the users to view and analyze reports on anomalous and suspicious activity: multiple failed sign-ins, sign-ins from suspicious IP addresses, sign-ins from possibly infected devices, detailed view of password reset in the AD owner's organization, a usage summary of all SaaS applications integrated with our AD, and so on.

Licenses – kinds of licensing to use AD: *Azure Active Directory Premium, Enterprise Mobility Suite*.

The Azure AD supports a lot of SaaS functionalities. It is possible for the user to add information on the application the user is developing. It is possible to enable single sign-on to simplify user access to thousands of cloud applications from Windows, Mac, Android, and iOS devices. Users can launch applications from a personalized Web-based Access Panel or mobile app using their company credentials. With the Application Proxy module, the user can go beyond SaaS applications and publish on-premises Web applications to provide secure remote access and single sign-on to them.

5.8   DEVELOPMENT OF MICROSOFT AZURE CLOUD SERVICES WITH MICROSOFT VISUAL STUDIO

This section covers the basics of the development of Microsoft Azure cloud service projects with Microsoft Visual Studio integrated development environment. The kinds of Visual Studio projects for Azure cloud services development are considered. Creating, debugging, publishing in Microsoft Azure cloud and the use of an Azure cloud service are covered.

Cloud Projects in Visual Studio. The Azure SDK

For my examples of Azure cloud services development, I use the version of Microsoft Visual Studio 2013 – not the latest but a well-known and tested version of the IDE. Please note that, by default, even in the "maximal" version – *Visual Studio Ultimate* – the cloud projects (having the *Cloud* type) are not included into the set of Visual Studio projects, and to have them appear and available we need to install the *Azure SDK* over the Visual Studio.

In Figure 5.68, creating a cloud project is depicted.

To make such project creation happen, it is necessary, on installing Visual Studio, to install the Azure SDK toolkit (the version number of the Azure SDK announced in the time of writing the book is 2.6). Figure 5.69 depicts the list of the installed components of the Azure SDK (see the upper part of the screenshot). The total size of downloads for Azure SDK is over 300 megabytes.

So let us install on our computer Visual Studio 2013, and then Azure SDK.

Creating a Cloud Service Project

Now let us create in Visual Studio 2013 a cloud project in C# (see Figure 5.68). With such configuration, we now can develop cloud services and publish them in the Azure cloud. To be able to develop other kinds of cloud projects – for example, *mobile services* – some extra installations are necessary (it will be explained later on in this section).

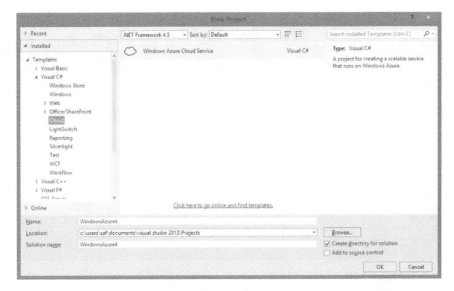

Figure 5.68   Creating a Microsoft Azure cloud service project in Visual Studio.

Figure 5.69   List of the installed components of the Azure SDK.

Let us continue creating our cloud project. Let us name it *WindowsAzure4*.

A very important detail: for creating and publishing a cloud service, the Visual Studio environment should be called under the name and the permissions of the *administrator*. How to do that in Windows 8.x operating system is explained in Figure 5.70.

In more detail, the following steps should be done sequentially. Go to the starting page of Windows 8 (with the tiles), find the Visual Studio 2013 icon, switch to

Figure 5.70   Calling Visual Studio under the name of the administrator.

the contextual menu (by the right click), and choose the menu item that calls Visual Studio under the name of the administrator. The contextual menu in such cases is depicted instead of the toolbar.

In Windows 7, similar actions are implemented in a slightly different way: in the toolbar, find the Visual Studio 2013 icon by the right click on it, switch to the contextual menu, and choose the menu item to call Visual Studio under the name of the administrator.

Please note that, if we call Visual Studio as an ordinary user (rather than as administrator), we will not have the necessary permissions even for the debugging call of our cloud services using the Azure cloud emulator, and also for publishing our service in the Azure cloud.

Now let us go back to creating our cloud project. We are in the Visual Studio 2013 integrated development environment. Let us press OK for creating a cloud project.

A window is opened to choose the *role* of the project. As we already know from the above, in specific Microsoft terms, *role* in Azure is a kind of cloud application. Intuitively, the term "role" in the context of Microsoft Azure denotes a kind of cloud application with some definite function (role) in the cloud and in the project considered. *Role* is the *code* of an application. An *instance* of the role is an instance (a call) of the application. The number of instances of the role is the number of calls of the cloud application running simultaneously. The number of role instances is very important. Actually, it somewhat expresses the degree of reliability of the cloud application. The developers of Azure recommend us to have at least 2–3 instances of each role, for better reliability of the cloud, since a cloud service is a server-side code that is subject to big workload (e.g., this code can theoretically be invoked at the same moment by a million cloud users. In Microsoft Azure, the following kinds of roles are supported:

- *Web role* – a cloud Web service.
- *Worker role* – a background process implementing some computations.
- *Virtual Machine (VM) role* – yet another kind of role added in the latest version of Microsoft Azure.

From this viewpoint, we can think of Web roles and worker roles as working in several instances (it is even recommended for better reliability), and each VM role always exists in one instance only. It could be hard to imagine that VMs would be cloned in multiple instances: a VM is very resource consuming, and the reliability of the VM is enabled by some other ways – by a server-side operating system that implements the virtual machine on a concrete computer of the data center (currently, with Microsoft Azure, such operating system is typically Windows Server 2013 R2, or some dialect of Linux).

The window for choosing the kind of role for our cloud service is depicted in Figure 5.71.

Here we see in more details what the possible kinds of roles are in the latest version of Microsoft Azure.

- *ASP.NET Web Role* – a cloud service with user Web interface implemented using ASP.NET technology, the most important of technology for Web application development for .NET platform;
- *WCF Web Role* – a Web role implemented by WCF. This technology is intended for creating Web services. In Microsoft Azure, most of the server-side functionality is implemented using WCF;
- *Worker Role* – a background process for making some kinds of computations;

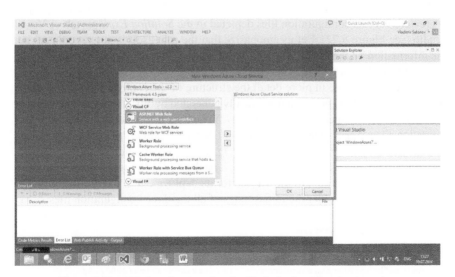

Figure 5.71   Window for choosing the kind of role of the cloud service.

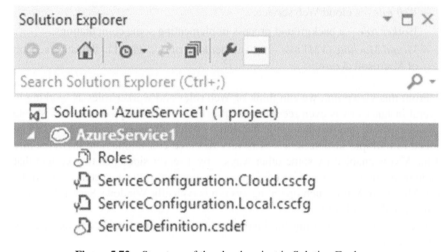

Figure 5.72   Structure of the cloud project in Solution Explorer.

- *Cache Worker Role* – a worker role that implements a cluster of cache memory available to all the instances of the role;
- *Worker Role with Service Bus Queue* – a worker role that implements processing of messages in the *Service Bus* queue.

So the kinds of Web roles considered above implement different kinds of Web interface, and the worker roles implement processing of different kinds of cloud resources shared by the instances of the roles.

Let us choose the variant most often used – *ASP.NET Web Role*. A cloud project is created, with its configuration files depicted in the *Solution Explorer* tab of Visual Studio (see Figure 5.72). Let us emphasize that the role itself is not yet created, but the information on the kind of the role was necessary at this moment for creating the configuration files of the cloud service.

Now let us examine in more detail the structure of the configuration files and the other files of the cloud project automatically generated by Visual Studio. The name of the cloud service created is *WindowsAzure4*. Visual Studio created for it the three configuration files: *ServiceDefinition.csdef.xml, ServiceConfiguration.Cloud.cscfg.xml*, and *ServiceConfiguration.Cloud.Local.cscfg.xml* – the definition of the service, the configuration of the service when invoking it on the local computer by the cloud emulator, and the configuration of the service for its deployment in the Azure cloud. For more detail, let us consider the initial states of all the three configuration files.

```
ServiceDefinition.csdef.xml:
 <?xml version="1.0" encoding="utf-8"?>
 <ServiceDefinition name="WindowsAzure4"
    xmlns="http://schemas.microsoft.com/ServiceHosting/2008/10/
ServiceDefinition"
```

```
    schemaVersion="2014-01.2.3">
 </ServiceDefinition>
```

```
ServiceConfiguration.Cloud.cscfg.xml:
 <?xml version="1.0" encoding="utf-8"?>
 <ServiceConfiguration serviceName=" WindowsAzure4"
    xmlns="http://schemas.microsoft.com/ServiceHosting/2008/10/
ServiceConfiguration"
    osFamily="4" osVersion="*" schemaVersion="2014-01.2.3">
 </ServiceConfiguration>
```

The *ServiceConfiguration.Local.cscfg.xml* file is identical to the previous file.

The content of the files is self-evident and does not require any extra comments: they define the name of the service, a reference to the namespace for the XML tags used, the version numbers of XML and XML schemes, and the version number of the operating system.

Now let us create a role in our cloud project. To do that, in the contextual menu of the *Roles* item, choose *Add* (adding a role)/*New Web Role Project*. The *Add New .NET 4.5 Role Project* window is opened (see Figure 5.73).

Of the two variants proposed, we choose *ASP.NET Web Role*. Yet another window is opened – *New ASP.NET Web project: WebRole1* (see Figure 5.74).

In this window, the following variants of templates for creating a Web role are offered:

– *Empty* – an empty role: a template of code to which the necessary actions for processing typical events should be added;

– *Web Forms* – implementation of the role based on a Web form with its typical GUI elements;

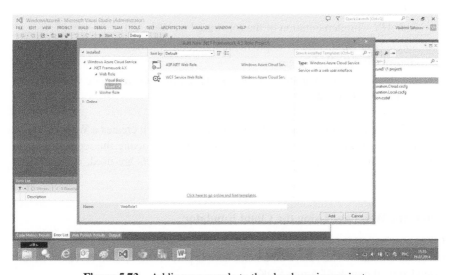

Figure 5.73 Adding a new role to the cloud service project.

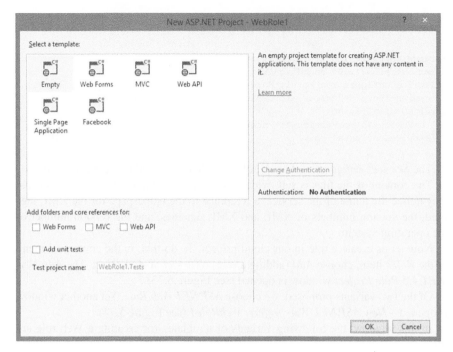

Figure 5.74   ASP.NET Web project: WebRole1 window.

- *MVC (Model – View – Controller)* – implementation of the role based on a commonly used paradigm *MVC* (*model* is a theoretical model of some data, *view* is a kind of most comfortably visualizing the data, *controller* is a way to enter the data);
- *Web API* – implementation of the role based on Web API;
- *Single Page Application* – implementation of the role based on code template to control the only Web page;
- *Facebook* – implementation of the role based on code template working with the Facebook social network.

We choose the option of *Single Page Application*, which creates a Web page with an opportunity to register on it and the subsequent login using the registered login name. To control the Web page, a set of JavaScript scripts are used, automatically generated by Visual Studio.

Debug the Web Page Using the Cloud Emulator

On generating all the project files, let us do the debugging run of the Web page on the cloud emulator. The Azure cloud emulator is part of the version of Visual Studio extended by the tools of Azure SDK.

To do debugging on the cloud emulator, choose in the Visual Studio environment the *Internet Explorer* item whose icon reminds us the traditional Play sign and which is located under the *Debug* item.

The environment performs building (compiling) the cloud project. Then it invokes the cloud emulator, with notification by a special message.

On the cloud emulator, a new page is browsed, under the traditional local URL address, with a special port number: *http://127.0.0.1:2289*, If we forget to invoke Visual Studio with administrator permissions, this debugging will not work because of not enough permissions.

Publishing the Cloud Service

For publishing the service in the Azure cloud, I recommend, first, the creation of an "empty" cloud service whose implementation will be enabled by Visual Studio. So, let us log in to the Azure cloud with our subscription, login, and password and create a cloud service named *saf-service*. How to do that is explained in this section.

The empty cloud service will be used to publish and deploy the created implementation of the Web page. To do that, in the *Solution Explorer* tab, enter the contextual menu of the *WebRole1* role item, and choose the action *Publish* (publish in Azure cloud).

Before publishing, Visual Studio requires us to enter the Azure cloud with the corresponding login and password. On logging in to the cloud, the environment gets the information on the empty service *saf*-service we already created, and proposes us to publish our Web page in the cloud under the corresponding URL address: http:// saf-service.cloudapp.net. Using this URL address, we can afterwards browse the Web page using any Web browser.

Let us emphasize that the new version of the IDE – Visual Studio 2013 – is much more comfortable for publishing services in the cloud that the previous ones. For example, the version of Visual Studio 2010, which I have used a lot for creating cloud services, requires to explicitly indicate the path to the directories where the cloud service configuration files *.csdef* and *.cscfg* are placed on the local computer (which is not so comfortable for cloud users). Now, starting with Visual Studio 2013, this is not required: the development environment "understands" by itself where to find the configuration files.

Publishing a service in the cloud can take long (the actual publishing time depends on the speed of the Internet connection). In my example, it took about half an hour. When publishing proceeds, a special tab is created and promptly updated, which displays the publishing information from the cloud, including information on the created and used Azure storage accounts. So, in the Visual Studio development environment, when publishing a service, a "window to the cloud world" is created through which the user can get necessary information related to publishing the service.

Finally, the service is published and deployed in the Azure cloud, and Visual Studio environment notifies the user about it.

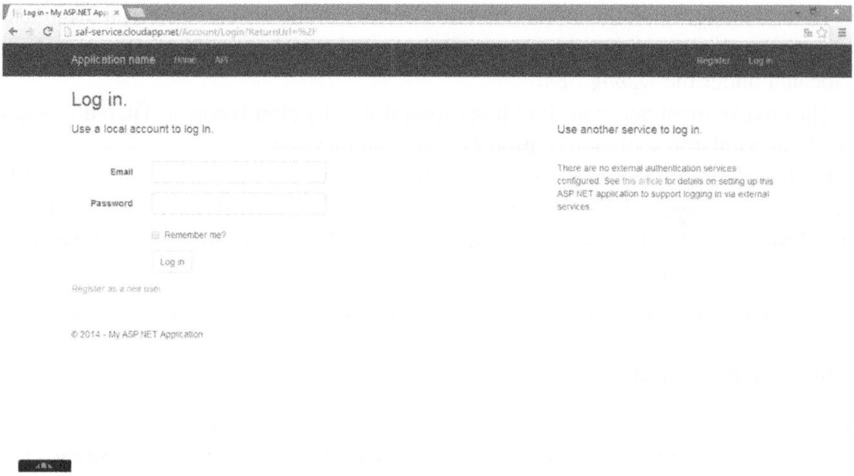

Figure 5.75   Result of browsing the new cloud service page in Google Chrome.

Now we can enter the cloud through the management portal http://manage
.windowsazure.com and make sure that our service is created, published, and
deployed.

Also we can just use the URL address of the published service; call the browser and
visualize the new Web page in it. In Figure 5.75, the result of visualizing the service
page in the Google Chrome browser (this browser is taken just for experiment to make
sure that everything works in this browser also).

Also, after publishing the service in the cloud, the Visual Studio environment
generates and stores in the local directories of the cloud project the following configuration files:

– *saf-serviceProduction.azurePubxml* – information on the service published in
  the cloud: the name of the service in the cloud (*saf-service*), its deployment
  label (*WindowsAzure4* – this is actually the name of the cloud project in Visual
  Studio), the options of the service, and so on.
– the updated configuration files after service publishing contain the following
  information: *ServiceDefinition.csdef* – specification of the published service
  interface in the WSDL standard; *ServiceConfiguration.Cloud.cscfg* and *Ser-
  viceConfiguration.Local.cscfg* – the number of the Web role instances (1, in
  our example).

Summary of Visual Studio Support of Cloud Service Development

The integrated development environment Visual Studio 2013 provides comfortable
features for development of cloud services for Microsoft Azure and for their publishing and deployment in the cloud. To enable it, besides the Visual Studio installation,

the installation of the Microsoft Azure SDK toolkit is required. The service is created as a Web role, that is, a cloud Web application. When creating the service code, a number of code templates for different variants of the service implementation, including the code template for one-page Web application, are used in our example. It is recommended, before publishing the service in the cloud, to enter the cloud and to create an "empty" cloud service using the Azure management portal. That guarantees creation of the cloud URL address. Then, the service is published in the cloud directly from the Visual Studio environment. When necessary, Visual Studio asks the user for the cloud login and password and enables the "window to the cloud" during the publication of the new service in it. In general, features of Visual Studio 2013 and later versions, even when compared with the previous versions of the environment, are just overwhelming by their convenience, self-explanation interface, and reliability. Let us emphasize again the tremendous work Microsoft has done on enhancement of the Visual Studio environment, which is especially sensitive in cloud projects.

5.9   VISUAL STUDIO ONLINE AND ITS RELATION TO MICROSOFT AZURE

Visual Studio Online is a cloud product by Microsoft implementing a functionality similar to that of *TFS*. Actually it is a cloud-hosted version of the TFS. It is intended for developing team projects. The advantage of Visual Studio Online is in its cloud nature. It does not require extra installations. Though it can be used in relation to a local version of Visual Studio, this is not required. The first version of Visual Studio Online was issued in November 2013.

Visual Studio Online is accessible from the management portal of Microsoft Azure via the *Visual Studio Online* section. This section allows the cloud user to create a Visual Studio Online account within the existing Microsoft Azure subscription.

Visual Studio Online can be used to create team projects, plan and track the work, collaborate with the project team, and manage the code online using Visual Studio client or other development tools. In particular, Visual Studio Online allows the users

- to create code repositories
- to manage work items and bugs
- to run cloud-based services, like build and load testing.

To create a Visual Studio Online account, let us go to the Visual Studio Online section of the Azure management portal and click *Create or Link to a Visual Studio Online Account*. Then, click *Quick Create*. In Figure 5.76, the page to create a Visual Studio Online account is depicted.

We chose the name of our account – *safonovvladimir*, and the full URL address of the account, as suggested by the cloud, will be as follows: *safonovvladimir. visualstudio.com*. We choose the alternative *Don't connect to a directory*, since otherwise the cloud requires access to the Microsoft Azure Pass active directory which we do not have. We choose the region for creating our Visual Studio Online

Figure 5.76   Page to create a Visual Studio Online account.

Figure 5.77   Visual Studio Online account created.

account as suggested by the cloud – *South Central US*. On clicking *Create*, in a few moments, our Visual Studio Online account is created. The result of creating the account displayed in the Azure dashboard is depicted in Figure 5.77.

To access our VS Online account, we click *Browse* (or the URL address displayed in the dashboard). To sign in to Visual Studio, a Microsoft account is required. We enter the information on our Microsoft account which we use for our Azure subscription. The result is shown in Figure 5.78: we have entered Visual Studio Online and are suggested to create our first team project.

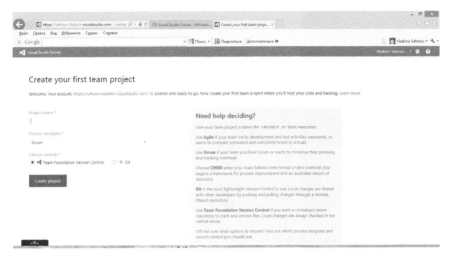

Figure 5.78   First login to Visual Studio Online.

We enter the name of our first team project – *saf_team_project*. Visual Studio online suggests several variants of project organization corresponding to modern project styles: *Scrum* (iterative project organization with minimal planning and tracking overhead), *Agile* (tracking development and testing activities separately), and *CMMI* (more formal and optimizing project development strategy). We choose the option of Scrum suggested by default. Also, Visual Studio Online suggests a source code control system for the project – either *Team Foundation Version Control* or *Git*. Both toolkits are quite popular now. We choose the TFVS and click *Create Project*.

The new project is now in the cloud. Visual Studio online suggests two directions of further activity on the project – *Manage work* and *Add code*. The project page is shown in Figure 5.79.

On the project page, information is available on possible further actions on the project – *Work, Code, Build, Test*, information on controlling the *Sprint* characteristic of the Scrum methodology – summarizing the intermediate results of the project in some definite planned moments of time (typically in 1–2 weeks), and information on the *Team Rooms* created for discussing the project between the members of the team. By default, currently one team room is created for the project, named *saf_team_project Team Room*. There is the only member of the project – me (with the initials *VS*).

To add a user to the project team, we click *Manage,* and, in the *Manage members of team project* window, choose the item *Add* (see Figure 5.80).

The *Add a user* window is opened. Let us enter a valid email address (related to Microsoft account) of Adel Safonova, whom we invite to become a new member of the project. As the result, Adel receives an email inviting her to join the project *saf_team_project*. Adel logs in to the project Web page and gets access to the project data. Visual Studio Online suggests Adel to start a 90-day free trial, which gives

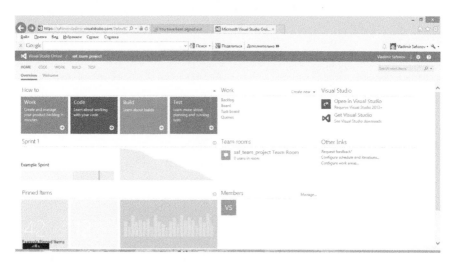

Figure 5.79   Page of the *saf_team_project*.

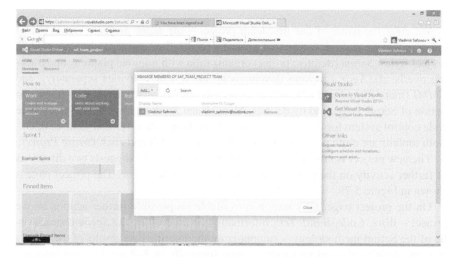

Figure 5.80   Managing project team members.

access to all the features of Visual Studio Online (as an invited person). By clicking *Start Free Trial*, she initiates her free trial. I do not illustrate those actions by
screenshots; you can do all of that by yourself.

Now let us enter the Team Room of the project. To do that, just let us click the
name of the team room. We have entered it. Another user, Adel, is not in the team
room yet. We post a message: *Let's start our project*! This situation is depicted in
Figure 5.81.

Now it is possible to open our project in Visual Studio, in its Team Explorer. To
do that, click *Open in Visual Studio*. The local installation of Visual Studio is called.

Figure 5.81   Working with the Team Room of the project and posting messages.

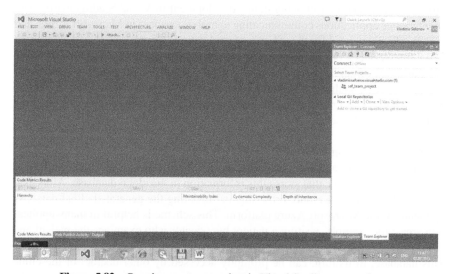

Figure 5.82   Opening our team project in Visual Studio team explorer.

Our credentials are requested. On logging in to Visual Studio using the same login and password as we used when we created the Visual Studio Online account, we get access to our project in Visual Studio. To open the project in the non-cloud version of Visual Studio, choose the menu item *Team Explorer* in which we can manage our project *saf_team_project* (see Figure 5.82).

The Team Explorer provides the following features (please check this by yourself as an exercise):

– *Configure workspace* of the project to get started developing;

- *Team Rooms* – access to the VS Online team rooms of the project (back link from Visual Studio to VS Online);
- *Connect* – connect to all the team projects we own;
- *Local Git repositories* – managing Git repositories to store the project sources;
- *Pending changes* – related work items, included changes, excluded changes;
- *Source Control Explorer* – explore the sources.

So, using cloud and non-cloud features jointly, we can manage team projects. The central point of this activity is the Microsoft Azure cloud, which provides access to the Visual Studio Online account we created. All three toolkits – Microsoft Azure, Visual Studio Online, and Visual Studio – work in cooperation to enable comfortable development of team projects.

5.10   DEVELOPING MOBILE SERVICES AND CONNECTED MOBILE APPLICATIONS FOR MICROSOFT AZURE

This section covers the following items: development in Visual Studio environment client mobile applications communicating to mobile services in Microsoft Azure, and push notifications used for those kinds of applications.

Mobile services on Microsoft Azure platform is one of the most modern and popular kinds of applications that can be developed in Visual Studio environment. A mobile service on the Azure platform is a server-side application managing a cloud database it uses to store the data coming from a mobile application working on some mobile device. The scheme of working of the chain "mobile application – mobile service" is as follows. The user (mobile client) on his smartphone can call a mobile application that communicates to a cloud mobile service in the Azure cloud. The mobile client enters necessary information into Web forms on his smartphone and calls the mobile service that stores this information in the cloud database. After that, it is possible to use the cloud, browsing and updating the generated cloud database by means of the Microsoft Azure platform. This scheme is helpful in many application areas: for example, visiting a patient by a doctor who examines the patient and sends the collected medical data by his smartphone into the medical cloud database. This database, in its turn, can be promptly accessed by other doctors of the clinic and its management, and so on. In many such cases, using cloud computing on the Azure platform provides really great opportunities, both from the viewpoint of the information stored in the cloud and from the viewpoint of convenience of its use.

In the latest version of the Azure platforms, the following popular mobile platforms are supported: *Windows Phone 8/8.1, iOS,* and *Android.*

Preparing a Computer with the Installed Visual Studio Environment to the Development of Mobile Services

Before considering in detail the development of mobile applications and mobile services, let us clarify the prerequisites for such kind of development. First, the Visual

Studio integrated development environment is necessary, with all available updates. As in the previous two sections, we will use Visual Studio 2013, whose version is dated back to summer 2014. In this version, development of mobile applications and mobile services is supported since *Visual Studio 2013 Update 2* (issued in May 2014). This update includes all necessary project types and tools for developing mobile applications and mobile services. For installation of Update 2 to Visual Studio 2013 on a middle-level computer (I used 6 gigabytes RAM, dual-core 64-bit processor Intel Core i5 3210M 2 * 2.5 GHz x64, with Windows 8 operating system) took me 10–12 h, including all the downloads via a 3G modem I used in 2014.

When checking the correctness of this update installation on the computer, it should be taken into account that it is *not* visualized by a separate line in the *Programs and components* section of the control panel; this section only contains the information on the Visual Studio environment itself.

Besides the update of the development environment, it is necessary to install a toolkit for developing mobile applications corresponding to your mobile platform. For Windows Phone, this is the *Windows Phone SDK*. There are also similar SDKs for the other mobile platforms – iOS and Android. For debugging mobile applications, smartphone emulators are included into the Windows Phone SDK. The approximate size of the downloads related to Windows Phone SDK is 1.2 gigabytes. The installation together with the downloads took me 15–20 h.

So please take into account before such experiments that, even if Visual Studio is already installed on your computer, the preparations may take you a few days. It should be noted either for planning your personal working time or for planning team projects on software development.

On completion of the Windows Phone SDK installation, I got a message that the emulators of mobile phones included into the Windows Phone SDK appeared to be uninstalled because the computer hardware did not support Hyper-V (hardware virtualization).

Example of Development of Mobile Service and the Connected Mobile Application for Windows Phone 8.x

As the basis for such development, I used the tutorial and the sample code of the mobile service published by Microsoft in the Azure cloud, in the *Mobile Services* section of the Azure management portal. I also used the templates for mobile projects, including the source code files and the configuration files from the above section of the Azure portal. It is interesting to note that, due to logging in to the Azure cloud before downloading the project samples, they appear to be already tuned to the concrete project under development, with their specific component names, which is quite comfortable. For example, the name of the mobile application project *saf_mobile* when visualizing the fragments of the tutorial appears to be already inserted into the corresponding points in the code and in the documentation. Such approach can be characterized as *user-centric computing* (the computing oriented to the concrete user and to his working environment, which is state of the art.

Figure 5.83 Empty mobile service *saf-mobile* created in the Azure cloud.

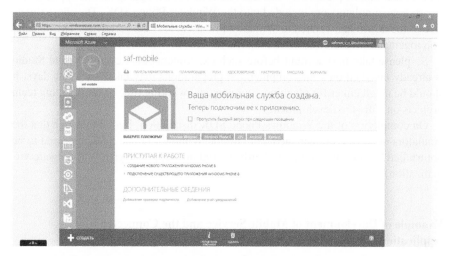

Figure 5.84 Azure cloud page to support development of mobile services for Windows Phone platform.

First, let us create in the Azure cloud an "empty" mobile service (see Section 5.3 for an example), with no implementation yet, named *saf-mobile* (see Figure 5.83). Please recall that, together with the mobile service, in the same region of the data centers, a cloud database is created and (if necessary) also a database server.

On clicking the name of the mobile service, we are redirected to the cloud page to support the development of mobile services (let us choose Windows Phone 8 as the mobile platform), see Figure 5.84.

By choosing the option "Creating a new mobile application for Windows Phone 8," we switch to the page containing a reference for downloading the mobile project

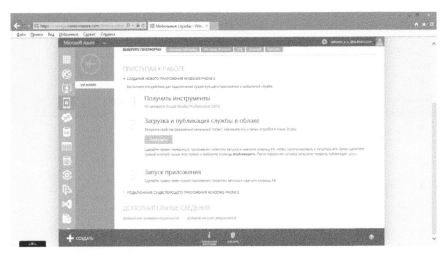

Figure 5.85   Azure cloud page with a reference to the mobile project and recommendations on the text steps of development.

for that platform and brief recommendation on the next steps of the development (see Figure 5.85).

The first step – installing Visual Studio 2013 Update 2 – is already completed.

Now we download the mobile project and find out that we now need to install the Windows Phone SDK.

It takes us only one day to download and install the Windows Phone SDK, and now we can open the mobile project.

We choose in the Solution Explorer of the Visual Studio the mobile service project *saf_mobileService*, build it, and do the debug run (as a Web site) on a local computer. The mobile service visualizes a simplified face picture, which reacts on any click in its windows by a "cry" – special mimic (please try it yourself).

Figure 5.86 shows the structure of the Visual Studio solution *saf_mobile* with the mobile service project *saf_mobileService*. The other component of the solution is a project with the corresponding mobile application.

Now let us compile (build) the mobile service: choose it as the basic project by the contextual menu, and then in the environment click F5 to do the build.

Now we publish our mobile service. In the contextual menu of the project, select the Publish item. A window is opened with the options for publishing the mobile service (see Figure 5.87).

Let us recall (see the previous section) that for publishing a mobile service (as well as for publishing an ordinary cloud service), the Visual Studio environment should be invoked with the permissions of the administrator.

Before publication of the mobile service, it is necessary to choose the profile of the publication (see Figure 5.88). An option of creating a new mobile service or using an existing mobile service can be chosen.

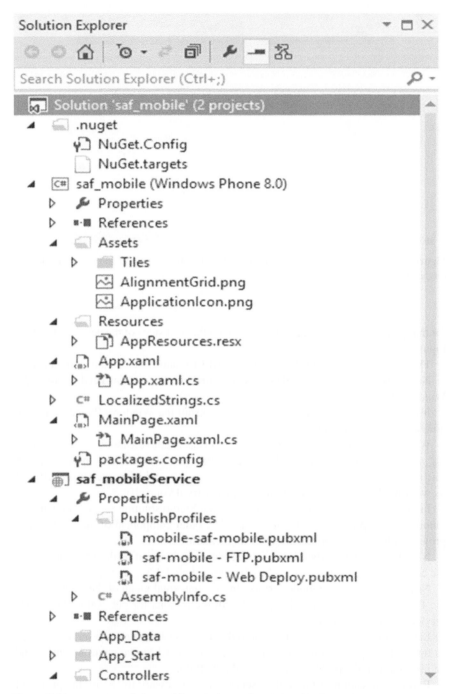

Figure 5.86   Structure of the mobile solution *saf_mobile* with the mobile service project *saf_mobileService*.

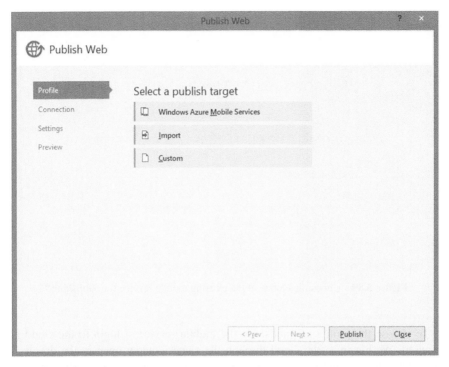

Figure 5.87 Window with the options for publishing the mobile service in the cloud.

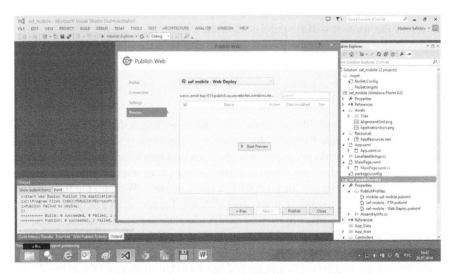

Figure 5.88 Choosing a profile for publishing the mobile service.

Figure 5.89   Choosing a name of the existing mobile service for publishing.

To choose the profile of publishing the mobile service, a login to the cloud is required. We log in to the cloud through the same window open in the development environment, and the cloud allows us to choose one of the existing mobile services for publishing. It is the "empty" mobile service *saf-mobile* we already created (Figure 5.89).

Choose the name of the service and click OK. The development environment contacts the cloud and visualizes, in a special window, detailed information on the mobile service in the form it will be published in the cloud (see Figure 5.90). The URL address under which the new mobile service will be accessible in the cloud is as follows:

http://saf-mobile.azure-mobile.net.

When choosing the profile for the mobile service, we use as the basis the XML file with the name *saf-mobile Publish Settings* generated by the development environment for our mobile service. As my experience has shown, if the default profile settings are used, the publication does not work: a network socket does not open for copying the files of the mobile service to the computer in the datacenter. We omit the full version of that XML file here to avoid extra technical detail. I propose, as a helpful exercise, that you explore that XML file by yourself. A template for the file can be found on the cloud page for recommendations on mobile services development.

Now click *Publish*. The publication of the mobile service is started.

Publishing the mobile service is logged in vast detail in special tabs in the development environment. On the *Web Publishing Activity* tab, writing to the cloud is displayed for the files that are components of the mobile service (see Figure 5.91).

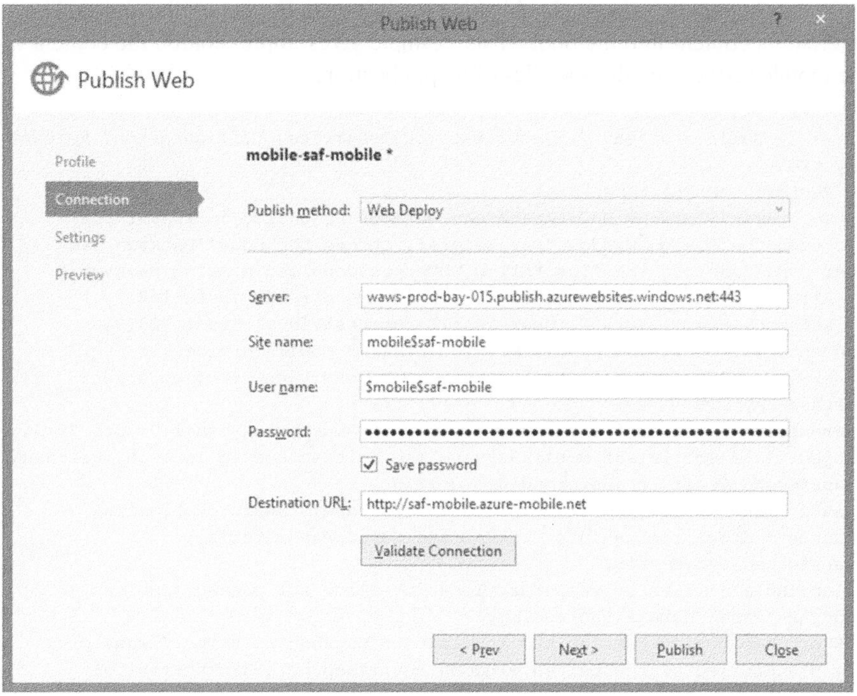

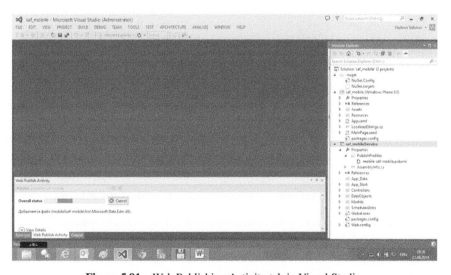

Figure 5.90   Visualizing detailed information on the mobile service being published.

Figure 5.91   Web Publishing Activity tab in Visual Studio.

In the *Output* tab, a detailed publishing log is issued. For better illustration, I have inserted its content into the book. This example gives impression on the content of the mobile service and the specifics of its publication.

```
1>------ Build started: Project: saf_mobileService, Configuration: Release
Any CPU ------
1> Restore the NuGet packages:
1> To prevent loading NuGet packages during the build, in Visual Stu-
dio open the dialog window "Parameters", choose the node "Package man-
ager" and deselect the flag "Allow NuGet to download missing packages".
1> All packages listed in packages.config are already installed.
1> saf_mobileService -> C:\Users\saf\Documents\Visual Studio 2013\
Projects\saf-mobile\saf_mobileService\bin\saf_mobileService.dll
2>------ Publish started: Project: saf_mobileService, Configuration:
Release Any CPU ------
2>Transformed Web.config using C:\Users\saf\Documents\Visual Studio 2013\
Projects\saf-mobile\saf_mobileService\Web.Release.config into obj\Release\
TransformWebConfig\transformed\Web.config.
2>Auto ConnectionString Transformed obj\Release\TransformWebConfig\
transformed\Web.config into obj\Release\CSAutoParameterize\
transformed\Web.config.
2>Copying all files to temporary location below for package/publish:
2>obj\Release\Package\PackageTmp.
2>Start Web Deploy Publish the Application/package to https://waws-prod-
bay-015.publish.azurewebsites.windows.net/msdeploy.axd?site=mobile$
saf-mobile …
2>Access control lists for the path (mobile$saf-mobile)
2> Access control lists for the path (mobile$saf-mobile)
2>Updated file (mobile$saf-mobile\bin\Microsoft.Data.Edm.dll).
2>Added file (mobile$saf-mobile\bin\Microsoft.Data.OData.dll).
2> Added file (mobile$saf-mobile\bin\Microsoft.Owin.dll).
2> Added file (mobile$saf-mobile\bin\Microsoft.Owin.Host.SystemWeb.dll).
2> Added file (mobile$saf-mobile\bin\Microsoft.Owin.Security.
ActiveDirectory.dll).
2> Added file (mobile$saf-mobile\bin\Microsoft.Owin.Security.Cookies.dll).
2> Added file (mobile$saf-mobile\bin\Microsoft.Owin.Security.dll).
2> Added file (mobile$saf-mobile\bin\Microsoft.Owin.Security.Facebook.dll).
2> Added file (mobile$saf-mobile\bin\Microsoft.Owin.Security.Google.dll).
2> Added file (mobile$saf-mobile\bin\Microsoft.Owin.Security.Jwt.dll).
2> Added file (mobile$saf-mobile\bin\Microsoft.Owin.Security.
MicrosoftAccount.dll).
2> Added file (mobile$saf-mobile\bin\Microsoft.Owin.Security.OAuth.dll).
2> Added file (mobile$saf-mobile\bin\Microsoft.Owin.Security.Twitter.dll).
2> Added file (mobile$saf-mobile\bin\Microsoft.ServiceBus.dll).
2> Added file (mobile$saf-mobile\bin\Microsoft.WindowsAzure.Mobile.
Service.dll).
2> Added file (mobile$saf-mobile\bin\Microsoft.WindowsAzure.Mobile.
Service.Entity.dll).
2> Added file (mobile$saf-mobile\bin\Microsoft.WindowsAzure.Mobile.
Service.Tables.dll).
2> Added file (mobile$saf-mobile\bin\Newtonsoft.Json.dll).
2> Added file (mobile$saf-mobile\bin\Owin.dll).
2> Added file (mobile$saf-mobile\bin\RazorEngine.dll).
```

```
2> Added file (mobile$saf-mobile\bin\saf_mobileService.dll).
2> Added file (mobile$saf-mobile\bin\System.Net.Http.Formatting.dll).
2> Added file (mobile$saf-mobile\bin\System.Spatial.dll).
2> Added file (mobile$saf-mobile\bin\System.Web.Http.dll).
2> Added file (mobile$saf-mobile\bin\System.Web.Http.OData.dll).
2> Added file (mobile$saf-mobile\bin\System.Web.Http.Owin.dll).
2> Added file (mobile$saf-mobile\bin\System.Web.Http.Tracing.dll).
2> Added file (mobile$saf-mobile\bin\System.Web.Razor.dll).
2> Added file (mobile$saf-mobile\Global.asax).
2> Added file (mobile$saf-mobile\packages.config).
2> Added file (mobile$saf-mobile\Web.config).
2>Access control lists added for the path (mobile$saf-mobile)
2> Access control lists added for the path (mobile$saf-mobile)
2>Publish Succeeded.
2>Site was published successfully http://saf-mobile.azure-mobile.net/
========== Build: 1 succeeded, 0 failed, 0 up-to-date, 0 skipped ==========
========== Publish: 1 succeeded, 0 failed, 0 skipped ==========
```

Finally, the publishing is finished. Next moment, the development environment launches the browser visualizing the Web page of the mobile service published in the cloud (see Figure 5.92).

Developing the Mobile Application

As a mobile application, we use the example of the *saf-mobile* solution presented by the cloud. It contains two projects: the mobile service *saf_mobileService* we have already published, and a template for the mobile application *saf_mobile*.

Following the recommendations of the Azure cloud developers on the mobile application development pages, first let us install the external software packages

Figure 5.92   Web page of the mobile service published in the cloud.

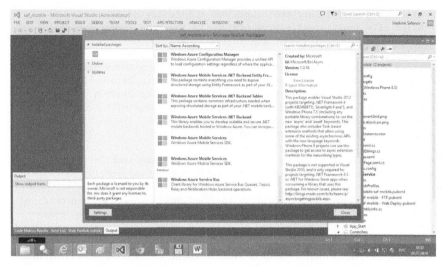

Figure 5.93 Searching and installing the *WindowsAzure.MobileServices* package by the NuGet utility.

used by the mobile application. As you may already know from your previous projects, external software package management in the Visual Studio development environment is performed by a special utility *NuGet*. With its help, we find on the network the package for developing mobile applications *Microsoft.WindowsAzure. MobileServices*. This package enables the interaction between the client mobile application and the mobile service.

In Figure 5.93, the process of searching and installing the *Microsoft.WindowsAzure. MobileServices* package is shown.

In Figure 5.94, the result of the installation of the *WindowsAzure.MobileServices* is depicted.

Below is the fragment of C# code of the mobile application (its file *App.Xaml.cs*), which enables calling the mobile service from the client mobile application:

```
public static MobileServiceClient MobileService =
  new MobileServiceClient(
     "https://saf-mobile.azure-mobile.net/",
     "..."
     // the password omitted for accessing the mobile service
);
```

The mobile application accesses the table of the current plans and to-do items – *TodoItems*, supported by the mobile service as a cloud database in Azure.

Using GUI of the mobile application *saf_mobile*, new rows can be entered into the *TodoItems* table. Then, the table can be browsed using the cloud.

Figure 5.94 *WindowsAzure.MobileServices* package installed.

To enable the access to the table from the mobile application, let us modify its code by inserting into the main method *Application_Launching* (launching the mobile application) the following code:

```
// Code to execute when the application is launching (eg, from Start)
// This code will not execute when the application is reactivated
private async void Application_Launching
    (object sender, LaunchingEventArgs e)
    {
    TodoItem item =
        new TodoItem { Text = "Awesome item", Complete = false };
    await
    App.MobileService.GetTable<TodoItem>().InsertAsync(item);
}
```

On updating the code of the client mobile application, let us build the application by selecting the item *Build* from the contextual menu.

Next, launch the mobile service and the mobile application by clicking F5.

The mobile service is launched as shown in Figure 5.92.

The result of selecting *Try It Out* on the mobile service page is shown in Figure 5.95, which shows the structure of the cloud database *TodoList* and the commands of the HTTP protocol (GET, POST, etc.) used to send information from the client to the server.

Unfortunately, on our computer we cannot launch the pair "mobile application – mobile service" which would enable us to watch their interaction on the local

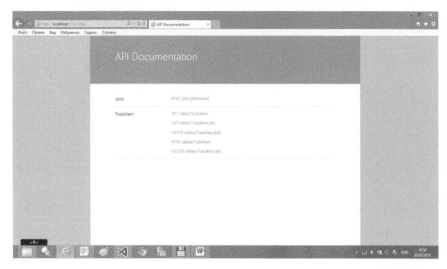

Figure 5.95 Visualizing by the mobile service of the structure of the cloud database.

machine. The reason is as follows: the computer does not support the *Hyper-V* technology of hardware virtualization. On computers with hardware support of Hyper-V, the emulators of the mobile phones are launched in their own virtual machines. On the other kinds of computers, development of mobile applications in the Visual Studio 2013 Update 2 is possible, but the debugging and launching mobile applications is possible only on real mobile phones on the platform Windows Phone 8/8.1. Please keep it in mind during your experiments.

Back Connection of the Mobile Service to Mobile Client: Push Notifications

It is possible to establish back connection of the mobile service to the mobile client in the form of the so-called *push notifications* – messages and screen forms sent by the mobile service to the mobile client, to remind that new information should be entered into the cloud database, or some changes should be made in the cloud database. For example, the mobile service can suggest to the mobile client to enter a new record (row) into the database or to change the values of some of its fields. An example is shown in Figure 5.96.

The necessary settings of the mobile service for sending push notifications to the mobile client can be dome in the cloud, in the *Push* menu item (see Figure 5.97).

Summary

The Visual Studio 2013 (Update 2) development environment, together with the Windows Phone SDK, enables the development, debugging, and use of mobile services and the connected mobile applications for the Microsoft Azure platform. Templates of mobile application projects are provided. Tutorials (including their textual parts

Figure 5.96 Examples of push notifications from the mobile service on the screen of the mobile device.

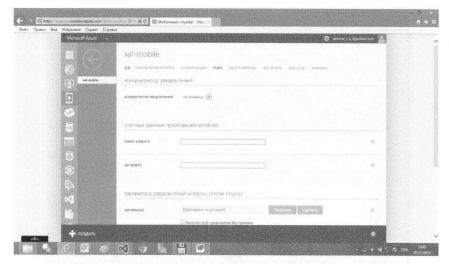

Figure 5.97   Setting the mobile service in the cloud for sending push notifications to the mobile client.

and the source codes), when accessing from the cloud, are tuned to the concrete user and the concrete project to make the life easier, according to the principles of user-centric computing. If the client computer supports the Hyper-V technology, debugging mobile applications on mobile phone emulators is possible; otherwise, debugging mobile applications is possible only using real phones on the Windows Phone 8/8.1 platforms. It should also be emphasized that the development environment is comfortable enough to organize communication between the mobile services and the connected mobile applications. Also convenient is the mechanism of push notifications that the mobile service can send to the mobile client.

5.11   MEDIA SERVICES

Media services allow the Azure users to create, deliver, stream, protect, and encode media content, in particular, video files.

For one Azure subscription, multiple media services can be created.

To create a media services account, it is necessary to provide the following information:

- A name of the media services account;
- A region to create the new account (choose the region from the drop-down list);
- A storage account. The general idea is to store media content as a blob, so the storage account is necessary to store this blob. The storage account must be created in the same region as the media services account.

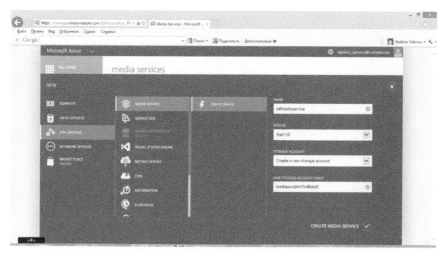

Figure 5.98 Cloud page for creating media services accounts.

Figure 5.99 Media services account created.

Now let us practice creating and manipulating media services accounts. To create the new account, we use the *Media Services* section of the Azure dashboard. Figure 5.98 depicts the cloud page for creating media services accounts.

For our account we choose the name *safmediaservice*, the region proposed by the cloud – *East US,* and the option *Create new storage account* – the storage account for the media blob will be created together with the media services account. The proposed name of the new storage account is *mediasvcq8ml7mllbkzl5*.

In a few moments, the new media services account is created and displayed in the Azure dashboard (see Figure 5.99).

Figure 5.100   Cloud page for starting to work with the media services account.

As usual, the status (active), the subscription ID, and location (East US) are visualized.

To use possible actions on the new media services account, click the name of the media services account – *safmediaservice*. We are switched to yet another cloud page for starting the work with the new account (see Figure 5.100).

The cloud allows us to manage media access keys, to upload a video file, or to start a project of uploading video programmatically, either in C# or in Java.

We choose the simplest action – upload a video file. The uploading content window is opened. It requires us to give a name to our video content (let us choose the name *my_video_file*), and to browse for a video file to be downloaded. The video file can be uploaded either from local disks on our computer or from the cloud storage. The maximum size of the video file uploaded from the local disks is 200 megabytes. The parameters for the media file to be uploaded are shown in Figure 5.101, which depicts the video file upload window.

The cloud issues a warning message on uploading the video file and displays a fragment of the cloud dashboard for the user to follow the process of uploading.

On finishing the upload, reference to the uploaded content (as a blob) is visualized in the Azure dashboard. Now we are invited to *publish* the media content in the cloud. Publishing means assigning the URL address to the video content under which the media file will be accessible on the Web for playback. On clicking *Publish*, we get the desired URL address in the Azure dashboard (see Figure 5.102).

Now we can click *Play* to playback the video file in the cloud, using the Media Services Content Player, part of Microsoft Azure. Only the published media can be played.

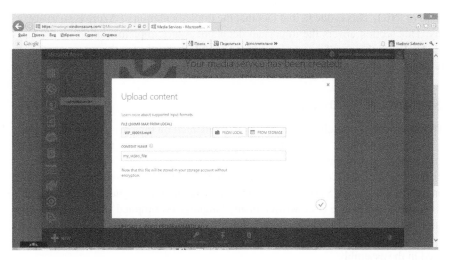

Figure 5.101   Video file upload window.

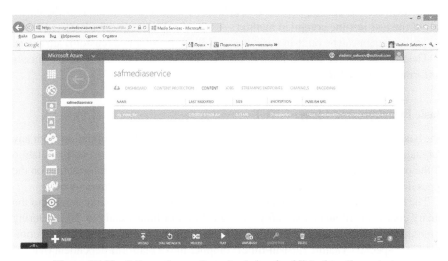

Figure 5.102   Information on the uploaded and published media content.

5.12   THE .NET PLATFORM – THE BASIS OF AZURE IMPLEMENTATION

In Chapter 3, I already briefly outlined the .NET platform as one of the most secure platforms in modern programming. The .NET platform is used as the foundation of the Microsoft Azure cloud platform. Most of Azure implementation is done on the basis of .NET. This is due to that fact that the implementation of Azure is so trustworthy. This section covers the important details of Azure implementation on the basis of .NET and the new features introduced in .NET, mostly for the purpose of more reliable and efficient implementation of Azure.

.NET Architecture Overview

The Microsoft Azure cloud platform is implemented on the basis of .NET.

As already stated in Chapter 3, .NET is a platform for reliable and secure multi-language programming.

It is based on the Common Language Infrastructure (CLI), used for all languages, on the Common Type System (CTS), and on the Common Language Runtime (CLR).

In .NET, the source code written in any language is compiled to an *assembly* containing the binary code in the Common Intermediate Language (CIL) – a postfix notation of the program, and the *metadata* – information on the types defined and used in the assembly.

Execution of a program in CLR is implemented as a sequence of method calls and just-in-time compilation of each method into native binary code during the first call of the method. The subsequent method calls are executed as execution of the native call of the just-in-time compiled method.

The metadata can be built-in attributes as well as user-defined (custom) attributes.

The metadata is the basis of runtime type checking and runtime security checks performed by the CLR.

Basic Principles and Ideas of .NET

The basic principles and ideas of .NET are as follows: It is the compilation from any language into the common intermediate binary code MSIL (CIL) – a postfix notation of the program, and generation by the compiler of the metadata – information on the types defined and used in any binary program module of the generated code.

The intermediate code, the metadata, and the *manifest* (the list of the content of the binary code) constitute an *assembly* – a logical unit of binary code in .NET. During program execution, when some method *M* is first called, its intermediate code is compiled by a special dynamic (just-in-time) compiler into a platform-dependent (native) code of the target hardware platform where the program is executed. A de facto standard used in .NET for configuration information and transferring information via the network is XML (extensible markup language).

The Advantages of the .NET Approach

The main advantage is the independence of the binary code of a concrete hardware platform. Also, the .NET virtual machine (CLR) executes the platform-independent binary code in a special mode – *managed execution* – which guarantees full checking of types and security. It enables reliability and security of programs, as opposed to many older languages and platforms, for example, C.

Multi-language programming is yet another important principle of .NET: the programmer can develop the modules of his program in any comfortable language, and .NET ensures *interoperability* of those modules within the framework of the same program.

Extended requirements to security is yet another characteristic feature of .NET. In addition, .NET has comfortable state-of-the-art mechanisms to support Web programming.

The .NET Framework Architecture

In Figure 5.103, the architecture of the Basic Class Library (BCL) of the .NET Framework is depicted.

The names of the namespaces and classes in BCL are self-evident. Very important is that each of the BCL classes can be used when programming in *any* language implemented for .NET – C#, Visual Basic, Managed C++, and so on.

The most important for this book are the namespaces *System.Web* – supporting of Web services – and *System.Security* – supporting installation, checking, and configuring the security permissions for the assemblies.

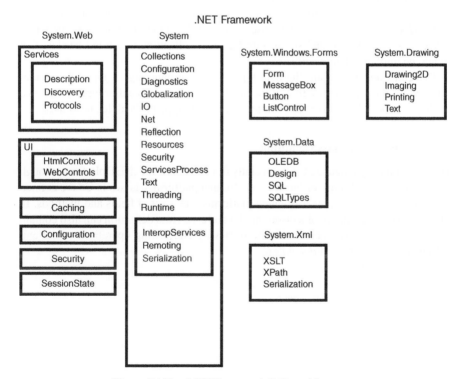

Figure 5.103   .NET Framework BCL architecture.

The Common Type System (CTS) of .NET

The common type system of .NET is an elegant unification of data type system in modern programming languages. I would like to emphasize that such kind of unification is just necessary in .NET since the CLR should "understand" all types of all languages in the same way.

The following kinds of types are available in the CTS.

The *value types* and the *reference types* are two main kinds of types in .NET, implementing the two different approaches to represent values and objects – the *container* approach and the *reference* approach.

The *simple* types (*int, double, unsigned int, native int,* etc.) are surely value types.

Structures (which is very helpful from practical viewpoint) are also classified as *value types* rather that reference types. It allows the developers to define in structures their own methods. The only feature lacking in structures (as compared to classes) is inheritance. Structures cannot inherit from each other. *Structures* are represented on the *stack* of the virtual machine, and *objects* (belonging to some classes) are allocated on the *heap.*

Managed pointer is a kind of pointers which are the basis for checking types and security in .NET. A managed pointer contains a reference to the type of the object (i.e., to metadata stored in this location of memory. Because of that, the type and the attributes of any object can be retrieved and checked at runtime.

Classes in .NET have similar meaning as in other object-oriented platforms.

Interface is also a commonly used concept for modern object-oriented languages – Java, C#, VB, and so on. Interface is a collection of method headers that should be implemented by some class.

Delegates and *events* are the data types for event handling. A type of the delegate defines the typical structure of the header for the event handler represented as a *callback method.* In an event declaration, a concrete type of the delegate is used.

The C# Language: Class Definition

The programming language C# is specially developed for the .NET platform, though it is not mandatory for use or the only one for that platform. Classes in C# are defined the way traditional for object-oriented platforms – as a set of fields and methods. In addition to other common object-oriented features, a class definition can also contain *properties* (generalized fields with the retrieving and setting operations of *set* and *get*), *indexers, events*, and *delegates.*

An example of a class:

```
public class Person :IPersonAge
{
private int YOB;
public Person()
{
}
public int YearOfBirth
{
```

```
   get { return YOB; };
   set { YOB = value; };
}
public int GetAgeToday()
{
   return Today()-
         YearOfBirth    };
}
```

Web Services in .NET

The concept of a Web service in .NET supports services as classes whose interface is available via the Web. Web services in .NET are based on the standards covered in the previous chapters (WSDL, SOAP, XML). Web services in .NET are based on the NET Framework class library.

In Figure 5.104, the structure of a distributed Web application in .NET is depicted.

The Web application consists of the client side and the server side. The Web service should satisfy some definite *contract* (i.e., should implement some definite interface).

The infrastructure of a Web service in .NET is depicted in Figure 5.105.

A .NET Web service can process several kinds of requests by the Web clients. When *discovering* (opening) the service, the client sends a request of the kind: *vsdisco*. Discovery services answer to the client by the information on locating the Web service – that can be the UDDI directory, the cloud, and so on. On answering another kind of request – *WSDL* – the service sends to the client the structure of its interface in XML format. The structure of that XML file is based on the WSDL (Web

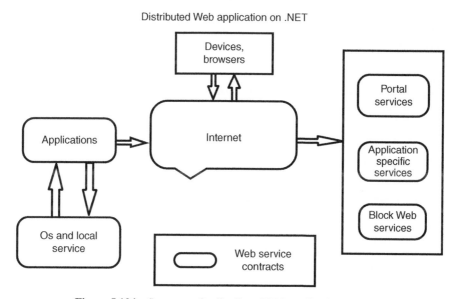

Figure 5.104 Structure of a distributed Web application in .NET.

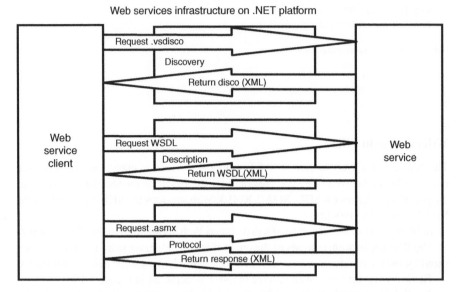

Figure 5.105   Infrastructure of a Web service in .NET.

Service Description Language) standard. On answering the third kind of requests, *asmx,* the Web service sends to the client its implementation (asmx) file in XML format.

In Figure 5.106, a simple example of the code of a Web service is shown that performs subtraction of two numbers and delivers the result.

In the listing below is the structure of the WSDL specification of a .NET Web service, consisting of *services*, *ports,* and *messages.*

```
<definitions name="serviceName">
<import namespace="http://namespacePath"
location="http://path/fileName.wsdl">
<portType name="serviceNamePortType">
<operation name="opName">
<input message="msgNameInput" />
<output message="msgNameOutput" />
</operation>
</portType>
<binding name="serviceNameSoapBinding">
<soap:operation soapAction="http://… " />
</binding>
<service name="serviceName">
<port name="serviceNamePort" binding="bindingName">
<soap:address location="http://… " />
</port>
</service>
</definitions>
```

Example of implementation of a Web service on .NET

```
<%@ WebService Language="C#" Class = "MathService" %>

using System;
using System.Web.Services;

public class MathService
{
   [WebMethod]
   public int Subtract (int a, int b)
   {
      return a - b;
   }

   public int Subtract_vs (int a, int b)
   {
      return b - a;
   }
}
```

Figure 5.106   Simple example of the code of a .NET Web service.

The use of .NET Web services is based on the following principles. The logics of implementation and call are fully separated. The service is represented as a pair of files: *.aspx* and *.aspx.cs* (or *.aspx.vb*). The *.aspx* files are intended for the designers, and the *aspx.cs* are for program developers. Because of that, it is easy to maintain the application.

A fragment of the code of a Web service:

```
<%@ Import Namespace="MathServiceSpace" %>
<script language="C#" runat="server">
public void Submit_Click(Object S, EventArgs E) {
service.Add(operand1, operand2);
…
</script>
…
<input OnServerClick="Submit_Click" runat="server" …>
```

New Features of the .NET Framework 4.5

As with Microsoft Azure, the .NET platform – one of the foundations for its implementation – is evolving rapidly: the performance is being improved, and new features are being implemented for parallel programming, networking communication, and so on. It is notable that the new features of NET 4.5, no doubt, are targeted mostly to the demand of enhancement of Microsoft Azure and impact deeply the performance and architectural enhancements of the Azure cloud. Let us consider those new features in more detail.

Major New Features of .NET 4.5

The following new features of .NET 4.5 are of especial importance for implementing Microsoft Azure:

- Support for development for .NET applications for Windows Store
- Support for development of portable class libraries (including those for ДЛЯ Windows Phone and for Windows Store)
- Support for large arrays (larger than 2 Gb)
- Background garbage collection for servers
- Background JIT compilation for multicore processors
- Improved performance when extracting resources of applications
- New features for parallel programming.

New Features of ASP.NET 4.5

ASP.NET is a set of libraries to support the development of Web applications and Web sites. The following new features of ASP.NET, implemented in version 4.5, are of especial importance for implementing Microsoft Azure:

- Support for new form types in HTML5 (please recall that one of the primary goals of HTML 5 is to support cloud computing)
- Support for model binders in Web forms. This feature allows the developers to bind data controls immediately to data access methods, and to automatically convert the user input into .NET Framework types
- Support using JavaScript in client-side checking scripts
- Improved client scripts processing by binding and minimization that improves performance when processing pages
- Integrated subroutines for encoding from the AntiXSS library (that library was an external library in earlier versions) for protection from site cross-scripting attacks
- Support for the WebSockets protocol
- Support for reading and writing HTTP requests and answers in asynchronous mode
- Support for asynchronous modules and handlers
- Support for reservation of the CDN in the *ScriptManager* control.

New Networking Features of .NET 4.5

The following new networking features of .NET are most important for implementing Microsoft Azure:

- .NET Framework 4.5 provides new application programming interface for HTTP-based applications. More information can be found in MSDN documentation for the namespaces *System.Net.Http* and *System.Net.Http.Headers*

- New APIs are implemented for interaction to *WebSocket* connections using the existing class *HttpListener* and the related classes. Extra information can be found in MSDN documentation on the namespace *System.Net.WebSockets* and the class *HttpListener*.

Besides that, in .NET Framework 4.5, networking features are enhanced as follows:

- RFC-compatible support of processing URI addresses. Extra information can be found in MSDN documentation of the *Uri* class and other related classes
- Support for parsing internationalized domain names (IDN). Extra information can be found in MSDN documentation for the *Uri* class and the related classes
- Support for internationalized email addresses (Email Address Internationalization (EAI)). More information can be found in MSDN documentation for the namespace *System.Net.Mail*
- Improved support for the IPv6 protocol (the new version of the Internet protocol). More information can be found in MSDN documentation for the namespace *System.Net.NetworkInformation*
- Support for dual-mode sockets. More information can be found in MSDN documentation for the classes *Socket* and *TcpListener*.

New Features of Windows Communication Foundation (WCF) in .NET Framework 4.5

In .NET Framework 4.5, some new features were added to simplify the development and maintenance of applications for WCF.

The following new features of WCF are most important for cloud computing in Microsoft Azure:

- Simplifying configuration files to be created
- Supporting development "from contract," that is, the contract becomes the starting point of the development. Let us recall that the contract of a service is a collection of its Web method headers. In WCF, Web methods are annotated by the attribute *[ServiceContract]*.
- Making settings for compatibility mode with ASP.NET simpler
- Changing the defaults for transportation properties to lower the probability of their settings
- Checking configuration files for WCF during the build of the service by Visual Studio, as part of the build process. Because of that, configuration bugs can now be detected before running the application
- New implementation of asynchronous stream transmission
- New feature of the HTTPS protocol implementation, simplifying the provisioning of the endpoint by HTTPS with the use of IIS services
- An opportunity to create metadata in one WSDL document by adding *?singleWSDL* to the URL address of the service

- Support of Websockets, to use really duplex connection by the ports 80 and 443, with performance characteristics similar to the TCP transport
- Support of setting the services in the code
- Pop-up helps of the XML editor
- Support of caching the *ChannelFactory*
- Support of compression by the binary coder
- Support of the UDP transport that allows the developers to write services using message transput according to the principle "send and forget." The client sends the message to the service and does not wait for an answer from the service
- An opportunity to support several authentication modes from one endpoint of the WCF service when using secure HTTP
- Support of WCF services using IDNs

Architecture of Microsoft Azure and the Implementation of Cloud Web Services

Now let us proceed with the Azure architecture and the implementation of cloud Web services using .NET.

The architecture of Microsoft Azure was covered in detail earlier in this chapter. Now let us recall some of its major features.

Fabric in Microsoft Azure is a network of interrelated nodes: commodity servers, high-performance routers, switches, fiber optic connectors.

Azure Fabric Controller is a service that performs monitoring and provides virtual machines for executing cloud applications.

The major services of Microsoft Azure are as follows:

- *Compute:* Hosting scalable cloud services on the server OS platforms of Windows Server 2012 R2 and Windows Server 2008 R2 (see above)
- *Storage:* Managing non-relational date (see above)
- *Network:* Resources for interaction with external applications (Service Bus).

The functions of *Fabric Controller* are the following.

- *Error handling*: *Fault Domains* are units of error handling in the datacenter (e.g., a cluster of servers).
- *Update Domains*: updating domains during the upgrades (of the operating system and the services).

The owners of cloud applications describe the required resources in the format of *resource descriptors* (models of services).

The Fabric Controller automatically provides the required resources.

Fabric Controller enables the tolerance of resources to errors, quick access to resources, early detection of faults in applications, and creation of extra instances on demand. The new instances are allocated over fault domains and update domains.

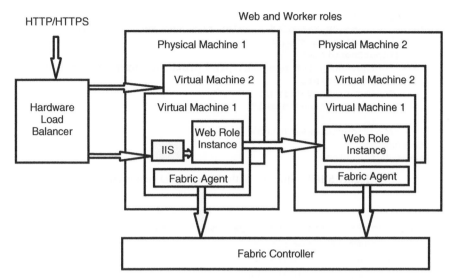

Figure 5.107   Web and Worker roles.

In Azure, the **Web** and **Worker** roles are distinguished. Essentially, each role in Azure is some kind of applications. The Web and Worker roles are depicted in Figure 5.107.

Web role is an interactive .NET application served by the IIS – a Web Application or a Web Service implemented in WCF.

Worker role is an independent isolated background process. Some ways are provided for accessing it from external applications.

The Fabric Agent keeps the metrics of the resources, such as their usage and the related errors.

The Service Model: The Service Definition

The file *ServiceDefiniton.csdef* defines the general structure of the service:

vmsize: CPU cores (1–8) and memory size for the virtual machine (1.7–15 GB)

full/partial trust: supporting execution of native code

Endpoint: internal and external communication points (HTTP, HTTPS, TCP)

LocalStorage: temporary storage on the server where the object is executed

ConfigurationSettings: the names of configuration parameters

The service definition file is processed during the deployment of the application.

The structure of the service definition file is depicted in Figure 5.108.

```
<ServiceDefinition name="MyService" ...>
  <WebRole name="MyWebRole" enableNativeCodeExecution="false"
           vmsize="Medium">
      <InputEndpoints>
          <InputEndpoint name="HttpIn" protocol="http" port="80"   />
      </InputEndpoints>
      <ConfigurationSettings>
          <Setting name="name1"   />
          ...
      </ConfigurationSettings>
  </WebRole>
</ServiceDefinition>
```

Figure 5.108   Structure of the file ServiceDefiniton.csdef.

```
<ServiceConfiguration serviceName="MyService"   xmlns="..."
   <Role name="MyWebRole">
       <Instances  count="3"   />
       <ConfigurationSettings>
           <Setting  name="name1"  value="value1"      />
       </ConfigurationSettings>
   </Role>
</ServiceConfiguration>
```

Figure 5.109   Structure of the file ServiceConfiguration.csdef.

Service Model: Service Configuration

The file ServiceConfiguration.csdef defines the configuration of the services. It contains the number of instances for each role and defines the values for configuration settings.

The content of the file ServiceConfiguration.csdef can be changes at execution time.

The structure of the service configuration file is depicted in Figure 5.109.

The class diagram of the Microsoft Azure Role API (to be used for implementing Web and Worker roles by cloud service developers) is shown in Figure 5.110.

In this diagram, the class *BasicEntryPoint* (with the descendants *MyWebRole* and *MyWorkerRole)* contains the lifecycle methods of a role – *onStart(), onStop(), run()*.

The class *RoleEnvironment* has two descendants – *Role* and *RoleInstance*.

The implementation of roles is depicted in Figure 5.111.

In the implementation of a role, the descendant class *RoleEntryPoint* is defined and the lifecycle methods are overloaded. Usually, the method *OnStart()* is overloaded. A handler is registered that listens to the changes in the configuration of the cloud storage account. When such change is registered, the role is restarted (reused).

Implementation of **Web** and **Worker** roles is shown in Figure 5.112.

In Web role implementation, there are no differences from the standards of ASP.NET Web Forms, ASP.NET MVC, and WCF applications.

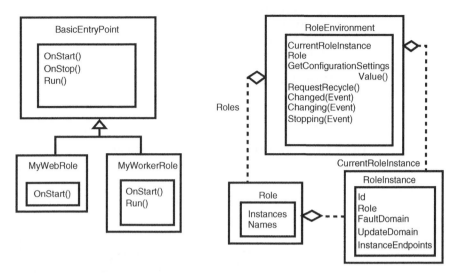

Figure 5.110 Windows Azure Role API class diagram.

```
public class MyRole: RoleEntryPoint {
  public override bool OnStart () {
    CloudStorageAccount.SetConfigurationSettingPublisher(
      (configName, configSetter) =>
        configSetter(RoleEnvironment.
          GetConfigurationSettingValue(coinfigName));
        RoleEnvironment.Changed += (sender, arg) => {
          if (arg.Changes.OfType
                <RoleEnvironmentConfigurationSettingChange> ()
                .Any((change) => {change.ConfigurationSettingName ==
                                  configName))) {
            if (!configSetter
                (RoleEnvironment.GetConfigurationSettingValue
                  (configName)))
              RoleEnvironment.RequestRecycle();
        }; // handler for Changed event
    }); // SetConfigurationSettingPublisher
    return base.OnStart();
  }
}
```

Figure 5.111 Implementation of roles.

In Worker role implementation, the method *Run()* is overloaded from the class *RoleEntryPoint*. This method serves as the main thread of execution for this role.

As an alternative implementation, is possible to listen to the external HTTP(S) or TCP communication points for incoming messages.

The interaction between roles is shown in Figure 5.113.

```
public class WorkerRole : RoleEntryPoint {
  public override void Run () {
    while (true) {
      // get next message
      // process message
      // delete message
      Thread.Sleep (1000);
    }
  }
}
```

Figure 5.112   Implementation of Web and Worker roles.

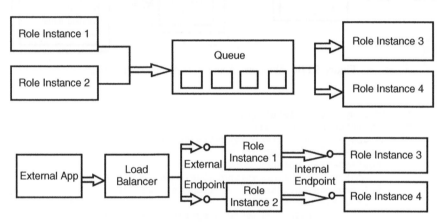

Figure 5.113   Interaction between the roles.

The instances of the roles can interact asynchronously by message queues. This is a preferable method of reliable message communication.

Also, the instances of the roles can interact immediately by TCP or HTTP(S) connections.

Interaction between the roles based on *WCF/TCP* is shown in Figures 5.114–5.116.

In the example, the service *xxx* is implemented. The attributes define the service contract. For configuring the worker role, external or internal communication points are added. The hosting of the WCF service is implemented. In implementing the client, when using internal communication points, the sender has to perform load balancing "by hand." To find those communication points, the construct *Environment.Roles["TargetRole"]* should be used.

Interactions between the roles based on WCF/TCP

```
[ServiceContract(Namespace="...")]
public interface ICalculator {
  [OperationContract]
  double Add(double a, double b);
}

public class CalculatorService: ICalculator {
  public double Add(double a, double b) {
    return a + b;
  }
}

<ServiceDefinition name="CalcService" ... >
  <WorkerRole name="CalcRole" enableNativeCodeExecution="true" >
    <EndPoints>
      <InputEndpoint name="CalcServiceEP" port="5000" protocol="tcp" />
      <InternalEndpoint name="MyInternalEP" protocol="tcp"/>
    </Endpoints>
  </WorkerRole>
</ServiceDefinition>
```

Figure 5.114   Interaction between roles based on WCF/TCP: Service.

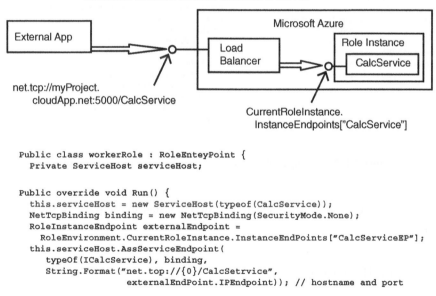

Interaction between the roles based on WCF/TCP

```
Public class workerRole : RoleEnteyPoint {
  Private ServiceHost serviceHost;

Public override void Run() {
  this.serviceHost = new ServiceHost(typeof(CalcService));
  NetTcpBinding binding = new NetTcpBinding(SecurityMode.None);
  RoleInstanceEndpoint externalEndpoint =
    RoleEnvironment.CurrentRoleInstance.InstanceEndPoints["CalcServiceEP"];
  this.serviceHost.AssServiceEndpoint(
    typeOf(ICalcService), binding,
    String.Format("net.top://{0}/CalcSetrvice",
                  externalEndPoint.IPEndpoint)); // hostname and port
```

Figure 5.115   Interaction between roles based on WCF/TCP: Hosting.

Interaction between the roles based on WCF / TCP

```
NetTcpBinding binding = new NetTcpBinding(SecurityMode.None, false);
using (ChannelFactory<ICalcService> cf =
  new ChannelFactory<ICalcService>(binding,
                                   "net.tcp://5000/CalcService")) {
  ICalcService calcProxy = cf.CreateChannel();
  double sum = calcProxy.Add(1, 2);
}
```

```
foreach(RoleInstance ri in RoleEnvironment.Roles["CalcRole"].Instances) {
  RoleInstanceEndpoint ep = ri.InstanceEndpoints["MyInternalEP"];
  string address = String.Format("net.tcp://{0}/MyService", ep.IPEndpoint);
  var cf = new ChannelFactory<IMyService>(binding, address);
```

Figure 5.116   Interaction between roles based on WCF/TCP: Client.

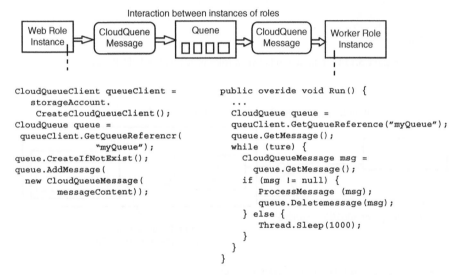

Interaction between instances of roles

Web Role Instance → CloudQuene Message → Quene → CloudQuene Message → Worker Role Instance

```
CloudQueueClient queueClient =            public override void Run() {
    storageAccount.                         ...
      CreateCloudQueueClient();             CloudQueue queue =
CloudQueue queue =                          queuClient.GetQueueReference("myQueue");
 queueClient.GetQueueReferencr(             queue.GetMessage();
               "myQueue");                  while (ture) {
queue.CreateIfNotExist();                     CloudQueueMessage msg =
queue.AddMessage(                               queue.GetMessage();
  new CloudQueueMessage(                      if (msg != null) {
      messageContent));                         ProcessMessage (msg);
                                                queue.Deletemessage(msg);
                                            } else {
                                                Thread.Sleep(1000);
                                            }
                                          }
                                        }
```

Figure 5.117   Example of code of interaction between instances of roles.

An example of code of interaction between instances of roles is shown in Figure 5.117.

5.13   AZURE TOOLS

Recently, during the period of publication of my Azure courses [3–6], great progress has been achieved in the development and enhancement of tools for cloud services development for Microsoft Azure.

Figure 5.118   Choosing the item in the main menu of Azure for downloading Azure tools.

Currently, the following kinds of Microsoft Azure tools are available:

– Azure SDKs – toolkits for developing cloud applications for Microsoft Azure in different programming g languages and for different platforms
– Scripting languages and commandlets for Azure (e.g., Windows Azure Power-Shell).

Downloading of Azure tools is possible via the appropriate main menu item [125] of the Azure cloud. Also, as seen from the previous content of the chapter, the Azure platform in many cases suggests to the user what kind of tools should be downloaded for development of some concrete kinds of cloud applications (e.g., mobile services).

Figure 5.118 shows which way it is possible to go to the main page for downloading Azure tools – choose the Downloads item of the main Azure menu.

Azure SDKs

Azure SDKs is a set of toolkits for development of Azure cloud services. Such development is possible in many languages and platforms. In the latest version of Azure, the collection of Azure SDKs has greatly increased. There are Azure SDKs available for the following platforms and languages:

– .NET (in the C#, VB, F#, Managed C++ and other .NET languages) – by means of Visual Studio 2015 or Visual Studio 2013
– Node.js – a toolkit for quick creation of Web sites using JavaScript language (there are Azure SDKs available for Windows, Mac, and Linux)
– PHP (there are Azure SDKs for Windows, Mac, Linux)
– Java (there are Azure SDKs for Windows, Mac, Linux)
– Python (there are Azure SDKs for Windows, Mac, Linux)

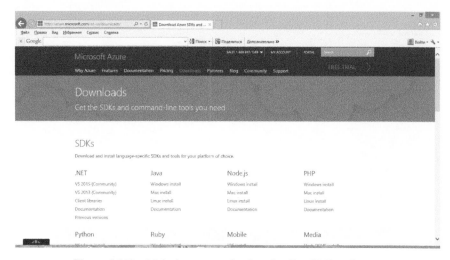

Figure 5.119 Main Azure page for downloading SDK packages.

- SDK packages for mobile platforms: Android, iOS, Windows Phone
- SDK packages for developing media services

In Figure 5.119, the main page for downloading SDK packages is depicted.

Command Line Tools for Microsoft Azure

There were no such tools in previous versions of Microsoft Azure. In the latest version, the following kinds of command-line tools for different platforms:

- *Windows Azure PowerShell* – a command-line toolkit for interaction with virtual machines and virtual networks for Microsoft Azure using *commandlets (cmdlets)*. This toolkit is similar to the new Windows PowerShell toolkit included into the latest server operating systems by Microsoft
- *Cross-platform Azure command line interface:*
- *Azure command-line interface for Windows*
- *Azure command-line interface for Mac*
- *Azure command-line interface for Linux.*

In Figure 5.120, the part of the main downloads page is depicted for downloading command-line Azure tools.

The latest achievement of the Azure team in this respect is a set of *Azure migration tools* targeted to migration of the existing user resources to Azure. Those are:

- *Virtual Machine assessment tools*
- *Virtual Machine optimization tools*
- *Azure Web site migration assistant.*

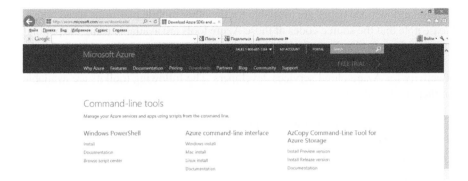

Figure 5.120   Part of the Azure page for downloading command-line Azure tools.

The references for downloading these tools are at the bottom of the Azure tools download page (not shown in the figures).

SDK Packages for Developing Mobile Services

In the latest version of Microsoft Azure, the following kinds of tools for developing mobile services are available:

- iOS
- Android
- Windows Store applications in C#
- Windows Store applications in JavaScript
- Windows Phone 8.

In Figure 5.121, a page for downloading tools for development of Azure mobile services for iOS is depicted.

Figure 5.121   Azure page for downloading tools for development of iOS mobile services.

Similar download pages are available for the other mobile platforms listed above. Please note that the source codes of those Azure tools are available using the popular source code control system *Git* [126].

Developing Azure services on the .NET platform is probably the most popular kind of activity for Azure cloud services developers. The following toolkits are available for them to download:

- Azure SDK for Visual Studio 2015
- Azure SDK for Visual Studio 2013
- Client libraries
- Documentation.

The Visual Studio development environment is in the state of active development and enhancement, in particular, for support of Microsoft Azure. In the latest version of Visual Studio 2015, the following new features are available:

- Support for developing projects that will work on .NET Framework 4.6 on Azure cloud virtual machines running on the latest server OS by Microsoft – Windows 2012 Server R2.

Azure SDKs for Java

Currently there are SDKs for developing Azure cloud services in Java for the following platforms:

- Windows
- Linux
- MacOS.

Detailed tutorials and textbooks are available on Java programming, and for popular Java development environment, for example, for Eclipse. There are also Azure client libraries for Java. Detailed documentation on all of these is available at [127].

For example, a textbook on Java Azure SDK describes how a virtual machine created in the Azure cloud can be configured for Java application server execution. In the Azure cloud, a virtual machine is created on which the Java Development Kit (JDK) is installed and then, with its help, a Java application server is launched. Thus, the Microsoft cloud helps further dissemination of the Java technology.

The source codes of the Azure SDK for Java and the client libraries for Java are available via the Git source code control system. I invite the readers to try those downloads and products.

Azure SDK Packages for Developing Cloud Media Services

This group of Azure tools is targeted to developing tools to playback media files in the Azure cloud using Azure media services (see above).

There are the following SDKs for developing cloud media services:

- SDK package for Windows 8;
- Pluggable module for OSMF (Open Source Media Framework – an open platform for developing media players);
- SDK package for iOS Media Player;
- SDK package for Silverlight;
- SDK package for Windows Phone 8.

The set of tools for creating various kinds of Microsoft Azure applications is growing fast.

5.14   MACHINE LEARNING IN THE CLOUD: AZURE MACHINE LEARNING STUDIO

Predictive analytics of big data and machine learning are one of the most popular topics of modern research in the area of computer science. Machine learning is part of *artificial intelligence* targeted at extracting data from knowledge. This section is an overview of a novel component of the Microsoft Azure platform – *Machine Learning Studio* [128].

Analysis of big data is very important for modern business and research. It is quite natural that cloud computing now includes machine learning tools, since it allows the developers to solve the issues of handling big data in the cloud, in the form of a cloud service. Azure Machine Learning is a technology available in the cloud that provides tools to import training data for machine learning, build, train and deploy the user's own training models using only a Web browser.

Azure Machine Learning provides a large collection of machine learning algorithms and supports the languages R and Python, which are quite popular in the area of data science. On developing a data model, it can be easily deployed and published in the form of a Web service. To work with machine learning, Microsoft Azure provides a studio that allows the developers to create data models, combining the forms together, to create an experiment that the user can run in Machine Learning Studio. If necessary, the user's own code can be added to it.

Development of machine learning applications in Java or in other modern languages from scratch is a very complicated task. Microsoft Azure Machine Learning Studio is an easy-to-use and simple tool for developing machine learning applications.

The architecture of the ML studio is shown in Figure 5.122.

ML Studio has the three major working zones. In the left part, the Saved Datasets, Data Input and Output, Machine Learning, and so on, tabs are located. Each of the tabs can be opened, the appropriate module can be chosen and dragged to the central zone. The central zone is named *Experiment*. This is a kind of interactive canvas. Here, the main drag-and-drop activities take place. On the right-hand side, details of the module chosen for the central zone are depicted.

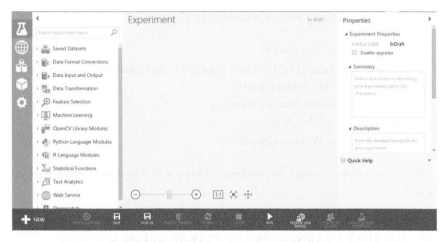

Figure 5.122   Architecture of Azure ML Studio.

The data for experiments can be generated by a user application, or can be taken from sample datasets provided by Azure. Among sample data sets are USA airport codes, automobile price data, bike rental dataset, blood donation data, and so on.

The stages of organizing a machine learning experiment in Azure ML Studio are as follows:

– getting data for the model from one or several sources
– preprocessing the model data (e.g., deleting some rows that have missing data)
– defining features (individual properties of the entities analyzed during an experiment)
– training the model: choosing and applying a learning algorithm
– scoring and testing the model.

The goal of an experiment is to predict some values of interest. For example, in the tutorial on Azure ML Studio [128], a sample experiment on predicting automobile prices is considered.

Azure ML studio supports various kinds of data formats, in particular:

– plain text
– comma-separated values
– tab-separated values
– hive table
– SQL database table
– OData values
– .zip file
– R object or workspace file (.RData).

R is a scripting programming language for statistical data processing and graphics applications whose implementation is available in Azure ML Studio. The advantages of R language are built-in analytics features and flexibility. R is an open-source product within the GNU framework.

A new experiment in ML Studio (see Figure 5.122) is created by clicking +NEW at the bottom of the ML Studio window. Then, the user is to select EXPERIMENT, and then *Blank experiment*. The default experiment name should be changed to something meaningful, for example, *Automobile price prediction*, as in the tutorial example.

The general idea of the ML Studio is that the components for the experiment should be connected together using their *input and output ports*. This selected sequence of the input and output ports determines the sequence of stages of the experiment.

There is a palette of datasets and modules to the left of the experiment canvas. The user can find an appropriate dataset, for example, *Automobile price data*, for the experiment.

Then, the chosen dataset should be dragged to the experiment canvas. To visualize the dataset, the user should click the output port at the bottom and select *Visualize*. The dataset is displayed in the form of the set of rows and columns.

At the stage of data analysis, the module *Missing Values Scrubber* is helpful to analyze which values are missing, to exclude the corresponding rows or columns from the experiment data.

On finishing the missing values analysis, the user can run the experiment by clicking RUN under the experiment canvas. When the experiment ends, all its modules will have a green check mark, which means they have completed successfully. Also, the *Finished running* status appears on the right upper corner of the canvas.

When the data for the experiment are ready, the user should construct a predictive model. It consists of *training* and *testing*. The model is trained using part of the input data, and the other part of data is used to *test* the model to estimate how close it is able to make predictions. The percentage of data to be used for training and testing can be defined in the *Fraction of rows in the first output dataset* field. For example, if this value is set to 0.75, it means that 75% of data will be used for training the model and 25% for its testing.

As for learning algorithms, there are two kinds of supervised machine learning techniques – *classification* (e.g., *Bayes* classifier that can be easily developed in R) and *regression*. Classification is used to make a prediction from a defined set of values (e.g., color – red, green, blue, etc.). Regression is used to make a prediction from a continuous set of values, for example, a person's age, or a price of a car. The most popular is *linear regression*.

The specifics of the formulas used for calculating the predictions are outside the scope of the book. See Ref. [128] for more details.

To start working with Azure ML Studio, it is necessary to create an ML workspace. To do that, the user should choose the *Machine Learning* item in the Azure dashboard. Next, create an ML workspace following the recommendations of the cloud.

In Figure 5.123, the Azure cloud page for creating an ML workspace is depicted.

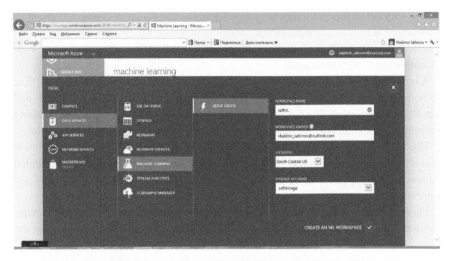

Figure 5.123   Creating an ML workspace in the Azure cloud.

The following information should be defined for creating an ML workspace:

- the *name of the workspace* (*safML*, in our example)
- the *name of the storage account* (*safstorage*, in our example)
- the *location (region)* where to create an ML workspace (in our example – *South Central US*, as suggested by the cloud.

The storage account should be created to keep the experimental data. The location of the storage account for the ML workspace and the location of the ML workspace itself should be the same.

In a few moments, our ML workspace is created. For the first experience, we will use the Gallery of experiments, part of ML studio. We choose the restaurant ratings recommended by Microsoft. The result of opening this experiment in Azure ML studio is depicted in Figure 5.124.

The My Experiments tab shows the scheme of the experiment. The Samples tab contains a plenty of samples prepared by Microsoft. All the samples from the Gallery have been recently created. The Gallery itself (at the moment of writing the book) is in the Preview stage. It confirms rapid evolution of Microsoft Azure. The Gallery contains

- machine learning APIs (e.g., for computer vision, text analytics, speech APIs, etc.)
- trending experiments by many companies
- Microsoft sample experiments.

In general, Azure Microsoft Machine Learning Studio is an elegant example of integration the latest achievements in cloud computing with state-of-the-art techniques of artificial intelligence. No doubt, this component of Azure will be very interesting for many users. I strongly advise the readers to learn the Azure ML studio using the Gallery.

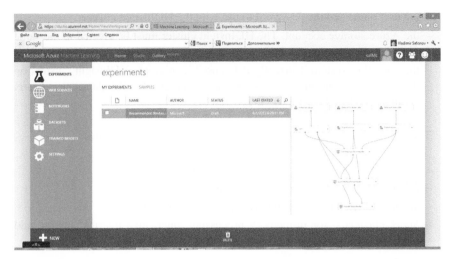

Figure 5.124 Opening an experiment from the gallery in our ML studio workspace.

5.15 PARALLEL PROCESSING OF BIG DATA IN THE CLOUD: USING APACHE HADOOP IN MICROSOFT AZURE

Apache Hadoop [129] is a popular technology for parallel handling big data. Because of the popularity of big data analysis, Microsoft included support of Hadoop into the new version of the Azure cloud. This section is a brief overview of Hadoop features in the Azure cloud.

Hadoop offers a distributed platform to store and manage large volumes of unstructured data, also known as Big Data.

Microsoft implemented Hadoop support as *HDInsight service*. The major features of the HDInsight are as follows:

- manage data of any type or size
- perform complex data analysis
- connect to the data using Microsoft Business Intelligence tools.

HDInsight uses Azure Blob storage for storing data. The user should specify the storage account in the appropriate region to locate the Hadoop cluster in the Azure cloud.

HDInsight makes Apache Hadoop available as an Azure cloud service.

When creating a new HDInsight service in Azure, the following information should be provided:

- Azure subscription name;
- the name of the instance;
- the number of data nodes to provision for the service (each data node is a *Compute* instance);

 – the user name and the password to use with the HDInsight cluster;
 – the Azure storage account. The HDInsight cluster must be created in the same region as the storage account;
 – the operating system. Currently it is possible to create HDInsight clusters on the following operating systems: Windows Server 2012 R2 Datacenter; Linux Ubuntu 12.04 LTS for Linux (in preview stage).

The following types of HDInsight clusters can be created in Azure:

 – *Hadoop clusters* – for query and analysis workloads;
 – *HBase clusters* – for NoSQL workloads;
 – *Storm clusters* – for real-time event processing workloads;
 – *Spark clusters* – for in-memory processing, interactive queries, stream, and machine learning workloads (currently in the preview stage).

To process big data, the cloud user should use *Hive* – a tool to make SQL-like queries.

The result of the query should be imported from Hive to Microsoft Excel for further use with other business intelligence tools.

An example of a Hive query is depicted in Figure 5.125.

As seen from the example, one of the versions of SQL is used in Hive.

As the further step, to connect to Microsoft Business Intelligence tools for Excel, cloud users should download and install the *Microsoft Power Query* add-in for Microsoft Excel 2010 or Microsoft Excel 2013.

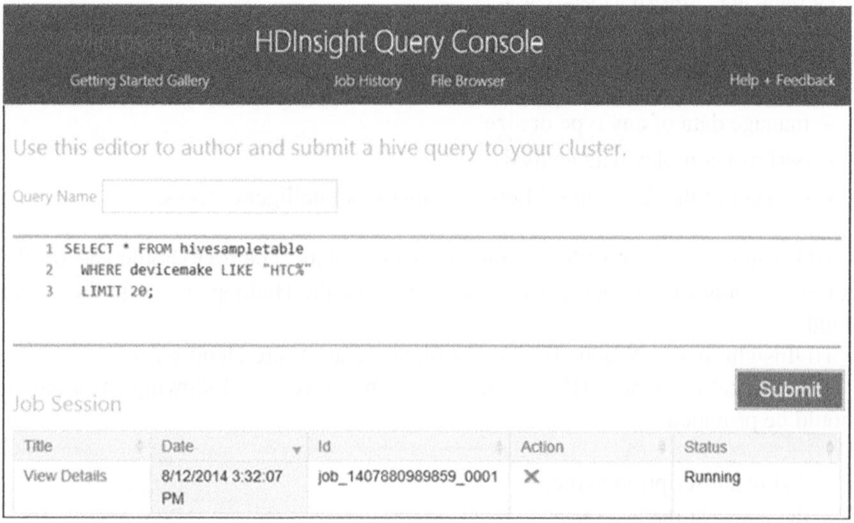

Figure 5.125   Example of a Hive query using Azure HDInsight.

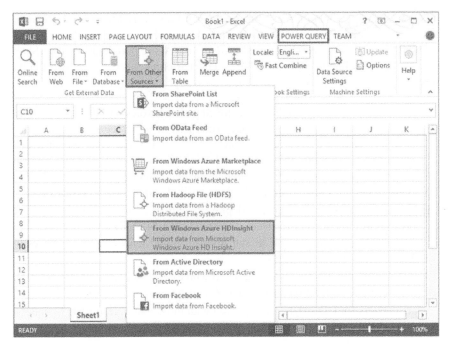

Figure 5.126 Importing the result of a Hive query from Azure HDInsight.

To import data from the HDInsight, the user should open the Power Query menu, then click *From Other Sources*, and then click *From Azure HDInsight*.

The result of running Excel with the Power Query add-in is shown in Figure 5.126.

Finally, to find and import the results of the query from Azure to Excel, the user should do the following:

– Enter the account name of the Azure Blob Storage account associated with the user's HDInsight cluster, and click OK.
– Enter the Account Key of the Azure Blob Storage account, and then click Save.
– In the right pane, double click the blob name. By default, the blob name is the same as the cluster name.
– Locate the result of the query by its name (e.g., *stdout*) in the *Name* column.
– Click *Close & Load* to import the Hive job output to Excel.

There are some other related tools available, for example:

– HDInsight Hadoop tools for Visual Studio
– HDInsight Emulator
– PowerShell commandlets for administering HDInsight.

The HDInsight emulator for Azure (formerly known as Microsoft HDInsight Developer Preview) supports only single-node deployments.

An HDInsight cluster can be created by using the Azure portal, or by PowerShell commandlets, or with the HDInsight .NET SDK. Different cluster types use different roles.

Hadoop clusters for HDInsight are deployed with two roles: Head node (2 nodes) and Data node (at least one node). The difference between the head nodes and the data nodes is as follows. The head node runs in just one machine – including the name node and the job tracker. They control where the data is and where the compute happens. Actually, the head node runs in one machine a few of the services, which make up the Hadoop platform.

HBase clusters for HDInsight are deployed with three roles: Head servers (2 nodes), Region servers (at least one node), and Master/Zookeeper nodes (3 nodes). Zookeeper is a tool to synchronize virtual machines and services in Microsoft Azure.

Storm clusters for HDInsight are deployed with three roles: Head node (2 nodes), Worker node (at least one node), and Zookeeper nodes (3 nodes).

Spark clusters for HDInsight are deployed with three roles: Head node (2 nodes), Worker node (at least one node), and Zookeeper nodes (3 nodes).

The nodes can have different sizes. Here are several typical examples of the node sizes:

- A3 (4 cores, 7 GB memory)
- A4 (8 cores, 14 GB memory)
- A6 (4 cores, 28 GB memory)
- A7 (8 cores, 56 GB memory)
- A10 (8 cores, 56 GB memory)
- A11 (16 cores, 112 GB memory)
- D12 (4 cores, 28 GB memory).

Configuring an HDInsight cluster is possible via the Azure portal, or via the PowerShell commandlets. The latter option is recommended by Microsoft Azure developers.

An example of configuring a HDInsight cluster in the Azure portal is depicted in Figure 5.127.

All in all, HDInsight is a state-of-the-art Azure component to manage big data in several ways. But Azure is not the only cloud platform to have such kind of functionality. The competitors – for example, IBM Bluemix cloud, have also developed similar features. It is very interesting and helpful for cloud users to track this competition and learn from it, which is what I recommend the readers to do.

In this big chapter on Microsoft Azure, however, I only overviewed some (not all) of the most interesting Azure features, and decided to finish it, not to test your

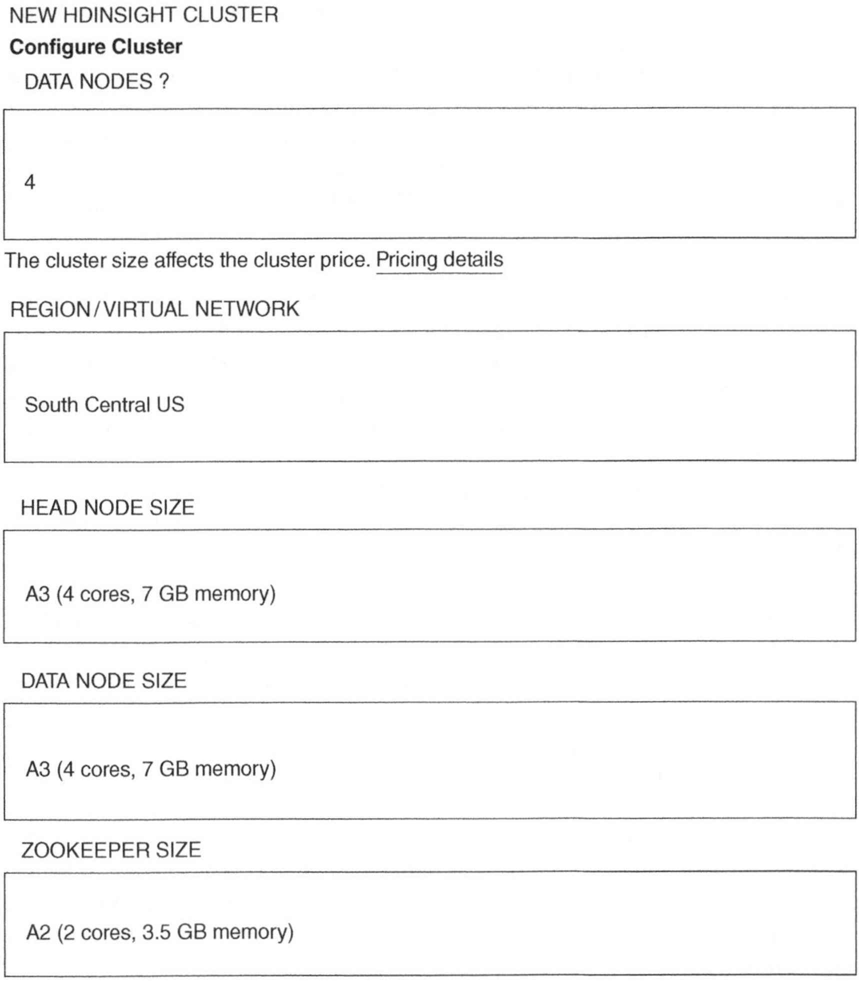

NEW HDINSIGHT CLUSTER
Configure Cluster
DATA NODES ?

```
4
```

The cluster size affects the cluster price. Pricing details

REGION / VIRTUAL NETWORK

```
South Central US
```

HEAD NODE SIZE

```
A3 (4 cores, 7 GB memory)
```

DATA NODE SIZE

```
A3 (4 cores, 7 GB memory)
```

ZOOKEEPER SIZE

```
A2 (2 cores, 3.5 GB memory)
```

Figure 5.127   Example of configuring a HDInsight cluster in the Azure portal.

patience any more with similar style descriptions of various Azure functionalities. As I am repeating throughout the book, cloud platforms, Microsoft Azure in particular, are rapidly evolving. So I leave it to the readers to have the pleasure to enjoy all features of Microsoft Azure.

5.16   PERSPECTIVES OF MICROSOFT AZURE

Based on my extensive experience of learning Microsoft Azure, using Microsoft Azure and teaching Microsoft Azure, in this section I summarize its perspectives and at least some trends in its development and enhancement.

The first development trend for all cloud platforms, including Microsoft Azure, is to port more and more non-cloud (on-premises) products of the software development company to the cloud. Recently, in the latest versions of Microsoft Azure, a number of on-premise Microsoft products have acquired their "second lives" in the cloud versions. Those products are SQL Azure database management system (SQL server, in non-cloud incarnation), Visual Studio Online (Visual Studio Team Foundation Server, in non-cloud version), Office 365 (Microsoft Office, in non-cloud version), and Azure Active Directory (Active Directory, in non-cloud version).

The second trend is to integrate Microsoft Azure with most of the existing non-cloud products by Microsoft (making bridges between Microsoft Azure and all other Microsoft products). For example, Visual Studio IDE is now linked with Visual Studio Online. Another example is BizTalk services, which allow the cloud users to use BizTalk in the cloud. A very important concept being implemented now in Azure is the idea of the Cloud OS, whose parts are Microsoft Azure and the Windows System Center.

The third trend is to create and make available SDKs targeted to development of applications for Azure in the most popular languages and platforms. Currently, SDKs are available for .NET, Java, Node.js, and many other software development platforms. This trend will surely continue in the future.

The fourth trend is getting available more and more cloud solutions and applications for Microsoft Azure. The commonly used portal for exchanging cloud solutions for Microsoft Azure is the *Marketplace*, available as one of the sections of the Azure portal.

This is just my personal opinion on the perspectives of Microsoft Azure. Plenty of publications do exist on the subject, many of which are cited in this book.

In general, I greatly appreciate the perspectives of Microsoft Azure as state-of-the-art, rapidly evolving, user-friendly cloud platform. I do think that the Microsoft Azure platform in the near future will be used in most areas of human activity. Based on my positive experience of working with Microsoft Azure for 5 years, I strongly recommend you to learn and use it, and wish you good luck in using Microsoft Azure.

EXERCISES TO CHAPTER 5

E5.1 Which portals are available to get access to Microsoft Azure?

E5.2 Which major components are available in the latest version of Microsoft Azure?

E5.3 What kind of functionality is enabled by the Microsoft Azure Compute component?

E5.4 What kind of functionality is enabled by the Microsoft Azure Data Services component?

E5.5 What kind of functionality is enabled by the Microsoft Azure Networking component?

E5.6   What kind of functionality is enabled by the Microsoft Azure App Services component?

E5.7   What kind of functionality is enabled by the Microsoft Azure Commerce component?

E5.8   What kind of cloud entities does the Compute allow the users to manage?

E5.9   What kind of cloud entities do the Data Services allow the users to manage?

E5.10 What is blob and for what kind of purposes are blobs used in Azure?

E5.11 What is SQL Database and in what form is it implemented in Azure?

E5.12 What is SQL Reporting and how is it used in Azure?

E5.13 What is SQL Data Sync and how is it used in Azure?

E5.14 What is HDInsight and how is it used in Azure?

E5.15 What is Microsoft Azure Connect and how is it used in Azure?

E5.16 What is Microsoft Azure Virtual Network component and how is it used in Azure?

E5.17 What is the Traffic Manager service and for what purposes is it used in Azure?

E5.18 What is ACS and for what purposes is it used in Azure?

E5.19 What is the Graph Control Library and how is it used in Azure, in relation to Azure Active Directory?

E5.20 What is CDN and how does it help to cache cloud objects in Azure to make their delivery to the users optimal?

E5.21 What are Storage Queues, and how and in which forms are they used in Azure?

E5.22 What is Service Bus and what kind of functionality does it perform in Azure?

E5.23 How and for which period is it possible to get trial access to Azure? Which Microsoft Web sites are used for registering new Azure users?

E5.24 How the Azure users are authenticated, and what is the starting point for logging into Azure? How the Azure management portal is organized?

E5.25 What kinds of cloud entities does Azure allow the users to handle?

E5.26 What kinds of features does Azure provide for managing Web sites?

E5.27 What kinds of features does Azure provide for managing virtual machines?

E5.28 What is a mobile service and what kind of functionalities does Azure provide for managing mobile services?

E5.29 What is a cloud service in Azure?

E5.30 How are cloud SQL databases are handled in Azure? Which tool is used for this purpose?

E5.31 What kind of cloud entities does the Azure Storage allow the users to manage?

E5.32 What is a media service in Azure? What kind of media files can be stored, and how? What kinds of tools are used for playing back media files in Azure?

E5.33 What is Visual Studio Online, and how is it related to non-cloud version of Visual Studio?

E5.34 What is Azure Cache and what kind of functionality does it provide?

E5.35 What is the BizTalk services component and how does it relate to on-premise Microsoft BizTalk product?

E5.36 What is Recovery Services in Azure? What is vault? How does Azure enable backups and recovery Web site functionality?

E5.37 What is an automation account in Azure? What is the goal of its components – runbooks, jobs, and assets? For what purposes are automation accounts used in Azure?

E5.38 What is Azure Scheduler and for which purposes is it used?

E5.39 What is the goal of the Azure API Management component?

E5.40 What is the goal of the Azure Machine Learning component?

E5.41 What is the goal of the Azure Stream Analytics component?

E5.42 What is the goal of the Azure Operational Insight component?

E5.43 What is the goal of the Azure Networks component?

E5.44 What is the goal of the Azure Traffic Manager component?

E5.45 What is the goal of the Azure RemoteApp component?

E5.46 What is the goal of the Azure Management Services component?

E5.47 What is the goal of the Azure Active Directory component?

E5.48 What is the goal of the Azure Marketplace component?

E5.49 What is the goal of the Azure Storsimple component?

E5.50 What is the principle of managing the Azure dashboard by the users? How do they create or delete a cloud item, or fulfill another typical Azure dashboard action?

E5.51 What is the structure and major functionalities of the Azure contextual menu?

E5.52 Where is the main menu in the Azure portal? How do you access it, and what are the major actions of the Azure menu?

E5.53 How do you get trial access to Azure for 1 month, how do you get a longer term trial access to Azure for university teachers and students of some courses?

E5.54 How is the help in Azure organized?

E5.55 How do you get documentation on Azure using the main menu?

E5.56 How do you get to the Download page of Azure using the main menu?

E5.57 What is the structure and content of the Azure Marketplace portal, and how do you get it from the main menu?

E5.58 Please define *role* in Azure. What kinds of roles do exist in Azure? Please explain their meanings.

E5.59 What are the advantages of Azure Compute, in relation to hosting applications?

E5.60 How do you create a Web site using Azure Compute? What is the system of domain names of the Web sites created in Azure?

E5.61 What kinds of actions are possible with Web sites using the Azure portal?

E5.62 How do you create a virtual machine in Azure using Compute? Please describe the process of creating a virtual machine and create it as a hand-on lab.

E5.63 What kind of network protocols can be used to connect to a virtual machine in Azure?

E5.64 What operating systems are available for creating virtual machines in Azure?

E5.65 How do you create an empty cloud service in Azure? Please do that in the Azure portal. By what kind of tools is it possible to implement the cloud service?

E5.66 How do you create a mobile service in Azure? Please do that in the Azure portal. What is the system of domain naming mobile services in Azure.

E5.67 Why is it necessary to create a database for the mobile service? What is it for?

E5.68 Please define and describe the three kinds of Azure Storage entities in Azure – Blob, Queue, and Table.

E5.69 Which communication protocol is used for communicating with Azure Storage entities?

E5.70 What is the system of domain naming Azure Storage entities?

E5.71 Please describe the features of Azure tables and their implementation.

E5.72 Please describe the features of Azure blobs and their implementation.

E5.73 Please describe the features of Azure queues and their implementation.

E5.74 Please describe how to create a Storage account and a Storage container in Azure.

E5.75 Please describe how to create an SQL database in Azure and explain the parameters of the database. Do it as a hand-on lab.

E5.76 Please describe the features of managing SQL databases in Azure using table constructor and built-in SQL interpreter. Do it as a hand-on lab.

E5.77 Please describe the NaaS features in Azure on creating a virtual network. Do it as a hand-on lab.

E5.78 Please describe the features of CDN in Azure.

E5.79 Please describe the features of Traffic Manager in Azure. Do it as a hand-on lab.

E5.80 Please describe how to implement a cloud service for Azure using Visual Studio: kinds of Azure projects, developing the cloud service, debugging it using Azure emulator, and publishing it in the cloud. Do it as a hand-on lab.

E5.81 Please describe the features of the Visual Studio Online: creating an account, creating more users and sending them notifications, creating a team room, communicating with the other users, managing the team project. Do it as a hand-on lab.

E5.82 Please describe how to develop a mobile service and a connected mobile application using Visual Studio: enhancing Visual Studio, kinds of cloud projects, developing and publishing the mobile service, and developing a connected mobile application. Do it as a hand-on lab.

E5.83 Please describe the features of Azure on creating and managing a media service: creating a media service account, uploading and playing a video file. Do it is a hand-on lab.

E5.84 Please explain the principles and major features of .NET as the basis for implementation of Azure – CLI, CIL, CTS, the C# language, the architecture of Web services, and the WSDL specification of Web services.

E5.85 Please explain new features of .NET 4.5 related to Azure and WCF.

E5.86 Please explain the concepts related to the implementation of Azure Web services: Fabric Controller, concept of roles, implementation of roles, Role API, and the ways of interaction between the roles and their instances.

E5.87 What is Azure PowerShell and commandlets? For what kind of cloud tasks are they recommended?

E5.88 What Azure SDKs are available for download, and for which languages and software development platforms, in particular, for mobile platforms?

E5.89 Please explain the command-line tools for Microsoft Azure.

E5.90 Please describe machine learning support in Azure: machine learning in general, its support in Azure, Azure ML Studio, creating an ML workspace, the concepts of experiment, dataset, its training, the basics of R language. Please perform one of the experiments from the ML Studio gallery as a hand-on lab.

E5.91 Please explain the big data processing feature support in Azure: HDInsight, Hadoop, HBase, Storm and Spark clusters, performing Hive requests to big data, and importing their results into Microsoft Excel. Please do it as a hand-on lab.

E5.92 Please explain and estimate the perspectives of Microsoft Azure.

6

CONCLUSIONS: PERSPECTIVES OF TRUSTWORTHY CLOUD COMPUTING

6.1 INTEGRATION OF CLOUDS. THE INTERCLOUD IEEE STANDARD

The *Intercloud* [21, 130, 131] is a prospective project on integrating the clouds. The idea of the project originated in 2007, in the early days of cloud computing [131]. It was formulated by Kevin Kelly: "Eventually we'll have the Intercloud, the cloud of clouds." Since that time, there has been a trend to integrate all clouds into one common cloud. This is not an easy task. Along with the related task of developing a standard for Intercloud, there is a serious issue that does not help implement this idea. Currently cloud computing is in the state of active rapid development in a highly and aggressively competitive environment. A number of major software companies develop their clouds using the principle "not worse than the competitors." Their interest is to win the competition on the cloud, rather than to obey to any standard of the cloud. Nevertheless, as you have already seen from the earlier content of the book (see Chapter 2), there are some trends on cloud standardization and using standard tools for cloud application development. So there is a hope that the idea of Intercloud will be finally accomplished, though, in my personal opinion, the work on developing a standard is not going fast enough.

The first draft version of the Intercloud standard [130] is developed by IEEE in 2012 and it is still unapproved.

Here is a brief history of the Intercloud concept. In 2009 in Japan the first Global Inter-Cloud Technology Forum (GICTF) was organized where the idea of Intercloud was officially formulated.

In 2010–2014, conferences on Intercloud took place in France, Turkey, Spain, and the United States. The first International Workshop on Cloud Computing Interoperability and Services (InterCloud 2010) took place in France. The second

Trustworthy Cloud Computing, First Edition. Vladimir O. Safonov.
© 2016 John Wiley & Sons, Inc. Published 2016 by John Wiley & Sons, Inc.

Intercloud forum was organized in 2011 in Turkey, the third in 2012 in Madrid, Spain, and the fourth in 2014 in Boston.

In 2011, IEEE started developing an international standard for Intercloud under the number of P2302, titled *Standard for Intercloud Interoperability and Federation (SIIF)* [21]. In 2012, the first version of the standard, Working Draft 1.0, was developed.

In 2011, the NIST Cloud Computing Reference architecture and NIST Cloud Computing Roadmap documents were published [18].

In 2012, IEEE announced on the InterCloud TestBed as a cloud infrastructure for testing clouds against the set of recommendations of the Intercloud standard P2302.

In 2013, IEEE announced a Global TestBed initiative. Twenty-one cloud academic and industry cloud service providers volunteered to share their expertise and the cloud implementations with the goal of creating a shared cloud test bed environment, and, finally, to develop a prototype of open source CloudOS neutral global Intercloud. The goal of the TestBed project is to create a *federation of clouds* so that the clouds can federate and interoperate.

Further initiatives on cloud integration were accomplished by Cisco. In 2014 they developed a product named Cisco Intercloud Fabric (ICF). This product provides the opportunity to migrate virtual machines between public and private clouds. This is not a complete solution of the Intercloud problem but an important step to it.

Now let us consider in more detail the key ideas of the IEEE Draft Standard for Intercloud [21, 130].

The goal of Intercloud is to enable a federation of clouds with common addressing, naming, identity, trust, presence, messaging, multicast, time domain, and application messaging.

The federation should enable dynamic workload migration between clouds.

Cloud applications in the Intercloud environment will be able to integrate services from multiple clouds.

According to the Intercloud model, there are public clouds which are similar to Internet Service Providers (ISPs). Also, there are private clouds – each of them is a cloud which some organization creates to serve itself.

In Intercloud, there should be *Intercloud Exchanges* where clouds can interoperate, and *the Intercloud Root* containing services such as *Naming Authority, Trust Authority, Directory Services,* and other root capabilities. Surely the Intercloud Root is not a physically single entity. It should use a global replicating and hierarchical system similar to DNS.

To enable the initial negotiating process between clouds, the concept of *Intercloud Gateway* is proposed. It will be similar to Internet router in functionality. The Intercloud Root and Intercloud Exchanges will facilitate and mediate the initial negotiating process among the clouds.

As the basic transport protocol for Intercloud communications, the Extensible Presence and Messaging protocol (XMPP) [132] will be used. XMPP, also known by the slang name as Jabber, is a middleware instant messaging and presence protocol based on XML format of messages, referred at as *stanza*. XMPP is one of the three popular instant messaging and presence protocols, along with SIMPLE/SIP and

Wireless Village. Due to XMPP's universal XML nature, it is a comfortable basis for such communications.

XMPP defines communication protocols for a group of entities registered with an XMPP server. Registration provides the basis for *presence*. XMPP servers are connected together. They support cross-domain *instant messaging* in XML formal.

XMPP servers support encrypted communication based on *Simple Authentication and Security Layer* (*SASL*) and *Transport-Level Security* (*TLS*). They can be restricted to accept only encrypted client-to-server and server-to-server connections.

Intercloud will use the cloud extension of XMPP.

Example of Initial XMPP Dialog between the Cloud, Intercloud Root, and Intercloud Exchange

To be more concrete, let us consider examples of XMPP stanza for Intercloud protocol communications [21].

Step 1. As the first step to initiate communication, a cloud starts a stream to Intercloud root, by the following XMPP message:

```
<stream:stream
xmlns='jabber:client'
xmlns:stream='http://etherx.jabber.org/streams'
to='intercloudexchg.com'
version='1.0'>
```

Step 2. As the second communication step, the Intercloud Root responds by sending a stream tag to client with the following XMPP message:

```
<stream:stream
xmlns='jabber:client'
xmlns:stream='http://etherx.jabber.org/streams'
id='cloud1_id1'
from='intercloudexchg.com'
version='1.0'>
```

Step 3. As the third step, the Intercloud Root sends the STARTTLS extension to cloud, with the following XMPP message:

```
<stream:features>
<starttls xmlns='urn:ietf:params:xml:ns:xmpp-tls'>
<required/>
</starttls>
</stream:features>
```

Here, STARTTLS means that the communication should be encrypted, in TLS form.

Step 4. As the fourth step of communication, the cloud sends the STARTTLS command to the Intercloud Root, as follows:

```
<starttls xmlns='urn:ietf:params:xml:ns:xmpp-tls'/>
```

Step 5. As the next, fifth, step of communication, the Intercloud Root sends the cloud a message that it is allowed to proceed:

```
<proceed xmlns='urn:ietf:params:xml:ns:xmpp-tls'/>
```

Step 5 (alternative). As an alternative to the proceed variant of the negotiations, the Intercloud Root can inform the cloud that the negotiation has failed, and close the stream and the TCP connection:

```
<failure xmlns='urn:ietf:params:xml:ns:xmpp-tls'/>
</stream:stream>
```

Step 6. As the sixth step of communication, the cloud and the Intercloud Root attempt to complete their TLS negotiation over the existing TCP connection.

Step 7. If the TLS negotiation is successful, the cloud initiates a new stream to the Intercloud Root:

```
<stream:stream
xmlns='jabber:client'
xmlns:stream='http://etherx.jabber.org/streams'
to='intercloudexchg.com'
version='1.0'>
```

Step 7 (alternative). If the negotiation is unsuccessful, the Intercloud Root closes the TCP connection.

Step 8. The Intercloud Root responds to the cloud by sending a stream header with a set of available stream features. The mechanism names listed below are the possible authentication mechanisms that can be used:

```
<stream:stream
    xmlns='jabber:client'
    xmlns:stream='http://etherx.jabber.org/streams'
    from='intercloudexchg.com'
    id=' cloud1_id2'
    version='1.0'>
<stream:features>
    <mechanisms xmlns='urn:ietf:params:xml:ns:xmpp-sasl'>
        <mechanism>DIGEST-MD5</mechanism>
        <mechanism> CRAM-MD5</mechanism>
        <mechanism>PLAIN</mechanism>
        <mechanism>ANONYMOUS</mechanism>
        <mechanism>EXTERNAL</mechanism>
        <mechanism>SAML20</mechanism>
    </mechanisms>
</stream:features>
```

Step 9. As the ninth step of communication, the cloud decides to continue with the SASL authentication mechanism.

Step 10. The cloud selects the SASL authentication mechanism with the following XMPP message:

```
<auth xmlns='urn:ietf:params:xml:ns:xmpp-sasl' mechanism='SAML20'/>
```

Step 11. As the 11th step of communication, the Intercloud Root sends to the cloud a BASE64 encoded challenge in the form of an HTTP Redirect to the SAML assertion consumer service with the SAML authentication request, as specified in the redirection URL.

Step 12. The cloud sends a BASE64 encoded empty response to the challenge:

```
<response xmlns='urn:ietf:params:xml:ns:xmpp-sasl'> = </response>
```

Step 13. The cloud sends the URL to a local Intercloud Gateway for processing. The Intercloud Gateway provides (similar to the browser) a normal SASL authentication flow like redirection to the Identity Provider. On authentication, the Intercloud Gateway is passed back to the cloud, which sends the AuthN XMPP response to the Intercloud Root, with the subject-identifier and the *jid* as an attribute.

Step 14. The Intercloud Gateway informs the cloud about successful authentication:

```
<success xmlns='urn:ietf:params:xml:ns:xmpp-sasl'/>
```

Step 14 (alternative). In case the authentication fails, the Intercloud Gateway informs the cloud about failed authentication:

```
<failure xmlns='urn:ietf:params:xml:ns:xmpp-sasl'>
<temporary-auth-failure/>
</failure>
</stream:stream>
```

Intercloud Exchange Service Invocation in XMPP

How should the cloud invoke a service from the Intercloud Root? The idea of the creators of the Intercloud standard is that, to keep the queries as general as possible, the queries from the cloud to the Intercloud Root should be formulated as a semantic query to databases, using *SPARQL* [133] – a semantic query language for databases that manipulates data stored in the *Resource Description Framework* (*RDF*) format. RDF was invented by the W3C consortium for use in Semantic Web. The meaning of the example of the SPARQL query below is as follows. One cloud requests the computing semantics catalog to find out if the service description of some other cloud meets the constraints of the first cloud interest. In the request below, the IO Data XMPP Extension Protocol (XEP) is used, XMPP Web Services for Java (xws4j):

```
<iq type='set'
    from='user@cloud1.org'
    to='service.intercloudexchg.com'
    id='cloud1_id1'>
    <command xmlns=
        'http://jabber.org/protocol/commands'
        node='constraint_catalog_resources'
        action='execute'>
        <iodata xmlns=
        'urn:xmpp:tmp:io-data' type='input'>
        <in>
        <constraints xmlns='http://www.csp/resOntology'>
        <constraint>
            <attribute>availabilityQuantity </attribute>
                <value>99.999</value>
            </constraint>
            <constraint>
                <attribute>replicationFactor</attribute>
                <value>5</value>
            </constraint>
            <constraint>
                <attribute>tierCountries</attribute>
                <value>JAPAN</value>
            </constraint>
            <constraint>
                <attribute>StorageReplicationMethod
                </attribute>
                <value>AMQP</value>
            </constraint>
            <constraint>
                <attribute>InterCloudStorageAccess
                </attribute>
                <value>NFS</value>
            </constraint>
        </constraints>
    </in>
    </iodata>
    </command>
</iq>
```

The result of this service invocation request is the following result set:

```
<iq type='result'
    from='service.intercloudexchg.com'
    to='user@cloud1.org'
    id='cloud1_id1'>
  <command xmlns=
    'http://jabber.org/protocol/commands'
    sessionid='RPC-SESSION-0000001'
    node='constraint_catalog_resources'
    status='completed'>
    <iodata xmlns=
    'urn:xmpp:tmp:io-data' type='output'>
```

```
            <out>
                <matchingClouds
                xmlns='http://www.csp/resOntology'>
                    <cloudName>cloud2</cloudName>
                    <cloudName>cloud5</cloudName>
            </matchingClouds>
        </out>
    </iodata>
    </command>
    </iq>
```

Let us analyze the above example. It may seem too general and too semantic level oriented. However, please do not forget that the task here is to organize *Intercloud* – a way of communication between clouds – so that the clouds understand each other in the most general format possible. In Chapter 2 an overview of different cloud models is presented. From this overview, it is clear that different cloud models differ in their implementation technologies and in architectures, so it is quite understandable that Semantic Web and RDF style is probably the most realistic communication style for different cloud models.

Intercloud Protocol: Presence and Dialog with XMPP

Suppose that the cloud that has made a request has found a target cloud suitable for interaction. In this case, the requesting cloud should work directly in dialog with the target cloud. Now let us describe this cloud-to-cloud presence and the scenario of their dialog. In the example below, the XMPP Java API from Google App Engine [134] is used. The example code tests for a service availability and then sends a message as part of the collaboration dialog:

```
// …
    JID jid = new JID("user@cloud2.com");
    String msgBody = "Cloud 2, I would like to use your resources for
        storage replication using AMQP over UDT protocol.";
    Message msg =
        new MessageBuilder()
            .withRecipientJids(jid)
            .withBody(msgBody)
            .build();
boolean messageSent = false;
    XMPPService xmpp = XMPPServiceFactory.getXMPPService();
    if (xmpp.getPresence(jid).isAvailable()) {
        SendResponse status = xmpp.sendMessage(msg);
        messageSent =
            (status.getStatusMap().get(jid) ==
            SendResponse.Status.SUCCESS);
    }
    if (!messageSent) {
        // Send an email message instead…
}
```

In the following code example, it is shown how the recipient cloud responds to the above message as part of the dialog. The Java technology used in the example is the *servlet* technology. Servlets are server-side Java classes for processing HTTP requests and sending back HTTP responses.

```
/* Handler class for all XMPP activity. */
public class XmppReceiverServlet extends HttpServlet {
    private static final XMPPService xmppService =
        XMPPServiceFactory.getXMPPService();
    public void doPost
        (HttpServletRequest request, HttpServletResponse response)
        throws IOException {
    Message message = xmppService.parseMessage(request);
    Message reply =
        new MessageBuilder()
            .withRecipientJids(message.getFromJid())
            .withMessageType(MessageType.NORMAL)
        .withBody("Cloud 1, please go ahead and use my resources for
                storage replication using AMQP/UDT protocol.")
            .build();
    xmppService.sendMessage(reply);
}
```

The Intercloud Trust Model

Now let us consider the trust model implied by the Intercloud protocol. It is based on *public key infrastructure (PKI)* [135]. According to it, the Intercloud Root systems will serve as the *Trust Authority*. In the commonly used trust architecture, certificates are issued by Certificate Authorities [136]. Those certificates should be utilized to establish a trust chain. Certificated are provided by Certificate Authorities in specific formats, should be subject to annual security audits, and conform to best practices of PKI. The requirements of certification may be different in different countries.

Certificates in the Intercloud trust model should not only identify the clouds but also the resources the clouds offer, and the workloads the cloud wishes to share with other clouds. The certificates should reflect all that dynamic information. The Intercloud Exchanges should work as intermediate "just-in-time" certificate authorities that generate certificates for limited lifetime trust needed to perform some transaction.

In the Intercloud topology, Intercloud Roots will provide *static* PKI functionality, whereas the Intercloud Exchanges will be responsible for the *dynamic* "Trust Level" model, based on PKI certificate trust model. All in all, the total trust model of the Intercloud will be like *Domain based trust* model. According to this, the cloud provider environment is divided into several trust domains. In the same domain, nodes are much more familiar to each other and have a higher degree of trust on each other.

So the Intercloud exchanges play the role of "custodians" of the domain-based trust systems environment for their cloud providers. Cloud providers rely on the Intercloud exchanges to manage trust. The Intercloud exchanges are domain trust agents. They store other domains' trust information for cooperation between the domains. The information stored by them reflects trust value for a concrete resource type (storage, compute, etc.). The other role of the Intercloud Exchanges is that they recommend to other domains the trust levels for initial interdomain interaction.

The Intercloud Identity and Access Management

From the viewpoint of identity and access, the Intercloud model can be characterized as *Trusted Federation*. As in the typical federation identity model, a cloud provider that would like to establish secure communication to another cloud provider asks the trust provider service for a trust token. The trust provider service sends two copies of secret keys, the encrypted proof token of the trust service, and the requested encrypted token.

If the recipient cloud is affiliated to another Intercloud Exchange, the XMPP server will send the message to the recipient XMPP server hosted by the affiliated Intercloud Exchange. So two XMPP servers communicate via the dynamically established link. A server accepts a connection from a peer only in case the peer supports TLS and presents a certificate issued by a root certification authority that is trusted by the server.

An RDF SPARQL and XMPP Approach to Intercloud Exchange Service Discovery

The authors of the draft Intercloud standard [21] proposed a method of description of cloud computing resources and a method of queries to this information in the form used in Semantic Web. It may be argued whether it is the right approach, since there are many opponents of the Semantic Web approach. But there is no doubt that this general approach is suitable for describing any cloud resources. Any kinds of resources can be described as a hierarchy of concepts and entities. The RDF model is based on the concept of a *triple* of the kind: *Subject/Property/Object*. Actually, in a triple, the resource is the subject, the property is a predicate (verb), and the object is the property value or another resource itself. An *ontology* is a hierarchy of concepts and instances of concepts. Ontology is a primary concept of Semantic Web. The authors of Semantic Web model from Stanford University developed and implemented *OWL* (*the Web Ontology Language*) [137] widely used in research community to represent ontologies. RDF, used in this standard, is yet another form to represent ontologies.

Here is an RDF example of ontology. In this example, *CloudDomain* is an instance of class *CloudDomainCapability*. It consists of three resources: *Cloud.1*, *Cloud.2*, and *Cloud.3*. Here is the RDF description of this ontology structure:

```
<http://cloud/domain> <http://www.csp/resOntology#hasCapability>
<http://cloud/domain/#cloud.1>.
<http://cloud/domain> <http://www.csp/resOntology#hasCapability>
<http://cloud/domain/#cloud.2>.
<http://cloud/domain> <http://www.csp/resOntology#hasCapability>
<http://cloud/domain/#cloud.3>.
<http://cloud/domain> <http://www.w3.org/1999/02/22-rdf-syntax-ns#type>
<http://www.csp/resOntology#ClouddomainCapability>.
<http://cloud/domain> <http://www.w3.org/2000/01/rdf-schema#label>
"Cloud Computing domain"^^<http://www.w3.org/2001/XMLSchema#string>.
```

In its turn, the resource *Cloud.1* consists of three tier instances, *tier.1*, *tier.2*, and *tier.3*. The RDF description follows:

```
<http://cloud/domain/#cloud.1> <http://www.csp/resOntology#hasCapability>
<http://cloud/domain/cloud.1#tier1>.
<http://cloud/domain/#cloud.1> <http://www.csp/resOntology#hasCapability>
<http://cloud/domain/cloud.1#tier2>.
<http://cloud/domain/#cloud.1> <http://www.csp/resOntology#hasCapability>
<http://cloud/domain/cloud.1#tier3>.
```

Similarly, the properties of cloud instances, such as *StorageReplicationMethod*, are described in RDF as ontologies. In the same way, the cloud resources such as storage, compute, and so on, are represented by ontologies in RDF. To avoid repeating similar and simple RDF descriptions, I omit them and refer the readers to the draft standard [21].

So, to summarize this section, the Intercloud model is based on the following standards and technologies:

- XMPP as the basic cloud communication model
- PKI and Federated Trust as the basis of the trust model
- RDF and SPARQL as the basis of the semantic model to represent cloud concepts and their instances.

The draft IEEE standard on Intercloud will no doubt be soon completed and accepted, and cloud computing providers and users will get the basis of further cloud unification, integration, and interaction, which becomes more and more necessary with the rapid growth of different cloud models by different companies.

6.2 THE TCLOUDS PROJECT BY THE EUROPEAN UNION

Trustworthy Clouds (TClouds) [138] is a prospective cloud computing research project by the European Union, funded by the European Program 7. Its duration was 3 years, and it successfully ended in September 2013. The goals of the project are

- to develop a cloud infrastructure with computing and storage capabilities with a new level of security, privacy, and resilience;
- to develop, as a proof of concept, a prototype cloud infrastructure in such socially significant areas as energy and healthcare.

The participants of the project are the following:

- The Technikon research company, Austria
- IBM Research, Switzerland
- Philips Electronics, the Netherlands
- Sirrix AG Security Technologies, Germany
- University of Lissabon, Portugal

- Unabhaengiges Landeszentrum fuer Datenschutz, Germany
- University of Oxford, United Kingdom
- Politecnico di Torino, Italy
- Friedrich-Alexander Universitat Erlangen-Nuernberg, Germany
- Foundazione Centro San Raffaele del Monte Tabor, Italy
- Electricidade de Portugal, Portugal
- University of Maastricht, Netherlands
- EFACEC Engenharia SA, Portugal
- Technical University Darmstadt, Germany
- Technical University Braunschweig, Germany
- INNOVA SpA, Italy
- Foundazione Centro San Raffaele, Italy.

One of the leaders of the TClouds project Dr Imad Abbadi published a book [8] that, in my opinion, can be regarded as one of the important results of the TClouds project, and surely is one of the best books on trustworthy cloud computing.

The following plan and strategy was followed by the participants of the TClouds project. The work plan consisted of four independent activities [138]:

Activity A1: Legal and Business Foundations for Cross-border computing. A1 is responsible for legal and regulatory guidance, the privacy impact assessment for cross-border clouds, and viable business models for cloud providers.

Activity A2: Trustworthy Internet-scale Computing Platform. A2 is responsible for the TClouds platform. This platform includes trustworthy individual clouds that are based either on extending commodity clouds or on strengthening cloud operation software.

Activity A3: Benchmark Application & User-centric Evaluation. A3 is responsible for delivering the Smart Lighting and Home Healthcare cloud scenarios as well as self-evaluation and self-improvement through end-user and expert feedback.

Activity A4: Programme Management and Dissemination. A4 is responsible for wide and effective dissemination as well as the proper programme management that ensures timely and high-quality delivery of all results while mitigating emerging conflicts.

Here are the objectives of the project, as formulated by its partners on the project site [138]:

Trustworthy Clouds (TClouds) aims to build a prototype Internet-scale ICT infrastructure, which allows virtualized computing, network, and storage resources over the Internet to provide scalability and cost-efficiency. The following objectives contribute to achieving the overall goal:

- Identifying and addressing the legal and business implications and opportunities of a widespread use of infrastructure clouds, contributing to building a regulatory framework for enabling resilient and privacy-enhanced cross-border infrastructure clouds.

- Defining an architecture and prototype for securing infrastructure clouds by providing security enhancements that can be deployed on top of commodity infrastructure clouds (as a cloud of clouds) and assessing the resilience and privacy benefits of security extensions of existing clouds.
- Providing resilient middleware for adaptive security on the cloud-of-clouds. The TClouds platform will provide tolerance and adaptability to mitigate security incidents and unstable operating conditions for a range of applications running on such clouds-of-clouds.

To demonstrate TClouds, scientists will prototype two scenarios involving critical IT systems:

- A smart lighting control system with Portugal's leading energy and solution providers Energias de Portugal and EFACEC: TClouds will exhibit a public-infrastructure solution as part of the smart grid and show how to migrate it to a secure cloud. This increases the resilience against hardware failures, adds privacy protection and protects from hacker attacks and other security problems.
- A patient-centric home healthcare service with San Raffaele Hospital in Milano, Italy: TClouds will demonstrate a cloud-supported solution that supports multiple different actors and remotely monitors, diagnoses and assists patients outside a hospital setting. The service respects security and privacy requirements and regulations governing patient data.

The results of the TClouds project were highly appreciated by the European Commission in 2013 [139]:

The TClouds project has improved the security and resilience of cloud computing platforms in response to widespread concerns about data privacy and robustness of services in the cloud model. It has realized a trustworthy cloud-computing platform, the TClouds platform, which integrates multiple advanced security technologies in a standard cloud distribution and in commercial cloud systems ...

Some of the TClouds systems are already being exploited commercially by the industrial partners of the project. The project has also organized many prominent and well-attended scientific workshops and technical events in Europe, which focus on the theme of cloud security. With these and through their technical contributions, the project partners have achieved global visibility for their leadership in this domain.

The TClouds (Trustworthy Clouds – Privacy and Resilience for Internet-scale Critical Infrastructure) project, co-funded by the European Union, has come to a successful conclusion at the end of September 2013. The multinational project consortium, led by the Austrian company Technikon, has developed a novel cloud infrastructure, which will lead to increased security and privacy-protection in data processing. Equally important, it will remain cost-efficient, scalable, and simple.

Protecting data and services in the cloud is a challenge of increasing importance for governments and organizations across all industries, including healthcare, energy utilities, and banking. In a cloud environment, all pertinent data is stored on remote hardware via the Internet instead of being kept on a local server or computer. Current cloud computing systems involve the disadvantage that users do not know where their data is stored and how it is processed. Focusing in particular on cross-border data processing, a number of legal questions arise concerning the protection of sensible information, such as person-related data.

Mission

This is exactly what the project TClouds focused on. During three years, its goal was to develop a trustworthy, reliable, and transparent cloud infrastructure allowing the processing of person-related as well as sensible company data in the cloud. The research focus was to design a secure cloud environment that meets European privacy protection requirements without compromising on the benefits of cloud computing, such as cost savings, scalability of services offered, and data availability. In addition, the project team worked on new open security standards and effective cloud management components.

Newly designed security mechanisms were also developed to remotely verify the security and resiliency of the cloud infrastructure, guaranteeing the integrity of a hardened cloud computing platform to users of cloud services.

Besides advanced technology, the TClouds consortium also studied the legal, business, and social aspects of cross-border cloud computing, such as country-specific privacy laws, writing cloud computing service agreements, and user–centric requirements, including languages and accessibility.

Results

The focus of the project was to prototype an advanced cloud infrastructure that can deliver a new level of secure, private, and resilient computing and storage that is cost-efficient, simple, and scalable. More specifically, two main results can be identified:

1. TClouds built a Trustworthy Cloud Platform where federations of standardized, resilient and privacy-protecting global infrastructure clouds offer virtualized computing, communication and storage resources. Therefore, novel resilient protocols, cloud security mechanisms, management components, and selected open source implementations could be created.
2. In order to evaluate the TClouds infrastructure empirically, TClouds worked on two scenarios comprising healthcare and smart lighting systems. These scenarios provided a set of critical IT-infrastructures through which the project team could demonstrate the applicability of their novel TClouds solutions in a real environment.

The project team has made significant progress towards realizing secure cloud computing systems, offering more security and reliability at low cost, scalability, and ease-of-use. Some of the achieved results are already state-of-the-art and published in the most prestigious conferences and journals."

The full list of publications on the TCloud project is shown on the project site [138].

The specifics of the project are best explained by its leaders in [140]. The rest of the section is mostly an overview of the content of [140].

The TClouds project has proposed several security and privacy protecting enhancements to existing commodity clouds as well as an own resilient cloud middleware. This is investigated as case examples from the healthcare and smart energy domains.

Another specific approach of the TClouds project is the use of standards (in particular open standards) in a cloud infrastructure.

Very interesting are the results of the survey on cloud computing [140] – the result of a poll of 60 interdisciplinary stakeholders.

The first question of the survey was as to why they would adopt cloud computing. The answers were as follows: Of the stakeholders, 84% answered that cloud computing is crucial because it helps in cost saving and reduction; 85.7% answered that cloud computing is crucial because it accelerates business processes. However, 60% answered that cloud computing is not important for them because of lack of skilled IT personnel. The latter answer should attract the attention of university teachers and industry companies' evangelists: it means that cloud computing should be disseminated and taught more intensively and deeply.

The second question of the survey was on the main barriers to adoption of cloud computing. According to 88% stakeholders the main barrier is privacy. It is quite understandable that the cloud user companies are primarily concerned about their confidential data, no matter how trustworthy a cloud model is. A related barrier is access and export of own data (as 51% answered).

Among the security risks related to the use of cloud computing, the polled stakeholders listed the following (indicating them as relevant or highly relevant):

– Cloud-specific attacks by externals (88%)
– Accidental leakage of data and credentials (82%)
– Insider attacks (e.g., by cloud administrators) (82%)
– Insufficient protection against more general IT security risks and attacks (75%).

The TClouds stakeholders expressed concerns about the dependences when working with single cloud provider. Most relevant of such concerns are the following:

– Breach of confidentiality (85%)
– Interruption of the service (85%)
– Impossibility to restore data or computation after a disruption (85%)
– Loss of data (78%).

The overall requirements to trustworthy cloud services selected by the survey respondents as relevant are as follows:

– Data portability support (98%)
– Support of open standards (75%)
– Support of de facto standards (e.g., Amazon APIs) (73%)
– Availability of components as open source (58%).

I would like to emphasize in the above information the importance of data portability expressed by the respondents. It means that most existing cloud providers do not support data portability, which is surely uncomfortable for cloud users. They would like to use their cloud data with any cloud provider. But the primary concern of cloud providers is to sell their own cloud model, so that they do not always care of data portability.

As one of the most important results of the TClouds project, the project consortium has developed a *trusted infrastructure cloud* solution based on trusted computing hardware to provide a high-security infrastructure cloud. In particular, this cloud can ensure full verifiable integrity of resource allocation, and it is immune against insider attacks or other attempts to compromise their resources.

The Trusted Infrastructure Cloud architecture, the main result of the project in the Activity 1 area, is as follows. The central management component, referred to as *Trusted Objects Manager* (*TOM*), manages a set of trusted servers (TSs). TSs run a *security kernel*. Security kernel runs the virtual machines (VM) of the users. Each virtual machine consists of the operating system (OS) and applications (App). The scheme of this architecture is depicted in [140, p. 17]. The TSs and the Trusted Object Manager are equipped with a Hardware Security Module (HSM). The HSM enables secure boot and integrity of the software, including the security kernel. The hard drives of the TSs are encrypted by a security key stored within the HSM. The local hard drives can be decrypted only when the HSM has cross-checked the integrity of the component. So only the untampered security kernel can be booted and can access the decrypted data. The security kernel enforces the security policy and the isolation.

The Trusted Objects Manager manages configuration data, including the keys and the security policies, and controls the virtual machines on the TSs. Encrypted communication of the TOM and a TS is accomplished via the *Trusted Management Channel* (*TMC*), which checks the integrity of the system using remote attestation before transmitting any data. All the administrative tasks performed on the TS is via the TMC. There is no other management channel for administrators.

Another key concept of this architecture is *trusted virtual domain* (*TVD*). TVD is a unit of isolation of the virtual machines. The VMs can only communicate if they are from the same TVD with the same TVD key. Remote communication between components of the same TVD over an untrusted network are secured via a Virtual Private Network (VPN).

A TS can run several VMs belonging to different tenants. But each tenant runs his own set of TVDs, thus ensuring isolation of tenants.

This architecture guarantees protection from insider attacks, and also isolation of tenants. The respondents of the survey, stakeholders, noticed, however, that such architecture is mostly suitable for specific critical application cases. Some of them have concerns that management complexity and price can be a road-blocking factor for the use of trusted computing technologies in cloud computing.

My personal opinion on the above Trusted Infrastructure Cloud is as follows. Surely this technology enables trustworthy cloud computing but it is very costly. It requires special kinds of hardware to be added to the cloud infrastructure specifically for the purpose of security checks, data encryption, decryption, and integrity checks.

Those complicated checks and attestations are implemented as part of hardware security modules. It can be regarded as a restrictive factor for wider use of the Trusted Infrastructure Cloud. Many other successfully and securely working cloud computing models (including Microsoft Azure, Amazon AWS, and Google cloud), to my knowledge, do not use such special hardware enhancements. The near future will show who has made the right choice and whose cloud computing architecture appeared more prospective and will be widely used.

In the Activity 2 area, the main result of the TClouds project is the analysis of the very popular OpenStack [78] cloud computing architecture – one of the de facto standards of cloud computing used, for example, for implementation of the HP Helion cloud (see Chapter 2). The analysis showed a number of security problems that may cause intrusion of security attackers to clouds built on the basis of the OpenStack technology. The result of this investigation is *Trustworthy OpenStack* – an enhancement of the OpenStack in the following directions: trust, integrity, confidentiality, resilience, and audit. Let us consider them in more detail.

Secure Logging and Log Resilience

This enhancement of OpenStack is an implementation of secure, confidential, and resilient logging and log entries. It is well known that logging is a popular object of attacks, since the attacker attempts to "leave no tracks" of his malicious actions. Due to this secure and resilient logging, the cloud administrator can access the log entries inside the logging sessions and, for each session, verify their integrity through the OpenStack Dashboard.

Advanced VM Scheduling Enhancement

This is an enhancement of the OpenStack scheduler, implemented as *Access Control as a Service* (ACaaS). It allows the cloud developers to add to the cloud nodes a set of key/value pairs defining some extra properties and requirements. When instantiating virtual machines, only the cloud nodes that have the required properties with the required values will be selected for the deployment of the VM.

Cloud Nodes Verification Enhancement

This enhancement of the OpenStack is a Remote Attestation subsystem. It defines the node *integrity level* of a cloud node. Virtual machines can be deployed for this node only if the node integrity level is appropriate (it can be one of five values). The integrity level is the number indicating that all running software is part of a Linux distribution and all packages are up to date. Also, the integrity level may indicate that some packages of the running software are not updated, since some improvements or security critical bug fixes are available. This security extension allows the customers to select the nodes to deploy a VM in a pool of Trusted Nodes.

Transparent Encryption Enhancement

This OpenStack enhancement provides a cryptography-as-a-service mechanism that encrypts data in VM instances and block storage devices. It enables storing a VM image in encrypted form and decrypting or encrypting it on the fly, thus protecting it from a malicious cloud administrator.

Trusted Virtual Domains Enhancement

This enhancement of OpenStack is implemented as an *Ontology-based reasoner* subsystem that allows to group together the virtual machines belonging to a single customer, to communicate to each other freely, but to be isolated from the VMs of the other customers. The confidentiality and integrity of the communication are enabled by secure communication protocols such as IPSec.

In the third area of research by the TClouds consortium, the main result is a set of *mechanisms to self-monitor and screen cloud security state* by the user. Several methods were developed to scan the virtual topology of the clouds and to investigate the security state from the user side.

Finally, in the fourth area of research by TClouds developers, the main result is *a highly resilient cloud service built on a cloud of clouds*. This approach allows the cloud users to consume multiple clouds at the same time to distribute stored data and for running services. For storage, *Key-Value Store* (*KVS*) interface was developed for storing and retrieving values associated with unique keys. This interface works securely for multiple clouds, which is a great achievement.

A Foundation for Critical Cloud Applications

To better understand requirements of customers to cloud services in different application areas, the TClouds team investigated two areas: health care (at San Faffaele hospital, Italy, at Philips healthcare) and smart energy (at Electridade de Portugal and EFACEC). The market of healthcare is big, so it offers great opportunity for specialized cloud computing services.

There is a set of specific requirements to cloud service providers for healthcare cloud applications, which was investigated and implemented by the TClouds team, as follows:

- *Mandatory security breach notifications – secure logs.* TClouds team implemented secure non-modifiable logs at cloud infrastructure level. These logs record any access, either authorized or non-authorized, at a granular level. So the users are notified on any breach in the cloud security system.
- *Conformity with HIPAA (Health Insurance Portability and Accountability Act) standards on medical data location and transfer.* This popular standard in the US healthcare system specifies in detail the treatment of electronic medical records and patient data and the prevention of fraud and abuse. One element is the granting of permissions by the data owner – for example, for data copy to different locations – as well as the logging of all such activities. In particular, standard cloud providers are not used to provide accountancy of data location as well as full transaction logging. TClouds demonstrates with the trusted infrastructure cloud and the secure log service that both is however implementable to infrastructure clouds in a way that would make them compliant to the high demands of health applications.

- *Encryption of data in transit and storage.* For hospitals and health systems to ensure an appropriate level of security they could leverage the supplied TClouds Platform libraries of security protocols. Application developers will be forced to ensure appropriate encryption of data during storage, transit and processing. That is, decryption should only be necessary when visualizing the data and results.

- *Granular data control.* With the increasing protection of patient information, there are concerns in the academic community about being deprived of data that is critical for medical research. Teaching hospitals, such as TClouds partner Hospital San Raffaele Italy, that have mandates for teaching and research while operating as a hospital, need to give physicians access to appropriate case studies and records whilst researchers also need to have access. Security is needed, but the huge body of data should still be accessible in some way for research and moving the medical science forward. TClouds has demonstrated that granular data control is possible to share only the data elements relevant e.g. to a research study. A secure log service would also document all use and access to data [140].

Requirements in a Smart Energy Grid Application

"Whereas in the healthcare domain the clear focus is on protecting the privacy of medical records and other patient data, in the smart energy domain, the focus has been stronger on protection against cyber-attacks. TClouds has investigated – with its partner EDP (Energias de Portugal) the linkage of cloud services to a critical physical infrastructure including a direct link to the SCADA (supervisory control and data acquisition) environment that controls street lighting units in major Portuguese cities. It is obvious that such infrastructures provides for multiple interests to be attacked and notably cloud providers need to prevent that the interfaces they have to such control services cannot be exploited in non-authorized ways. The functionalities realized in the TClouds Smart Lighting example allow power grid operators to act upon public lighting with more information, ensuring the most efficient control. Also, municipalities are able to directly monitor the system, which allows them to make more specific and strategic decisions. The Smart Lighting system is based on a cloud environment, which brings to the utility the scalability and computational power needed to manage a system with this level of geographic expansion and constant integration of new assets. Smart Grid components in general and public lighting in particular involve many different kinds of technical devices which, in many cases, are vulnerable to failures or damage. With a cloud based solution using TClouds' security components this impact is reduced, bringing a higher reliability to the system. From the utility point of view, cloud computing adds flexibility to hardware investment plans. It allows lower starting investments and also the possibility to evolve the solution to follow changing requirements." [140].

Open Standards for Trustworthy Clouds

Yet another area of investigation by the TClouds team was on the role and need for open standards in trustworthy cloud computing. The survey respondents, stakeholders of the TClouds project, noticed the importance of the open standards in cloud computing, since the missing elements in trustworthy cloud computing should be standardized. However, standards in this area are a complex subject, because of the complexity of cloud computing architecture.

The TClouds team formulated the set of levels of standards in trustworthy cloud computing. They are as follows:

– *Organization level.* This level unites the standards related to management process and organization level security. First of all, it relates to cloud service providers and the related procedures in cloud data centers. Also, this level may apply to the corresponding management procedures by cloud users.
– *Semantic level.* This level of standards is related to definitions of entities, roles, terms, concepts, and logical relations in cloud computing infrastructure. So these standards support semantic correspondence of organization level requirements to the entities of the cloud infrastructure.
– *Services and application level.* This level unites the standards related to description, orchestration, and deployment of applications, processes, and services built on top of cloud infrastructure.
– *Infrastructure topology and validation level.* This level contains the standards related to the topology description of the cloud infrastructure and of the security goals as corresponding directly to the cloud infrastructure. At this level, a distinction is made between the "desired" topology, the description of security goals (for example, isolation and encryption), and the description of the "actual" topology, as it is implemented in the cloud.
– *Infrastructure level.* This level unites the standards related to all aspects of the cloud infrastructure, with its technical operation such as interface specifications and data formats. In this respect, the following subareas of the infrastructure level are distinguished:
  • *Infrastructure management.* Those are interface standards concerned with the management of infrastructure. They include switching the actions by the infrastructure (such as deployment or migration of virtual machines). They also include access to security information from the infrastructure.
  • *Virtual machines management.* This subset of standards is related to data standards for virtual machine images and metadata standards for deployment and execution of a virtual machine.
  • *Hypervisor configuration.* This subset of standards is related to definition of the direct configuration of the virtualization software used (e.g., Hyper-V by Microsoft).
  • *Cloud storage.* This subset of standards is concerned with data storage in the cloud and the related metadata standards, for example, for the lifecycle of data in the cloud and the type and object structure of the cloud data.
  • *Authentication.* Those standards are related to the management of secure user credentials to access the cloud and its services. The related authorization standards are concerned with the description of access level of a cloud

user – for example, his authorized activities, access to specific secure domains, etc.

- *Key management.* This subset of standards is related to handling encryption security keys used to access the encrypted data or to process encrypted virtual machine images in the cloud. Also, authentication and key management areas provide a link to enterprise – wide infrastructure for authentication and key management.

- *Remote attestation.* This subset of standards relates to integrity verification of components of the cloud infrastructure and verification of this.

Surely there are a number of other standards, such as those for secure data transmissions such as HTTPS that apply to the trustworthy cloud but are not specific to the area of cloud computing. So these standards are not included in the above classification.

To conclude this section, I would like to emphasize that the TClouds project is state-of-the-art in trustworthy cloud computing domain. The European consortium of organizations that successfully performed this project has shown that security and privacy in cloud computing are key concepts and can be implemented in an innovative trustworthy cloud computing project. The following are the most important achievements of the TCloud project:

- Guaranteeing integrity of the resources and data locations
- Encrypting data in storage and in transit
- Methods of prevention of insider attacks
- Non-modifiable logging activities.

These achievements are covered in this section in more detail.

As the developers of the TClouds project notice, in many critical areas such as healthcare the domain experts are still reluctant to adopt cloud computing because of the specific requirements of these domains regarding security and privacy. However, the results of the TClouds project have proved that in those critical areas trustworthy cloud computing is implementable and comfortably applicable.

The authors of the TCloud project notice that the first commercial successes have grown out of TClouds. They include

- the SAVE technology for security analysis of virtual systems commercialized by IBM;
- the enhanced Trusted Management Components and Trusted Cloud Nodes in the Trusted Infrastructure by Sirrix;
- open source toolkits such as DeepSky being adopted by academic and commercial users.

The results of the TClouds project, on the one hand, can be regarded as specific solutions for specific clouds, and on the other hand as a toolkit and architectural approach of secure cloud infrastructure in general. In future, as the project developers hope, much more security and privacy cloud services will be created that offer different levels and toolkits for cloud security and privacy.

6.3 FURTHER DEVELOPMENTS AND TRENDS OF TRUSTWORTHY CLOUD COMPUTING

During the recent years, a number of very important initiatives, alliances, trends, and tools related to trustworthy cloud computing have appeared. Two of them are worth mentioning for the first turn: the *Cloud Security Alliance (CSA)* [141] and the *Cloud Security Readiness Tool (CSRT)* by Microsoft [142, 143].

Cloud Security Alliance

The Cloud Security Alliance is a global not-for-profit organization. Its main goals, as written in the CSA mission statement [141], are as follows: "To promote the use of best practices for providing security assurance within Cloud Computing, and provide education on the uses of Cloud Computing to help secure all other forms of computing." The members of the Cloud Security Alliance are several dozen companies – Microsoft, HP, EMC, and many others, large as well as small.

The Cloud Security Alliance provides two kinds of certification:

- *CSA Security Trust and Assurance Registry (STAR)*
- *Certificate of Cloud Security Knowledge (CCSK)*.

Security Trust and Assurance Registry (STAR)

The STAR program is targeted at several categories of experts: users of cloud services, cloud service providers, IT auditors, security solution providers, and consultants. For cloud users, the STAR program helps them to appropriately assess their cloud providers and the related offerings. STAR consists of three levels of assurance.

Cloud Control Matrix

The main informational structure used in STAR is the *Cloud Controls Matrix (CCM)* [144]. Informally speaking, the CCM is a big list of descriptions of cloud-specific security controls mapped to leading standards, best practices, and regulations in cloud computing. This list helps cloud users to make a better assessment of cloud providers and helps cloud providers to implement better and secure cloud services. The CCM provides fundamental security principles to guide cloud vendors and to help cloud users to make assessment of the overall security risk of a cloud provider. CCM provides a controls framework in 16 domains related to industry accepted security standards, regulations, and controls frameworks to reduce audit complexity. Here is the list of the CCM domains (version 3.0.1):

- Application and Interface Security
- Audit Assurance and Compliance

- Business Continuity Management and Operations Resilience
- Change Control and Configuration Management
- Data Security and Information Lifecycle Management
- Datacenter Security
- Encryption and Key Management
- Governance and Risk Management
- Human Resources Security
- Identity and Access Management
- Infrastructure and Virtualization
- Interoperability and Portability
- Mobile Security
- Security Incident Management, E-Disc, and Cloud Forensics
- Supply Chain Management, Transparency, and Accountability
- Threat and Vulnerability Management.

Here is an example of a CCM control specification.
Control domain: Application and Interface Security. Data Integrity.
The specification (control ID - AIS 03):

Data input and output integrity routines (i.e., reconciliation and edit checks) shall be implemented for application interfaces and databases to prevent manual or systematic processing errors, corruption of data, or misuse.

In the subsequent columns of the CCM table the corresponding numbers of NIST and other standards are provided.

The CCM is organized as a table in Microsoft Excel format.

The *Consensus Assessments Initiative Questionnaire* (*CAIQ*) is a questionnaire based on CCM. It provides a set of Yes/No questions a cloud consumer and cloud auditor may wish to ask of a cloud provider to assure their compliance to the CCM and CSA best practices.

The three above-mentioned levels of the STAR certification program are as follows:

Level 1: Self-assessment–The idea of this level is as follows. The cloud service providers either fill out and submit the Consensus Assessment Initiative Questionnaire (CAIQ) or submit a report documenting compliance to the CCM. Then, this self-assessment information becomes publicly available. It helps the cloud users to make assessment of their cloud providers or the cloud providers they are just considering to use.

Level 2: CSA STAR Attestation–CSA STAR Certification, and *CSA C-STAR Assessment* – This level consists of rigorous third-party independent assessment of cloud providers; rigorous third-party independent assessment of the security of a cloud service providers; robust third-party independent assessment of the security of a cloud service provider for the Greater China market that unites best practices of CSA with Chinese national traditions. The attestation and certification procedures are based on CCM and some other standards.

Level 3: CSA STAR continuous monitoring–This new level, being implemented for the 2015 release, automates the current security practices of cloud service providers. Providers publish their security practices according to CSA formatting and specifications, and customers and tool vendors can retrieve and present this information in a variety of contexts.

The *CCSK* is an exam for IT professionals on cloud security knowledge. The exam can be passed online using the CSA Web site. This exam is considered very important and prestigious and was listed as number one exam on the list of Top Ten Cloud Computing Certifications.

As for the research area, the Cloud Security Alliance is very active in this respect: it maintains working groups in 28 (!) domains of cloud security.

The CSA also supports several kinds of training on cloud security: intensive training courses and regular CloudBytes webinars, and runs the APAC (Asia Pacific) Education Council for Higher Learning and Research institutes from the Asia Pacific region.

The CSA is a rapidly growing organization. It contains several dozen regional chapters in all parts of the world, including the Americas, Europe, Africa, Middle East, Indochina, and one chapter in Russia.

CSA organizes more than 10 events – summits and congresses each year in different regions of the world.

Cloud Security Readiness Tool (CSRT) [142, 143]

This tool was announced by Microsoft in 2012. This tool is actually a brief interactive, easy-to-use survey whose goal is to analyze the maturity level of the IT infrastructure of an organization. This survey helps the organizations to better understand their IT systems, processes, policies and practices. Due to that, they can analyze and improve their current IT state, get information on the industry standards on cloud computing, and get recommendations on how to evaluate different cloud features.

The CSRT tool uses information obtained from the respondents to provide relevant guidance in a report that helps organizations to better understand their IT capabilities, evaluate cloud services in critical areas, and to learn about compliance issues. The critical areas considered by CSRT are

- security policy capabilities;
- personnel capabilities;
- physical security capabilities;
- privacy capabilities;
- asset and risk management capabilities;
- reliability capabilities.

The four levels of maturity assessed by the CSRT have the following names and meanings:

– *Getting Started.* Undocumented, ad hoc state. Reactive and incident or event response driven.
– *Making Progress.* Response driven, following trends, and somewhat repeatable with limited automation in segments.
– *Almost There.* Scaled response, using programs. Limited scaling still segmented.
– *Streamlined.* Centralized, automated, self-service, and scalable. Can allocate resources automatically.

These maturity levels are calculated, based on the answers provided to the CSRT. Here are some sample CSRT questions and possible answers for each maturity level.

Question 1. Which of these statements best describes your security policies and procedures?

Possible answers for each level of maturity [142]:

Getting started: Policies and procedures exist within an organization, but they are not uniformly coordinated and enforced.

Making progress: The organization has identified and assigned some information security responsibilities across the organization.

Almost there: The organization has formalized information security responsibilities into a program across much of the organization.

Streamlined effort: The organization formally measures, audits, and improves a security program across all of the organization.

Of the above four possible answers to each question, the users of the CSRT should choose only one and mark it. On analyzing the answers, a clear general picture of the maturity level of the respondent organization will be available.

To my mind, this style of naming and separating maturity levels in cloud computing security used by the CSRT developers is very similar to the style of the Capability Maturity Model (CMM) by Carnegie-Mellon University Software Engineering Institute [145], with its initial, repeatable, defined, managed, and optimizing maturity levels. This is quite understandable: CMM and CMMI models of software process are world famous and well recommended themselves in many successful software projects, so why not to use them as the basis for cloud computing assessment?

All in all, 27 questions are used in the CSRT questionnaire. The full list of CSRT questions is available as appendix to [142]. The questions are related to the Cloud Security Alliance's CCM [144]. Each question relates to a control area in the CCM.

The CSRT tool was used by many organizations since 2012 till 2013. The results of the survey were carefully analyzed. Here are some of the most interesting [142]:

Enterprise organizations (more than 500 PCs) show a solid maturity trend toward physical security adoption. This trend is evident for antimalware, firewalls, and patch management capabilities.

- 66 percent of enterprise organizations have advanced antimalware capabilities
- 49 percent have vulnerability/patch management
- 56 percent have advanced capabilities that include management and auditing of the organization's security policy.

In contrast, enterprise organization security policy distribution data indicates that 55 percent of enterprise organizations have security policies that are not uniform, but that some information security responsibilities have been identified and assigned across the organization.

In general, 35% of organizations all over the world have not yet established stable security policies and procedures in their environments. There is a trend of creating security policies; however, currently only about 17% of organizations have security programs that are formally managed, reviewed, audited, and regularly enforced.

In this respect, the advantage of using a cloud provider is as follows. Cloud providers have an explicit security update plan and provide careful notifications to their customers.

As for *physical access* issues, it is an inherent part of informational security. Physical access to datacenters should be strictly controlled through security mechanisms and limited to authorized personnel whose identities can be verified. In practice, adoption of role-based user access policies is still at the Getting Started level with about one-third of the respondents.

In this respect, there is an evident advantage of using a cloud provider: for the cloud providers, strict control over important systems is typical, and authorization for access is typically granted to a relatively small set of trusted staff members.

In the area of security architecture, necessary measures to avoid or mitigate attacks are patch management, antivirus software, using firewalls, and segmentation of the network. Also, all computer systems should be updated on a regular basis. So it was surprising to learn from the results of the CSRT survey that, worldwide

- 68% of organizations do not even attempt to ensure that patches are configured and installed automatically;
- 64% of organizations do not run a centrally managed and scheduled antivirus software;
- 66% of organizations do not use a stateful firewall.

In this respect, there is a great advantage of using cloud providers. The cloud providers use automated tools and procedures to scan systems for vulnerabilities. Also, they use the latest information obtained from security experts and software vendors. If a vulnerability is discovered, mitigations and workarounds are applied at the cloud datacenter to reduce the risk for the systems and data.

To conclude this section, for any organization the benefits of using trustworthy cloud computing should be carefully weighted. As the results of the CSRT survey showed, small and mid-sized business organization have maximal benefits from cloud computing.

In general, to sum up the perspectives of trustworthy cloud computing, we can consider cloud datacenters and cloud providers as schools of trustworthiness, security, and privacy. Trustworthy cloud computing teaches cloud users – organizations and individuals – to carefully handle their data, machines, and other computing resources, and use them for their benefits in their problem domains. Trustworthy cloud computing widens the horizons of everyday thinking for cloud users. It organizes the users very strictly and carefully in their way to the culture of trustworthy computing. The cloud users get accustomed to thinking in worldwide scope, to choose optimal regions for distributed computing, and to combine clouds and cloud services when seeking an optimal decision for their problems. Actually, trustworthy cloud computing is a state-of-the-art way of uniting professionals in many areas worldwide.

I wish the readers happy and secure trustworthy cloud computing, with any cloud or clouds they use or develop, with any cloud provider or toolkit, with any integrated development environment.

I hope my book and my experience that I shared with you on using, learning, and teaching state-of-the-art cloud platforms were interesting and helpful for you to feel the usefulness, power, and beauty of modern cloud computing.

EXERCISES TO CONCLUSIONS

E6.1 What is Intercloud, and what are its main idea and goals?

E6.2 Which standard covers Intercloud, which organization developed it, and what status does it still have?

E6.3 What is Intercloud TestBed, and what is the goal of this project?

E6.4 Which companies are the most active players in Intercloud area? Which approaches and tools do they offer?

E6.5 What are the goals of federation of clouds?

E6.6 What are Intercloud Roots, Intercloud Exchanges, and Intercloud Gateways? Which roles do they play in the Intercloud architecture?

E6.7 Which network protocol is the basis for Intercloud communications between clouds and integration components of Intercloud?

E6.8 Please overview the specifics and advantages of XMPP.

E6.9 What is instant messaging and presence?

E6.10 Please overview a typical scheme of communication between the clouds, Intercloud Root and Intercloud Exchanges using XMPP protocol.

E6.11 Please overview the Intercloud trust model.

E6.12 What is PKI and which role does this play in Intercloud trust model?

E6.13 What are certificates and Certificate Authorities and how do they help in establishing the Intercloud trust model?

E6.14 What is Domain Based Trust Model and how is it used in Intercloud architecture?

E6.15 What is semantic Web and how is it and its major concepts used in Intercloud architecture?

E6.16 What is RDF and how is it used in Intercloud?

E6.17 What is ontology and what are the most common ways (tools, languages) for implementing this concept?

E6.18 What is the TClouds project, and what are its main goals?

E6.19 Which organizations are currently the participants of the TClouds project?

E6.20 Please list the main experts and leaders on TClouds and overview their contribution, results, and publications.

E6.21 Which stages (activities) are in the working plan of the TClouds project?

E6.22 Please overview the main results and contributions of the TClouds project.

E6.23 What kind of survey have the TClouds leaders organized among the stakeholders (users) of the project? Please overview the most interesting results of this survey.

E6.24 What is Trusted Infrastructure Cloud solution and how was it implemented in TClouds project?

E6.25 What is Trusted Object Manager as part of the Trusted Infrastructure Cloud architecture?

E6.26 What is TS as part of the Trusted Infrastructure Cloud architecture?

E6.27 What is Hardware Security Module and which roles does it play in Trusted Infrastructure Cloud architecture?

E6.28 What is TVD as part of the Trusted Infrastructure Cloud architecture?

E6.29 Which enhancements have the TClouds participants proposed and implemented in the OpenStack cloud software?

E6.30 What is the idea of secure logging and log resilience, and how was it implemented as OpenStack enhancement in TClouds project?

E6.31 What is advanced VM Scheduling Enhancement and how was it implemented as OpenStack enhancement in TClouds project?

E6.32 What is cloud nodes verification enhancement and how was it implemented as OpenStack enhancement in TClouds project?

E6.33 What is transparent encryption enhancement and how was it implemented as OpenStack enhancement in TClouds project?

E6.34 What is TVD enhancement and how was it implemented as OpenStack enhancement in TClouds project?

E6.35 What is Key-Value-Store (KVS) interface and how is it used in TClouds project?

E6.36 Please overview the specific requirements to cloud service providers in the area of healthcare clouds.

E6.37 Please overview the specific requirements to cloud service providers for smart energy grid clouds.

E6.38 Please overview the open standards for trustworthy clouds investigated in TClouds project, their levels, kinds, and meanings.

E6.39 What is Cloud Security Alliance, its goal and its role in worldwide trustworthy cloud computing?

E6.40 What is STAR program?

E6.41 What is CCM and its outstanding role in worldwide trustworthy cloud computing and its assessment?

E6.42 What is CSRT by Microsoft? What is its role in worldwide cloud computing?

E6.43 Please overview and analyze the results of the CSRT survey by Microsoft in 2012–2013.

E6.44 Please give your personal assessment of perspectives of trustworthy cloud computing.

APPENDIX A

EXAMPLE OF MICROSOFT AZURE CLOUD SERVICE: FILEMANAGER

This appendix contains example of trustworthy cloud service *FileManager* [146] developed for the Microsoft Azure cloud platforms. The sample cloud service is developed by Evgeny Korolev, my bachelor student, in 2015 as his bachelor's thesis [147] developed and proved under my supervision at St. Petersburg University. The cloud service is available at [146] for free use. The service provides functionality for upload and temporary storage of files in Microsoft Azure cloud. The appendix contains description of the cloud service architecture, implementation, functionality, and the source codes of the most important classes and methods of the cloud service. The full source code of the cloud service is available at [148].

Surely the FileManager cloud service is very simple and is not a real life commercial application. But I have included it in the book as a helpful educational example. There are many other cloud commercial services that provide similar functionality. But, nevertheless, the cloud service does some useful job and can be used for its goal of uploading and storing files in the Azure cloud. The FileManager cloud service can be regarded as an example of a successful project performed by a good fourth year student for 1–2 months who just did not know cloud computing before the project. During his work on the project, the author used free academic access granted by Microsoft Research. I, as the scientific advisor, and the author of the project are very grateful to Microsoft Research for this great opportunity.

The goal of the FileManager bachelor project is to overview and learn the features of the Microsoft Azure platform, and then to implement a simple cloud service for

Trustworthy Cloud Computing, First Edition. Vladimir O. Safonov.
© 2016 John Wiley & Sons, Inc. Published 2016 by John Wiley & Sons, Inc.

temporary storing of files using Azure Storage (see Chapter 5) and synchronizing with an SQL Azure database.

The main requirements and criteria for the cloud service to be developed are as follows:

- Functionality that enables uploading a selected file from the user's computer to Blob (Binary Large Object Service) storage in Microsoft Azure cloud
- Automatic deletion of the file from the cloud after the time interval indicated by the user (1, 5, or 10 days) when this interval expires
- Adding information on the uploaded file into a database and deletion of this information when the indicated time period expires
- Implementation of a simple and comfortable user interface of the Web site for using the developed cloud service.

The cloud service is implemented using the integrated development environment Microsoft Visual Studio 2013, on the ASP.NET Model-View-Controller (MVC) 5 platform, using Azure SDK. The Web site [146] intended to manipulate with the FileManager application is implemented using the following languages and technologies:.NET/C#, HTML, CSS, Bootstrap Framework, JavaScript and jQuery library.

Below is a detailed description of the most important parts (directories and files) of the implementation of the FileManager cloud service.

A.1   MODELS: MyFile.cs

Models is one of the directories of the FileManager source code that contains the source code of the classes implementing data models, according to the Model – View – Controller paradigm. *MyFile.cs* is the class containing the information on the file that the user selected and is uploading to the cloud.

The class has the following *properties*:

- *string Key* – a unique key used to identify the file
- *string Name* – the name of the file
- *int Time* – the number of days the file will be stored in the cloud
- *Stream FileStream* – the representation of the file as a sequence (stream) of bytes
- *int Downloads* – the number of downloads of the file
- *string URI* – the Web reference (URL address) for downloading the file.

A.2   MODELS: FileManagerBlobAccess.cs

FileManagerBlobAccess is the class intended for handling blob objects of the Microsoft Azure platform.

This class uses the following APIs from Microsoft Azure:

- *CloudStorageAccount* – the class that allows the developer to get information on the Azure Storage account from configuration files or to create an object that represents the Azure Storage account using its parameters
- *CloudBlobClient* – the wrapper class for getting references to components of the Blob objects Azure Storage. The class contains the following methods: *GetContainerReference(),* and *GetBlobReference()*
- *CloudBlobContainer* – the class implementing the operations on Blob objects
- *CloudBlockBlob* – the class defining the methods of handling blocked Blob objects.

The methods of the *FileManagerBlobAccess* class from the FileManager service are as follows:

- The class constructor *FileManagerBlobAccess* – gets from the *Web.*config configuration file the connection string for the Azure Storage and initializes the objects of the classes *CloudStorageAccount, CloudBlobClient,* and *CloudBlob-Container.* Creates the container *fmcontainer* if it is not yet created.
- The method *GetContainerUri()* returns the URI address of the container *fmcontainer* represented as a string.
- The method *AddFile(MyFile)* – stores in the cloud the file from the indicated input stream using the method *UploadFromStream(FileStream)* of the class *CloudBlockBlob.*
- The method *DeleteFile(MyFile)* – deletes the file using the method *Delete()* of the class *CloudBlockBlob.*

A.3   MODELS: FileManagerDataBase.cs

The class *FileManagerDataBase* is intended for handling an SQL Azure cloud database using SQL queries. It assumes that, on the management portal of Microsoft Azure, a cloud database is created with the table *MyFiles* containing the information on the uploaded file.

To connect to the SQL Azure database, we used the ADO.NET technology, which is the most popular for such purposes nowadays. Since the Microsoft Azure platform fully supports such way of connection to the cloud database, it is not necessary for us to use the REST API provided for SQL Azure. Connection using ADO.NET to the SQL Azure cloud database is similar to local (on-premises, using the cloud slang), with the following exception: the developer must take into account the regulations or other bugs that can terminate the connection or temporarily block new connections. This state can be characterized as *unstable* fault. To solve this problem, in the Microsoft Enterprise Library Integration Pack [106] some strategies of detection are implemented, which determine the state of instability. These strategies are parts of the block *Transient Fault Handling Application Block*. If the database, for any reasons, will be unavailable for a few seconds, the query will be repeated.

To determine the strategy of repeating the queries to the database, the class *ExponentialBackoff* is used, which enables a correct way of delaying of the service workload.

The class *RetryManager* sets up the exponential delay as the default strategy.

The objects of the class *RetryPolicy* determine the policy of repeating the queries and the SQL commands used by default.

The class *ReliableSqlConnection* provides functionality for repeating the attempts of the connection to the database and the attempts of executing SQL queries.

To connect to the SQL Azure database, it is necessary to get the appropriate connection string. It can be obtained on the SQL Azure portal or be built programmatically using the class *System.Data.SqlClient.SqlConnectionStringBuilder*. To do this, the properties *Server*, *UserID*, *Password,* and *Database* of the object of this class were given the following values: the name of the server, the user identifier, the password, and the name of the instance of the cloud database. After creating the connection string, we can connect to the SQL Azure database using the method *Open()* of the class *ReliableSqlConnection*. Next, the transactions on the database are performed using the class *System.Data.IDbCommand,* which actually represents the appropriate SQL statements.

The methods of the class *FileManagerDataBase* are as follows:

Add(MyFile) – adds to the table *MyFiles* the information on the file uploaded to the Blob objects store using the *Insert* SQL statement.

Delete(MyFile) – deletes from the *MyFiles* table the string containing the information on the uploaded file using the Delete SQL statement.

DownloadsInc(string key) – adds one to the value of the column FileKey for the string whose *FileKey* is equal to the key parameter. The SQL statement Update is used for this purpose.

A.4   CONTROLLERS

This is yet another directory of the FileManager project containing the sources of the classes implementing the controllers (according to the MVC paradigm).

Controllers: HomeController.cs

The class *HomeController* implements the logic of the cloud service. It contains static objects of the classes *FileManagerBlobAccess* and *FileManagerDataBase* to manage the storage data and the cloud database.

The methods of the *HomeController* are as follows:

– The method *UploadFile(HttpPostedFileBase, int)* gets from the client a POST request containing the file that the client uploads to the cloud, and the time period for its store. Then, the method uploads the file to the store and adds to the database the information on the uploaded file. Then, the method creates a separate thread that calls the method *DeleteFile(MyFile)*.

- The method *DeleteFile(MyFile)* suspends the thread for the indicated time period, and then deletes the file and information about it from the store and from the database.
- The method *Download(string key)* calls the method *DownloadsInc(string key)* and downloads the file.

A.5   REPRESENTATION AND USER INTERFACE

The representation file *Index.cshtml* contains the code of the user interface. The user interface of the FileManager cloud service is very simple: it is a Web page [146] with a schematic picture of the cloud. Please see also Figure A.2. To initiate uploading a new file to the cloud, the user is invited to *click the picture of the cloud*. When clicking this picture, a traditional file dialog appears that allows the user to choose the file to be uploaded to the cloud from local directories on his or her computer. When uploading a file, the user is invited to indicate the maximal number of days to store the file in the cloud – 1 day, 5 days, or 10 days. Please note that the messages to the user are issued in Russian but they are so self-evident that they do not require any explanations.

When downloading the file uploaded to the cloud, the representation file sends an AJAX request to the server and, as the answer to it, gets a reference that calls the *Download(string key)* of the class *HomeController*.

The UML diagram of the most important classes of the FileManager cloud service is depicted in Figure A.1.

The user interface of the cloud service FileManager is shown in Figure A.2.

The FileManager cloud service, as specified above, works well and can be used by the readers for experiment using the Web reference [146]. The readers are also invited, as a helpful exercise, to download the full source code from [148] and to extend or change the functionality of the cloud service.

Further work on this project by its author Evgeny Korolev is planned in the following directions:

- Improvement of the user interface
- Adding a functionality to sign up and sign in for the users
- Adding connections to other accounts to make the information on the file to be uploaded more comfortable.

A.6   THE FRAGMENTS OF THE SOURCE CODE

Below, the most important parts of the source code of the FileManager cloud service are depicted. The full source code is available at [148]. All necessary explanations to the source code are given in this section.

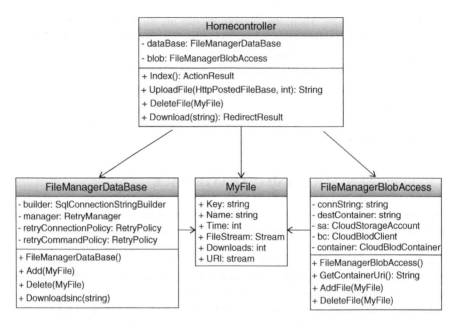

Figure A.1   The UML diagram of the classes of the FileManager cloud service.

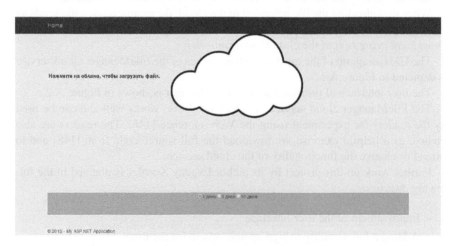

Figure A.2   The user interface of the FileManager cloud service.

The FileManagerDataBase.cs Source Code

```
private SqlConnectionStringBuilder builder =
    new SqlConnectionStringBuilder();
private RetryManager manager;
```

```
private RetryPolicy retryConnectionPolicy;
private RetryPolicy retryCommandPolicy;
public FileManagerDataBase()
{
  builder["Server"] = "j7is9tex2d.database.windows.net";
  builder["User ID"] = "SQLAdmin@j7is9tex2d.database.windows.net";
  builder["Password"] = "Gg90879087";
  builder["Database"] = "filemanager12345_db";
  builder["Trusted_Connection"] = false;
  builder["Integrated Security"] = false;
  builder["Encrypt"] = true;
  int retryCount = 4;
  int minBackoffDelayMilliseconds = 2000;
  int maxBackoffDelayMilliseconds = 8000;
  int deltaBackoffMilliseconds = 2000;
  ExponentialBackoff exponentialBackoffStrategy =
   new ExponentialBackoff("exponentialBackoffStrategy",
    retryCount,
    TimeSpan.FromMilliseconds(minBackoffDelayMilliseconds),
    TimeSpan.FromMilliseconds(maxBackoffDelayMilliseconds),
    TimeSpan.FromMilliseconds(deltaBackoffMilliseconds));
  manager = new RetryManager(new List<RetryStrategy>
  {
    exponentialBackoffStrategy
  }, "exponentialBackoffStrategy");
  RetryManager.SetDefault(manager);
  retryConnectionPolicy = manager.GetDefaultSqlConnectionRetryPolicy();
  retryCommandPolicy = manager.GetDefaultSqlCommandRetryPolicy();
}

public void Add(MyFile file)
{
  string sqlCommand =
    "INSERT INTO MyFiles (FileKey, Name, Time, Uri, Downloads) VALUES
('" + file.Key + "', '" + file.Name + "'," + file.Time.ToString() + ",
'" + file.URI + "', " + file.Downloads.ToString() + ");";
  retryConnectionPolicy.ExecuteAction(() =>
  {
    using (ReliableSqlConnection connection = new
ReliableSqlConnection(builder.ConnectionString))
    {
      connection.Open();

        IDbCommand command = connection.CreateCommand();
        command.CommandText = sqlCommand;
        connection.ExecuteCommand(command);
    }
  });
}
}
```

The FileManagerBlobAccess.cs Source Code

```
private string connString;
private string destContainer;
private CloudStorageAccount sa;
private CloudBlobClient bc;
private CloudBlobContainer container;
public FileManagerBlobAccess()
{
   connString =
      ConfigurationManager.ConnectionStrings["StorageConnectionString"]
   .ConnectionString;
   destContainer = ConfigurationManager.AppSettings["destContainer"];
   sa = CloudStorageAccount.Parse(connString);
   bc = sa.CreateCloudBlobClient();
   container = bc.GetContainerReference(destContainer);
   container.CreateIfNotExists();
}


public String GetContainerUri()
{
   return container.Uri.ToString();
}


public void AddFile(MyFile file)
{
   CloudBlockBlob b = container.GetBlockBlobReference(file.Key);
   b.UploadFromStream(file.FileStream);
}
}
```

The HomeController.cs Source Code

```
static FileManagerDataBase dataBase = new FileManagerDataBase();
static FileManagerBlobAccess blob = new FileManagerBlobAccess();

public ActionResult Index()
{
   return View();
}

[HttpPost]
public String UploadFile(HttpPostedFileBase upload, int time)
{
   string key = DateTime.UtcNow.ToString("yyyy-MM-dd-HH:mm:ss") + "-" +
upload.FileName;

   string containerUri = blob.GetContainerUri() + @"/";

   MyFile file = new MyFile { Key = key, Name = upload.FileName, Time =
time, FileStream = upload.InputStream, Downloads = 0, URI = containerUri
+ key };
```

```
    blob.AddFile(file);
    dataBase.Add(file);
    Thread thread = new Thread(delegate() { DeleteFile(file); });
    thread.Start();
    return key;
}

public void DeleteFile(MyFile file)
{
    Thread.Sleep(file.Time * 24 * 60 * 60 * 1000);
    blob.DeleteFile(file);
    dataBase.Delete(file);
}

public RedirectResult Download(string key)
{
    string uri = blob.GetContainerUri() + @"/" + key;
    dataBase.DownloadsInc(key);
    return Redirect(uri);
}
}
```

REFERENCES

1. Safonov, V.O., *Using Aspect-Oriented Programming for Trustworthy Software Development,* John Wiley and Sons, Inc. Hoboken, 2008, 352 pp.

2. Safonov, V.O., *Trustworthy Compilers,* John Wiley and Sons, Inc. Hoboken, 2010, 295 pp.

3. Safonov, V.O., *The Microsoft Windows Azure Cloud Computing Platform,* BINOM Knowledge Laboratory. Moscow, 2012, 235 pp. (in Russian).

4. Safonov, V.O., *Enhancements and New Features of Microsoft Windows Azure Cloud Computing Platform,* BINOM Knowledge Laboratory. Moscow, 2013, 304 pp. (in Russian).

5. Safonov, V.O. 2011. The Microsoft Windows Azure Cloud Computing Platform. Educational course. Available at http://www.intuit.ru/studies/courses/2314/614/info (in Russian). Accessed 2015 Oct 9.

6. Safonov, V.O. 2013. Enhancements and New Features of Microsoft Windows Azure Cloud Computing Platform. Educational course. Available at http://www.intuit.ru/studies/courses/11007/1117/info (in Russian). Accessed 2015 Oct 9.

7. Safonov, V.O. 2014. Features of Visual Studio 2013 and Their Use for Cloud Computing. Educational course. Available at http://www.intuit.ru/studies/courses/13805/1223/info (in Russian). Accessed 2015 Oct 9.

8. Abbadi, I.M., *Cloud Management and Security,* John Wiley and Sons, Inc. Hoboken, 2014, 216 pp.

9. Erl, T., Puttini, R., Mahmood, Z., *Cloud Computing: Concepts, Technology & Architecture*, Prentice Hall, 2013. 489 pp.

10. Kavis, M., *Architecting the Cloud: Design Decisions for Cloud Computing Service Models*. John Wiley and Sons, Inc. Hoboken, 2014, 200 pp.

11. Yeluri, R., Castro-Leon, E., *Building the Infrastructure for Cloud Security: A Solutions View*. APress Media, 2014, 216 pp.

12. Rhoton, J., De Clercq, J., Graves, D., *Cloud Computing Protected: Security Assessment Handbook*. Recursive Press, 2013, 390 pp.

13. Safonov, V.O., *Modern Operating Systems Basics,* BINOM Knowledge Laboratory. Moscow, 2011, 583 pp. (in Russian).

14. Safonov, V.O. 2004. Microsoft.NET Architecture and the C# Language. University course curriculum. Available at https://www.facultyresourcecenter.com/curriculum/5911-MicrosoftNET-Architecture-and.aspx?c1=en-us&c2=0. Accessed 2015 Oct 9.

15. Safonov, V.O., *Introduction to Java Technology*, Lambert Academic Publishers. Saarbrücken, 2011, 232 pp.

16. Protégé Web site. 2015. Available at http://protege.stanford.edu. Accessed 2015 Oct 9.

17. Knowledge.NET Web site. 2015. Available at http://www.knowledge-net.ru. Accessed 2015 Oct 9.

18. NIST Cloud Computing Standards Roadmap. 2013. Available at http://www.nist.gov/itl/cloud/upload/NIST_SP-500-291_Version-2_2013_June18_FINAL.pdf. Accessed 2015 Oct 9.

19. International Standard ISO/IEC 17788. *Information Technology – Cloud Computing – Overview and Vocabulary*, ISO/IEC 2014, 16 pp.

20. International Standard ISO/IEC 17789. *Information Technology – Cloud Computing – Reference Architecture*, ISO/IEC 2014, 58 pp.

21. IEEE P2302/D0.2 Draft Standard for Intercloud Interoperability and Federation (SIIF). 2012. Available at https://www.oasis-open.org/committees/download.php/46205/p2302-12-0002-00-DRFT-intercloud-p2302-draft-0-2.pdf. Accessed 2015 Oct 9.

22. REST vs. SOAP: How to choose the best Web service. 2015. Available at http://searchsoa.techtarget.com/tip/REST-vs-SOAP-How-to-choose-the-best-Web-service. Accessed 2015 Oct 9.

23. Jung, E.-S., Kettimuthu, R. Challenges and opportunities for data-intensive computing in the cloud. *IEEE Computer Magazine*, 2014, pp. 82–85.

24. Microsoft Cloud-Scale Datacenters. 2012. Available at http://download.microsoft.com/download/B/9/3/B93FCE14-50A2-40F6-86EE-8C1E1F0D3A95/Cloud_Scale_Datacenters_Strategy_Brief.pdf. Accessed 2015 Oct 9.

25. Microsoft Datacenter sustainability strategy brief. Microsoft Press, 2015, 9 pp. Available at http://download.microsoft.com/download/1/1/9/119CD765-0CEE-4DA6-B396-20603D3F4701/Datacenter_Sustainability_Strategy_Brief.pdf. Accessed 2015 Oct 9.

26. The Blade Server article in Wikipedia. Available at http://en.wikipedia.org/wiki/Blade_server. Accessed 2015 Oct 9.

27. Hwang, K., Fox, G., Dongarra, J., Distributed Computing: Clusters, Grids and Clouds. Chapter 7, Cloud Architecture and Datacenter Design, 2010.

28. The NetBeans project site. Available at http://www.netbeans.org. Accessed 2015 Oct 9.

29. The IBM Tivoli Storage Manager Web site. Available at http://www-03.ibm.com/software/products/en/tivostormana. Accessed 2015 Oct 9.

30. IEEE Transactions on Cloud Computing Web site. Available at http://www.computer .org/web/tcc. Accessed 2015 Oct 9.

31. The portal of IEEE Computing Magazine. Available at http://www.computer.org/ computer. Accessed 2015 Oct 9.

32. The Web site of the Journal of Cloud Computing. A Springer Open Journal. Available at http://www.journalofcloudcomputing.com/. Accessed 2015 Oct 9.

33. The Web site of the International Journal of Cloud Computing. Available at http://hipore .com/ijcc/. Accessed 2015 Oct 9.

34. The Web site of the SYS-CON company's Cloud Computing Journal. Available at http:// cloudcomputing.sys-con.com/. Accessed 2015 Oct 9.

35. IEEE Cloud Computing Community Web site. Available at https://www .ieee.org/membership-catalog/productdetail/showProductDetailPage.html? product=CMYCC738. Accessed 2015 Oct 9.

36. The IEEE Web portal on cloud computing. Available at http://cloudcomputing.ieee.org/. Accessed 2015 Oct 9.

37. IBM Cloud Computing Community portal. Available at https://www-304.ibm.com/ connections/communities/service/html/communityview?communityUuid=fa3a3fd5- 6d7b-48b9-b13b-ba25f3325dda&lang=en. Accessed 2015 Oct 9.

38. Oracle Cloud Computing Community portal. Available at http://www.oracle.com/ technetwork/topics/cloud/community/index.html. Accessed 2015 Oct 9.

39. Microsoft Azure in Education portal. Available at http://azure.microsoft.com/en-us/ community/education/. Accessed 2015 Oct 9.

40. The portal of IEEE Cloud 2014 international conference. Available at http://www .thecloudcomputing.org/2014/. Accessed 2015 Oct 9.

41. Microsoft TechEd Europe 2014 Web site. Available at http://europe.msteched.com/# fbid=XC5F-f27KMS. Accessed 2015 Oct 9.

42. TechDays Russia conference Web site. 2014. Available at https://www.techdays.ru/ videos/TechEd%20Russia. Accessed 2015 Oct 9.

43. The Web site of the "Cloud in Russia" Microsoft's conference. 2015. Available at http:// events.techdays.ru/msitconf/2015-02/. Accessed 2015 Oct 9.

44. Collier, M., Shahan, R., *Microsoft Azure Essentials. Fundamentals of Azure*. Microsoft Press, 2014. Available at http://aka.ms/697225pdf. Accessed 2015 Oct 9.

45. Oracle cloud e-books portal. Available at https://cloud.oracle.com/ebooks. Accessed 2015 Oct 9.

46. Wessler, M., *Cloud Architecture for Dummies*. Oracle special edition. John Wiley & Sons, 2012, 51 pp. Available at http://www.dummies.com/Section/id-811854.html. Accessed 2015 Oct 9.

47. Wessler, M. *Enterprise Cloud Infrastructure for Dummies*. Oracle special edition. John Wiley & Sons, 2015, 51 pp.

48. Wessler, M. *Server Virtualization for Dummies*. Oracle special edition. John Wiley & Sons, 2015, 67 pp.

49. IBM Private, *Public and Hybrid Cloud Storage Solutions*. 2014, 146 pp. Available at http://www.redbooks.ibm.com/redpapers/pdfs/redp4873.pdf. Accessed 2015 Oct 9.

50. HP collection of commercial cloud books by HP Press. Available at http://h10120.www1 .hp.com/ExpertOne/hp_press.html. Accessed 2015 Oct 9.

51. Cohen, M., Hurley, K., Newson, P., *Google Compute Engine. Managing Secure and Scalable Cloud Computing*. O'Reilly Media, 2014, 246 pp.

52. Cloud Computing Wire portal. Available at http://cloudcomputingwire.com/cloud-computing-universities/. Accessed 2015 Oct 9.

53. Microsoft Azure management portal. Available at https://manage.windowsazure.com. Accessed 2015 Oct 9.

54. Microsoft Azure preview portal. Available at http://portal.azure.com. Accessed 2015 Oct 9.

55. Amazon AWS cloud portal. Available at http://aws.amazon.com. Accessed 2015 Oct 9.

56. Oracle cloud portal. Available at https://cloud.oracle.com. Accessed 2015 Oct 9.

57. IBM Cloud portal with free trial offer for one month. Available at http://www.ibm.com/cloud-computing/us/en/why-cloud.html. Accessed 2015 Oct 9.

58. IBM Cloud marketplace portal. Available at http://www.ibm.com/marketplace/cloud/us/en-us/. Accessed 2015 Oct 9.

59. Amazon AWS Cloud documentation: Getting Started with AWS. Available at http://aws.amazon.com/ru/documentation/gettingstarted/. Accessed 2015 Oct 9.

60. Amazon AWS Cloud documentation: Hosting a Static Website. Available at http://aws.amazon.com/ru/documentation/gettingstarted/. Accessed 2015 Oct 9.

61. Amazon AWS Cloud documentation: Hosting a Web Application. Available at http://aws.amazon.com/ru/documentation/gettingstarted/. Accessed 2015 Oct 9.

62. Amazon AWS Cloud documentation: Deploying a Web Application. Available at http://aws.amazon.com/ru/documentation/gettingstarted/. Accessed 2015 Oct 9.

63. Amazon AWS Cloud documentation: Hosting .NET Web Apps. Available at http://aws.amazon.com/ru/documentation/gettingstarted/. Accessed 2015 Oct 9.

64. Amazon AWS Cloud documentation: Analyzing Big Data. Available at http://aws.amazon.com/ru/documentation/gettingstarted/. Accessed 2015 Oct 9.

65. Wikipedia article on Amazon Web Services. Available at http://en.wikipedia.org/wiki/Amazon_Web_Services. Accessed 2015 Oct 9.

66. Amazon Relational Database Service User Guide. Available at http://aws.amazon.com/documentation/rds. Accessed 2015 Oct 9.

67. Amazon DynamoDB database engine. Available at https://us-west-2.console.aws.amazon.com/dynamodb/home?region=us-west-2. Accessed 2015 Oct 9.

68. Amazon DynamoDB Developer's Guide. Available at http://docs.aws.amazon.com/amazondynamodb/latest/developerguide/dynamodb-dg.pdf. Accessed 2015 Oct 9.

69. Bluemix cloud documentation. Overview of the IBM Bluemix Cloud. Available at https://www.ng.bluemix.net/docs/#overview/overview.html#overview. Accessed 2015 Oct 9.

70. The Cloud Foundry portal. Available at http://cloudfoundry.org. Accessed 2015 Oct 9.

71. The Oracle cloud sign-in page. Available at https://cloud.oracle.com/sign_in. Accessed 2015 Oct 9.

72. The Oracle cloud try-it page. Available at https://cloud.oracle.com/tryit. Accessed 2015 Oct 9.

73. The Oracle cloud marketplace page. Available at https://cloud.oracle.com/marketplace/faces/homePage.jspx?_afrLoop=1308113152150430_afrWindowMode=0_adf.ctrl-state=u5o7wffug_4. Accessed 2015 Oct 9.

74. Google Cloud Platform portal. Available at https://cloud.google.com/. Accessed 2015 Oct 9.

75. Google Developers Console. Available at https://console.developers.google.com. Accessed 2015 Oct 9.

76. HP Helion Public cloud portal. Available at http://www.hpcloud.com/. Accessed 2015 Oct 9.

77. HP Helion overview (in Russian). Available at http://www8.hp.com/ru/ru/cloud/helion-overview.html. Accessed 2015 Oct 9.

78. OpenStack – Open source software for creating private and public clouds. Available at https://www.openstack.org/. Accessed 2015 Oct 9.

79. HP Helion cloud landing page. Available at https://horizon.hpcloud.com/landing/. Accessed 2015 Oct 9.

80. Getting Started with HP Helion Cloud. Available at http://docs.hpcloud.com/publiccloud/hpcloudconsole. Accessed 2015 Oct 9.

81. HP Helion Cloud documentation. Available at http://docs.hpcloud.com/. Accessed 2015 Oct 9.

82. The Salesforce cloud login page. Available at https://login.salesforce.com/. Accessed 2015 Oct 9.

83. The Salesforce cloud starting page. Available at https://eu5.salesforce.com/servlet/servlet.Integration?lid=01r24000000Kcc6&ic=1. Accessed 2015 Oct 9.

84. The Salesforce AppExchange portal. Available at https://appexchange.salesforce.com/. Accessed 2015 Oct 9.

85. The Salesforce developers portal. Available at https://developer.salesforce.com/. Accessed 2015 Oct 9.

86. The Force.com IDE for develop APEX applications. Available at https://developer.salesforce.com/page/Force.com_IDE. Accessed 2015 Oct 9.

87. The Salesforce All Tabs page. Available at https://eu5.salesforce.com/home/showAllTabs.jsp. Accessed 2015 Oct 9.

88. The APEX developer console in the Salesforce cloud. Available at https://eu5.salesforce.com/_ui/common/apex/debug/ApexCSIPage. Accessed 2015 Oct 9.

89. Safonov, V.O. *Trustworthy Computing // Encyclopedia of Information Science and Technology*, Third Edition — IGI Global Publishers, 2014. pp. 3598–3606.

90. Microsoft Trustworthy Computing portal. Available at http://www.microsoft.com/en-us/twc/. Accessed 2015 Oct 9.

91. Schneider, F.B. Ed., *Trust in Cyberspace*. Committee on Information Systems Trustworthiness, National Research Council, Washington, DC, 1999.

92. Howard, M., LeBlanc, D., *Writing Secure Code*, Second edition, Microsoft Press, 2002, 800 pp.

93. Mundie, C., et al. (2002). Trustworthy Computing white paper, http://download.microsoft.com/download/a/f/2/af22fd56-7f19-47aa-8167-4b1d73cd3c57/twc_mundie.doc. Accessed 2015 Oct 9.

94. Howard, M., & Lipner, S. (2006). *The Security Development Lifecycle*, Microsoft Press, Redmond, WA.

95. FxCop Web page. Available at https://fxcopinstaller.codeplex.com/. Accessed 2015 Oct 9.

96. Microsoft Security Response Center Progress Report, July 2012–June 2013. Available at http://aka.ms/msrcprogressreport. Accessed 2015 Oct 9.

97. Rosenberg, L., Hammer, T., Shaw, J., *Software Metrics and Reliability*. NASA Software Assurance Technology Center. Awarded best paper, 1998.

98. Bernstein, L., & Yuhas, C.H., *Trustworthy Systems through Quantitative Software Engineering*, John Wiley & Sons, Hoboken, NJ, 2005.

99. Sahinoglu, M., *Trustworthy Computing: Analytical and Quantitative Engineering Evaluation*, John Wiley & Sons, Hoboken, NJ, 2007.

100. Safonov, V.O., *Parametrized Data Types: History, Theory, Implementation, and Applications*. St. Petersburg University Press, 2013, 116 pp. (in Russian).

101. Lukan, D. The top cloud computing threats and vulnerabilities in an enterprise environment. 2015. Available at http://www.cloudcomputing-news.net/news/2014/nov/21/top-cloud-computing-threats-and-vulnerabilities-enterprise-environment/. Accessed 2015 Oct 9.

102. Security Management in Microsoft Azure. White paper. Published November 2014 by Microsoft Corporation, 17 pp. Available at http://eqinc.com/images/white-papers/azure/security-management-in-microsoft-azure-11062014.pdf.

103. Tulloch, M., *Introducing Windows Server 2012 R2 Technical Overview*, Microsoft Press, 2013, 229 pp. Available at http://blogs.msdn.com/b/microsoft_press/archive/2013/11/08/free-ebook-introducing-windows-server-2012-r2-technical-overview.aspx. Accessed 2015 Oct 9.

104. The Web site of Enterprise Library 5.0 Integration Pack for Microsoft Azure. Available at http://entlib.codeplex.com/wikipage?title=EntLib5Azure. Accessed 2015 Oct 9.

105. *Aspect.NET Web site*. Available at http://www.aspectdotnet.org. Accessed 2015 Oct 9.

106. Grigoriev, D.A., Grigorieva, A.V., Safonov, V.O. (2012). Seamless integration of aspects to cloud applications based on the Enterprise Library Integration Pack for Microsoft Azure and Aspect.NET. *Computer Tools in Education*, 4, 3–15. (in Russian).

107. Safonov, V.O. (2003) Aspect.NET – a new approach to aspect-oriented programming. *.NET Developers Journal*, 1(*4*), 36–40.

108. Safonov, V.O. (2004). Aspect.NET – concepts and architecture. *.NET Developers Journal*, 2(*9*), 44–48.

109. Safonov, V.O. (2005). Presentation on Aspect.NET at the Web site of Microsoft Research SSCLI (Rotor) Seminar, Redmond, September 2005. Available at http://research.microsoft.com/en-us/events/sscli2005/safonov.ppt. Accessed 2015 Oct 9.

110. Safonov, V.O. (2005). Presentation on Aspect.NET at Microsoft Faculty Summit, Redmond, July 2005. Available at http://research.microsoft.com/en-us/um/redmond/events/fs2005/presentations/FacultySummit_2005_Safonov.ppt. Accessed 2015 Oct 9.

111. Safonov, V.O., Grigoriev, D.A. (2005). Aspect.NET: aspect-oriented programming for Microsoft.NET in practice. *.NET Developers Journal*, 3(*7*), 28–33.

112. Safonov, V.O., Gratchev, M.K., Grigoriev, D.A., Maslennikov, A.I. (2006). Aspect.NET – aspect-oriented toolkit for Microsoft.NET based on Phoenix and Whidbey. In: J. Knoop, V. Skala (Eds.), .NET Technologies 2006 International Conference. Univ. of West Bohemia Campus Bory, May 29 – June 1,2006, Pilsen, Czech Republic. Full Paper Proceedings (pp. 19–29). Available at http://dotnet.zcu.cz/NET_2006/NET_2006.htm. Accessed 2015 Oct 9.

113. Safonov, V.O. Aspect-Oriented Programming and Aspect.NET as security and privacy tool for Web and 3D Web programming. Chapter 11 (40 pp.) In: Rea, A. Ed. *Security in Virtual Worlds, 3D webs and Immersive Environments: Models for Development, Interaction and Management*, IGI Global Publishers, 2010.

114. Aspect.NET 1.0. September 2005. Available at https://www.facultyresourcecenter.com/curriculum/6219-AspectNET-10.aspx?c1=en-us&c2=0. Accessed 2015 Oct 9.

115. Aspect.NET 1.1. March 2006. Available at https://www.facultyresourcecenter.com/curriculum/6334-AspectNET-11.aspx?c1=en-us&c2=0. Accessed 2015 Oct 9.

116. Aspect.NET 2.0. September 2006. Available at https://www.facultyresourcecenter.com/curriculum/6595-AspectNET-20.aspx?c1=en-us&c2=0. Accessed 2015 Oct 9.

117. Aspect.NET 2.1. April 2007. Available at https://www.facultyresourcecenter.com/curriculum/6801-AspectNET-21.aspx?c1=en-us&c2=0. Accessed 2015 Oct 9.

118. Aspect.NET 2.2. April 2010. Available at https://www.facultyresourcecenter.com/curriculum/8658-AspectNET-22.aspx?c1=en-us&c2=0. Accessed 2015 Oct 9.

119. The Web site on Hand-on Labs for Enterprise Library Integration Pack for Microsoft Azure. Available at http://www.microsoft.com/en-us/download/details.aspx?id=28785. Accessed 2015 Oct 9.

120. The Mono.Cecil project site. Available at http://www.mono-project.com/Cecil. Accessed 2015 Oct 9.

121. The PostSharp project site. Available at http://www.postsharp.net. Accessed 2015 Oct 9.

122. I. Aracic, V. Gasiunas, M. Mezini, K. Ostermann. An overview of CaesarJ. Transactions on Aspect-Oriented Software Development I, Springer, Berlin, Heidelberg, New York, 2008, 135–173.

123. Storage Services REST API Reference. Available at https://msdn.microsoft.com/en-us/library/azure/dd179355.aspx. Accessed 2015 Oct 9.

124. Microsoft Azure Storage Client Library for .NET. Available at https://msdn.microsoft.com/en-us/library/azure/dn261237.aspx. Accessed 2015 Oct 9.

125. Azure tools downloading page. Available at http://azure.microsoft.com/en-us/downloads/. Accessed 2015 Oct 9.

126. Azure tools for developing iOS mobile services. Available at https://github.com/Azure/azure-mobile-services/blob/master/CHANGELOG.ios.md#sdk-downloads. Accessed 2015 Oct 9.

127. Documentation on Azure client libraries for Java. Available at https://azure.microsoft.com/en-us/documentation/articles/java-download-windows/?rnd=1. Accessed 2015 Oct 9.

128. Microsoft Azure Machine Learning Studio. Available at https://studio.azureml.net/. Accessed 2015 Oct 9.

129. Apache Hadoop tutorial. Available at https://azure.microsoft.com/en-us/documentation/articles/hdinsight-hadoop-tutorial-get-started-windows/. Accessed 2015 Oct 9.

130. The Intercloud Web site. Available at http://cloudcomputing.ieee.org/web/ieee-cloud-computing/intercloud. Accessed 2015 Oct 9.

131. The Intercloud article in Wikipedia. Available at https://en.wikipedia.org/wiki/Intercloud. Accessed 2015 Oct 9.

132. Extensible Messaging and Presence Protocol (XMPP). Available at http://xmpp.org/rfcs/rfc3920.html. Accessed 2015 Oct 9.

133. The SPARQL article in Wikipedia. Available at https://en.wikipedia.org/wiki/SPARQL. Accessed 2015 Oct 9.

134. The Google App Engine. The XMPP Java API. Available at http://code.google.com/appengine/docs/java/xmpp/. Accessed 2015 Oct 9.

135. Internet X.509 Public Key Infrastructure, Certificate Policy and Certification Practices Framework. Available at http://tools.ietf.org/html/rfc3647. Accessed 2015 Oct 9.

136. The Certificate Authority article in Wikipedia. Available at http://en.wikipedia.org/wiki/Certificate_authority. Accessed 2015 Oct 9.

137. The Web Ontology Language. Available at http://www.w3.org/TR/owl-features/. Accessed 2015 Oct 9.

138. The TClouds project site. Available at http://www.tclouds-project.eu/. Accessed 2015 Oct 9.

139. TClouds boosts security and adds trustworthiness to Cloud Computing. Available at http://ec.europa.eu/digital-agenda/en/news/tclouds-boosts-security-and-adds-trustworthiness-cloud-computing. Accessed 2015 Oct 9.

140. Burger, R.A., Cachin, C., Hussman, E. (eds.) *Cloud, Trust, Privacy. Trustworthy cloud computing whitepaper*. Available at http://www.tclouds-project.eu/downloads/TClouds_12_final_150dpi.pdf. Accessed 2015 Oct 9.

141. Cloud Security Alliance (CSA) Web site. Available at https://cloudsecurityalliance.org/. Accessed 2015 Oct 9.

142. Trends in Cloud Computing: Cloud Security Readiness Tool. Available at http://www.microsoft.com/en-us/download/details.aspx?id=39043. Accessed 2015 Oct 9.

143. Cloud Security Alliance Recommends the Cloud Security Readiness Tool. Available at https://cloudsecurityalliance.org/media/news/csa-recommends-cloud-security-readiness-tool/. Accessed 2015 Oct 9.

144. The Cloud Control Matrix. Available at https://cloudsecurityalliance.org/group/cloud-controls-matrix/. Accessed 2015 Oct 9.

145. The Capability Maturity Model article in Wikipedia. Available at https://en.wikipedia.org/wiki/Capability_Maturity_Model. Accessed 2015 Oct 9.

146. The FileManager Azure Web service. Available at http://filemanager12345.azurewebsites.net/. Accessed 2015 Oct 9.

147. Korolev, E.N., Cloud application for temporary storage of files on Microsoft Azure Platform. Bachelor's thesis, St. Petersburg State University, 2015.

148. Korolev, E.N. (2015) The source code of the FileManager cloud service. Available at https://drive.google.com/folderview?id=0B-Js7wY30irnM0RhS241Q2JyOW8&usp=sharing. Accessed 2015 Oct 9.

INDEX

Printed and bound by CPI Group (UK) Ltd, Croydon, CR0 4YY

27/10/2024

14580277-0003